The IMF and the World Bank at Sixty

Advance Reviews

'If the Bretton Woods Institutions did not exist, they would have to be invented – or so many experts would have us believe. However, the real question is, would they be designed differently? The contributors to this volume provide cogent arguments for substantial reforms, not only to the IMF and World Bank, but to the entire financial system, to make it less prone to crisis and more supportive to developing countries.'

Roy Culpeper, Ph.D.
President and CEO, The North-South Institute, Canada

'This book combines a well-informed critique of IMF and World Bank activities by spokespeople for a group of developing countries, with proposals to improve the situation. It contains a valuable critique of the current power-based international monetary system, the unrepresentative governance system of the IMF and World Bank, the IMF's mission creep, and existing indices of policy and institutional quality. It also contains proposals to reduce the risk of developing country financial crises, apply industrial policy, increase world cocoa prices, and introduce fiscal insurance in the Eastern Caribbean. It should have an impact on global policy discussion. It will supply ammunition to all those sceptical about the benefits to developing countries of current global economic policies and institutions. It will also be useful reading for courses on global governance, development economics, and international finance.'

Professor Michael J Ellman
Department Chair, Economics, Faculty of Economics and Econometrics,
Universiteit van Amsterdam

'More than ever the International Financial Institutions like World Bank and IMF are in need of the creative and well documented thinking of developing countries. In this book, Ariel Buira and his group of co-authors provide such thinking, based on their work for the G-24, the powerful group of upcoming nations (today developing, tomorrow the world leaders, like India and Brazil). These "voices of the poorer" are excellent challenges and extensions of present development thinking, whether they are concerned with debt management in developing countries, with conditionalities of the IMF or (my favourite) industrial competitiveness.'

Jozef Ritzen
President of the Universiteit Maastricht and former Vice President of the
World Bank's Development Economics Department (2001–3)

'The current volume is indicative of the range of significant second opinions, reflective of developing countries' concerns, that emanate from the G-24's continuing research programme. Its papers should stimulate debates that, on the occasion of the IFIs' 60th anniversary, deserve to take place both within these institutions and throughout the broader community of financial and development analysts and policymakers.'

Gerry Helleiner
Professor Emeritus, Economics and distinguished Research Fellow,
Munk Centre for International Studies, University of Toronto

The IMF and the
World Bank at Sixty

Edited by
ARIEL BUIRA
for the G-24 Research Programme

Anthem Press

Anthem Press
An imprint of Wimbledon Publishing Company
75-76 Blackfriars Road, London SE1 8HA

or

PO Box 9779, London SW19 7ZG
www.anthempress.com

This edition first published by Anthem Press 2005

British Library Cataloguing in Publication Data
A catalogue record for this book is available from the British Library.

Library of Congress Cataloging in Publication Data
A catalog record for this book has been requested.

1 3 5 7 9 10 8 6 4 2

ISBN 1 84331 196 8 (Pbk)

Typeset by Footprint Labs Ltd, London
www.footprintlabs.com

Printed in Malta

CONTENTS

The G-24

The Intergovernmental Group of 24 for Intentional Monetary Affairs and Development was constituted in 1972 as a result of a mandate given in Lima by the Group of 77 to their Chairman, to consult member governments on the establishment of an intergovernmental group on monetary issues. Its members, nine African, eight Latin American and seven Asian countries are as follows:

Algeria, Argentina, Brazil, Colombia, Côte d'Ivoire, Democratic Republic of Congo, Egypt, Ethiopia, Gabon, Ghana, Guatemala, India, Iran, Lebanon, Mexico, Nigeria, Pakistan, Peru, Philippines, South Africa, Sri Lanka, Syrian Arab Republic, Trinidad and Tobago, and Venezuela.

The purpose of the G-24 is to further the interests of the developing countries and their effective participation in the discussions of monetary, financial and development issues at the Bretton Woods institutions and other fora. It seeks to provide technical support to its members and to the G77 in their consideration of these issues. To this effect, the G-24 Secretariat, supported by its members and other sources, runs a research programme in which academics and other researchers from countries in the North and South address the main issues of concern to the developing world in their areas of competence. To ensure intellectual freedom in their work, the results of their research and the views expressed in the papers presented to the G-24 are the sole responsibility of the authors.

LIST OF CONTRIBUTORS

Sarah Babb is Assistant Professor of Sociology at Boston College. She is author and co-author of a number of articles in political and economic sociology, as well as 'Managing Mexico: Economists from Nationalism to Neoliberalism', which traces the history and social structure of the Mexican economics profession over the course of the 20th century.

Ariel Buira, Editor, is Director of the G-24 Secretariat. He has been Special Envoy of the President of Mexico for the UN Conference on Financing for Development, Ambassador of Mexico, Senior Associate Member of St. Anthony's College, Oxford, Member of the Board of Governors of the Bank of Mexico, Staff member and Executive Director of the IMF. He is author of numerous articles on macroeconomics and international economics. He edited *Challenges to the World Bank and IMF* (Anthem Press, 2003).

Randall Dodd is the founder and director of the Financial Policy Forum in Washington, D.C. He previously worked as an economist for the Commodity Futures Trading Commission and the U.S Congress. He received his Ph.D. in economics from Columbia University where he specialized in international trade and finance.

Ilene Grabel, Ph.D., is Associate Professor of International Finance at the Graduate School of International Studies of the University of Denver. She is the co-author (with Professor Ha-Joon Chang) of *Reclaiming Development: An Alternative Economic Policy Manual* (Zed Books, 2004). She has written widely on financial crisis and reform in the developing world.

Irfan ul Haque holds a B.A. and M.A. in Economics from the University of Panjab, and a B.A., M.A. and Ph.D. in Economics from the University of Cambridge. He worked for UNCTAD 1967–69 and for the World Bank 1970–97. He also served at the South Centre, Geneva, during 1998–99. He has written a number of publications on issues of trade, finance and development.

Barry Herman is a Senior Advisor in the Financing for Development Office in the United Nations Department of Economic and Social Affairs, New York. He was part of the Secretariat that prepared the Monterrey UN Conference on Financing for Development in 2002. Earlier, he led the team that produced the UN's annual *World Economic and Social Survey*. He has edited three books and published articles and chapters in books on North-South financial issues.

Devesh Kapur is the Frederick Danziger Associate Professor of Government at Harvard University. He is a faculty associate at the Weatherhead Center for International Affairs and the Center for International Development at Harvard University, a senior associate of the Global Economic Governance Programme at the University of Oxford and a Non-Resident Fellow at the Center for Global Development in Washington, D.C.

Tim Kessler, an independent consultant, wrote the present contribution when he served as Director of Research for the Network on Essential Services. He has also worked as a social science consultant at the World Bank, where he helped develop tools for social and institutional analysis used to conduct *ex ante* evaluations of the impact of structural adjustment programs. Kessler has a doctorate in political science from the University of California, Berkeley.

Sanjaya Lall, educated in India and Oxford, is Professor of Development Economics at the Department of International Development at Oxford University. He has also been a staff member of the World Bank for several years and consultant to various international organizations and governments on technology, foreign direct investment and competitiveness. He is chief editor of *Oxford Development Studies*.

Aziz Ali Mohammed is Advisor to Executive Director at the IMF, and G-24 Deputy for Pakistan. He served on IMF staff from 1961 to 1990, his last position being Head of the External Relations Department. He served as Alternate Executive Director representing the Middle East constituency on the IMF Executive Board from 1991 to 1992. He has co-authored two books on Pakistan and contributed to several academic journals.

Laura dos Reis is Research Associate at the G-24 Secretariat in Washington, D.C. She has been a consultant for the World Bank (2002) and the Research department of the Inter-American Development Bank (1999–2001) on issues related to macroeconomics and international finance. She previously worked as an analyst for the Ministry of Economics in Argentina (1995–97). She holds an M.A. in International Development from the Kennedy School of Government at Harvard University and an M.A. in Economics from Di Tella University, Argentina.

Shari Spiegel is Managing Director of Initiative for Policy Dialogue. Previously, she was a Director of Lazard Asset Management LLC. Ms Spiegel was one of the founders and CEO of Budapest Investment Management Company. She worked at Citibank and Drexel Burnham Lambert in fixed income research, cross-currency interest-rate-swap trading, and credit research. Ms Spiegel has an M.A. in economics from Princeton University and a B.A. in applied mathematics and economics from Northwestern University. She is an Adjunct Associate Professor at Columbia University's School of International and Public Affairs.

FOREWORD

Gerry Helleiner*

Professor Emeritus, Economics and Distinguished Research Fellow,
Munk Centre for International Studies,
University of Toronto

Sixty years after their creation, the IMF and World Bank play roles quite different from those their original founders had envisaged. The founders would undoubtedly be astounded to learn that these international financial institutions (IFIs) have emerged as, above all else, significant financiers, analysts and advisors for the developing (and, more recently, transition) countries. As purveyors of current 'knowledge' about stabilization and development issues, and gatekeepers to external sources of finance, the IFIs are dominant influences in macroeconomic and development policy formation in much of the developing (and transition) world, particularly in the economically most vulnerable parts of it. The policies and practices of the Fund and Bank are far more important to these countries than they are to the developed countries that created them and whose interests they were presumably created primarily to serve. Yet the influence of the developing countries' governments and citizenry upon the functioning of these institutions and the policies they prescribe remains very small.

Thousands of economists toil in the IFIs. Many come from developing countries (though almost all were trained in North America and Europe). Despite their various origins and economists' notoriously divergent views on both theoretical and policy matters, the views expressed in their public writings

---

*Gerry Helleiner O.C., Ph.D., L.L.D., F.R.S.C., an eminent development economist, well known for his scholarly writings on trade, finance and development, was awarded the Order of Canada in October, 2002. Professor Helleiner has worked in Canada and Africa to promote the interests of developing countries and shared his expertise with numerous international bodies and governments. Professor Helleiner served as Research Coordinator for the G-24 in the period 1991–99.

and in these institutions' public documents remain quite narrowly constrained within current (albeit sometimes changing) IFI 'orthodoxies'. Why are the views of Fund and Bank staff at any one time apparently so uniform and so 'orthodox'? Certainly, some self-selection in the decision to seek employment in the IMF and the well-known tightness of its internal institutional discipline keep IMF economists from ever stepping very far out of line. At the World Bank, there is greater room for internal debate and freedom of expression, both inside and externally; but even in the Bank there are decided limits to the degree of unorthodoxy that can be tolerated, at least in public expression, by its principal owners and managers. Not only are IFI analyses and policy approaches typically constrained by the 'group-think' atmosphere within which they are formulated, but these analyses and approaches also enjoy ready access, through well-oiled channels of communication, to the most influential media and to key decision-makers, both at the global level and within individual countries. When critical views of the IFIs do circulate in the global financial community, they usually originate in the academic, governmental and business sectors of the industrial countries; and most frequently build on conservative principles rather than, except in the case of recent NGO assaults, on the more appropriate pre-eminence of developmental objectives. Critiques emanating from the developing countries, most often registered at the level of individual borrowing countries, rarely percolate up to the global financial community or media, and if they do, they are assigned very little relative weight by key IFI or other decisionmakers. Yet developing (and transition) economies are where the IFIs now do the bulk of their work and carry the greatest influence.

Clearly, the developing world has not been well served by such heavy concentration of influence and power (and economists) in the two Bretton Woods financial institutions, the management of which remains, despite rising clamour for reform, firmly under the control of the major industrial powers. In the spheres in which the IFIs operate, alternative professional analyses and, in particular, professional voices from the developing countries have not as yet been sufficiently heard or, if heard, sufficiently seriously considered. Both at the global and at national levels, professional 'second opinions' (indeed, third and fourth ones) in the spheres of developing country finance and overall development policies and, in particular, professional voices from the developing countries, must be encouraged and provided with more opportunities not only to be heard but also to be listened to. Agencies of the United Nations, e.g., UNCTAD, UNDP, UNICEF – more responsive to developing countries' concerns – have played significant roles in this respect over the past 30 years or so. In recent years, some NGOs, primarily based in the North, have also been able to provide some alternative, and increasingly professional, voices. It has often been difficult for these divergent analyses, however, to penetrate the intellectual and administrative 'silos' of the IFIs.

Since the creation of the Intergovernmental Group of 24 on International Monetary Affairs (the G-24) in 1971, its research programme has endeavoured to provide such 'second opinions' and to make them available within the very heart of the Fund and Bank – to developing country Executive Directors, Governors and their staffs. Originally, G-24 research papers were made available only to developing country governments. For many years, however, they have been made more widely available, albeit often with something of a time lag. The analyses of these papers, which have always met professional standards, have often been far ahead of the orthodox mainstream, as for instance in their consideration of such issues as the need for growth-oriented adjustment programmes, local ownership of programmes, debt relief, and the potential downside of capital account liberalisation. But they have not circulated widely, or received much attention in the policy corridors or the financial media of the developed world. When the G-24 celebrated the 50th anniversary of the Bretton Woods institutions with a conference (and a volume) offering developing country perspectives on the international monetary and financial system, containing many analyses that were well 'ahead of the curve' (and ahead, in time, of more mainstream celebrations), it was virtually ignored. Now, happily, the G-24 research papers are widely available on the Internet and in real time (at www.g24.org). Greater mainstream attention, one hopes, will have to be paid to them. The current volume is indicative of the range of significant second opinions, reflective of developing countries' concerns, that emanate from the G-24's continuing research programme. Its papers should stimulate debates that, on the occasion of the IFIs' 60th anniversary, deserve to take place both within these institutions and throughout the broader community of financial and development analysts and policymakers.

1

INTRODUCTION

As the Bretton Woods institutions turn 60, they face a number of challenges, some new resulting from the changes that have occurred in the world economy, others the outcome of their approaches to the problems of stabilization and development, and of their own governance structure. This book presents a selection of research papers prepared for the G-24 that address these challenges and suggest the need for reform. The introductory essay presents a critical overview of the functioning of the IMF and the international monetary system and underscores a number of shortcomings that could be remedied through changes in its governance.

The next two papers examine IMF conditionality. Babb and Buira consider its evolution, the factors behind the redefinition of the Fund's mission, and the dramatic increase in the number of conditions attached to Fund-supported programmes. They note that pressures from major countries gave rise to the expansion of the Fund's mandate, and that the resulting increase in conditionality causes high rates of programme non-compliance. This in turn calls for discretionary decisions and leads to an absence of rules. The consequent increase in the discretionary decisions by staff and management makes it easier for the Fund's most powerful members to influence the appraisal of particular countries' performance in cases where, as is usual in programmes with a large number of conditions, the country in question does not meet a number of them.

Professor Kapur considers the reasons for conditionality, and reviews the evolution of IMF conditionality as a mechanism for managing creditor risks and obtaining concessions from borrowers. He notes the relative ineffectiveness of the conditionality of the international financial institutions, reviews the intrinsic limitations of conditionalities, seen as incomplete contracts, and explores the reasons for their extension to development assistance. Given the shortcomings of this mechanism, Kapur explores options for its reform and concludes that there is greater potential for seeking alternatives outside the framework of conditionalities, arguing that risk-sharing development contracts offer considerable long-term potential.

The next three papers develop proposals for the prevention of financial crisis. Since 1997, at the instance of the USA,[1] the Fund has promoted the total elimination of restrictions on capital movements, in the belief that this would improve resource allocation and promote growth. To this effect, the Fund undertook a campaign to amend the Articles of Agreement[2] in order to gain jurisdiction over the capital account. There was no empirical research to support this policy. Six years later, after the Asian crisis, the Fund's own Research Department found that 'If financial integration has a positive effect on growth, there is as yet no clear and robust empirical proof that the effect is quantitatively significant.' Moreover, while 'international financial integration should, in principle, also help countries to reduce macroeconomic volatility … the process of capital account liberalization appears to have been accompanied in some cases by increased vulnerability to crises.'[3]

The papers by Randall Dodd and Shari Spiegel, and by Ilene Grabel present complementary approaches to the prevention of financial crises. In an innovative paper Dodd and Spiegel develop a proposal for lending in local currency by international financial institutions, that would allow countries to deal with the 'original sin' – the exchange risks of borrowing in foreign currency, as well as with interest rate changes in creditor countries. They show that this can be done through a portfolio of emerging-market local-currency debt that employs the risk-management technique of diversification to generate a rate of return-to-risk that competes favourably with other major capital market security indices.

Professor Grabel develops an ingenious system of 'trip wires and speed bumps' for managing financial risks and reducing the potential for financial crises. This allows the authorities of a borrowing country to adopt appropriate preventive measures, such as adjusting financial regulation, in order to reduce the risks arising from volatility of capital movements. Laura dos Reis then proposes an original fiscal group insurance scheme that allows a group of countries with a common currency to deal with temporary, exogenous shocks without the disruptions arising from abandoning their currency peg, thereby enhancing the viability of the currency union. The author shows that fiscal insurance produces welfare gains for all members of the group, in terms of lower volatility at a significantly lower cost than resorting to self-insurance. The proposal, which is tested for members of the Eastern Caribbean Monetary Union, can be applied in other regions.

In 'Who Pays for the World Bank?' Aziz Ali Mohammed addresses a number of fundamental questions related to the operations and policies of the World Bank Group. He argues that the burden-sharing issue is best viewed through the lens of the allocation of net income. He notes that over time, as the share of retained earnings has risen while the share of paid-in capital has declined, the distribution of voting power no longer reflects the borrowing members' contributions to Bank equity. Secondly, he shows that the major shareholders have used their political control to allocate significant portions of IBRD earnings to serve their own interests at the expense of the borrowing members, and points out that the continuation of a stagnant loan portfolio in nominal terms – declining in real terms – is likely to constrain the Bank's income from lending operations and make it increasingly dependent on its operations as a financial trader and arbitrageur rather than as a development finance institution. In order to regain its role as a provider of development finance, the Bank should revise the pricing and conditions attached to its loans and lift the restraints applied to the purposes for which it lends.

In looking at the private provision of basic services, Tim Kessler considers certain risks associated with market-based approaches to the distribution of such essential services as water and electricity. In particular, Kessler notes the risk that private service providers will not deliver essential services to low-income people who cannot afford commercial rates. The paper raises important questions, such as: to what extent will the private provision improve existing levels of quality, reliability and access? He notes that the standards for investment in other sectors are insufficient for essential services, and that too often the success of the private provision model is based on a social bargain that excludes the poor. When attracting private investment requires financial incentives, guarantees or subsidies, how do the costs of these compare with that of reforming the provision of services by the public sector? What is the balance of payments impact of the outflow of profits and dividends to investors?

In 'The Role of Government Policy in Building Industrial Competitiveness' Sanjay Lall addresses the question of whether there is a role for industrial policy in developing countries. To this purpose he reviews the experiences of a small number of countries that have been successful in achieving industrial development and of many more who have not. Professor Lall evaluates the approach that considers that the best strategy for all countries and all cases is to liberalize and integrate into the world economy, allowing the free play of market forces to promote the best allocation of resources, in line with their comparative advantage. He also considers the structuralist argument that puts less faith in markets and more in the ability of governments to intervene effectively, in order to overcome market failures in building the capabilities required for industrial development. The paper describes the strategies followed by the Asian Tigers to build industrial competitiveness, pointing out the pervasiveness of selective intervention and the strategic differences between them. He draws lessons for other developing countries, concluding with the need to reconsider the rules of the game that constrain the exercise of industrial policy, and calls for international assistance in designing and implementing appropriate policies.

Official donors and private investors focus increasingly on the quality of developing country policies and seek to appraise the role of institutions in development. Barry Herman examines the World Bank's Country Policy and Institutional Assessments, a set of governance indicators developed at the Bank, and the World Economic Forum's Global Competitive Indices. He points out the weaknesses of such indicators, which are often used as a means of allocating scarce official assistance, their subjectivity and inability to discriminate among countries or over time. More robust elements in these indicators might complement descriptive narrative analysis of countries and stimulate public discussion on institutional and policy development.

Exports of three or fewer commodities account for over half of the export revenues of 50 low-income countries and of a number of middle-income countries. Whereas the problems of commodity markets and commodity producers figured prominently in discussions of international finance and development for several decades, today these issues receive little attention in the BWIs, which no longer provide support for dealing with this issue. Irfan ul Haque provides a case study of the impact of market liberalization on the cocoa price and on producers of cocoa. The paper shows that improvements in productive efficiency cannot be attributed to market liberalization, which was one of its goals, and it finds no evidence that liberalization contributed to increase the farmers' share of the export price. The focus on liberalization, however, diverted attention from the main problems faced by cocoa producers – i.e. market volatility, low prices, and the producers' low share in the value chain. The paper goes on to suggest how an alliance of producers could address these problems.

The Editor

Notes

1   See the series of four articles in the *New York Times* by Nicholas D. Kristoff and David E. Sanger 'Global Contagion: A Narrative', published 15–18 February 1999. The article published on 16 February is particularly relevant.
2   Article VI, Section 3 allows members to 'exercise such controls as are necessary to regulate international capital movements'.
3   See page 5 of Prasad, E., K. Rogoff, S. Wei and M. Kose, 'Effects of Financial Globalization on Developing Countries: Some Empirical Evidence', IMF, 2003.

2

THE *IMF* AT SIXTY:
AN UNFULFILLED POTENTIAL?

Ariel Buira

Abstract:

The governing structure of the Bretton Woods institutions – that is, the International Monetary Fund and the World Bank – was determined sixty years ago. In 1944, a few industrial countries accounted for the bulk of world output, trade, and capital flows. This is no longer the case. Developing countries and economies in transition, the more dynamic elements of the world economy, account today for the same volume of output as the Group of Seven (G-7) countries in terms of purchasing power parity, and for 84 per cent of the world's population. They can no longer be dismissed as minor partners in the global economy.

The lack of adequate representation of the developing countries and emerging market economies in the governance of the global economy and the declining commitment of major countries to a multilateral rules-based system of international monetary cooperation has resulted in short-sighted, and politically motivated, decisions by major shareholders which undermine the efficacy of the IMF and World Bank and have adverse consequences for world economic growth and stability. Indeed, the non-representative character of the governance of these institutions increasingly threatens the integrity of the international monetary system, as countries in Asia and elsewhere move away from the IMF and take distance from the World Bank, leaving the institutions to deal mainly with low-income countries.

This paper provides an overview of the international monetary system, briefly discussing six key problems[1] in which the concentration of power in a few countries and the limited participation of developing countries in the discussion of systemic issues leads to poor results:

- the correction of global imbalances;
- the role of the IMF in the adjustment process;
- combating deflation through countercyclical policies;
- financial crises prevention and resolution;
- the management of international liquidity; and
- responding to commodity shocks.

Overcoming these problems requires a renewed commitment of industrial countries to a rules-based multilateral system and the participation of developing countries in decision-making in a manner commensurate with their economic importance.

Global Economic Transformation

Over the past half-century the world economy has become increasingly interdependent. Developments in the economy of one country or region are transmitted to other countries through increased international trade and financial flows. This integration differs from the patterns of a century ago in that a growing number of multinational firms have spread their production processes over a number of countries. As a result intra-firm trade and intra-industry trade have risen sharply as a proportion of international trade. Developments in information technology have erased distances and the integration of capital markets has proceeded in a way that essentially creates a single international capital market. The volume of financial transactions has grown exponentially and now greatly exceeds the volume of flows in trade of goods and services. The close integration of the global economy presents new and difficult economic challenges.

The transformation of the global economy has not been matched by a parallel evolution of the mechanisms and institutions of global economic governance. The current government structure of the World Bank and the IMF is the result of a political settlement at the Bretton Woods Conference in 1944. But given the changes that have taken place in the world economy since then, the current structure is not representative of the size and importance of the economies of the member countries in terms of GDP, population, share of world trade, reserves, or of their ability to contribute financial resources. Moreover, because the 'basic votes' of members – intended to ensure that countries with small quotas would have a sense of participation in the affairs of the Fund – have not increased while quota-based votes have increased 37-fold, the resulting erosion in basic votes has diminished the influence of developing countries in the IMF. This inadequate representation of their membership undermines the effectiveness, credibility, and legitimacy of the two institutions.

The most important changes that have taken place in the world economy since 1944 include:

- The United States, which was the only large capital-surplus country up to the 1960s and thus the main provider of resources for the IMF and World Bank, has become a net debtor as its external liabilities have exceeded its assets abroad. Today it is the world's largest debtor country.
- The European Common Market, now become the European Union, has introduced a common currency, but the voting shares of countries in the euro-area have not been adjusted to reflect this change. According to the 1944 Bretton Woods formulas, international trade is a major factor in determining IMF quotas. This resulted in the small open economies of EU members having a 74 per cent greater voting power than the United States, despite having a smaller combined GDP. However, trade within a single currency area is akin to trade within a domestic market and cannot give rise to balance of payments imbalances. When the calculated quotas of the euro-zone countries are adjusted to exclude intra-euro-zone trade, their voting power declines by 40 per cent.[2]
- The G-7 industrial countries, which have effective control of the IMF and World Bank, represent less than 14 per cent of the world population and yet accounted for about 44 per cent of world output in 2002. The developing countries and economies in transition account for more than 84 per cent of the world's population and the same proportion of world output as the developed countries measured in terms of purchasing power parity.[3] For this reason, decisions made by the G-7 countries without the participation of the major developing countries are often perceived by the developing world as having limited legitimacy.
- From 1950 to 2002, the developing countries have registered higher GDP growth rates than the industrial countries and have increased their share of world GDP, measured in terms of purchasing power parity (PPP), from 30 per cent to 39 per cent – and to 44.2 per cent if economies in transition are included (World Bank 2003). The developing countries have increased their share of world exports from 26 per cent in 1972 to 37 per cent in 2002 (IMF 2003). Particularly noteworthy is the rise of output of the Asian economies excluding Japan: Asian output accounted for only 9 per cent of world output in 1950 but today represents some 23 per cent of global GDP.
- Reserves held by non oil developing countries have risen from SDR 33.3 billion in 1972 to SDR 1,315 billion at the end of June 2004[4] – a figure that greatly exceeds the reserves of the industrial countries, which stood at

SDR 749.5 billion on the same date. The reserves of Asian countries recorded an extraordinary increase, from SDR 7.9 billion in 1972 to SDR 947 billion at the end of June 2004.

The growing breach between world economic and financial realities and the governance structure of the Bretton Woods institutions argues for reform to enhance the legitimacy and restore the effectiveness of these institutions. A more representative and inclusive governance structure of the World Bank and the IMF – achieved by enhancing the participation of developing countries in resolving the major monetary and financial problems confronting the world economy – would improve global economic performance. It would secure a more effective international adjustment process and achieve a more efficient use of global resources, higher rates of growth and employment, and greater macroeconomic stability. It would also increase support for primary-producer countries subject to commodity shocks and contribute to the elimination of world poverty.

Correcting Global Payments Imbalances

Under the Bretton Woods system, structural balance of payments disequilibria were to be corrected by exchange-rate movements. Surveillance over exchange rates and exchange-rate arrangements was to be one of the IMF's key functions. Following the breakdown of the Bretton Woods system of fixed parities, the world moved to a 'non-system' in 1973, in which each country was free to pursue the exchange-rate regime of its choice. Surveillance is the means by which the international community aims to ensure that all countries – and particularly those that exert a major influence on the world economy – pursue policies conducive to sustained growth with stability, avoiding policies that might lead them into problems or have detrimental effects on other countries. Through its surveillance function, the IMF, acting on behalf of the international community, assesses a country's economic circumstances by reviewing its monetary, fiscal, exchange-rate, trade and other policies, and offers advice on appropriate policy measures for the country to adopt. Article IV consultations – periodic reviews of member country economies, as prescribed in Article IV of the IMF's Articles of Agreement, or charter – are the IMF's main instrument of surveillance.

More recently, the effectiveness of the IMF is being questioned with regard to its ability to:

• persuade the United States to undertake measures to reduce its large fiscal and balance of payments deficits;

- persuade the EU countries to tackle labour market and other economic rigidities that have constrained their GDP growth rates;
- suggest measures to correct the growing payments imbalances between China and other Asian countries (which peg their currencies to the US dollar) and the United States, and to reduce the impact of the dollar's depreciation on the euro-area and others, which operate a floating currency regime; and
- to prevent financial crises in emerging market economies. The fact that these have recurred on average at the rate of more than one a year over the last decade suggests that the IMF has not been successful in either preserving the confidence of financial markets or inducing countries to make timely changes in their policies.

The effectiveness of IMF surveillance has been weakened by asymmetries in power and compliance and by the fact that surveillance has not been applied in an evenhanded way. Paul Volcker, former Chairman of the Federal Reserve System, has observed, 'When the Fund consults with a poor and weak country, the country gets in line. When the Fund consults with a big and strong country, the Fund gets in line' (Volcker and Gyoten 1992).

The growing asymmetries in IMF surveillance are reflected in the way it is conducted today.[6] Bilateral surveillance (that is, oversight of the policies of individual member countries) is the most direct one and has been exercised primarily over developing countries, particularly those that have adjustment programmes supported by IMF resources and that require IMF support in seeking debt relief. In addition, in the 1990s the recurrence of financial crises that ended often in major currency depreciations encouraged the reorientation of surveillance to prevent financial crisis. It was then that the international community gradually accepted the IMF public dissemination of country surveillance appraisals. As a result, countries with open capital accounts have become more sensitive to changes in 'market sentiment'. Thus, with the publication of its bilateral surveillance conclusions, IMF increasingly influences countries wishing to gain or maintain market access. 'Multilateral' and 'regional' surveillance are more analytical than operational in character, since they have not had a direct impact on member country domestic policies, especially in larger countries or groups of countries with greater influence on the global economy.

Through its 'multilateral' surveillance, the IMF highlights for example, the risks for the international economy of growing US fiscal and payments imbalances in the 2002 and 2003 editions of the IMF's *World Economic Outlook*. In a recent report (IMF 2004) on the increasing world dependence on US growth, the IMF highlights how the US current account deficit and growing indebtedness, if not corrected, could have a negative impact not only on the United States but also on the global economy (ibid. p. 9):

> Although the dollar's adjustment could occur gradually over an extended period, the possible global risks of a disorderly exchange rate adjustment, especially to financial markets, cannot be ignored. Episodes of rapid dollar adjustments failed to inflict significant damage in the past, but with US net external debt at record levels, an abrupt weakening of investor sentiments vis-à-vis the dollar could possibly lead to adverse consequences both domestically and abroad. ...

The response of the US Treasury to the IMF report made it clear that the Treasury did not consider any correction in its domestic policy necessary.[7] Since the persistence of large imbalances in the reserve currency country pose significant risks to the system, the US response weakens the authority of the IMF and its ability to exert influence over other countries. As a result, the world moves away from a rules-based multilateral system to a power-based system in which the size of countries largely determines whether they abide by the rules and large powers feel free to go their own way, based on their short-term interests.

In recent years, growing US fiscal[8] and current account deficits have been financed mostly through sales of government paper to Asian central banks whose currencies have been pegged to the US dollar and which have been accumulating high levels of international reserves. As a result, the burden of dollar depreciation has fallen on countries with floating exchange-rate regimes, which have seen their currencies appreciate substantially (that is, the euro-area and a few industrial countries and developing countries, mostly in Latin America). In contrast, countries with managed and fixed exchange-rate regimes – such as most Asian countries – have been able to keep their currencies undervalued, generating growing demands for protection from European and US labour unions and some industrial sectors that are losing jobs and market share. In order to ease global adjustments, the IMF has recommended not only a correction of US imbalances but also greater exchange-rate flexibility among Asian countries.

In a recent paper, Dooley, Folkerts-Landau and Garber (2003) explain why countries in Asia may not be willing to follow IMF recommendations. They suggest that in order to maintain export-led development strategies, Asian countries – and China in particular – fix the exchange rate to the dollar to ensure a competitive edge. As a result, they have run large current and capital account surpluses and are accumulating international reserves at a fast pace. In the case of China, this policy has been sustained without giving rise as yet to overheating and inflation. Dooley *et al.* believe that the primary motivation in China's export-led strategy has been the absorption into the modern sector of a substantial proportion of the labour force from an underemployed farming sector.

Global payments imbalances can no longer be corrected by exchange-rate adjustments among the major industrial countries with flexible exchange rates. Dooley *et al.* consider that with the collapse of communism, the decline in protectionism and the ensuing integration of Asia and Latin America into the world economy, these countries must now be seen as a new driving force (Dooley *et al.* 2003):

> Now the Asian periphery has reached a similar weight [as Europe-Japan in the 1950s]: the dynamics of the international monetary system, reserve accumulation, net capital flows, and exchange rate movements, are driven by the development of these periphery countries. The emerging markets can no longer be treated as small countries, weightless with respect to the center.

Asian countries have maintained very high rates of export growth and large trade surpluses, which have attracted private investment flows. As a result they have run large trade and capital account surpluses and, since their currencies have not been allowed to appreciate, they have accumulated high levels of international reserves that have been heavily invested in US Treasury paper. They have thus financed the US twin deficits and have made them sustainable, for the time being.

A number of problems and risks are apparent in this situation:

- The depreciation of the US dollar, vis-à-vis non-Asian currencies appears insufficient to address the US external deficit; it also poses an impediment to the recovery of the European Union and other countries with floating currencies.
- The dollar depreciation has precipitated rising trade tensions and calls for protection in Europe and other countries whose currencies have appreciated in dollar terms.
- The rapid growth of Asian exports of textiles and other goods has also given rise to calls for protection in the United States. Thus, pressures for protectionism are rising in response to unemployment and political pressures in countries whose industries are unable to compete with Asian goods.
- There is the risk that at some point the demand for dollars as a reserve currency will decline as monetary authorities and private investors choose to hold reserve assets that maintain their value – possibly euros, yen or gold.

This decline in dollar demand could take place among the industrial, oil-exporting and developing countries that cannot justify capital losses arising from a declining dollar, with gains from higher rates of growth, employment and industrialization.

- A disorderly depreciation of the dollar would lead to a sharp rise in dollar interest rates that would put a sharp brake on the US recovery and on the growth of Asian and other countries dependent on the US market.
- Although flexible exchange rates contribute to the international adjustment process, the volatility of exchange rates among major currencies discourages trade, and, above all, investment flows that require a medium-term planning horizon, since hedging instruments are unavailable for longer maturities. The euro/dollar rate has fluctuated by more than 50 per cent (from 0.82 to 1.36) since the euro's introduction.

The correction of global imbalances through agreements among a few industrial countries (such as the Plaza Accord of September 1985) is no longer feasible and solutions arrived at without the full participation of developing countries are unlikely to work.[9] The resolution of major global imbalances requires the involvement of both deficit and surplus countries, in this case of key developing countries, in accordance with basic rules and in a manner commensurate with their economic importance. To overcome the current risks and correct major imbalances in an orderly manner, the IMF's governance must become more representative and its surveillance more effective and even-handed. The impact of surveillance could be enhanced through discussions with the participation of all relevant developing country players. A larger, more representative IMF could be firmer and more effective in dealing with global imbalances than an IMF run by a few industrial countries. However, the stability of the international system requires a degree of self-discipline by major countries. A lack of discipline by the reserve currency country was at the root of the demise of the par value system.

The Role of IMF Financing in the Adjustment Process

To be effective and in keeping with its mandate, the Fund has to provide member countries with technical advice and financial support to address their payments imbalances in a manner that sustains the level of economic activity to the greatest possible extent. Recall that the purposes of the Fund include:

(ii) To facilitate the expansion and balanced growth of international trade, and to contribute thereby to the promotion and maintenance of high levels of employment and real income and to the development of the productive resources of all members as primary objectives of economic policy

and

(v) To give confidence to members by making the general resources of the Fund temporarily available to them under adequate safeguards, thus providing them with the opportunity to correct maladjustments in their balance of payments without resorting to measures destructive of national or international prosperity[10]

Thus, in addressing each case, the Fund should seek to strike a fine balance between adjustment and financing. When a country has unlimited financing, like the United States at present, it may well be able to resist adjustment, however necessary, for long period of time. At the other extreme, developing countries undertaking adjustment without adequate financial support face increased economic costs as well as political resistance to necessary measures, which are likely to be politically unpopular. Consequently, the risk of programme failure rises. The Fund must therefore be able to encourage the adoption of adjustment programmes in a timely manner by offering a level of financing that limits the undesirable short-term effects of an adjustment programme. A Fund without adequate financial resources will not be able to perform its role. It cannot provide incentives to adjustment, nor can it be seen as a friend to which countries can turn for support and guidance in uncertain times. Rather, it will be seen as a harsh taskmaster to be held at bay, particularly when the countries know that the IMF is dominated by a few industrial country creditors who are blocking a badly needed expansion in its financial resources.

The IMF was established to combat a market failure – that is, the collapse of domestic demand – and to counter attempts by countries seeking to emerge from balance of payments problems through the adoption of protectionist measures, competitive depreciations, and other 'beggar-thy-neighbour policies'. Circumstances led to the industrial countries' drawing on its resources during the early decades of the IMF. However, with industrial country members no longer needing to use IMF resources, these were allowed to decline as a proportion of world trade. IMF resources thus fell sharply, from 58 per cent in 1944 to 15 per cent in 1965, and further to an estimated 4 per cent at present.

As a result of the relative decline in the IMF's resources, the balance between adjustment and financing in Fund-supported programmes necessarily shifted toward less financing and more severe adjustment. As resources declined, a hardening of conditionality ensued – defined as the number of measures and policies that a country has to adopt to gain access to Fund resources – and as a result, the rate of success of Fund-supported programmes declined. In fact, the rate of non-compliance with Fund programmes, measured by the IMF's failure to fully disburse approved drawings, rose sharply, reaching 86 per cent in the late 1990s.

Because the increase in conditionality made the IMF dysfunctional, a revision of its guidelines on conditionality became necessary and was undertaken. However, in any discussion about revised conditionality, a key question arises. Should conditionality be determined by the availability of resources, even as these decline sharply over time, or, in keeping with the IMF's purposes as an institution for international monetary cooperation, should its resources increase in step with the liberalization and growth of world trade and the integration and volatility of international capital markets?

This is not to ignore that in some cases, large, systemically or strategically important countries (such as Mexico, Brazil, Russia, Korea and Turkey) have received Fund financial support far in excess of their quota access limits. But the circumstances under which these countries obtained such exceptional support are neither transparent nor predictable. It is not available to all IMF members and at times comes with questionable conditions imposed by countries that contribute to the financial rescue package (Feldstein 1998).

IMF officials often make references to the 'catalytic role of the IMF' as a means of justifying its limited financing to members. The rationale here is that the IMF provides a 'seal of approval' to a borrower country's policies that then spurs other sources of financing. Since there is no reference in the IMF's Articles to the Fund's playing a 'catalytic' role, this is a strange argument to put forward. Nevertheless, the argument that a member's access to the Fund's more conditional resources is sufficient to induce additional private capital flows could be acceptable if, in fact, it assured that market financing was actually forthcoming. Unfortunately, this is not the case. While the Fund did play a role in inducing capital flows to Latin America during the debt crisis of the 1980s, empirical studies of the catalytic effect conclude that there is little evidence to support its existence in the 1990s (Bird and Rowlands 1997). A similar conclusion is reached by a recent IMF study:[11]

> All in all catalytic effects do not appear to be strong, which is the more remarkable since most empirical studies fail to control for actual policy change, thereby biasing results in favour of catalytic official finance.

Unfortunately, as is often the case when the conclusion of negotiations on an IMF-supported programme does not bring forth market financing in sufficient amounts, the programme may be underfinanced to allow an adjustment that is not sharply contractionary. Indeed, as Bird and Rowlands point out:

> Structural adjustment is unlikely to succeed if starved of finance. The Fund appears to have assumed – perhaps on the basis of partial and, in the event, unrepresentative evidence – that finance would come from elsewhere, catalysed by its own involvement. In practice the catalytic effect was largely unforthcoming and IMF programmes showed an increasing tendency to break down. Significantly, the likelihood of breakdown appears to vary inversely with the amount of finance provided by the Fund.

Bird and Rowlands add that 'The premise of a universally positive catalytic effect will lead to inappropriate conditionality and will have adverse consequences for its effectiveness.'

Since a large majority of Fund members support an increase in its resources, why have quotas not kept pace with members' needs, in a manner related to the expansion of international trade and capital movements? Under the Articles, an increase in quotas requires an 85 per cent majority of votes, under the weighted voting system. The question thus becomes, what countries have blocked the increase in Fund resources? Industrial countries no longer resort to IMF support and are no longer willing to contribute to its resources, as shown by the Fund's failure to agree to adopt a quota increase since January 1998. However, in order to preserve their political control of the IMF these countries do not wish to see their share of quotas and voting power reduced. Thus, the industrial countries have been reluctant to allow more dynamic emerging-market countries and other developing countries to increase their quotas and voting power. A different structure of governance and decision-making – one not constrained by an 85 per cent majority requirement for quota changes,[12] which gives a veto on quota increases to a single country, the United States – would have led to a very different outcome.

Table 1. Quota distribution by groups of countries

Total quotas (in millions SDR)	212,666	100.00%
24 industrial countries	130,567	62.04%
Developing and transition economies	82,009	37.96%

Source: IMF, *International Financial Statistics*, April 2003.

The unrepresentative character of current quotas is shown by the following table[13] comparing the GDPs and quotas of selected countries. These quotas limit Fund resources and, save in a few exceptional cases, member countries' access to financing of adjustment programmes.

Table 2. Are quotas representative?

	GDP 2002 (SDR)	GDP ppp 2002 (share in world)	Actual quota (SDR)
Small European Countries			
Austria	158,691	0.50	1,872
Belgium	188,939	0.58	4,605
Denmark	133,111	0.34	1,643
Finland	101,613	0.28	1,264
Norway	147,245	0.36	1,672
Sweden	186,183	0.50	2,396
Switzerland	206,772	0.43	3,459
Total	**1,122,555**	**2.99**	**16,910**
Asian Countries			
China*	1,080,192	12.07	4,687
India	384,907	5.59	4,158
Indonesia	133,539	1.44	2,079
Korea	422,396	1.67	1,634
Pakistan	49,441	0.63	1,034
Philippines	60,203	0.69	880
Thailand	97,675	0.88	1,082
Total	**2,228,353**	**23.00**	**15,554**
Latin American Countries			
Argentina	78,922	0.82	2,117
Brazil	349,415	2.80	3,036
Chile	52,027	0.31	856
Colombia	62,243	0.57	774
Mexico	500,804	1.87	2,586
Peru	43,581	0.28	638
Venezuela	73,695	0.27	2,659
Total	**1,160,687**	**6.92**	**12,667**

*Following the accession of Hong Kong SAR, China's GDP was $1,237 billion converted at market exchange rates; its share of world GDP rose to 12.67 per cent, and its quota was increased to SDR 6,369 billion.
Source: IMF and World Bank, World Economic Indicators 2003.

Combating Deflation and Low Levels of Aggregate Demand

A number of major industrial countries (United States, France, Germany, Japan, United Kingdom and others) have actively pursued their own countercyclical policies and an economic recovery appears to be on the way in these countries. Most developing and emerging market countries have been unable to adopt countercyclical policies, and the Fund has been ineffective in combating the recession prevailing in the international economy in recent years.

The IMF's recent passivity in the face of international recession can be contrasted with the active counter-cyclical stance it adopted in the mid-1970s. With the world economy emerging from three years (1969 to 1971) of a combination of recession and high rates of inflation, the sharp increase in oil prices in 1973 and 1974, which deepened the recession and fueled inflation, posed for the Fund what was perhaps its greatest challenge to that date.

In addition, the ensuing massive transfer of wealth from oil-importing to oil-exporting countries posed another grave problem for the international economy. It was recognized at an early stage that very poor countries would not be able to borrow from private markets to pay for the increased cost of oil imports and there were doubts as to the ability of the banks to recycle the large sums involved.

The IMF's then Managing Director, Johannes Witteveen, a man of vision and an outstanding economist, understood the challenge and proposed the establishment of an Oil Facility in the Fund in 1974 for one year to recycle the surplus from oil-exporting to oil-importing countries. This recycling would help poor countries finance their external imbalances without further restricting economic activity and gain time for devising energy-saving and other adjustment strategies to reduce their external imbalances. The proposal, initially resisted by the United States, was put into place with the strong support of European and developing countries – several of which intended to resort to it – as well as that of oil-exporting developing countries who would finance it.

The sole requirement for access to the Oil Facility by oil-importing countries was the existence of a balance of payments need. There was virtually no other conditionality than for potential users to refrain from imposing or intensifying restrictions on trade and payments without the approval of the Fund. As in other cases of the use of resources, the country was expected to consult with the Fund in order to give it the opportunity to determine whether the member's policies were conducive to its balance of payments adjustment. The 1974 Oil Facility proved useful and was followed by another such facility in 1975.

Under the 1975 Oil Facility the IMF applied stricter conditionality. Members making drawings were to describe to the Fund their policies to achieve medium-term solutions to their balance of payments problems and have the Fund assess the adequacy of these policies. The borrowing countries were also required to describe the measures they had adopted or proposed to adopt to conserve oil and/or develop alternative energy sources in order to reduce their oil imports.

With this strong response, the Fund helped recycle the surpluses from oil-exporting to oil-importing countries, many of which would not have had access to capital markets. This allowed borrowing countries to avoid deflating aggregate demand unduly, which would have compounded the problems besetting the international economy.

In recent years (1998–2002), the developed economies have been able to adopt countercyclical monetary and fiscal policies to deal with recession and the risk of deflation. However, the failure of countries in large surplus to expand or appreciate, coupled with the absence of a mechanism to recycle their surpluses, has obliged emerging market economies and low-income countries to adopt contractionary measures to protect their balance of payments and avoid crises of confidence. Given their importance in international output and trade, this has contributed to a protracted recession in a large group of developing countries and to a deeper contraction of world trade.

At a time of net negative capital flows to the developing and emerging market countries, why didn't the IMF recycle the large (Asian) surpluses, as it had done in the 1970s, to sustain higher levels of economic activity, investment, and structural reform in developing and emerging-market countries that could not pursue anti-cyclical policies on their own? Perhaps the main reason is that back in the 1970s, several industrial countries wishing to resort to IMF financial support under the Oil Facility supported its role in recycling. More recently, however, the developed countries' lack of interest in helping the developing countries by recycling surpluses and their inadequate representation in Fund decision-making has doomed these countries' ability to pursue anti-cyclical policies.

Financial Crisis Prevention and Resolution

Borrowing from international financial markets has become more dangerous for developing countries. While capital account volatility has been increasing since the late 1980s, the volatility became more pronounced in the late 1990s. This is illustrated in Chart 1.

The Mexican crisis of 1995, which was followed by those of Thailand, Indonesia, and Korea in 1997, and later by those of Russia, Brazil, Venezuela, Turkey, Argentina and Uruguay, are best-known cases in which the loss of market confidence gave rise to massive capital outflows. Although the problems posed by the volatility of financial flows are well recognized, even countries with sound economic policies that experience short-term pressures on their balance of payments or exchange rate do not have a ready source of emergency financing.

In 2002, the international community agreed that 'Measures that mitigate the impact of excessive volatility of short-term capital should be considered.'[14] Moreover, the IMF's own research studies have concluded that capital account liberalization does not promote growth and that market-friendly capital

Chart 1. Latin America: private flows, external current account and real exchange rates

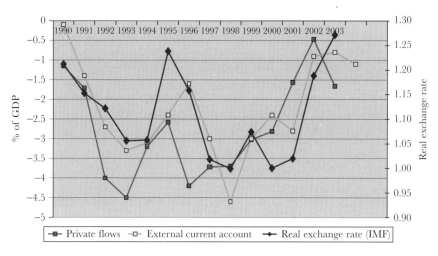

Source: IMF

controls have been effective in crisis prevention in a number of countries (Prasad *et al.* 2003). Nevertheless, the use of capital controls is still discouraged and there has been little by way of Fund reaction to US efforts to proscribe the use of controls in the context of bilateral trade agreements (i.e. with Chile and Singapore).

The IMF's Contingent Credit Line (CCL) was established in 1999 as a precautionary facility, intended to give emerging market countries with sound policies and good fundamentals the assurance of IMF financial support to discourage, and protect countries from, speculative attacks. But it was designed in such a restrictive manner that, despite the high costs of self-insurance and the many difficulties developing countries have encountered, none has resorted to it in its five years of existence. Although most IMF Executive Directors, particularly those representing potential users, supported the continuation of a reformed CCL that would fulfil the original purpose of discouraging speculative attacks, they did not constitute a qualified majority of the vote (85 per cent) required to keep it in existence. So on 30 November 2003 the IMF terminated the CCL. The official statement said that many emerging market countries had reduced their vulnerability to speculative attacks by building up their reserves and adopting flexible exchange rates and other reforms.

The risks posed by capital market volatility remain high and new financial crises may recur as financial flows return to emerging markets. Following the cancellation of the CCL, Tim Geithner, currently President of the Federal

Reserve Bank of New York but previously Director of the IMF's Policy Development and Review Department, criticized the Fund's economic review and lending policies towards emerging market nations and advocated an alternative policy aimed at crisis prevention. He said that the Fund's policy of monitoring the performance of countries and then lending after a crisis develops is not well suited for emerging markets. Geithner argued that these nations would be better served through an insurance fund that could be 'mobilized quickly and on a sufficiently large scale'. A similar criticism had been made several years earlier by this writer (Buira 1999).

If market confidence cannot be maintained, and no financing is available, there are essentially two ways other than default of dealing with a crisis arising from the volatility of capital:

- the temporary suspension of debt service payments – that is, through the declaration of a 'standstill' leading to a debt restructuring; and
- the use of capital controls to prevent excessive inflows of short-term money.

To deal with this issue the IMF proposed a Sovereign Debt Restructuring Mechanism (SDRM).[15] This mechanism called for a 'standstill' on payments that would give countries in crisis legal protection against creditor suits for a limited time to allow them to negotiate the restructuring of their debt in an orderly manner. After initially supporting the SDRM, the United Sates withdrew support for the standstill proviso that was essential to make it operational, thus effectively eliminating it. Most emerging market countries had reservations regarding the SDRM. They feared that their support would be read by markets as indicating their intent to restructure their debt, which would raise the cost of borrowing and hinder their access to markets instead of providing an insurance mechanism, as it was meant to do.

Recent months have seen a sharp fall in the spreads for emerging market borrowers – that is, a sharp rise in their asset prices that responds to the US Federal Reserve's policy of monetary easing, which has pumped large amounts of liquidity into financial markets. As a result, after years of withdrawal, investors in search of higher yields are again attracted to emerging markets.

If the global economy continues to gain strength and US interest rates remain low, emerging market countries will be able to borrow with little risk. However, when these conditions change, as they will in time, the risk of financial crisis will again loom large – particularly for those countries whose borrowing is sustained by market momentum rather than by their fundamentals. In that event, the recurrence of financial crisis will simply be a matter of time. Because the emerging market countries that are potentially at risk did not command sufficient votes in the IMF to retain a modified and effective precautionary facility, and controls on short-term capital flows are discouraged, the international financial system has no mechanism to prevent the devastation wrought by financial crises in emerging market countries. The alternative, including collective action clauses[16] in bond contracts, takes a long time to take effect (only after existing contracts expire).

The Creation and Management of International Liquidity

International liquidity creation depends on the expansion of capital markets, and in today's US-dollar-based payments system, on the balance of payments deficit of the United States.

Concern that global liquidity would not expand in step with the needs of the world economy, thereby creating a deflationary bias, led the international community in 1969 – under the IMF's auspices – to create the SDR as a supplemental reserve asset. The subsequent rapid expansion of financial markets, starting in the late 1970s, led the major countries to believe that it was not necessary to expand liquidity through the allocation of additional SDRs, since creditworthy countries could resort to market borrowing. This was always a dubious argument, however, since, at best, access to financial markets was limited to the industrial countries and to only a few emerging market economies.

As noted earlier, access to financial markets for a number of emerging market countries is improving currently, the result of increased market confidence and the low demand for credit in industrial countries. Nonetheless, more than 140 developing countries still have virtually no access to international financial markets. For these countries the accumulation of international reserves (or export of capital) comes at the cost of reduced imports of consumer and investment goods, which means reduced consumption and investment.

Arguing that an SDR allocation would give rise to inflationary pressures, several major industrial countries have opposed even a modest allocation. As a result, no SDRs have been allocated since 1981. This concern about the inflationary consequences of an SDR allocation, however, was not valid amid the recessionary global economic circumstances that prevailed in 2000 to 2002 – in fact, an SDR allocation would have contributed to economic recovery.

Should the international community leave the creation of liquidity entirely to market forces? No Central Bank does. Nor was this the view of the founding fathers of the IMF. Nor is it the view implicit in Article XVIII of the IMF's Articles of Agreement, which empowers the IMF to create international liquidity to promote its purposes. In fact, a system that depends on the reserve currency country running huge deficits is inherently unstable, as discussed above. (See the section on correcting global payments imbalances.)

The international community accordingly gave itself the capability to counter contractionary forces by expanding international liquidity through the IMF's capacity to create international reserve assets through SDR allocations. In this way, the international community could help developing countries build up their international reserves.

In times of recession or of an incipient international economic recovery, an allocation of some SDR 70–100 billion would not only not pose no inflationary risks and be helpful to recipients of SDRs, it would also further the recovery of the world economy. But approval of an SDR allocation requires an 85 per cent majority of the IMF's Executive Board. This means that it is subject to a US veto (the US share of the vote is now 17.2 per cent) and may also be blocked by other industrial countries, such as the EU countries. In the past, however, several European countries with a strong interest in Africa have been favourable to an SDR allocation, and one can assume that, in the current circumstances, they would again be supportive. If this were the case, could a coalition of developing and EU countries be able to persuade the United States to overcome its reluctance to put the matter to Congress?

Under the Articles of Agreement, SDRs are to be allocated to Fund members in proportion to their quotas; consequently, over 60 per cent of any SDR allocation would accrue to the industrial countries. However, short of an amendment of the Articles, industrial country recipients could donate the SDRs they are allocated to developing countries at no cost to them, on the condition that the recipients pay the low interest rate due on the SDRs they receive.

Since the SDR interest rate is equal to the average of the short-term interest rates on a basket of currencies that compose the SDR, it is market-determined. And although it would be below the developing country cost of borrowing, it would not impose any resource transfers or costs on other countries. The liquidity provided as a result of SDR transfers would be on terms much more attractive to recipients than market borrowing, even for those few countries that have access to financial markets, as these countries normally pay a significant spread or premium over interest rates on developed country Treasury papers. Moreover, the cost of holding international reserves for recipients of SDRs would decline, since the return they can obtain on the investment of their international reserves would be similar to the SDR interest rate (with no quasi-fiscal costs). For those countries unable to borrow in financial markets, the benefits of an SDR allocation – plus transfers of SDRs originally allocated to industrial countries – are unquestionably larger.

Responding to Exogenous Shocks

More than 50 developing countries depend on three or fewer commodities for most of their merchandise export earnings. The poorest countries with less diversified economies are the ones most affected by commodity shocks. Whether they are the result of price shocks or those arising from droughts, floods or other natural disasters, countries with incomes per capita of $1,000 or less are those that suffer the most. Developing countries with incomes of $2,000 per capita or higher are less seriously affected in relative terms. This is because the greater diversification of their productive structure and exports make them better equipped to absorb commodity shocks.

The cost of the average commodity shock has been estimated at some 2.5 per cent of GDP (IMF 2003) and by another estimate at 7 per cent of GDP, and if indirect costs are considered, as much as 20 per cent of GDP (Collier 2002). On average, shocks occur every two to three years, and there is reason to believe that natural disasters, particularly those related to extreme weather, are on the rise.

The IMF has a facility to assist countries to cope with commodity price shocks and excess costs of cereal imports. The Compensatory Financing Facility (CFF), whose purpose is to provide countries with finance for export revenue shortfalls relative to a medium-term trend, was introduced in 1963 and liberalized in 1966 and again in 1975.[17] In principle, access to the CFF is virtually unconditional since exogenous shocks – whether attributable to a fall in the price of commodity exports to such natural disasters as a drought – are not the result of government policies. Countries suffering from a shortfall in

Chart 2. Indices of non-fuel primary commodity prices (1995 = 100)

1/ Indices comprise 60 price series for 44 non-fuel primary commodities. Weights are based on the 1995–97 average of world export earnings.

2/ Deflated by the export unit value index for manufactures of industrial countries

Source: IMF

their export earnings as a result of such shocks could therefore have access to the CFF, provided the IMF determines that there is assurance of repayment and that the commodity problem is not the result of a secular deterioration in the borrower country's terms of trade. Drawings on Fund resources, however, are limited to 45 per cent of a member's quota for commodity shocks and 45 per cent for excess import costs in any 12-month period, with a cumulative total of no more than 55 per cent of quota. Given the small size of IMF quotas relative to world trade and the high dependency of some countries on exports of a single commodity, this limit is by itself very restrictive.

The CFF was much used by low-income countries in the 1970s and early 1980s. However, Executive Directors of industrial countries, wishing to limit the facility's use, argued that drawings on the CFF allowed countries to postpone adjustments. As a result, the Executive Board imposed heavy conditionality on the use of the CFF in 1983.[18] The conditionality introduced has greatly discouraged use of the CFF, and for practical purposes the facility has virtually ceased to exist. A more representative governance structure at the IMF would be more sympathetic to the needs of countries affected by exogenous shocks.

Conclusion

Sixty years after the establishment of the Bretton Wood Institutions, a review of the major monetary and financial problems confronting the world economy, suggests that existing arrangements fall short of providing an enabling environment for financial stability and economic growth, particularly for the developing countries. The IMF is not able to influence the adjustment of global imbalances, sustain market confidence to reduce volatility of capital flows and prevent costly financial crises,[19] does not support countercyclical policies in emerging markets, nor compensatory financing to assist primary producers deal with exogenous shocks, and has little influence over the creation and distribution of international liquidity.

Since the issues are well understood and the potential for improvement exists, the deficiencies of current arrangements must be seen as a political problem resulting from a non-representative governance structure that fails to address the concerns of most of the world and a lack of commitment on the part of major industrial countries to abide by the rules of a multilateral system.

In the BWIs, decision-making power is vested in a small group of industrial countries which, having dealt with their own monetary problems and financial imbalances over the last quarter-century outside the Bretton Woods system, are no longer committed to it as a multilateral cooperative enterprise.

As a result, decisions on major policy issues are rarely rules-based. More often than not, they are opportunistic and short-sighted, giving inadequate consideration to the interests of developing countries, which account for an increasing share of the world economy and for the great majority of the world's population. The major shareholders of the IMF (and World Bank) have shown themselves unwilling to yield power in order to allow a representative governance structure to emerge – one in which developing countries would play a role commensurate with the size of their economies, assume greater responsibilities, and increase their financial contributions to the international financial institutions. Consequently, the major shareholders have witnessed a decline in the resources, prestige, and authority of the institutions.

Industrial countries no longer pay much heed to the Bretton Woods institutions. Following the United States and Europe, emerging countries in Asia have also largely walked away. Other emerging economies may also be expected to reduce their reliance on the Fund and Bank over time. Thus, the multilateral system for international monetary and financial cooperation painfully constructed at Bretton Woods is becoming irrelevant to all except the very low-income countries, mainly in Africa, where their record is mixed.

Since the multilateral institutions for monetary cooperation and development have a great potential to contribute to the better functioning of the international economy by helping achieve more stable growth and a fuller utilization of economic resources, the decline in their resources, role and legitimacy are much to be regretted and call out for a bold and immediate solution.

Appendix 1

Adjustment of European Quotas for Intra-euro-zone Trade

1 The 15-member European Union (EU), with a smaller GDP than the United States has 74 per cent greater voting power and is currently represented by nine Executive Directors in the IMF Executive Board (see Table 1).[20] In addition, the EU has 56 per cent greater voting power than the United States in the World Bank and eight Executive Directors on the World Bank Executive Board. The over-representation of EU members comes at the expense of other members. The excessive weight of the EU group of countries is partly attributable to the treatment of intra-EU trade in goods and services in the formula used for quota calculations.

Table 1. Quotas and voting power of selected industrial countries in 2000

	GNI[1] (PPP)	GNI[1] (billion $) at market exchange rates	IMF Quotas (million SDR)	Votes	As a proportion of total
Austria	214	204.5	1,872.3	18,973	
Belgium	282	251.6	4,605.2	46,302	
Denmark	145	172.2	1,642.8	16,678	
Finland	127	130.1	1,263.8	12,888	
France	1,438	1,438.3	10,738.5	107,635	
Germany	2,047	2,063.7	13,008.2	130,332	
Greece	178	126.3	823.0	8,480	
Ireland	97	86.0	838.4	8,634	
Italy	1,354	1,163.2	7,055.5	70,805	
Luxembourg	20	19.2	279.1	3,041	
Netherlands	412	397.5	5,162.4	51,874	
Portugal	170	111.3	867.4	8,924	
Spain	760	595.3	3,048.9	30,739	
Sweden	213	240.7	2,395.5	24,205	
United Kingdom	1,407	1,459.5	10,738.5	107,635	
European Union (15 above)[26]	8,864	8,459.4	64,339.5	647,145	29.79
United States	9,601	9,601.5	37,149.3	371,743	17.10
Japan	3,436	4,519.1	13,312.8	133,378	6.14
Memorandum items					
World	44,459	31,315	212,666	2,172,350	100
All industrial countries	24,793	24,994	130,567	1,347,885	62.04
Developing countries and transition economies	19,666	6,321	82,099	824,465	37.96

[1] In 2000.

Source: World Bank, *World Development Indicators* 2002. IMF *Survey Supplement* 2002.

2 A number of European countries formed a monetary union in 1999. This fact gives rise to a new situation calling for a revision of the calculated quota of the 12 euro-zone members. Since trade within a single currency area cannot give rise to balance of payments problems among its members, it is more akin to domestic trade than to international trade. Thus, trade between California and New York, or between Delhi and Calcutta is not regarded as international trade. Similarly, since trade between euro-zone members cannot give rise to balance of payments problems, it cannot be regarded as international trade for the purposes of the IMF quota calculations.[21]

3 Recognizing the impact of intra-EU trade on quota calculations, an IMF staff report, *External Review of the Quota Formulas*, EBAP/00/52 Sup. 1, 1

May 2000, shows what would be the hypothetical adjustments needed to exclude intra-trade in goods. The reason given for exclusion is that intra-trade is seen as entrepôt trade[22] in a free trade area. The report explains that if this adjustment were made 'EU-15 countries' share would be reduced by 9.2 percentage points (from about 37.1 per cent to about 28.0 per cent). The largest declines in percentage points are for Germany, the Netherlands, France and Belgium.' Note that IMF staff estimates do not include trade in services in these results because of lack of data.

4 Following the methodology of the 12th Quota Review, we have made a new estimate of the calculated quota for the euro-zone countries adjusted for intra-trade in goods and services.[23] The new estimate refers only to the 12 euro-zone members.[24] When this adjustment is made, the share in calculated quotas for the 12 euro-zone countries declines, from 28.3 per cent to 16.9 per cent, a fall of 11.4 percentage points (or 40.3 per cent) (see Table 2). In addition, if one reduces the actual quotas by the same proportion as the decline

Table 2. Current and adjusted calculated quotas for the EU-12 countries

	Current Calculated Quota (in millions SDR)	Share (per cent)	Adjusted calculated quota (excluding intra-trade in good and services) (in millions SDR)	Share (per cent)
EU-12	**234,860**	**28.3**	**120,926**	**16.9**
Austria	9,572	1.2	4,177	0.5
Belgium	17,709	2.1	6,649	0.8
Finland	4,955	0.6	2,592	0.3
France	38,652	4.7	21,593	2.6
Germany	62,854	7.6	34,872	4.2
Greece	3,087	0.4	2,031	0.2
Ireland	9,323	1.1	6,494	0.8
Italy	30,286	3.6	17,407	2.1
Luxembourg	12,903	1.6	3,580	0.4
Netherlands	24,562	3.0	10,990	1.3
Portugal	4,433	0.5	1,844	0.2
Spain	16,522	2.0	8,697	1.0
United States	**138,060**	**16.6**	**138,060**	**19.3**
Japan	**70,364**	**8.5**	**70,364**	**9.8**
Other countries	**387,271**	**46.6**	**387,271**	**54.0**
Total	**830,556**	**100.0**	**716,622**	**100.0**

Note: OECD data on trade in services was converted from US dollars to SDR at the average rate for each year taken from IMF's *International Financial Statistics*.

in calculated quotas, the quota shares of the EU-12 countries would fall from 23.3 per cent to 14.1 per cent, a reduction of 9.2 percentage points.[25]

5 Since total quotas shares add up to 100 per cent, the decline in the shares of a group of countries results in an increase in the relative share of IMF quotas of all other countries. With a single exchange rate and a single monetary policy, there is a lot to be said for members of the euro-zone having a single representative on the IMF's Executive Board. This would allow room for an increase in representation by the developing countries. Note that the recently signed Constitutional Treaty of the European Union, which is yet to be ratified, calls for the development of a single external policy for the European Union and a single EU representative in international organizations.

Notes

1 For reasons of space, other important problems – such as the issue of negative net transfers of resources to developing countries – and the problems of the low-income countries will not be discussed.

2 See Appendix on the adjustment of European Union quotas for intra-euro-zone trade. If basic votes were restored to the original level of 11.3 per cent and quotas were solely based on GDP in terms of PPP, developing countries would account for 49 per cent and industrial countries for 51 per cent of total voting power.

3 Developing countries alone account for over 39 per cent of world GDP (IMF 2003).

4 On 2 July 2004, 1 SDR was equivalent to 1.466 US dollars.

5 Article I Section V.

6 Three levels of surveillance are described in the 2003 IMF *Annual Report*: 1) country or 'bilateral' surveillance, 2) global or 'multilateral' surveillance, and 3) 'regional' surveillance – for example, of the European Union. Each type of surveillance addresses a different economic arrangement and thus has an impact in surveillance enforcement and effectiveness.

7 The Treasury considered the report was a 'breathless hyperbole', adding 'The paper seems to conclude that if everything goes wrong in the US economy, and no one does anything about it, that would be bad. That's not exactly groundbreaking analysis.' Treasury press release, as quoted by IMF, *Morning Press*, 9 January 2004.

8 Of nearly 6 per cent of GDP, including the social security surplus that is currently being spent.

9 Witness such initiatives as the Contingency Credit Line, the Sovereign Debt Restructuring Mechanism and the Highly Indebted Poor Countries Initiative to reduce debt levels.

10 IMF, Articles of Agreement, Article I, Section II.

11 See page 42 of Carlo Cotarelli and Curzio Giannini, 'Bedfellows, Hostages, or Perfect Strangers? Global Capital Markets and the Catalytic Effect of IMF Crisis Lending', IMF Working Paper 02/193 , November 2002.

12 See Article III, section 2(c).

13 Moreover, by converting GDPs at market exchange rates rather that in PPP terms, current quota formulas significantly underestimate the size of developing countries' economies. This is because in these countries there is a significant difference in the level

of prices and wages in the traditional sector vis-à-vis the modern export sector, which PPP estimates correct.

14 Paragraph 25 of the Monterrey Consensus, the outcome of the UN Conference on Financing for Development, Monterrey, Mexico, 18–22 March 2002.

15 The proposal was made by Anne Krueger, Deputy Managing Director of the IMF in 2001.

16 Collective action clauses allow bondholders to modify repayment terms of bonds, subject to the approval of a qualified majority of bondholders.

17 Executive Board Decision No. 4912 (75/207), 24 December 1975.

18 Executive Board Decision No. 7528 (83/140), 14 September 1983.

19 As the catalytic role played by its seal of approval has lost credibility.

20 In addition, the ECB representative participates in Article IV consultations on surveillance of the euro-area members and on the use of resources of the 13 accession countries, as well as in discussions on the world economic outlook, the international capital market reports, the role of the euro in the international monetary system, and world economic and market developments.

21 See also IMF staff report *The European Monetary Union and the IMF – Main Legal Issues Relating to Rights and Obligations of EMU Members in the Fund*, SM/98/131, dated 8 June 1998. R. Sroits, *The European Central Bank, Institutional Aspects*, page 443, argues that once the European Community has a common currency, a single monetary and exchange rate policy, a single monetary authority (the European Central Bank), and a single external position in terms of payments and other financial transactions to and from third countries, it will have assumed the characteristics of a 'country' for the purposes of Article II, Section 2 of the Fund's Articles of Agreement. Sroits further refers to various expressions of the opinion that euro-area member states may no longer qualify for membership in the IMF since they no longer possess the necessary characteristic of monetary sovereignty in the international order. J. V. Louis, in 'Governing the EMU or Governing the EU', in the Symposium on Monetary Policy and Globalization of the Markets, June 2002, observes that the European Monetary Union is 'irreversible and irrevocable', and that 'the Member States are not able any more to comply individually with the commitments inherent to their participation in the IMF.'

22 IMF adjustments of entrepôt trade is in order to consider only the domestic value added in international transactions.

23 The OECD dataset for services and the same formula and methodology used in the 12th Quota Review.

24 The 12 countries considered in the calculation are: Austria, Belgium, Finland, France, Germany, Greece, Ireland, Italy, Luxembourg, the Netherlands, Portugal and Spain.

25 Actual quotas as of 14 July 2003.

26 Since trade among countries with a common currency cannot lead to balance of payments problems, when the use of a single currency is taken into account, the calculated quotas of the 12 euro-zone countries fall by 40 per cent.

References

Buira, Ariel, 1999, 'An Alternative Approach to Financial Crises', Essays in International Finance No. 212, International Finance Section, Dept. of Economics, Princeton University, Princeton, NJ.

Chang, Ha-Joon, 2002, *Kicking Away the Ladder*, London: Anthem Press.

Collier, Paul, 2002, *Primary Commodity Dependence and Africa's Future*, World Bank, April, p. 3.

Cotarelli, Carlo and Curzio Giannini, 2002, 'Bedfellows, Hostages or Perfect Strangers? Global Capital Markets and the Catalytic Effect of IMF Crisis Lending', IMF Working Paper 02/193, Washington, D.C.

Dooley, M., Folkerts-Landau, D. and Garber, P., 2003, 'An Essay on the Reveived Bretton Woods System', NBER Working Paper Series, Working Paper 9971, September.

Fedelino, Annalis and Alina Kudina, 2003, 'Fiscal Sustainability in African HIPC Countries: A Policy Dilemma?', IMF, WP/03/187.

Gunter, Bernhard, 2003, 'Achieving Long-Term Debt Sustainability in Heavily Indebted Poor Countries', in Ariel Buira (ed.), *Challeges to the World Bank and the IMF*.

Helleiner, Gerry, 2002, 'Marginalization and/or Participation: Africa in Today's Global Economy', Lecture to CASS Conference, published in *Canadian Journal of African Studies*, Vol. 36, No. 3.

International Financial Statistics Yearbook 2003, IMF.

IMF, 2004, Occasional Paper 227, January.

IMF, 2003, 'Fund Assistance for Countries Facing Exogenous Shocks', prepared by PDR, August.

IMF, 2003, World Economic Outlook Database, IMF.

Prasad, E., K. Rogoff, S. Wei and M. Kose, 2003, 'Effects of Financial Globalization on Developing Countries: Some Empirical Evidence', Harvard University/IMF.

Volcker, P. and T. Gyoten, 1992, *Changing Fortunes*, New York: Random House.

World Bank, 2003, *World Development Indicators*, World Bank, Washington, D.C.

3

CONDITIONALITY AND ITS ALTERNATIVES

Devesh Kapur

Abstract:

The paper examines the rationale and growth of conditionalities in international development assistance (in particular the IMF) despite their limited effectiveness and options for reform. It first examines risk management mechanisms that mitigate creditor risk and align the behaviour of the agent (borrower) more closely to the objectives of the principal (creditor). It then discusses why international creditors, in particular international financial institutions (the IMF and the multilateral development banks), have been prone to deploying conditionalities, and why these grew despite continued uncertainty about theirs effectiveness. It examines the evidence on the effectiveness of conditionalities, with a focus on the intrinsic limitations inherent in conditionalities when viewed as incomplete contracts. Given the limitations of this mechanism, the paper subsequently examines options to reform conditionalities – their scale, scope and mechanics. The paper argues that while there is certainly room on this front, there is much greater potential in seeking alternatives outside of conditionalities, in particular the development of risk-sharing development contracts.

Introduction

In the post-Bretton Woods era conditionality emerged at the heart of international development assistance. Its expansion in scale and scope poses a puzzle: why did an international institutional mechanism designed to change the behaviour of governments expand, despite continued uncertainty about the effectiveness of this mechanism? Recently, there has been a shift in the regime. While loan conditionalities of International Financial Institutions (IFIs) have been scaled back modestly, conditionalities as a meta-regime are becoming more, not less, important in development assistance.

Several explanations have been advanced to understand these trends. Some would challenge the assertion that conditionality 'does not work'. It could be argued that the yardsticks used to measure success fail to specify viable counterfactuals and that the expansion of conditionality simply reflects the development community's 'learning' from prior experience. Another set of explanations focuses on the preferences and interests of principal actors (the USA, the G-7, the industrialized countries, the International Financial Institutions or the financial markets). Yet a third set focuses on the perceived 'agency' of the IFIs arising from their financial characteristics: an expansion of conditionalities reflects not just the preferences and interests of the institutions' principals but of the agents themselves – the management and staff of these institutions. Finally (and more recently), a fourth set of explanations for expansion has focused on the demand side, arguing that borrowers often want more conditionality.

The criticisms of conditionality are that they are intrusive and politically costly for the borrower. More troubling, however, is the evidence that conditionality is simply not a very effective instrument of development. While these criticisms are undoubtedly valid, it must be acknowledged that taxpayers of donor countries require some reassurance that their financial contributions to another country are achieving their objectives. It is one thing to say that there are many problems with conditionalities. But in an imperfect world are they the second (or even third) best option, or are there indeed more viable options that would address the concerns of the major stakeholders?

The structure of the paper is as follows. It first discusses conditionality as a mechanism for risk management that attempts to align the behaviour of the borrower more closely to the objectives of the creditor. It then discusses why international creditors – in particular, international financial institutions – are more prone to deploying conditionalities. The paper subsequently traces the evolution of conditionality in the International Monetary Fund (IMF), and the factors underlying the growth of conditionalities. The next section examines the evidence on the effectiveness of conditionalities, with a focus on the intrinsic limitations inherent in conditionalities when viewed as incomplete contracts. Given its limitations, the paper examines options to reform conditionalities. The paper argues that although there is certainly room on this front, there is much greater potential in seeking alternatives outside of conditionalities. Subsequently, it examines some of these alternatives and argues that risk-sharing development contracts offer the greatest long-term potential.

Why Conditionality?

Any agreement between a creditor and a borrower must deal with the risk of non-compliance that can arise by accident or opportunism. Different mechanisms have evolved for managing that risk. One consists of *ex ante* demands on borrowers. By requiring prior concessions, a party to the agreement may improve the expected outcome by enough to compensate for the risk of a breach. A second approach is to structure the agreement in ways that reduces the level of risk, often through stipulations that restrict a party's freedom of action.

Private lenders use a variety of mechanisms to limit default risk. Lenders can monitor borrowers and employ increasingly sophisticated methods of screening risks. Credit risk is reflected in loan agreements in the form of higher risk premiums, greater collateral, and shorter maturities to reduce the risk of non-compliance. Where these mechanisms are not feasible, such as microfinance banks, creditors use social groups to screen and monitor loans, rely on refinancing threats in the absence of alternative sources of credit to provide repayment incentives, and create collateral substitutes such as self-insurance by borrowers against default. The potential for repeated loans, together with the credible threat to cut off future lending when terms and conditions are not met, can be exploited to help ensure borrower compliance.

While international and domestic creditors face similar conceptual problems, there are important differences as well. Problems of asymmetric information, but especially contract enforcement, are much greater in the case of the former. For sovereign lending these problems are amplified since while the agent (the sovereign) has a clear legal entity as a sovereign state, in reality it is a much more complex and amorphous entity. In practice this means that the incentives facing the borrowing country depend on which actor is the dominant interest group in the borrowing state. To address these problems creditors can threaten to seize the overseas assets of debtor countries, refuse to engage in trade with debtors, or convince debtors that in the case of default the negative effects on reputation would adversely affect both future access and risk premiums.

Prior to Bretton Woods, international lending had been characterized by boom-bust cycles, in which private banks used both conditionalities and the potential coercive power of their national governments to ensure debtor country compliance. The US government, for instance, played a behind-the-scenes role in supervising conditioned loans by private bankers in the 1920s and 1930s (Rosenberg 1999). Nonetheless, the limitations of these strategies – reflected in the widespread sovereign bond defaults in the 1930s – exposed the inherent market failures in international credit markets and were a primary reason behind Bretton Woods.

The Evolution of IMF Conditionality[1]

Debates at Bretton Woods on how the IMF and World Bank should manage risk were divisive, especially with regard to the former. Discussions on the World Bank were muted because by focusing on specific projects, especially infrastructure projects with clear cash flows, rather than on programmes with national policy ramifications, its lending was less contentious. Since World Bank lending was principally for projects, conditionality took the form of covenants in investment loans. Although the Bank did not formally make loans with the specific purpose of policy reform – with attached conditions – it did condition *the decision to lend* and *the volume of lending* to a country to a conducive policy environment (Kapur, Lewis and Webb 1997). This changed after 1979 when the Bank launched 'structural adjustment lending', a quick disbursing loan with the specific objective of promoting policy reforms. That turn took the Bank closer to the Fund, exposing it to much greater external criticism. As we shall note later in the case of the Fund, the Bank's record with promoting policy reform though structural adjustment lending has been modest. A recent World Bank evaluation aptly sums up the record: 'Conditionality is effective in linking Bank support to reform only in certain circumstances' (World Bank 2004).

The real debutante at the Bretton Woods ball was the IMF and the heated debates on conditionality centred on this institution, the USA insisting that the Fund review applications and establish mandatory conditions for borrowing nations. The US position was based both on its own experience and the fact that as the key net creditor to the IMF, its resources were most at risk. Keynes led the counter-charge, arguing that conditionality was an attempt by the USA to establish 'grandmotherly influence and control' over central banks and, in turn, to influence economic and social policy in borrowing countries. Although Keynes' position prevailed initially, the final text of the IMF agreement incorporated sufficient leeway under the provision that, as a financial institution, the IMF had to be satisfied that a borrower could meet its repayment obligations to the Fund.[2] The US view ultimately prevailed in the practice of the IMF after 1948 and especially after 1952, when the practice of 'stand-by' agreements commenced (Horsefield 1969; Gold 1981; Dell 1981).

The design of the Fund as a financial cooperative for member countries, most of which were poor, lacking the wherewithal to provide meaningful collateral, ruled out the basic mechanism used by the private sector to secure lending. Conditionality emerged as a substitute for collateral assuring that the borrowing country would be able to rectify its macroeconomic and structural imbalances and repay the loan. Over time other International Financial Institutions developed market-mimicking mechanisms. The World Bank created the International Finance Corporation (IFC) to lend to the private sector and other multilateral development banks developed similar institutional mechanisms. But the Fund has been limited by its purpose and mandate to lend to sovereign governments. For a long time the only market mechanism that it could use to address non-compliance risks was to structure its programmes over a short duration and (more recently) charge a higher risk premium in exceptional cases.[3] Nonetheless, as public institutions and financial cooperatives, there are limits to their use of these mechanisms, and their reliance on conditionalities was a way to overcome borrower incentives that might lead to commitment failure.

The original rationale of conditionality as a mechanism to protect the financial integrity of the Fund was gradually supplemented and even supplanted by additional justifications. In its first quarter-century, the Fund's lending horizon was short and loan conditions were narrow in scope, limited to exchange rates, budgets, and monetary targets aimed at demand management. Thus while its programmes would typically insist on tax increases and expenditure cuts, the precise composition of these fiscal changes was left to governments. Supply-side policies and conditions were confined to gradual trade and investment liberalization.

However, as documented in Figure 1, conditionalities in IMF programmes increased significantly after the mid-1970s and again after 1990. The data exclude prior actions and cover only the number of performance criteria in the stand-by arrangement.[4] The 1999 data is from Kapur (2000) and is based on a sample of 25 countries with programmes initiated in 1999 and which did not have programmes in the preceding three years. However, in the case of East Asia, the programmes initiated in the aftermath of the Asian Crisis in 1997 were examined rather the 1999 programmes, since the latter were a continuation of the former.

While the numbers may not be strictly comparable, the upward trend until the end of the 1990s was quite evident. Through 1982, less than 5 per cent of the Fund's upper tranche arrangements contained eleven or more performance criteria (Figure 1). By the end of the 1980s, more than two-thirds of such arrangements had eleven or more criteria, and by 1999, 92 per cent of programmes sampled had eleven or more criteria. The average number of criteria rose from about six in the 1970s to ten in the 1980s (Boughton 2001) and 23 (26 if prior actions are included) in 1999.

However, these figures severely underestimate the sharp increase in the quantum of conditionalities in this period. The increase is much larger for the latter period if conditionality is more loosely defined than performance criteria (see Table 1). For one, some of the most important conditions are not reflected in these numbers at all. They are found in 'side letters' and

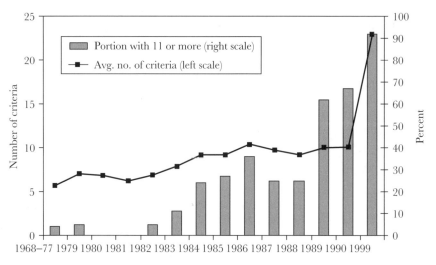

Source: Boughton (2000), Kapur (2000)

Figure 1. IMF performance criteria 1968–1999

Table 1. The burden of conditionality 1999

Region	Total conditionalities	
	Strictly defined	*Loosely defined*
Africa	23	114
Asia	17	84
East Europe and Central Asia	36	93
Latin America	33	78

Source: Kapur (2000).

'pre-programme' conditions, the latter being particularly important in the case of the poorest aid-dependent countries, for which they are put in place at meetings of Consultative Groups (aid coordination groups comprising bilateral and multilateral agencies).

Second, conditionalities extend well beyond traditional quantitative 'performance criteria', including 'prior actions', 'quantitative targets', and 'structural benchmarks'. IMF programme documents have numerous 'programme objectives' and lay out 'strategies and measures' to meet them. Sticking to the narrowest definition would be seriously misleading. However, including them creates other problems of interpretation. In most cases they are dated covenants, but unlike quantitative performance criteria, they are not explicitly tranche release conditions. A government may promise to do *a*, *b*, *c*, but the consequences of not doing so are unclear. Crucially, there are many subjective elements in interpreting what constitutes conditionality. By the narrowest criteria, the controversial Indonesia programme of 1997 had 18 conditionalities. A closer look reveals figures ranging from 80 (Feldstein 1998) to 81 (Kapur 2000) to 140 (Goldstein 2000).

The change in the scale of IMF conditionality has been parallelled by its burgeoning scope over time. The early focus was on variables that would help restore equilibrium in a country's balance of payments. These were principally monetary and fiscal aggregates and the exchange rate. This narrow focus was gradually expanded in the 1980s and 1990s. In recent years the Fund's performance criteria encompasses actions covering a wide range of structural policy areas including 'financial-sector reform, privatization and public enterprise reform, social safety nets, tax and expenditure policies (including so-called "unproductive" public expenditures, like high military spending), labour market policies, pricing and marketing/distribution policies, agricultural policies, environmental policies, and policies to combat corruption and money-laundering' (Goldstein 2000). The conditionalities in the World Bank have also expanded significantly into new areas including environmental, social and governance-related policies (Kapur 2000).

Factors Underlying the Growth of Conditionalities

A range of factors has been advanced to explain the growth of conditionalities in the IMF. During the 1970s the IMF's response to the gradual erosion of quotas relative to world trade was to allow countries to borrow greater percentages of their quotas. Cumulative access limits increased from 100 to 600 per cent of quotas over the 1970s. Although they declined somewhat (to 300 per cent), the perceived loosening of credit discipline was counterbalanced by increasing conditions.[5] This link was even more evident in the 1990s, when the size of Fund programmes (relative to quotas) sharply increased.

The move to stiffer conditionality was facilitated by the disappearance of industrialized countries as IMF borrowers. The last substantial programme of the industrialized countries took place in 1976. This altered the risk perceptions of the major shareholders. The creation of the General Agreement to Borrow (GAB) and swap facilities through the Bank of International Settlements (BIS) drastically reduced the liquidity function of the IMF for its major shareholders. The demise of the fixed exchange rate regime in the early 1970s, the rise of the G-7 as an institutional mechanism to informally manage exchange rates between key currencies in the 1970s and 1980s, and the move to market-determined exchange rates since the late 1980s meant that the IMF was of little direct relevance to the richer countries.

The de facto exit of industrialized countries had three important consequences. First, the Fund's loan portfolio became concentrated in higher-risk countries, and the the prudent course for any financial institution facing the prospect of a riskier portfolio would be to either cut back new lending or be tougher on any new loans. A worsening global environment and its position as lender of last resort meant that the first option was not viable. A second consequence was that the exit of industrialized countries as potential borrowers reduced their exposure to political risk inherent in a substantial expansion of conditionality. Concomitant with the decline of political risk, the *ex ante* financial risk arising from the contingent liabilities inherent in financing IMF programmes that drew on currencies of 'structural creditors' also declined as financial risk was transferred from major shareholders to borrowers (by increasing loan charges) and to the institution's own balance sheets (in the form of higher reserves). And third, the IMF's own *raison d'être* shifted – from an institution whose primary goal was to facilitate international monetary cooperation, to one that facilitated economic globalization, especially in diffusing the norms and institutions of capitalism. All these factors affected the scale and content of the Fund's conditionality.

Conditionality in IMF operations took on a particularly central role after the introduction of new guidelines that loosened restrictions on the IMF as a lender of last resort in 1979. The Fund had been heavily criticized (especially in Latin America) for being fixated on the demand for money and the fiscal balance while ignoring structural supply-side issues. Mainstream criticism questioned whether the Fund's focus on overall targets ignored the political reality that governments would cut politically expedient expenditures, leaving the politically powerful unscathed. As a result, critics claimed, the burden of expenditure cuts fell on much-needed social expenditures and reductions in government investments.

In the 1980s, in response to criticisms that its programmes focused unduly on demand-based stabilization measures, the IMF began to pay greater attention to structural measures that would enhance supply-side responses. This spawned a new set of corresponding lending conditions (de Vries 1985). Traditional fiscal and monetary conditions became increasingly fine-tuned as sub-criteria (both ceilings and floors) proliferated. Additionally, new macro conditions with their own sub-criteria were set on debt ceilings and arrears. The rapid proliferation of economic growth theories bursting with causal variables also played a role in rationalizing and legitimizing the expansion of conditionality. This is particularly worthy of note given the strong networks between the IMF and the economics research community.[6] After the collapse of the Soviet Union, the reticence on politically sensitive issues waned, triggering new governance-related conditionalities.

The sharply enhanced role of private capital markets provided new rationale for conditionality. It was argued that conditionality gave confidence not only to the IMF but to private creditors as well by serving as a screening device that enabled creditors to discriminate between debtor countries willing to subject themselves to IMF discipline and others which were not (Marchesi and Thomas 1999). The signalling effects of conditionalities on financial markets were highlighted to stress the growing *demand* for conditionalities by borrowers. According to this rationale, countries needed to establish a reputation for predictable behaviour, and conditionality was the mechanism to bridge the 'predictability gap'. Instead of being imposed, the new argument went, conditionality was a sought-after instrument that governments used to signal the predictability of their policies to private creditors. This new rationale for conditionality was interpreted as implying a substantially 'far-reaching extension in the scope of needed reforms', especially a 'strengthening of the whole civil administration, in particular the judiciary' (Dhonte 1997). A more direct role of financial markets in shaping IMF conditionality put the onus on the Fund's growing role as a debt collector for financial markets. Gould (2003) offers an argument on these lines, based on the supplementary financing that is a necessary part of all IMF loans (since IMF loans are only a fraction of the total resources involved in a Fund programme). As the source of supplementary financing has changed – from states to multilateral institutions to private banks to equity flows – so have Fund activities and conditionalities in response to the shifting preferences of the financiers of its programmes.

A different rationale puts the onus on the domestic politics of borrowing country governments. Vreeland, borrowing from Schelling ('a government may, by tying its hands domestically, gain bargaining leverage abroad') and Gourevitch ('the second image reversed' – that is, the international sources of domestic politics), argues that borrowing governments seek conditionality to tie their hands internationally; by doing this, they gain domestic bargaining leverage. If politicians act not to bind themselves but their opponents, then governments may seek IMF programmes (and associated conditionalities) not to tie their own hands but to tie the hands of their domestic opponents (Vreeland 2003).

The expansion of IMF conditionalities can also be understood with reference to the agency problems inherent in *public* institutions. Theories of incentives underlying principal-agent models broadly assume that while *outcomes* are verifiable, *actions* are not. In the case of the IFIs (as with other public institutions), the opposite is generally the case. Hence the principals focus much more on outputs as a mechanism to shape the agency: in the case of the multilateral development banks, it is the volume of lending; in the IMF's case, the outputs are conditionalities. The more attractive the IMF is to its major shareholders, the greater the focus on conditionality as indicator of output. Thus the expansion of IMF conditionality is, in part, a function of the greater importance of the institution to major shareholders, in turn the result of three key financial features of the Fund:

1 The IMF's financial structure has allowed it to transfer the incidence of risk from the major shareholders to borrowers and to its own balance sheet (in the form of higher reserves), thereby changing the cost-benefit ratio for major shareholders. The relative contribution of creditors (based on the total of actual and imputed costs) declined from 72 per cent in 1982 to 25 per cent in 2002 with a corresponding increase in the share of debtors (Mohammed 2003). This altered cost-benefit ratio has resulted in greater risk-taking by major shareholders vis-à-vis the Fund and, in turn, by the Fund, vis-à-vis the borrowers. It was only in the aftermath of the Asian Crisis when it became evident that the burgeoning conditionality agenda could precipitate a breakdown in the programme (as in Indonesia), thereby triggering a systemic crisis with significant implications for major shareholders as well, that conditionalities began to ebb.

2 Unlike most international organizations, the IMF's administrative budgets are independent of its shareholders' budget appropriations. The budgetary aspect of financial agency allows the IMF to not only underwrite the many purposes of international organizations (transnational cooperation and collective action, lowering information costs for members, etc.) but also co-opt multiple and changing interest groups, including reputational institutions, such as academia and think-tanks.

3 The substantially longer cycles (compared to other international organiza-tions) between potential veto points on quota expansion and the ability to borrow with only broad limits gives the IMF greater agency from its principals. Not only is the size of its access to resources quite substantial, automatic and rule-based, but the structure of the quota system gives the institution access to substantially greater *liquid* resources. Liquidity allows for a quicker institutional response and helps address a missing dimension in existing theories of international institutions. The latter stress the coor-dination role of international institutions in establishing equilibrium, but have little to say on how fast equilibrium is attained. The greater and more liquid resources of the IFIs (and especially the IMF) permit a speedier response, allowing them to edge out other organizations when crises occur and new demands are made on international institutions.

Another factor, much favoured by public choice theorists, places the onus of the expansion of the IFIs' conditionalities on the intrinsic pathology of bureaucracies. More conditionalities may be the result of self-interested IMF managers that are inherently 'empire'/budget-maximizing agents. There is modest support for this proposition in the 'mission-creep', even in the IMF's Surveillance and Article IV consultations (IMF 1999). Alternatively, if managers are risk-averse agents, then conditionalities in current programmes reflect the lessons and criticisms emanating from the last crisis. Conditionalities may therefore simply accrete with each crisis.

The Limitations of Conditionalities

Numerous studies of the effectiveness of IMF conditionalities have found that conditionalities have not been an effective instrument for changing borrower behaviour. Even as structural conditionality increased during the 1990s, the rate of compliance declined significantly. During 1993–97 just over a quarter of 141 arrangements could be considered in compliance. (Buira 2003). According to the Fund's own analysis of implementation rates during the 1990s, '69 per cent of prior actions, 58 per cent of performance criteria and 56 per cent of structural benchmarks [were] fully implemented.'[7]

Joyce (2004) reviews the empirical literature on the impact of IMF programmes on the economies of borrowing countries. Most of the work finds that Fund programmes improve the balance of payments but may have a negative impact on growth and income distribution. They do not appear to have a catalytic effect on private capital flows to programme countries, but do seem to somewhat increase moral hazard in private capital flows (with the latter expecting to get bailed out by an IMF programme).

An important reason why conditionality generates much controversy is that definite conclusions on its effects are hard to reach. Analytically, it is difficult to establish viable counterfactuals and the time-frame in question makes judgements problematic. The IMF's defence of the limited success of its programmes rests on several factors. First, there is the 'adverse selection' in its clientele since many countries come to the Fund only when in a crisis. The success rate of a hospital's emergency ward cannot be compared with its outpatients department. The counter-argument is that it is the steady expansion of its loan conditions that prevents countries from seeking help from the Fund unless stricken. This may explain both the institution's poor record in crisis prevention and why its medicine has had limited impact, undermining institutional credibility. On the other hand, there is also ample evidence of countries' ignoring warning signals passed out by annual Fund 'surveillance' missions.

A related argument centres on Fund programmes that fail when countries do not complete the full dose of the IMF's medicine as agreed upon in the loan conditions. In many cases, countries sign onto IMF programmes often when they are severely pressed, and in that sense loan contracts with the IMF are signed under conditions of duress. Do the programmes fail because of a failure to take the full dosage, or because of the high cost of medication itself? Equally, however, criticisms of Fund programmes have frequently masked the actions of member states whose own limitations were often responsible for their countries' predicaments.

The contentious debates were in full evidence in the IMF's handling of the Asian Crisis. Both the Fund and its critics agreed on the significance of panic in amplifying the crisis. But they sharply disagreed on how best to address the crisis and restore confidence.[8] The Fund's strategy was two-pronged: assembling a massive financial package together with sweeping policy changes that included fiscal and monetary tightening; radical structural reform, including the breaking up of monopolies and the closure of bankrupt financial institutions. Critics charged that the Fund misunderstood the rationale underlying the region's highly leveraged corporate sector; that its strategy of sudden bank closures, sharp hikes in interest rates, and deep budget cuts stoked panic rather than moderate it.

The Fund defended its actions given both how highly leveraged the corporate sector was in these countries as well as the high component of foreign exchange liabilities in the balance sheets of domestic financial institutions and corporations. The former meant that while high interest rates could potentially defend the currency, it would exacerbate the economic slowdown and magnify debt-servicing problems of the corporate sector. The latter meant that lower interest rates would increase the debt-servicing burden of external liabilities if the currency depreciated rapidly. The IMF chose the former risk – indicating that at the margin at least the IMF errs more on the side of ensuring the servicing of foreign liabilities over domestic liabilities.

It is possible that analysis of the effectiveness of Fund conditionality is deficient in that it does not capture changes in economic behaviour that may result to avoid the political costs of going to the Fund. Thus conditionality may be more effective when it is a contingent threat rather than when it is actually applied. A parallel with the literature on sanctions is instructive. That literature points to a similar paradox – the recurrent use of an instrument whose effectiveness has been questioned in innumerable studies (Pape 1997; Elliott and Hufbauer 1999). Like the case of sanctions, the hardening of the conditionality regime constitutes a contingent threat – and countries could be setting their economic house in order simply to avoid becoming ensnared by that regime.

In the mid-1980s, the regional contagion effects of the Latin American debt crisis dragged down Colombia's economy, but a history of deeply strained relations with the IMF precluded the country from entering into a formal programme with the IMF. Colombia undertook an adjustment programme with the World Bank that had many features similar to what a formal Fund programme would have required. Similarly, during the 1997–98 Asian Crisis, even while Prime Minister Mahathir of Malaysia railed against the IMF, his government undertook economic reforms that had many features similar to those that would have been arranged if the country had entered into a formal agreement with the Fund. And one reason for the burgeoning foreign-exchange reserves of developing countries in the last few years is that countries would rather pay the financial costs of self-insurance than risk the political costs of a Fund programme (Kapur and Patel 2003).

A wide range of research suggests that conditionality *per se* has been ineffective in linking aid with reform. There are several reasons why this is the case. Conditionality creates resentment since it smacks of external imposition rather than of something that has emerged out of domestic debate. It is intrinsically difficult to specify precise conditions with regard to reform given the uncertainties inherent in policy reform processes. During a crisis countries are prone to accept onerous conditionalities even if they know there is no possibility of fulfilling them. Countries that do not want to reform find ways to avoid a serious loss of funding, aware that the incentive structure makes it difficult for donors to disengage when conditions are not met.

Additionally, it has become apparent that conditionalities have grown in part to appease domestic interest groups in industrialized countries, where the appearance of good policy (embodied as conditionalities) has a greater political immediacy than eventual outcomes. Thus the weakness of conditionalities arose not from what they could or could not do in borrowing countries, but the logic inherent in the incentives stemming from the IMF's governance structure. Fund conditionality began to respond more to the pressures emanating from its major shareholders. In the USA, both conservatives and liberals denounce the IMF's conditionalities. Conservatives argue that IMF conditionalities are not tough enough while liberals argue that conditionalities are misplaced in their priorities, emphasizing fiscal and monetary aggregates rather than distributional, environmental and social issues. In explaining why this has occurred Goldstein (2000) puts the onus on the 'political' demand for structural performance criteria.

Finally some conditionalities don't work because the IFIs are not the appropriate institution for the objectives sought to be addressed by the conditionalities. The IFIs' 'governance' agenda is a case in point. In September 1997 the World Bank adopted a policy statement that 'corruption should be explicitly taken into account in country risk analysis, lending decisions, and portfolio supervision if it affects project or country performance.' The inclusion of governance-related conditionalities (GRCs) in the Bank's agenda was amplified by IDA-12, negotiated in 1998, which stated unambiguously, 'good governance is *critical* to the development process and to the effectiveness of development assistance; this is a *key* concern of the IDA Deputies' (IDA-12, 1998, emphasis added).

In the Fund's case, in 1996 its Board of Governors enjoined it to 'promote good governance in all its aspects. These included strengthening the rule of law, improving the efficiency and accountability of the public sector, and tackling corruption, all expressed by the IMF as essential elements of a framework within which economies can prosper.'[9] Since then, according to the Fund, its 'role in promoting good governance has expanded considerably' and the underlying assumption has been that this agenda is positive for the economy as well as for democracy. For operational purposes, however, the Executive Board interpreted the Governors' guidelines by emphasizing that 'the IMF's judgements should not be influenced by the nature of a political regime of a country.'[10] Consequently, the IMF has largely defined its 'governance' role to improve the 'quality of government', and in particular the reduction of corruption. However, there is a fundamental limitation to the IFIs' promoting *institutions* of good governance, since the time horizon of their programmes are much shorter than the minimum reasonably needed for institution-building. All prior experience of political and social reengineering suggests that the road to better governance – and the emergence of liberal democracies – is likely to be long and uneven.[11]

Conditionality as Incomplete Contracts

The limitations of conditionalities can be analytically supplemented by viewing Fund programmes through the lens of contract theory. Changes in the content of Fund programmes and Fund conditionalities could reflect an attempt to move towards more 'complete' contracts as the Fund (as principal) tries to change the borrowing government's (the agent's) behaviour. In a strict legal sense IMF conditionalities are not contracts (in that they cannot be adjudicated in a court of law). However, the analytical framework of contract theory provides insights into the inherent limitations of the instrument.

First, these contracts are inherently *incomplete and renegotiable*. Contract theory often assumes that contracts are complete. This is a strong assumption in normal circumstances. In the case of development-linked financial flows (such as IMF conditionalities), the assumption is untenable. Neither the IMF nor the borrower can fully anticipate all possible contingencies that might arise during their relationship. By 'incomplete' I mean that in some cases a Fund programme may leave something out or be ambiguous while in other cases contracting may be constrained by limited information and the fact that complicated states of nature cannot be verified. Although the contracting literature justifies incomplete contracting due to transaction costs (identified as unforeseen contingencies, costs of writing a complete set of contingencies, enforcement costs, and renegotiation), this view has its critics. Maskin and Tirole (1999) for instance argue that there is 'no well accepted incomplete contracting paradigm, unlike for the phenomena of moral hazard and adverse selection'. They are not impressed with the recourse to transaction costs in explaining renegotiation, arguing 'it is not obvious why rational agents must allow renegotiation to constrain them – i.e. why they cannot simply write an irrevocability clause into their contracts.'

This view seems rather extreme. My view is more in line with the argument offered by Hart and Moore (1999) who argue that the 'degree of commitment is something about which reasonable people can disagree'. Segal (1999) identifies environmental complexity in which all four elements of 'transaction costs' are important factors in explaining contractual incompleteness. The contracting parties are unable to verify publicly observable information and prevent renegotiation; further, the complexity of the environment explains the actors' bounded rationality. The parties' inability to foresee all possible trades *ex ante* and the cost of describing them *ex post* imposes additional costs on contracting. In such complex environments, the transaction costs of formal communication leads the players to *ex ante* strictly prefer to write an incomplete contract and leave open the option of renegotiation than to complete a non-renegotiable contract.

What are the effects of renegotiation? Maskin and Moore (1999) argue that with renegotiation, non-verifiability may become a more binding constraint.[12] The likelihood of renegotiation makes contracting between the Fund and the borrower easier. Why fight to the last detail when one knows one will be redoing this again – and soon? This is particularly the case when the country programme has systemic implications, such as during a financial crisis with contagion possibilities. In a crisis, reaching an agreement quickly is more important than considering how the agreement is likely to be implemented. There may be reputation costs for the government and the Fund – but given the number of times IMF programmes are renegotiated, at the margin, they are likely to be quite low.[13]

Second, even where outcomes are observable they are *imperfectly verifiable*. Although the Executive Boards of IFIs are meant to serve as the third-party verification mechanism, in practice this is not the case. Executive Directors are themselves interested actors, and even when there is little self-interest, it is difficult to confirm or contradict management's position, especially since the borrower is not there to argue its case.

Third, there is *no risk-sharing in the contracts*. The risks of an IFI loan, both financial and political, are borne only by the borrower. In the case of concessional loans, the financial risks are much less, but the political or economic risks for the borrower are still high. The 'residual rights of control', specifying which party will have the authority to make critical decisions when unforeseen contingencies arise, rest with the lender. The IMF's stress on capital account liberalization just prior to the Asian Crisis illustrates the behavioural effects when risk is borne asymmetrically. Unlike the case of trade, when the IMF began pressing for capital account liberalization, the analytical foundations for its claims were weak (Bhagwati 1998). The absence of theoretical models in this area as well as limited empirical work on the relationship of trade in financial assets to growth is well known (Rogoff 1999; Bosworth and Collins 1999). Indeed, at the time the evidence was ambivalent about the benefits of capital account liberalization (Rodrik 1998).[14] In countries with weak institutions – a common characteristic of low-income countries – free capital mobility can as easily magnify distortions and generate costly crises as they can increase investment and consumption (Cooper 1999). Conversely, the IMF's strictures on capital controls lacked the contextual qualifications that it admitted after following a more rigorous empirical examination of the issues (Ariyoshi *et al.* 2000; Prasad, Rogoff *et al.* 2003). Nonetheless, the IMF was insistent on the issue, even going to the extent of pressing for an Amendment of its Articles. It stressed 'constraints on reforms and the limited capacity of countries to reform themselves in the absence of external pressures for reform; this view favours early capital account liberalization, which can serve as a catalyst for broader economic reform and overcome vested interests' opposition to reforms' (Johnston 1998). Arguments stressing the role of 'vested interests' (in borrowing countries) opposing policy change rarely acknowledge the possibility of 'vested interests' in those arguing *for* policy change. It is hardly likely that the Fund could have moved as strongly on the issue of capital account liberalization if the incidence of risk fell either to the institution itself or to its key principals.

Reform Proposals

Alternatives to Traditional Conditionality: Reforming Conditionality from Within

Reforms of conditionality run in several directions. First there is the 'what' which tries to address the scope of conditionality which has expanded massively, from narrow financial issues to broader economic, administrative, social and political issues. The second issue is the scale, which addresses the number of conditions, the 'how much'. The third issue is the 'how', which tries to address the issue of mechanism design, in particular instruments that are flexible, recognizing the inherent uncertainties about the future.

Following the Asian Crisis, the Fund was criticized for its 'Christmas tree' approach to adding conditions to its programmes that had little to do with immediate programme goals. In response to a widespread perception of a 'conditionality Laffer curve' (Bird 1999), the IFIs began to scale back conditionalities. The IMF established new guidelines on conditionality in 2002, replacing the earlier ones issued in 1979. The new guidelines reduced the emphasis on structural conditionality and stressed that conditionality would be applied 'parsimoniously'. They recognized that conditions should be tailored to the administrative capacity of each borrower and called upon the institution to focus on its core areas of responsibility (macroeconomic policymaking and implementation) while leaving other more sectoral, social, or microeconomic issues to the World Bank and other regional multilateral development banks (IMF 2002).

The other trend has been to try to tinker with the mechanics of conditionality. Even where a programme has been negotiated with the best of intentions, the inflexibility of conditionality has been a source of frustration. One innovation has been to introduce floating tranches and flexible timing. Instead of dated covenants, governments would choose the timing of the implementation of reforms and would receive a tranche when that occurred. This would allow the borrower to fulfil its obligations in its own time which would automatically trigger a release of the agreed-upon resources. This principle underlay the design of the High Impact Adjustment Lending (HIAL) programme implemented by the World Bank in Africa in the mid-1990s. These adjustment loans had multiple smaller tranches specified to certain sectors, with flexible timing for the release of resources, depending on the sector. This programme provided borrowers with greater flexibility, reducing pressure on the World Bank to release funds even when conditions were not met. Such flexibility increased country ownership and control and the flexible tranches were associated with positive policy outcomes in terms of fiscal adjustment and exchange and interest-rate policy (Khan and Sharma 2001). Another suggestion has been the need for programmes to have built-in contingency arrangements to cope with external shocks. A fast-disbursing low-conditionality facility to provide liquidity in the event of a temporary external shock could address this concern. This would give more time to develop a domestic consensus on reforms and a more realistic programme (Bird 2003).

A different approach seeks to link the degree of conditionality to a country's track record. This would provide an additional incentive for governments not to abandon programmes in mid-course and would help alleviate the moral hazard problem that arises where previous failure does not exert any adverse effect on future access to fund resources. Alternatively, access to resources could be limited to countries that already have good policy environments. However, this would often imply penalizing citizens for actions of their governments – over which they often have little influence. Countries could also be offered combinations of conditionality and interest rates, allowing them to trade off the political costs of conditionality against higher financial costs stemming from higher rates of interest.

A different set of reforms to address some of the ownership, accountability, incentive and ambiguity problems with conditionality is to focus on conditions in terms of variables nearer the outcome end of the results chain rather than input or intermediate steps (Koeberle 2003). In principle, they could also provide more flexibility to the borrowing country to meet objectives by tailoring the means to their own institutional context. An important limitation is that most outcome indicators change only very gradually (especially those related to poverty, social indicators and institutional change) and can be buffeted by factors outside the government's control. Moreover, in practice it also increases uncertainty as regards the future availability of funds. Nonetheless, the less intrusiveness would certainly increase country ownership (Khan and Sharma 2001).

A major criticism of Fund programmes and conditionalities is their lack of transparency. The Fund has argued that there is a limit to the amount of confidential information that can be disclosed to the public, and that it is up to the borrower to decide how much information to make public. However, as the Independent Evaluation Office of the IMF argues, this argument is increasingly less and less tenable. A lack of transparency 'contributes to the perception that the prescriptions are arbitrary and prevents a serious debate on the issues involved' (Ahluwalia 2003). By increasing transparency other actors would be able to comment on the technical merits of the programme and would also force the government to 'sell' the programme to the domestic electorate. Making the process more transparent is messy, but involving civil society is likely to facilitate implementation.

Both the Bank and Fund have begun to recognize the limitations of conditionality for programme success, and instead have begun to stress the importance of borrower 'ownership' for successful implementation of programmes. The concept of 'ownership' is recognition that successful implementation of economic policy changes requires strong input and participation of the principal stakeholders in society and cannot be parachuted in from outside the country. Recent Fund guidelines state rather judiciously that it 'will encourage members to seek to broaden and deepen the base of support for sound policies in order to enhance the likelihood of successful implementation [of a Fund programme]' (IMF 2002, para 3). Nonetheless, 'ownership' is a nebulous difficult-to-measure characteristic, especially during crises when borrowing governments face a Hobson's choice or, in the case of non-democratic governments, when there can be a large divergence between 'government ownership' and 'country ownership'. This is particularly the case in countries with weak democratic systems.

The most ineffective Fund programmes (and the most onerous conditions) have been in small low-income countries with weak administrative capacity. Since the mid-1970s, the IMF's programmes to these countries have provided concessional financing, beginning with the Trust Fund, and then the Structural Adjustment Facility (SAF) in 1986 and the Enhanced Structural Adjustment Facility (ESAF) in 1987. In 1999 the IMF replaced the ESAF, the principal vehicle for concessional lending, with the Poverty Reduction and Growth Facility (PRGF). Internal and external evaluations conducted in 1997 and 1998, respectively, identified a number of problems that hindered the effectiveness of programmes supported by this facility. In particular, the external evaluation highlighted significant weaknesses in national ownership, in the analytical and empirical bases of the social policy content of programmes, and in attention to trade-offs involving policy choices that imply significantly different paths for growth and social welfare.

The new approach to supporting reform and adjustment programmes in low-income countries was set out in a new vehicle, the Poverty Reduction Strategy Paper (PRSP). The core principles of the PRSP approach were that the programmes would: a) be country-driven, with broad-based participation of civil society; b) be results-oriented; c) have a long-term perspective; d) be comprehensive (to address the multi-dimensional nature of poverty and the policies needed to reduce it); and e) partner with all stakeholders, especially all donors.

Given the limited period that has passed, it is difficult to reach firm conclusions on the just how much PRSPs have achieved. 'Ownership' is a complex concept. Preliminary indications are that it is more likely when consultations are conducted in tandem with and through the country's normal political processes and institutions. However, limited technical capabilities in many poor countries, the inherent power asymmetries between a borrower and a lender, and the PRSP's multiple roles (as a process for building domestic consensus and ownership, its role in triggering debt relief as well as access to aid resources), are bound to limit what it can achieve.

Alternatives to Traditional Conditionality: Reform from Without

While the conditionality regime has stepped back from its micro-detailed orientation, the trend appears to be towards a meta-regime with transparent *ex ante* criteria or prior actions. Thus, rather than insist on conditionalities in specific IFI loans, donors began imposing conditions on the concessional windows of the IFIs, beginning with IDA in the 1980s and continuing later with the ESAF and PRGF. The success of the IDA replenishment itself became increasingly conditional on the World Bank's agreeing to reshape its lending priorities to accommodate donor demands. For example, in IDA-13, even as the donors insisted that stakeholders be involved in Bank projects, they were more reticent when it came to stakeholder involvement in Bank policies, especially lending priorities. A survey of preferences of opinion leaders from IDA borrowing countries, found that the 'Northern' donor agenda was near the bottom of the list (IDA 2001, Tables 3 and 4). The donors wanted IDA to put greater stress on post-conflict countries but to ensure that the funds were spent wisely, 29 progress indicators were added. IDA-13 had a total of 23 objectives, and its recommendations/actions added up to 62 – one of which was 'increasing selectivity'![15]

The Highly Indebted Poor Countries (HIPC) initiative to reduce the debt of 41 'debt distressed' countries (33 in Africa) to a 'sustainable' level is another example. While the argument for debt reduction for these countries was straightforward, countries had to meet a set of criteria to qualify. In retrospect it appears that the bar was set too high and as a result the programme ran into problems because of the rigid and excessive conditionalities that accompanied the debt-relief measure. In the case of Uganda, which was the first country to qualify under the enhanced HIPC Programme, the creditors postponed debt reduction because they were worried about the government's conflict with Rwanda and feared that any escalation of conflict would force the government to spend more on defence and put debt servicing at risk.

The trend towards *ex ante* conditionality is exemplified by the new US foreign aid regime. Under the new Millennium Challenge Account programme, the USA has promised to double its aid commitments to $5 billion annually by 2008. Countries will have to meet certain criteria to qualify for this aid. Their per capita income levels should be below $1,415; they should not be listed by the State Department as sponsors of terrorism; and their inclusion will be based on their report card on 16 independent indicators (many of them from outside government) to indicate that their countries leaders are, in the words of the US president, 'ruling justly, investing in their people, and establishing economic freedom'.[16] The indicators include areas such as budget deficits, trade policy, immunization rates, primary-school completion rates, control of corruption, and the protection of civil liberties. To qualify, a country must score above the median on half of the indicators in each of the three categories, and it must score above the median on corruption. The design is meant to limit (but not eliminate) discretion in the allocation of US foreign aid (Radalet 2003). Selected countries will then have the flexibility to set their own priorities, propose specific activities, and establish benchmarks that will be used to measure progress. However, they then risk funding being cut off if the programmes fail. It is, however, unclear whether a country which meets the criteria but which votes against the USA in an important international forum will not face pressure. Moreover, there simply is no guarantee that the US Congress will be bound by the promise of the executive branch, especially with a ballooning fiscal deficit.

The European Community has begun to use a reward-based system of 'positive conditionality' or 'reinforcement by reward'. One example is granting additional preferences within the General System of Preferences (GSP) programme to countries that comply with certain specified environmental or labour standards (Barlets 2003). Under a strategy of 'reinforcement by reward', the EU withholds the reward if the target government fails to comply with its conditions, but does not intervene either coercively or supportively to change the cost-benefit assessment of the target government by inflicting extra costs ('reinforcement by punishment') or offering unconditional assistance ('reinforcement by support'). In the case of EU democratic conditionality, countries that failed to fulfil the political criteria were simply denied assistance or the upgrading of their institutional ties. (Schimmelfennig, Engert and Knobel 2003).

The three examples discussed above all share a common problem. There is nothing to hold the more powerful party to its commitments. Woods (2000) stresses three aspects of donor behaviour that especially need to be monitored: the keeping of pledges; the tying of aid and resources (often inappropriate to development needs); and the failure to live up to rhetoric about national and local ownership. IFI conditionality has a similar intrinsic weakness since the design, lending and monitoring functions are embedded in the same institution, thereby creating an inherent conflict of interest. A recent innovation is to separate the monitoring function through a peer-review mechanism. The latest example is the New Partnership for African Development (NEPAD) launched in 2001. This commits African governments to democracy and good governance in return for greater aid and investment from the developed economies. Countries in the 53-member African Union can join NEPAD by signing up to its Democratic and Political Governance Initiative – a set of 12 commitments and eight actions – and by agreeing to an external review every three years by a panel of eminent Africans. This peer-review system marks an unprecedented development in the most stressed region in the world. Thus far 17 countries have agreed to be reviewed. The first round of reviews examining compliance with NEPAD's standards will focus on Ghana, Kenya, Rwanda and Mauritius, and are scheduled for completion by 2006.

The African peer-review mechanism (APRM) has drawn wide interest. It represents an ambitious attempt to subject African leaders to an ongoing examination by other Africans in priority areas and to shift from donor-imposed conditionalities to peer monitoring. Nonetheless, NEPAD faces many challenges. The reluctance of Africa's leaders to criticize Robert Mugabe whose poor political leadership and abject economic mismanagement has ruined a once-promising economy is undermining a key principle of NEPAD. On the other hand, it is unclear that if there is real ownership by developing countries, donors will increase resource flows and reform aid policies, programmes and practices. Donor countries may also use adherence to the peer-review standards as another way of attaching yet more conditions to their support.

The emergence of NEPAD highlights the importance of developing countries' recognizing their own role in the growth of conditionalities. For instance, in recent years it has become a matter of dogma that the MDBs' principal goal of poverty alleviation is best achieved through broadly defined 'social development' projects. Developing countries should have serious misgivings about the *instruments* to exercise universally-accepted goals. International organizations will invariably impose universal standards and norms. And more than ever before, the universal standards that come attached to external resources bring with them their own priorities, consultants, values and technologies. It is one thing to deploy these resources for physical infrastructure, for knowledge production, but it is quite another for the resources to be focused almost exclusively on social development, which is much more context-specific and deeply rooted in a society's culture, norms and values.

It is unclear, however, if developing countries have drawn the necessary lessons. For a long time, obtaining greater concessional resources has been their highest priority. In the process they have been paying increasingly higher non-pecuniary costs that have offset any gains in additional 'concessional' resources. Developing countries need to reevaluate their priorities and ponder whether their cause would be better served by asking rich countries not for more 'positive freedoms' (through, say, additional financial resources) but fewer 'negative freedoms' allowed them in the international system (e.g. lower barriers to their exports; lower greenhouse gas emissions; weaker insistence that they conform to imposed artificial high standards, be it those on intellectual property rights or MDB lending; a strong international regime controlling exports of small arms; etc.). The relative benefits of these measures are likely to far exceed those from any modest increase in concessional flows.

A bold option – one more realistic in the long run than in the immediate future – is to develop risk-sharing contracts for development on the lines proposed by Shiller (2003). Commercial examples of such contracts, while rare, are not unknown. The most obvious form is to tie the rate of interest on sovereign loans to GDP growth. For instance, in 1994 Citibank arranged a loan of US $1.865 billion to Bulgaria on which the higher Bulgaria's growth rate, the greater the interest rate. Shiller's proposals are much more ambitious, and an example of a contract he has in mind would run as follows: Country A pays other countries if its GDP does better than expected relative to other countries' performance during the contract period, whereas other countries pay Country A if A's economy does less well. These arrangements would work best between countries that are both geographically and economically distant, since this would result in a lower risk correlation in their economic fortunes. The contract could be made not between Country A and Country B, but between each of them and an international agency. For this to work the contracts would have to be long-term (50 or more years) and would require prior agreement on expected per capita growth rates for each country. The effect would be tantamount to an exchange of unexpected GDPs. Shiller's plan would also include a fixed annual fee paid between countries, regardless of GDP. This extremely ambitious proposal can only emerge in the long run. Even then it will require concerted political will. Nonetheless, it represents an out-of-the-box thinking that LDCs must engage in if they are to transcend the straightjacket of conditionalities.

Conclusions

Although there are many factors that explain the growth of conditionality, their limited effectiveness is now widely recognized. Nonetheless, as long as a transaction has a lender and a borrower, conditionalities are inevitable. They may be implicit or explicit, narrow or expansive, but they cannot be wished away. This paper gives several suggestions that can improve the conditionality regime. Peer-monitoring mechanisms like NEPAD and greater emphasis on country 'ownership' of programmes (as envisaged in the PRGF) are steps in the right direction. It is also important that there be a separation of powers between the agencies that lend the money and impose conditions and those that monitor compliance. As long as the actions of lenders separate risks from rewards (both political and financial), they will induce a 'conditionality moral hazard'. Nonetheless, the paper argues that conditionalities are akin to incomplete contracts and there are inherent limitations to what the instrument can achieve. A more viable, albeit drastic, change would be to institute broad-ranging risk-sharing contracts between individual developing countries and the wealthier countries, mediated through the IFIs.

Notes

1 This section draws on Kapur (2000).

2 Article V, Section 3(a) states: 'The Fund shall adopt policies ... that will establish adequate safeguards for the temporary use of the general resources of the Fund.' However, although conditionality helps the repayment of sovereign debt, when anticipated by lenders it can get international financial institutions and sovereign debtors into a trap where the debt overhang persists, debt rescheduling takes place periodically, and conditionality continues indefinitely (Fafchamps 1996).

3 For instance, access to the IMF's Supplemental Reserve Facility (SRF) – created in the aftermath of the 1994 Mexican crisis to provide financial assistance to member countries experiencing balance of payments difficulties due to a large short-term financing need resulting from pressure on the capital account and the member's reserves – is at 300–500 basis points above IMF loan charges with a repayment period ranging from 1½ to 2½ years.

4 Data through 1990 are from Boughton (2001), who used data until 1987 from an internal Fund document, while data for 1988–90 were provided him by PDR staff. The latter were unable to replicate precisely the 1987 data, so he spliced the two series. James Boughton, personal communication, 11 August 2000.

5 Table 1, Report to the IMF Executive Board of the Quota Formula Review Group, IMF, 28 April 2000.

6 The counterfactual – that research findings have played *no role* in the Fund's changing agenda (and related conditionalities) – would be itself noteworthy.

7 IMF, 'Structural Conditionality in Fund-Supported Programmes', February 2001, para 80.

8 For a sharp critique of the Fund's handling of the Asian Crisis, see Stiglitz (2002). For a robust non-technical defence, see Rogoff (2003).

9 http://www.imf.org/external/np/exr/facts/gov.htm

10 See 'The Role of the IMF in Governance Issues: Guidance Note', approved by the IMF Executive Board, 25 July 1997.

11 For a skeptical view of outsiders trying to jump-start democracy in developing countries, see Carothers (2002).

12 More precisely, the possibility of renegotiation not only constrains the set of implementable social choice rules but the nature of the renegotiation may be crucially important.

13 Lee and Rhee (1999) examined a set of 455 IMF programmes to non-OECD countries negotiated between mid-1973 and mid-1994 and classify a programme as independent if there has not been another programme to the country within four years of its initiation. Else, the programme is counted as a consecutive approval of previous programmes and identified by the first year of the previous independent programme. This procedure yielded a total of 159 independent programmes among 455 programmes – implying that nearly two-thirds of all Fund programmes were renegotiated contracts.

14 Rodrik found (after controlling for factors) that capital restrictions have no significant effects on macroeconomic performance. Research by the World Bank also found a lack of correlation between capital account convertibility and growth in general: http://www.worldbank.org/prospects/gep98-99/ppt/sld019.htm

15 IDA, 'Additions to IDA Resources: Thirteenth Replenishment', IDA/SecM 2002-0488, 17 September, Annex 3.

16 Christopher Marquis, 'New System Begins Rerouting US Aid For Poor Countries', the *New York Times*, 22 February 2004. Under these criteria 63 countries are eligible to compete for the first round of the Millennium Challenge funds.

References

Ahluwalia, Montek, 2003, Statement by Montek S. Ahluwalia, Director, Independent Evaluation Office of the International Monetary Fund at the General Assembly of the Club de Madrid, 1 November 2003.

Akira Ariyoshi, Karl Habermeier, Bernard Laurens, Inci Otker-Robe, Jorge Iván Canales-Kriljenko and Andrei Kirilenko, 2000, 'Country Experiences with the Use and Liberalization of Capital Controls', IMF Occasional Paper No. 190.

Aylward, Lynne and Rupert Thorne, 1998, 'Countries' Repayment Performance vis-à-vis the IMF: An Empirical Analysis', *IMF Staff Papers*, Vol. 45, December, 595–618.

Bartels, L., 2003, 'The WTO Enabling Clause and Positive Conditionality in the European Community's GSP programme', *Journal of International Economic Law*, 6 (2): 507–532, June.

Bhagwati, Jagdish, 1998, 'The Capital Myth: The Differences Between Trade in Widgets and Trade in Dollars', *Foreign Affairs*, 77, 7–12.

Bird, Graham, 1999, 'IMF Programmes: Is there a Conditionality Laffer Curve?', mimeo.

Bird, Graham, 2003, 'Restructuring the IMF's Lending Facilities', *The World Economy*, 26 (2).

Bosworth, Barry P. and Susan M. Collins, 1999, 'Capital Flows to Developing Economies: Implications for Saving and Investment', *Brookings Papers on Economic Activity*, 1.

Boughton, James, 2001, *Silent Revolution: The International Monetary Fund, 1979–1989*, Washington D.C.: International Monetary Fund.

Buria, Ariel, 2003, 'An Analysis of IMF Conditionality', in Ariel Buria (ed.), *Challenges to the World Bank and IMF*, London: Anthem Press.

Carothers, Thomas, 2002, 'The End of the Transition Paradigm', *Journal of Democracy*, 13 (1), January.

Cooper, Richard, 1999, 'Should Capital Controls Be Banished?', *Brookings Papers on Economic Activity*, 1.

Dell, Sidney, 1981, 'On being Grandmotherly', *Princeton Essays in International Finance*, No. 144, Princeton.

Dhonte, Pierre, 1997, 'Conditionality as an Instrument of Borrower Credibility', IMF Paper on Policy Analysis and Assessment, PPAA/97/2, February.

de Vries, Margaret, 1985, *The IMF, 1972–78: Cooperation on Trial*, Washington D.C.: International Monetary Fund.

Elliott, Kimberly A. and Gary Hufbauer, 1999, 'Ineffectiveness of Economic Sanctions: Same Song, Same Refrain? Economic Sanctions in the 1990s', *American Economic Review*, Papers and Proceedings, Vol. 89 (2), May, 403–8.

Fafchamps, Michael, 1996, 'Sovereign Debt, Structural Adjustment, and Conditionality', *Journal of Development Economics*, 50: (2), August, 313–335.

Feldstein, Martin, 1998, 'Refocusing the IMF', *Foreign Affairs*, March/April.

Gold, Joseph, 1981, 'Keynes and the Articles of the Fund', *Finance and Development*, 18 September, 38–42.

Goldstein, Morris, 2000, 'Strengthening the International Financial Architecture: Where Do We Stand?', IIE Working Paper 00-8.

Hart, Oliver and John Moore, 1999, 'Foundations of Incomplete Contracts', *The Review of Economic Studies*, 66 (1), January, 115–138.

Gould, Erica, 2003, 'Money Talks: Supplementary Financiers and International Monetary Fund Conditionality', *International Organization*, 57: 3 (Summer).

Horsefield, J. Keith (ed.), 1969, *The International Monetary Fund 1945–65*, Vol. 1, Washington D.C.: IMF, pp. 69–77.

IDA, 1998, 'IDA-12'.

IDA, 2001, 'Sounding Out Borrowers about IDA's Policy Framework', May.

IMF, 1999, *Report on the External Evaluation of Fund Surveillance.*

IMF, 2002, 'Guidelines on Conditionality', September.

Johnston, R. Barry, 1998, 'Sequencing Capital Account Liberalization', *Finance and Development,* December.

Joyce, Joseph P., 2004, 'The Adoption, Implementation and Impact of IMF Programs: A Review of the Evidence', *Comparative Economic Studies,* Vol. 46, No. 2, May.

Kapur, Devesh, John Lewis and Richard Webb, 1997, *The World Bank: Its First Half Century. Volume 1: History.* Washington D.C.: The Brookings Institution.

Kapur, Devesh, 2001, 'Expansive Agendas and Weak Instruments: Governance-Related Conditionalities of International Financial Institutions', *Policy Reform,* Vol. 4 (3), pp. 207–241.

Kapur, Devesh and Urjit Patel, 2003, 'Large Foreign Currency Reserves: Insurance For Domestic Weaknesses And External Uncertainties?', *Economic and Political Weekly,* XXXVIII (11), 15–21 March, pp. 1047–1053.

Khan, Mohsin and Sharma, 2001, 'IMF Conditionality and Country Ownership of Programs', IMF Working Paper WP/01/142, September.

Koeberle, Stefan, 2003, 'Should Policy-Based Lending Still Involve Conditionality?', *World Bank Research Observer,* 18 (2): 249–73.

Lee, Jong-Wha and Chanyong Rhee, 1999, 'Macroeconomic Impacts of the Korean Financial Crisis: Comparisons with the Cross-country Patterns', Paper prepared for a conference on the Korean Financial Crisis, Harvard University.

Marchesi, S. and J.P. Thomas, 1999, 'IMF Conditionality as a Screening Device', *Economic Journal,* 109 (454) C111–C125, March.

Maskin, Eric and John Moore, 1999, 'Implementation and Renegotiation', *The Review of Economic Studies,* 66 (1), January, 39–56.

Maskin, Eric and Jean Tirole, 1999, 'Unforeseen Contingencies and Incomplete Contracts', *The Review of Economic Studies,* 66 (1), January, 83–114.

Messick, Richard, 1999, 'Judicial Reform and Economic Development: A Survey of the Issues', *The World Bank Research Observer,* Vol. 14, No.1, February.

Mohammed, Aziz Ali, 2003, 'Who Pays for the IMF?', in Ariel Buria (ed.), *Challenges to the World Bank and IMF,* London: Anthem Press.

Pape, Robert, 1997, 'Why Economic Sanctions Do Not Work', *International Security,* Vol. 22, 90–136.

Prasad, Eswar, Kenneth Rogoff, Shang-Jin Wei and M. Ayan Kose, 2003, *Effects of Financial Globalization on Developing Countries: Some Empirical Evidence,* IMF, 17 March.

Radelet, Steve, 2003, 'Bush and Foreign Aid', *Foreign Affairs,* September/October, pp. 104–117.

Rodrik, Dani, 1998, 'Who Needs Capital Account Convertibility?', Princeton Essays in International Finance, No. 207, 55–65.

Rogoff, Kenneth, 1999, 'International Institutions for Reducing Global Financial Instability', *Journal of Economic Perspectives,* 13 (4), Fall, 21–42.

Rogoff, Kenneth, 2003, 'The IMF Strikes Back', *Foreign Policy,* January–February.

Rosenberg, Emily, 1999, *Financial Missionaries to the World: The Politics and Culture of Dollar Diplomacy, 1900–1930,* Cambridge: Harvard University Press.

Schimmelfennig, F., S. Engert and H. Knobel, 2003, 'Costs, Commitment and Compliance: The Impact of EU Democratic Conditionality on Latvia, Slovakia and Turkey', *Journal of Common Market Studies,* 41 (3), June, 495–518.

Segal, Ilya, 1999, 'Complexity and Renegotiation: A Foundation for Incomplete Contracts', *The Review of Economic Studies*, 66 (1), January, 57–82.

Shiller, Robert, 2003, *The New Financial Order*, Princeton: Princeton University Press.

Stiglitz, Joseph, 2002, *Globalization and its Discontents*, New York: W.W. Norton.

Vreeland, James, 2003, *The IMF and Economic Development*, Cambridge: Cambridge University Press.

Woods, Ngaire, 2000, 'Improving Accountability and Governance in Global Financial Institutions', mimeo, University College, Oxford, available at http://users.ox.ac.uk/~ntwoods/wg3%20december%20report.PDF.

World Bank, 2004, *2003 Annual Review of Development Effectiveness*.

4

MISSION CREEP, MISSION PUSH AND DISCRETION: THE CASE OF *IMF* CONDITIONALITY

Sarah Babb and Ariel Buira

Abstract:

The most important thing about organizations is that, though they are tools, each nevertheless has a life of its own.
                    Philip Selznick, *TVA and the Grass Roots*, 1949, p.10.

In recent years, the Bretton Woods organizations have been subjected to intense scrutiny and pressure to change. Founded at the end of World War II to help lay the foundations of a new era of stability and prosperity, the World Bank and the International Monetary Fund (IMF) are widely viewed as having evolved in ways that would have surprised their founders. A term that has gained popularity among World Bank and IMF critics is 'mission creep', meaning the systematic shifting of organizational activities away from original mandates (IFI Advisory Commission 1998; Stiglitz 2002; Einhorn 2001; Bretton Woods Project 2003).

The case of the IMF is arguably the more dramatic of the two. The IMF's original purpose as it was conceived in 1944 was to establish a code of conduct that would enhance economic cooperation, and avoid the 'beggar-thy-neighbour' policies that led to the economic turbulence of the 1930s. This code of conduct required members to establish par values (which could only be changed with international agreement in cases of 'fundamental disequilibrium') and to work toward lifting restrictions on current payments. Lending the currencies of members in strong balance of payments and reserve positions to countries in weaker positions was intended to insulate the latter from the need to undergo deflations.

Over time, however, the functions and activities of the IMF changed along with the introduction and expansion of 'conditionality' – the policy measures member countries must adopt in order to have access to the IMF's resources. Initially, the IMF's conditions were aimed at reducing excess demand by cutting fiscal deficits and restricting the growth of the money supply. But over time, conditionality expanded to include the adjustment of national currencies and the terms of repayment of private creditors. Most recently, they have come to include the privatization of public enterprises, trade liberalization, the reform of banking and bankruptcy legislation, anti-poverty measures, and the prevention of money-laundering and terrorist financing – to name some of the most prominent items. Clearly, the IMF has changed considerably.

The issue of mission creep in international financial institutions is often treated by its critics as if it were a problem unique to these organizations in particular, attributable to perverse and unusual circumstances (Stiglitz 2002; Einhorn 2001). For sociologists who study organizations, however, the phenomenon of mission creep is neither new nor unusual. Since Michels' (1959[1915]) classic study of the German Social Democratic Party, sociologists have observed that public service organizations are not just means to pursue predetermined ends, but rather tend to become ends in themselves, more preoccupied with their own survival than with fidelity to the intentions of their founders (Selznick 1949; Zald and Denton 1963; Messinger 1955; Gouldner 1954). Missions, these studies all observed, have a tendency to creep – a tendency that is fuelled both by internal organizational dynamics and by the co-opting of organizations by powerful forces in their environments.

In this paper we examine the historical evidence of mission creep at the IMF and explore the organizational dynamics that may have contributed to this process. To this end we draw on an eclectic array of sources, including Letters of Intent from borrowing governments, secondary literature, and IMF staff analyses. Synthesizing this evidence, we describe and account for three separate phases in the expansion of conditionality:

- the establishment of fiscal and monetary conditions in the 1950s;
- the introduction of debt-related conditions in the 1970s; and
- the introduction of liberalization, governance, and a host of other reforms since the 1980s.

We argue that during the earliest phase, the IMF underwent a process of bureaucratic consolidation commonly observed in complex organizations, in which its procedures were standardized and routinized (Weber 1946). During the second phase, the IMF developed a mutually beneficial relationship with private creditors, a development that had an additive rather than a transformative effect on its practices.

In contrast to these two first phases, we argue that the most recent phase has marked a significant break with the past. Whereas the first period in the IMF's evolution was associated with the development of standardized rules, this latest stage is linked to the rise of 'discretional conditionality': the increased dependence of disbursements and lending arrangements on the judgements of management and staff, rather than on clear and predetermined rules. We conclude that this reversal cannot be attributed primarily to internal bureaucratic factors, but rather that it responded to the demands of the IMF's most powerful organizational constituent: the US Treasury. Thus, 'mission push' seems to be the most accurate way of describing recent developments in IMF conditionality.

Mission Creep: The Evidence

The IMF's original purposes, as outlined in Article I of its 1944 Articles of Agreement, were both to promote international trade and economic integration (through removing barriers to trade and current payments), and to 'contribute … to the promotion and maintenance of high levels of employment and real income and to the development of the productive resources of all members as primary objectives of economic policy' (IMF 1944). The IMF's two principal intellectual influences – John Maynard Keynes and Harry Dexter White – had been convinced by the experience of the Great Depression that international financial markets could not be trusted to govern themselves, and that space needed to be created for national governments to conduct relatively autonomous economic policies. In contrast to the early twentieth-century gold standard, the Bretton Woods regime was supposed to enable national policymakers to pursue the goals of economic growth and high levels of employment and real income at home, rather than simply reducing the money supply in order to defend the exchange rate (Ruggie 1983; Ikenberry 1992). Recently, however, Joseph Stiglitz has argued that the IMF ended up doing exactly the opposite of what it was intended to do: in his estimation, 'Keynes would be rolling in his grave were he to see what has happened to his child' (Stiglitz 2002).

Stiglitz and other critics focus primarily on the IMF's policy of conditionality, which was not part of the original Bretton Woods plan: the 1944 Articles of Agreement contained no provision for conditions to be placed on lending arrangements. During the 1950s, the IMF developed a practice whereby access to its resources would be contingent upon agreement to implement certain policies, and the Stand-by Arrangement became the legal vehicle through which these policy promises were made and enforced. It was not until 1969 that the Fund's de facto policy of conditionality was given *de jure* legal sanction, through an unassuming amendment to Article V, section 3(a).[1] It was not until a decade later that the IMF published a set of *Guidelines on Conditionality*. These *Guidelines* recommended that conditions be kept to a minimum, but imposed little obligation on IMF staff to adhere to them. Only a decade later, as we will see, the number of conditions had expanded dramatically (Gold 1996: 169, 361; Polak 1991:53). Prompted by this proliferation of conditions, as well as high rates of programme failure, a new set of *Guidelines* was published in 2002.

Because of the legal peculiarities mentioned above, conditionality cannot be studied through an exegesis of the Articles of Agreement. An alternative means of studying changes in IMF conditionality over time is through examining Letters of Intent: the quasi-contractual documents outlining the terms of IMF lending arrangements. Letters of Intent contain 'performance criteria' – formal conditions that must be met by borrower countries in order for the loan disbursements not to be suspended – and provide concrete evidence of the expansion of conditionality over time. For example, the first Stand-by Arrangement with Peru in 1954 was only two pages in length and contained no explicit performance criteria. The 1963 Peruvian Stand-by was six pages long and contained fiscal and monetary targets, as well as prohibitions on exchange restrictions and multiple currency practices. By 1993, Peruvian officials were signing a Stand-by Arrangement that was 13 pages in length and included not only the types of conditions required by the 1963 agreement, but also targets for the international reserves of the central bank, limits on external debt, a prohibition on implementing import restrictions 'for balance of payments reasons', and explicit provisions for trade liberalization, privatization, and the deregulation of Peruvian labour law (Peru LOI 1954, 1963, 1993).

In the following sections, we draw on Letters of Intent and other sources to show that conditionality expanded in three cumulative stages, each of which built upon its predecessor in a pattern resembling geological stratification. The first stage was the development of the monetary approach to the balance of payments in the 1950s, which made fiscal and monetary conditions a standard element of IMF-supported programmes. The second stage, which emerged in the 1970s, was the increasing involvement of the IMF with private creditors, and the inclusion of conditions designed to ensure the prompt and orderly repayment of debts. The third stage, which began in the 1980s, was the development of 'structural' conditionality. This most recent phase has been associated with an increased reliance on the discretion of IMF management and staff.

The Monetary Approach: 1950s to the Present

Developed over the course of the 1950s, the IMF's 'monetary approach to the balance of payments' identified credit expansion – often the result of financing fiscal deficits through central bank emissions – as the primary cause of persistent external imbalances. If a national government increased domestic credit too rapidly, causing a deficit in the balance of payments and a loss in central bank reserves, the real value of its currency would inevitably decline, and balance of payments pressures would eventually force governments to devalue. Significantly, devaluation alone might not be sufficient to bring about external balance; rather, the government needed to crack down on excess demand by reducing the money supply (Alexander 1952; Polak 1957; de Vries 1987).

This theory was associated with the development of 'financial programming': the technique used by IMF staff to estimate the domestic demand for money, set a target for international reserves, and use these figures to calculate fiscal and monetary targets a government needed to reach to stem inflation (Cline 1981; Williamson 1982). While the fiscal and monetary conditions applied in the 1950s and 1960s tended to assume the form of ceilings on fiscal deficits and net domestic credit, from the 1970s onward lending arrangements also typically included direct targets for international reserves. These prescriptions were first put into practice in Latin America and the Caribbean under the jurisdiction of the IMF's Western Hemisphere Department, and were later applied by other regional departments, as the IMF became more standardized (Finch 1997).

The Alliance with Private Creditors: 1970s to the Present

With the collapse of the Bretton Woods system at the beginning of the 1970s, the IMF was no longer responsible for upholding the par value system. Meanwhile, access to international credit allowed many developing countries to avoid resort to IMF conditionality entirely by borrowing from private sources. As a consequence, the number of Fund-supported lending programmes decreased dramatically. Desperate for customers, the IMF even found itself having to soften some of the conditions required for its loans (Polak 1991).

This temporary softening of fiscal and monetary conditions notwithstanding, the 1970s also marked the beginning of a second phase of expansion, in which conditionality began to address relations between governments and their private creditors. The IMF's relationship to private banks during its first several decades had been arms-length in character (Gold 1988). But by the end of the 1970s, Letters of Intent routinely included the requirement that governments be making regular payments to their private creditors (i.e. minimizing arrears), and limiting their incurring of new external debt.[2] With the outbreak of the Third World debt crisis in 1982, the IMF played an instrumental role in averting disaster by keeping governments from defaulting, while simultaneously requiring banks to grant new loans and restructure existing debt.[3] From that time forward, the IMF and the private banks would have a close working relationship, and lending conditions relating to private creditors were ubiquitous. For example, in Letters of Intent for six Latin American and Caribbean countries from 1982 to 1996, nearly 80 per cent contained the performance criterion that governments not fall into external payments arrears – compared to less than 20 per cent from 1972 to 1981.[4]

Structural Reforms and Beyond: 1980s to the Present

The third phase in the expansion of conditionality began in the 1980s and when lending arrangements began to require 'structural' reforms. Earlier generations of IMF conditions tended to focus on transitory variables having a bearing on a nation's short-term balance-of-payments: price stabilization, the reduction of the fiscal deficit, net domestic credit, the level of external debt, etc. Structural conditionality, in contrast, was aimed at the fundamental transformation of the underlying institutions governing national economies.

Structural conditionality represented a major departure from past practices. The conditions of prior decades were both circumscribed and temporary: they mostly left underlying institutional arrangements untouched, and once the IMF lending arrangement expired, a government could in theory go back to whatever fiscal and monetary policies it wanted. In contrast, structural conditionality was oriented toward making deep changes that were much more difficult to reverse, such as privatization and trade liberalization. The philosophy behind this new generation of reforms was also new. During the postwar period, the IMF had focused primarily on promoting an agenda of fiscal and monetary austerity, and generally stayed away from the issue of free-market reforms (Webb 2000). Thus, earlier generations of IMF critics focused on the negative impact of fiscal and monetary contraction on economic growth and employment (Felix 1961; Thorp and Whitehead 1979; Dell 1981); it has only been in recent decades that the IMF has also been accused of promoting an agenda of 'market fundamentalism' (Stiglitz 2002).

The ostensible justification for structural conditions was that the IMF's organizational mandate was not only to promote balance-of-payments stability but also to promote growth (Camdessus, quoted in Polak 1991). In theory, this was consistent with the original Articles of Agreement, which stated that a purpose of the Fund was '... to contribute thereby to the promotion and maintenance of high levels of employment and real income and to the development of the productive resources of all members as primary objectives of economic policy' (IMF 1944 I(ii)). In practice, however, structural conditionality was based on a contestable premise – namely, that in all cases the best recipe for growth lay in the liberalization of market forces,[5] privatization and the reduction of the role of the state, irrespective of the structural and constitutional and regulatory framework,[6] in the context of monetary stability.

Significantly, the expansion of the IMF's mandate to include structural conditionality was viewed with scepticism by some among the IMF staff's 'old guard'. Joseph Gold, the long-time director of the IMF's Legal Department, asserted that 'In neither logic nor law is it defensible to transform the [Fund's] purpose into jurisdiction over economic growth' (Gold 1996). The most controversial element of the new conditionality was the requirement that governments remove controls on the free movement of capital, a goal endorsed by the IMF's chief advisory body, the Interim Committee, in 1997. Jacques Polak (the renowned author of the IMF's original 'monetary approach to the balance of payments') has pointed out that 'The promotion of the worldwide flow of capital is not listed among the purposes of the Fund in Article I,' and opposed the revision of the Articles of Agreement to include this as part of its mission (Polak 1998). The original Articles of Agreement not only asserted the right of governments to maintain capital controls as a buffer against speculative capital inflows and outflows, but had actually encouraged them (Boughton 1997).

Such objections notwithstanding, the IMF's involvement in promoting structural reforms expanded rapidly. In keeping with the IMF's new 'growth-oriented' philosophy, new varieties of lending programmes were introduced for low-income countries: the Structural Adjustment Facility (SAF), introduced in 1980,[7] and the Enhanced Structural Adjustment Facility (ESAF), introduced in 1987. In 1999, the ESAF was replaced by the Poverty Reduction and Growth Facility (PRGF). Like the ESAF, PRGF-supported programmes are designed exclusively for very-low-income countries, last three years, and carry a low rate of interest. Unlike ESAF-supported programmes, PRGF arrangements have somewhat fewer structural conditions, and include 'pro-poor' performance criteria (IMF 2002a). However, although their name suggests a complete change in focus, in most respects PRGF-supported programmes resemble those of other lending facilities, and contain the standard elements of fiscal and monetary, debt-related, and structural conditionality.

In contrast to traditional stand-by arrangements, which typically lasted only one year, these new types of arrangements were all 'medium-term' facilities lasting several years, in recognition that structural reforms might take longer than balancing internal and external accounts. However, stand-by arrangements also soon came to include structural conditions, with the result that the difference between stand-bys and the newer lending arrangements today lies primarily in the length of the programme and the terms of repayment – not in the content of conditionality. The average number of structural performance criteria per programme rose sharply during the late 1980s and 1990s, going from two in 1987 to six in 1990, 12 in 1995, and 16 in 1997, before declining to 12 by 1999. The number of structural policy commitments peaked during the Asian financial crisis, the programmes with Korea including 94 structural conditions at their peak, 73 structural conditions applied to Thailand, and 140 to Indonesia (IMF 2002a)

Structural conditionality has not been confined to market liberalization. In recent years, IMF conditionality has been expanded to include such diverse elements as institutional reforms, poverty reduction, and the fight against global terrorism. The Asian financial crisis of 1997 contributed to a new recognition within the IMF that without a solid legal and institutional framework – strong bankruptcy laws, independent bank regulation and supervision, etc. – markets could not function efficiently. Like the market-liberalizing elements of conditionality, 'governance-related' conditions were intended to create deep and long-lasting changes in national economic structures – in marked contrast to the relatively ephemeral fiscal and monetary conditions of previous years (Kapur and Webb 2000). Most recently, the IMF has come to include combating money-laundering, corruption, and terrorism as factors in conditional lending programmes (IMF 2003c). For example, in 2003 Gabon committed to the appointment and financing of a National Commission to Combat Illicit Enrichment (LOI Gabon 2003).

From Rules to Discretion: 1990s to the Present

Over time there has not only been an increase in the volume and the scope of lending conditions, but also a significant change in the *vehicles* of conditional lending. During the past two decades, IMF lending programmes have come to depend less on the precise and formal rules laid out as performance criteria in the Letters of Intent, and more on the discretion of management and staff.

Since early in the IMF's history, its management and staff have exercised considerable authority in determining the contents of conditional lending arrangements. In 1948, it was decided that it was unwieldy to have Executive Board members head negotiations with member governments, since such negotiations took place off-site (i.e. in the member nations) rather than at IMF headquarters in Washington, D.C. (de Vries 1969; Horsefield 1969). The pragmatic justification for this practice was that it would have been prohibitively inefficient for management and staff to spend weeks negotiating with governments and then have to go back and renegotiate because the programme had been rejected by the Executive Board. From that point onward, the Board exerted authority over lending arrangements only at the 'endpoint' – that is, it could threaten to veto future IMF-supported programmes that it found undesirable but would rarely fail to approve programmes already negotiated (de Vries 1974; Southard 1979). This rule had an important exception: the US Executive Director continued to be consulted before bringing a lending arrangement up for consideration by the Board (Woods 2001).

These practices notwithstanding, during the IMF's first decades, the discretion of management and staff over lending conditions was distinctly circumscribed. Discretion was minimized both by the limitation of conditionality to a standardized set of fiscal and monetary performance criteria and by the formal review of these performance criteria by the Executive Board. Today, in contrast, although 'informal' Board briefings on 'problem' countries also occur, this formal procedure has largely been circumvented through the enhanced use of prior actions, structural benchmarks, programme reviews and waivers.

Prior actions are conditions that governments must fulfil in order to be eligible to receive IMF financing in the first place. Prior actions have been present in IMF-supported arrangements since at least the 1970s, when governments were often required to devalue their currencies in order to qualify for IMF financing. In recent years, however, prior actions have become both much more numerous and more ambitious in scope. For example, a recent stand-by arrangement with Turkey contains 17 prior actions, covering such diverse policy issues as introduction of legislation governing foreign investment and laying off government workers (LOI Turkey 2003). IMF-supported arrangements averaged less than half a prior action in 1987–90, but in 1997–2000, they averaged more than five (IMF 2002a). The use of prior actions has been particularly evident in credits for economies undergoing post-socialist transitions: for example, the stand-by with Ukraine in 1997 was tied to a startling 45 prior actions (IMF 2002a).

Prior actions considerably enhance the leverage of IMF management and staff vis-à-vis the governments of developing countries. In earlier decades, a Letter of Intent to the IMF committed a government to a series of fiscal and monetary reforms to be implemented in the near future. Today, in contrast, a government in the throes of a balance-of-payments crisis may have to agree to implement a series of policy actions even before a Letter of Intent is signed. Failure to reach agreement by refusing to implement prior actions means not only losing access to IMF resources but also to the resources of other multilateral agencies (e.g. the World Bank and regional development banks); it also means a loss of access to those private investors who look on an IMF arrangement as 'a seal of approval' signalling a borrowing government's creditworthiness.

Structural benchmarks are policy promises, which often take the form of incremental steps toward structural reforms, such as sending a privatization bill to Congress. They were introduced to IMF-supported programmes in the 1980s (IMF 2002). Benchmarks tend to be more numerous than performance criteria. Deviations from structural benchmarks are not formally considered to be grounds for suspending disbursements (Gold 1996). However, the IMF's Policy Development and Review Department recently concluded that there was no clearly developed policy on the extent to which deviation from benchmarks affects the ability of a government to continue to draw on the IMF's resources (IMF 2001):

> The delay of one or a few benchmarks would rarely if ever by itself interrupt a programme or lead to a requirement for additional measures to complete a review. However, delays in a substantial number of benchmarks could interrupt a review or, at least, would likely require compensating actions. But it is not clear how the staff would determine what constitutes a critical mass.

Thus, it is up to management and staff to decide whether deviation from benchmarks causes the interruption of an IMF arrangement. They may also decide whether deviation from benchmarks may lead to additional programme reviews, as discussed below.

Over the past decade and a half, the IMF has also increasingly turned to programme reviews and waivers in determining whether lending programmes are continued or terminated before disbursement is complete. Reviews consist of staff visits to member nations to monitor whether policy conditions are being met; they can be held at biennial, quarterly, or even monthly 'test' dates, or at unscheduled dates if deemed necessary by management and staff. A recent IMF report on the tools of conditionality acknowledges the enhanced importance of programme reviews and documents their growing frequency from 1992 through 2000 (IMF 2002a). Waivers are decisions to allow disbursements under Fund-supported programmes to continue in spite of deviations from performance criteria. Since the 1970s the use of waivers has increased remarkably, with a particularly notable increase between 1987 and 2000 (IMF 2002a).

Programme reviews and waivers expand IMF management and staff discretion because performance criteria – the formal terms of the loan – are usually not met. In a study of IMF-supported programmes from 1973 through 1997, Mussa and Savastano (1999) found that in a majority of cases borrowing governments were unable to meet performance criteria. Upon discovering such a deviation, it is up to management and staff to decide whether to make a recommendation to the Executive Board that the government be granted a waiver – recommendations that are usually followed by the Board (Mussa and Savastano 1999). Under these circumstances it is in the borrowing government's best interests (and also in the interest of the Executive Director representing the borrowing government) to cultivate the goodwill of the IMF staff members with which it is negotiating. A government that is caught deviating from performance criteria can enhance its chances of receiving a waiver if it can demonstrate compliance with structural benchmarks (IMF 2001). Another way governments can cultivate good relations with management and staff is to comply with the less precisely specified 'policy understandings' (e.g. an informal acknowledgement that it would be a good idea to privatize a state-owned firm: Williamson 1982).[8]

The increased use of prior actions, structural benchmarks, programme reviews and waivers has increased the authority of management and staff at the expense of the Executive Board. The Board normally meets three days a week, when it is supposed to discuss and approve, among other things, IMF-supported programmes. In anticipation of these meetings, Board members are normally provided with staff reports some four weeks ahead of time, which include detailed descriptions of the country's situation and the loan's performance criteria. However, a considerable component of conditionality is negotiated 'on the ground' between staff and borrowing governments. Executive Directors are kept informed of these negotiations through periodic informal Board meetings, and a representative from the office of the Executive Director is normally present during negotiations with the country. But much of what a borrowing country is required to do in order to receive and maintain a lending arrangement may not be subject to the Board's formal review and approval (except as an *ex post* formality). This is particularly obvious with prior actions, which do not appear consistently in the Letters of Intent and are not approved by the Board (although they are known to the Executive Director representing the country) (Buira 2003b). Thus, conditionality and access to IMF resources has evolved away from a predictable rules-based system in which required policies are explicit at the outset and formally approved by the IMF's governing body, to one that is heavily dependent on discretion.

Mission Creep in Sociological Perspective

In the previous section we saw evidence of significant changes in the IMF's activities over time, the most dramatic of which occurred during the past two decades. The emphasis on 'growth', the explosive increase in the number of lending conditions, and the move away from rules toward management and staff discretion are well documented trends, the seriousness of which has been acknowledged by former as well as current IMF staff members (Gold 1996; Polak 1998; IMF 2001, 2002a, 2002b). Indeed, the IMF published a new set of *Guidelines on Conditionality* in 2002 precisely to address widespread concerns over excess conditionality (known to the outside world as 'mission creep').

To successfully address the problem of mission creep, however, it is important to begin with a serious analysis of its causes. For sociologists concerned with organizations, mission creep in international financial institutions is only a single instance of a commonly-observed phenomenon, in which an organization's original goals are 'displaced' over time (Selznick 1949; Zald and Denton 1963; Messinger 1955; Gouldner 1954; Barnett and Finnemore 1999). A number of dynamics commonly observed in complex organizations cause organizational missions to evolve in this way. In the interests of simplifying a large sociological literature, we distinguish between two types of dynamics implicated in unexpected organizational change. The first dynamic is organizations' perennial need to adapt to pressures in their environments. The second dynamic is the internal logic of organizations, which change their practices to meet the challenge of changing problems.

When organizations depend on more powerful organizations for resources, they become subject to control by these organizations and behave accordingly (Michels 1959[1915]; Pfeffer and Salancik 1977). In the case of the IMF, the controlling organization has clearly always been the government of the United States. The IMF's dependence on the United States has historically been manifested in two different sorts of control: that exercised through the institutional mechanism of the Executive Board, and that exercised through non-institutional channels (the so-called 'Treasury effect'). Since the IMF's founding, voting has been weighted according to capital contributions using an arcane and arbitrary formula that has not been widely publicized (Buira 2003b). Although the United States has never had a majority of Board votes, its influence has always been magnified by its power to veto lending and other proposals, as well as the tendency of representatives from other industrial countries to follow the US lead in voting. The United States has always been the IMF's largest contributor, and the largest lender to the IMF through the General Arrangements to Borrow. Most important, as the former Director of the IMF's Legal Department observed, 'The United States, as the issuer of the currency in greatest demand, exercised an irresistible influence on the interpretation of the Articles and the practice of the IMF' (Gold 1996).

The influence of the United States on the early development of the IMF is probably the best-known and best-documented episode in the organization's history (Block 1977; Dell 1981; Dam 1982; Southard 1979; Mikesell 1994; Boughton 2002). Because of US opposition, the IMF was endowed with less than a quarter of the resources John Maynard Keynes had considered necessary for it to be an international lender of last resort (Boughton 2002). Thus handicapped at the outset, the IMF's resources (measured both as a percentage of world GDP and as percentage of world imports) continued to decline over time (Buira 2003a). The United States also was instrumental in developing the principle of conditionality: during the Fund's first decades, the USA used its veto to prevent loans until the IMF adopted a policy of requiring substantive guarantees from debtor nations (Horsefield and Lovasy 1969; Southard 1979; James 1996).

However, although the United States was instrumental in promoting the principle of conditional lending, the *practice* of conditionality evolved more gradually, and was not solidified into a set of clearly-defined performance criteria until the mid-to-late 1950s. Although the intellectual antecedents of the IMF approach are well known (Alexander 1952; Polak 1957; de Vries 1987), we would like to suggest that there was also a pragmatic logic at work – namely, that of a young organization attempting to carve out a 'market niche' so as to guarantee its own survival (Brint and Karabel 1991). Forbidden by the United States from making loans to Marshall Plan recipients, the IMF was simultaneously blocked by the US government from making loans without defining a strict policy of conditionality. The result was that drawings on the IMF's resources fell to zero in 1950 (Block 1997). In large measure because of US pressures, the IMF began to specialize in lending to developing nations, particularly in Latin America (Finch 1997). These nations suffered from chronic and related problems of inflation, balance-of-payments deficits and complex systems of currency controls.

From the perspective of a young organization attempting to justify its existence, the application of fiscal and monetary conditionality to these countries had a number of advantages. For one thing, it provided the IMF with a role that was wholeheartedly supported by its most powerful client. Furthermore, financial programming allowed for the setting of concrete, attainable goals with straightforward means of measurement – the current account deficit, reserve levels, the price level, the fiscal deficit, and so on. It had a well known and well understood historical precedent, since coalitions of private bankers, central banks, and the League of Nations had imposed similar fiscal and monetary conditions during the era of the gold standard (Gisselquist 1981; Clarke 1967; Eichengreen 1996). Finally, it assumed the form of a set of routine, categorical and universal rules of the sort favoured by bureaucracies – and inevitably bemoaned by their clients, who prefer more personal treatment (Weber 1946; Barnett and Finnemore 1999).

These fiscal and monetary conditions remain at the core of IMF financing arrangements and continue to be a primary target of IMF critics, who often focus on the damage that fiscal and monetary austerity inflicts on economic growth (Barro and Lee 2002; Stone 2002). But today's IMF does a good deal more than this: it serves an ally of private creditors and as a promoter of market-oriented structural reforms. The alliance with private creditors is relatively easy to explain as a straightforward case of organizations' joining in a mutually-beneficial symbiosis (Scott 1981). As the IMF's resources, as a proportion of world GDP declined, 'most members in need of balance of payments financing [found] it necessary to negotiate loans by banks, coupled with the restructuring of existing debt, to take care of the gap left unfilled by the IMF and other official agencies' (Gold 1988). The symbiotic relationship that developed over the decades benefited both the IMF and private creditors: the IMF because it gained both assistance in balance-of-payments lending and enhanced authority over borrowing governments, and the creditors because the IMF helped organize their claims and insure them against default. In short, it was widely recognized 'that the IMF and the banks had common interests, and that cooperation between them was essential to defend those interests' (Gold 1988).

The explanation for the rise and expansion of structural conditionality is more elusive, both because there are a number of likely causes and because the internal discussions of management and staff are not available for public scrutiny. Nevertheless, three pieces of circumstantial evidence stand out as relevant. First, IMF resources declined dramatically – from the equivalent of 14 per cent of world imports in 1970 to 6 per cent in 1990, to less than 4 per cent today (Buira 2003a). This created an organizational need to 'ration' resources in some way through more stringent policy conditions. Second, in the 1970s and 1980s there was an important intellectual shift among economists and policymakers, which IMF historian James Boughton (2001) refers to as the 'Silent Revolution'. The emergent neoliberal consensus rejected the view that there was a trade-off between growth and price stability – as the Phillips curve had supposed – and endorsed the view that price stability was actually a *precondition* to growth. Economics has moved well beyond this belief.[9] This 'silent' intellectual revolution meant that the IMF's rediscovery of growth as an organizational purpose would no longer appear to be in contradiction to the IMF's prescription of fiscal and monetary austerity (Boughton 2001).

The third circumstance was the arrival in office of the administrations of Ronald Reagan and Margaret Thatcher, which made no secret of their desire to promote free-market reforms and open the developing world to foreign trade and investment. In 1985 US Treasury Secretary James Baker called on the World Bank and the IMF to help liberalize market institutions and strengthen the private sector. The IMF supported the Baker initiative, which included provisions for structural conditionality and stronger collaboration between the IMF and the Bank (Boughton 2001).[10] The neoliberal emphasis in US policy continued with the Clinton administration: under the leadership of Treasury Secretary Robert E. Rubin, the United States pressured the IMF to amend the Articles of Agreement so that it could require borrowing governments to remove capital controls (Kristof and Sanger 1999).

Which of these factors has played the greatest role in shaping the direction of IMF conditionality over the past two decades? Without downplaying the importance of the decline in resources and the 'intellectual revolution' in economics, we conclude that the third factor has been most salient: external pressures from the IMF's key constituent, the US Treasury, pushed the Fund to assume jurisdiction over such an extraordinary variety of policy areas.[11] Thus we believe that the dominant trend in recent years is best described as 'mission push'.

One piece of evidence that supports this conclusion is the growing disjuncture between the IMF's prescriptions and the views of academic economists. In the 1980s US objectives and the views of mainstream economists were more difficult to disentangle. Today, however, while the IMF continues to promote Washington Consensus-style liberalizations, economists are subjecting the Washington Consensus to extensive critique and revision (Naím 1999; Stiglitz 1998, 2002; Williamson 2003). Thus some of the IMF's current prescriptions contain an ideological legacy of the intellectual environment of two decades ago. Indeed, the head of the IMF's Research Department recently conceded that the liberalization of capital movements does not contribute to higher growth, and that market-friendly capital controls have been effective in preventing crises in a number of countries (Prasad et al. 2003). This suggests that the IMF's ongoing promotion of capital-account liberalization may derive more from outside pressures than from intellectual conviction.

Another reason to consider 'mission push' to be the predominant factor is that recent additions to conditionality have been so far removed from the IMF's purposes and organizational capacity. The fight against money laundering and global terrorism, while laudable, are activities that have more to do with police and security cooperation than with the purposes of the IMF in the fields of economic growth and balance-of-payments stability. Moreover, there is little reason to believe that IMF staff possess expertise concerning such matters.[12]

'Mission push', in turn, helps explain the recent trend toward discretional conditionality. Whereas during its first decades the IMF developed a standardized set of fiscal and monetary performance criteria, for at least a decade it has been rapidly moving in the opposite direction. In any lending arrangement today, the performance criteria formally approved by the Executive Board are only the tip of the iceberg; what may lie beneath is a complex set of prior actions, structural benchmarks, reviews and waivers, the full significance of which may be known only to a few Executive Directors, management and staff. In the absence of clear rules, borrowing governments no longer have a secure understanding of the actions that will prevent their disbursements from being interrupted. Management and staff exercise a wide degree of discretion in deciding whether lending arrangements will be interrupted, and what sorts of conditions must be met.

Such a move from rules to discretion is a dynamic commonly observed in organizations facing challenging circumstances. Bureaucratic organizations ordinarily become more rule-based and routinized over time (Weber 1947). But where tasks become unusually complex and environments uncertain, formally specified rules may not be flexible enough to deal with contingencies. In these cases, tasks are increasingly removed from the restrictions of automatic rules and delegated instead to experts (or professionals) possessing high levels of discretion (Scott 1981). Where such organizations are formally accountable to representative bodies, this may lead to a shift in authority away from representative authorities and toward technocratic experts, according to a process Robert Michels termed the 'iron law of oligarchy' (Michels 1959[1911]).

It would be difficult to deny that the Fund's job today is both more uncertain and more complex than it was during the postwar period. Uncertainty has resulted in part from the decrease in the predictability of key macroeconomic variables. In the more stable 1950s and 1960s it was easier to foresee the macroeconomic environment over the coming year, and hence to determine and meet a circumscribed set of performance criteria set at the outset of a lending arrangement.[13] Today, with the increased volatility of exchange rates, interest rates, and short-term capital flows, it is more likely that performance criteria will have to be modified (IMF 2002a).[14]

More important, both uncertainty and complexity have been heightened by the recent and unprecedented proliferation of lending conditions. Fiscal and monetary performance criteria are relatively easy to measure and enforce, and hence relatively congenial to being formally specified at the outset of a lending arrangement. Structural conditions, in contrast, are difficult to enforce, 'due to the vagaries of the political process involved in bringing them to completion' (IMF 2002a). In other words, they have to go through Congress or Parliament; what ultimately gets approved may be a compromise that does not fully meet an initially-specified performance criterion. Structural reforms are also difficult to break down into manageable, measurable targets (Gold 1996). For example, whereas it is relatively easy for IMF staff to set a quarterly goal for a fiscal deficit, and to check whether a government has complied, how can the IMF measure whether a government has gone a quarter of the way toward privatizing a state-owned firm? The logical solution to this organizational dilemma has been to make lending arrangements less dependent on formally-specified rules, and to enforce them at the discretion of management and staff. Unfortunately, this move to technocratic discretion raises serious questions of transparency and accountability.

Some Implications of Recent Trends

Some observers may suggest that the proliferation of IMF lending conditions is the lesser of two evils – the greater being the failure of governments to implement much-needed reforms. But we identify four reasons to believe that mission creep creates more serious problems than it solves:

1 Mission creep greatly increases borrowing governments' uncertainty as to whether they may continue to draw on IMF resources. The proliferation of performance criteria, benchmarks, and prior actions in such diverse fields as governance, privatization, legal reforms, anti-corruption efforts, money laundering and the financing of terrorism, and so on, has decreased the probability that governments will be able to keep all or even most of their original commitments. It then is up to IMF management and staff to decide which conditions are important and which are not. In short, under the current system, it is hard for governments to know where they stand – and for investors to know what the outcome will be. The resulting lending arrangements, in the language of the Articles of Agreement, do not 'give confidence to members'.

2 In ambiguous bargaining situations where one party has discretionary power, political considerations often influence organizational goals.[15] Since the mid-1990s, the IMF has abandoned lending limits related to quota size, allowing for larger support packages 'in exceptional circumstances' (IMF 1999). In practice, such 'exceptions' have been made for significant emerging-market economies in which foreign portfolio investors have a large stake. For example, Turkey's maximum access in excess of 1,700 per cent of quota in 2003; Brazil's was 628 per cent that same year (IMF 2003c). The 1997 stand-by with South Korea was widely criticized for including bilateral trade conditions tailored to benefit American and Japanese companies (Pollack 1997). The promotion of geopolitical interests is also facilitated by discretion. It is widely understood among Executive Directors and borrowing governments that strategically-placed nations such as Turkey and Afghanistan are much more likely to receive sympathetic consideration than geopolitically less important nations.[16]

3 The Fund's expanded mission is based largely on the questionable assumption that Fund-supported programmes are an effective means to economic growth. Unlike fiscal, monetary, and liberalizing conditions, indicators of economic growth are not included as benchmarks or performance criteria. Rather, IMF-supported programmes implicitly assume that lowering inflation and implementing free-market reforms are necessary and sufficient preconditions for economic growth. However, recently a number of studies, from both inside and outside the IMF, have recognized that while IMF-supported programmes improve the balance of payments, and often reduce inflation, they do not increase growth rates, and indeed often have a contractionary effect (Stone 2002; Barro and Lee 2002; Selowsky *et al.* 2003). This is no surprise since Fund-supported programmes continue to require sharp fiscal and monetary cutbacks and the prioritization of debt repayment.

4 Another problem with mission creep is the twofold problem of accountability. First, because of the rise of discretional conditionality, the IMF's accountability to its own governing body – the Executive Board – has declined significantly. The developing countries that make up the IMF's client base have always had very little power and representation on the Executive Board, owing to the IMF's weighted voting structure and their need not to antagonize staff and management to be able to secure flexibility or leniency for their countries. But because the Board has become less relevant, the developing countries' influence has been further diminished. Second, the IMF lacks accountability to national electorates at a time when it both claims jurisdiction over a much wider range of national policies and possesses greater leverage to implement them.

In response to concerns over the proliferation of conditionality and the high rate of programme failure, the IMF adopted a new set of *Guidelines on Conditionality* in 2002, which recommend the limited use of prior actions and programme reviews, and the scaling down of performance criteria. However, there is little reason to expect that these will reverse or even stem the trend of mission creep. The 1979 *Guidelines*, which put considerably greater limits on conditionality than the current ones, were unsuccessful in checking the explosive growth of conditions in the 1980s (Polak 1991). History seems to be repeating itself. The 2003 stand-by arrangement with Turkey is associated with 38 prior actions and 42 structural benchmarks, most of them oriented toward an ambitious programme of free-market reforms (IMF 2003).

Conclusion

The IMF was originally founded for the purpose of helping countries weather balance-of-payments crises by providing them with temporary financing. But the IMF's tasks have expanded steadily over time. By the early 1960s these included the crusade against inflation and fiscal irresponsibility, a goal that could be seen as directly related to balance-of-payments objectives. By the early 1980s the tasks also included helping avoid defaults and collecting the debts of developing countries. Today, the IMF's concerns range from free-market reforms to institution-building, and to measures to combat terrorism. More than any other development in the IMF's history, this latest phase represents a revolutionary shift. It has been associated with a redefinition of the IMF's mission, a dramatic rise in the number of lending conditions, and a significant increase in the discretionary power of IMF management and staff. The absence of rules appears to have resulted in part from the expansion of the IMF's mandate – which, in turn, seems to have resulted from heightened pressures from the US Treasury. The diminished importance of rules makes it easier for the IMF's most powerful clients to push for a further expansion of its mission, and for more exceptions to the rules. Thus 'mission push' and discretion are mutually reinforcing.

For Michels, such developments are inevitable liabilities of public interest organizations. To stem the tide of mission creep and technocratization, he recommends adopting more open communication and implementing broader systems of participation. We are similarly led to the conclusion that it is only by increasing the Fund's transparency, and beginning to address issues of accountability, that the problems of mission creep can be addressed. Two separate levels of reform would be required.

- Lending conditions would have to be scaled back to include only items that can be measured or evaluated and approved in an objective manner. Diminishing technocratic discretion in favour of formal, bureaucratic rules would contribute to making lending policies truly transparent.
- The IMF's system of formal governance would have to be reworked in such a way that the IMF's stakeholders could have a greater say in the Fund's policies. This would require an extensive revision of the voting structure of the Executive Board, which currently gives the United States veto power and developing countries very little say (Woods 2001; Buira 2001, 2003b).

Such calls for enhanced transparency and accountability are nothing new – in fact, they are among the relatively standard recommendations advanced by the IMF's most prominent critics and would-be reformers (International Financial Institution Advisory Commission 1998; Stiglitz 2002). The fact that there has thus far been no move to follow these recommendations attests to the powerful vested interests and forces that have contributed to pushing the IMF's mission in the first place.

Notes

Paper presented at the XVIII G-24 Technical Group Meeting, 8–9 March 2004, Geneva, Switzerland.

1 This amendment stated that 'The Fund shall adopt policies on the use of its general resources, including policies on stand-by or similar arrangements, and may adopt special policies for special balance of payments problems that will assist members to solve their balance of payments problems in a manner consistent with the provisions of this Agreement, and that will establish adequate safeguards for the temporary use of the general resources of the Fund' (IMF 1969).

2 Source: Letters of Intent from Argentina, Bolivia, Brazil, Haiti, Jamaica, and Peru, 1970–79.

3 In a sense, the approach followed on this occasion constituted a major departure from the normal IMF approach to programme formulation. The previous standard operating procedure had been to estimate the availability of financial resources as the starting point for the design of the programme, and on that basis working out the permissible credit expansion and fiscal balance. In response to the debt crisis, however, the IMF constructed programmes based on an estimate of how much debtors could be expected to adjust without resorting to default. Thus, the usual approach to programme design was reversed.

4 Source: Letters of Intent from Argentina, Bolivia, Brazil, Haiti, Jamaica, and Peru, 1971–96.

5 Three recent Nobel laureates have challenged this 'first best' belief, showing that it rests on very restrictive assumptions about perfect information that are rarely met, and that even small deviations from this paradigm lead to very different outcomes. See Nobel lectures by Ackerlof, Spence and Stiglitz. Other Nobel laureates to challenge the paradigm include Douglas North and Daniel Kahneman.

6 The sharp fall in output in Russia, Moldova, and other former Soviet republics underscores the importance of the institutional and legal framework. Contrast this with the high growth experience of China, where management was reformed to foster competition but the property of many enterprises remains that of the state.

7 The SAF was phased out in 1995.

8 Rumours of this sort of bargain have led to speculation that some governments 'trade' fiscal and monetary performance criteria for structural reforms (such an informal deal is believed to have been struck between IMF staff and the Menem government in Argentina in the 1990s, for example: *Latin American Newsletters* 17/10/96, 18/11/96). A recent IMF report on conditionality acknowledges that 'some critics see the Fund as pressing countries to agree to ambitious programmes that it does not expect to be implemented, in order to obtain leverage over the countries' policies ...' (IMF 2002a).

9 While high levels of inflation are harmful to growth, several studies, including IMF studies, have concluded that inflation rates below 40 per cent are not (Bruno and Easterly 1996; Fischer 1993; Stiglitz 1998; Khan 2002). Ackerlof, Dickens and Perry (1996) find that low levels of inflation may actually improve economic performance relative to what it would have been if it had been eliminated altogether.

10 Over the course of the 1980s, IMF staff brought numerous proposals for the introduction of structural conditionality to the Executive Board; while resistance to these proposals was initially fierce (particularly among developing-country representatives), over time opposition was eroded (Boughton 2001).

11 Recently, the Director of the IMF's External Relations Department responded to concerns about 'creeping conditionality' by noting that 'we as an institution are being asked to do much, much more in the economic, social, and political arenas' (*Book Forum*, 16/2/04:36).

12 However, including these items in IMF financing arrangements fits remarkably well with US geopolitical objectives since September 11, 2001.

13 Even during this more stable period, however, it was impossible to predict crop failures in agricultural economies.

14 The IMF is partly responsible for this more volatile macroeconomic environment, since it has been promoting capital account liberalization without providing the necessary protections (i.e. automatic lending) that the resulting risks demand.

15 This despite of the fact that Article XII, Section 4(c) directs management and staff to 'respect the international character [of the Fund's activities] and [to] refrain from all attempts to influence any of the staff in the discharge of these functions'.

16 Although a nation such as Argentina may have little geopolitical importance, its status as a major debtor to the IMF (owing about $17 billion) has recently allowed it to bargain for more flexible conditions; the Fund is thus able to save itself the embarrassment of default and large non-performing assets.

References

Akerlof, George, William Dickens and George Perry, 1996, 'The Macroeconomics of Low Inflation', Brookings Papers on Economic Activity.

Alexander, Sidney S., 1952, 'Effects of a Devaluation on a Trade Balance', *IMF Staff Papers*, 2, pp. 263–278.

Babb, Sarah, 2001, *Managing Mexico: Economists from Nationalism to Neoliberalism*, Princeton, NJ: Princeton University Press.

Barnett, Michael N. and Martha Finnemore, 1999, 'The Politics, Power, and Pathologies of International Organizations', *International Organization*, 53 (4), pp. 698–721.

Barro, Robert J. and Jong-Wha Lee, 2002, 'IMF Programs: Who is Chosen and What Are the Effects?', National Bureau of Economic Research Working Paper 8951.

Bernstein, Edward, 1984, 'Epilogue: Reflections on the Fortieth Anniversary of the Bretton Woods Conference', Paper presented at the 40th Anniversary of the United Nations Monetary and Financial Conference of 1944, Mt Washington Hotel, Bretton Woods, pp. 97–115 in Black (ed.) 1991 (see below).

Bird, Graham, 1997, 'External Financing and Balance of Payments Adjustment in Developing Countries: Getting a Better Policy Mix', *World Development*, 25 (9), pp. 1409–1420.

Black, Stanley (ed.), 1991, *A Levite Among the Priests: Edward M. Bernstein and the Origins of the Bretton Woods System*, Boulder, CO: Westview.

Block, Fred, 1977, *The Origins of International Economic Disorder: A Study of United States International Monetary Policy from World War II to the Present*, Berkeley: University of California Press.

Book Forum, 16/2/04, *IMF Survey* 33 (3), pp. 33, 35–37.

Boughton, James M., 1997, 'From Suez to Tequila: The IMF as Crisis Manager', IMF Working Paper 97/90.

——, 2001, *Silent Revolution: The International Monetary Fund, 1979–1989*. Washington, D.C.: IMF.

——, 2002, 'Why White, Not Keynes? Inventing the Postwar International Monetary System', IMF Working Paper 02/52.

Bruno, Michael and William Easterly, 1996, 'Inflation and Growth: In Search of a Stable Relationship', *Federal Reserve Bank of St Louis Review*, 78 (3), pp. 139–146.

Buira, Ariel, 2003a, 'An Analysis of IMF Conditionality', Paper prepared for the XVI Technical Group Meeting of the Intergovernmental Group of 24, Port of Spain, Trinidad and Tobago, 13–14 February 2003.

——, 2003b, 'The Governance of the International Monetary Fund', in Inge Kaul, Pedro Conceição, Katell Le Goulven and Ronald U. Mendoza (eds), *Providing Global Public Goods: Managing Globalization*, New York: Oxford University Press, pp. 225–244.

Bretton Woods Project, 2003, 'IMF Mission Creep'. http://www.brettonwoodsproject.org/update/14/14b.html#creep.

Clarke, Stephen V. O., 1967, *Central Bank Cooperation 1924–31*, New York: Federal Reserve Bank of New York.

Dam, Kenneth W., 1982, *The Rules of the Game: Reform and Evolution in the International Monetary System*, Chicago: The University of Chicago Press.

Dell, Sydney, 1981, *On Being Grandmotherly: The Evolution of IMF Conditionality*, Princeton, NJ: International Finance Section, Department of Economics, Princeton University, Essays in International Finance, No. 144.

de Vries, Margaret G., 1974, *The International Monetary Fund, 1966–1971: The System Under Stress*.

——, 1987, *Balance of Payments Adjustment, 1945 to 1986: The IMF Experience*, Washington, D.C.: IMF.

de Vries, Margaret and J. Keith Horsefield (eds) 1969, *The International Monetary Fund 1945–1965: Twenty Years of International Monetary Cooperation*, Washington, D.C.: IMF.

Edwards, Sebastian, 1995, *Crisis and Reform in Latin America: From Despair to Hope*, New York: Oxford University Press.

Eichengreen, Barry, 1996, *Globalizing Capital: A History of the International Monetary System*, Princeton, NJ: Princeton University Press.

Einhorn, Jessica, 2001, 'The World Bank's Mission Creep', *Foreign Affairs*, 80 (5), pp. 22–35.

Felix, David, 1961, 'An Alternative View of the "Monetarist"– "Structuralist" Controversy', in A. O. Hirschman (ed.), *Latin American Issues*, New York: The Twentieth Century Fund, pp. 81–93.

Finch, C. David, 1997, *Werribee to Washington: A Career at the International Monetary Fund*, unpublished manuscript.

Fischer, Stanley, 1993, 'The Role of Macroeconomic Factors in Growth', *Journal of Monetary Economics*, 32, pp. 485–512.

Gisselquist, David, 1981, *The Political Economics of International Bank Lending*, New York: Praeger.

Gold, Joseph, 1988, 'Mexico and the Development of the Practice of the International Monetary Fund', *World Development*, 16 (10), pp. 1127–1142.

——, 1996, *Interpretation: The IMF and International Law*, London: Kluwer Law International.

Gouldner, Alvin W., 1954, *Patterns of Industrial Bureaucracy*, Glencoe, IL: Free Press.

Hirschman, Albert O., 1963, *Journeys Toward Progress: Studies of Economic Policy-Making in Latin America*, New York: Norton.

Horsefield, J. Keith, 1969, *Chronicle*, Volume 1 of de Vries *et al.* (eds).

Horsefield, J. Keith and Gertrud Lovasy, 1969, 'Evolution of the Fund's Policy on Drawings', in de Vries *et al.* (eds), pp. 381–427.

Ikenberry, G. John, 1992, 'A World Economy Restored: Expert Consensus and the Anglo-American Postwar Settlement', *International Organization*, 46 (1), pp. 289–321.

International Financial Institution Advisory Commission (Meltzer Commission), 1998, Summary of Findings and Report, http://csf.colorado.edu/roper/if/Meltzer-com-mission-mar00/.

International Monetary Fund, 1944, Articles of Agreement.

——, 1969, First Amendment to the Articles of Agreement.

——, 1999, 'Access Policy – Guidelines on Access Limits', Executive Board Decision No. 11876-(99/2), 6 January 1999.

——, 2001, 'Conditionality in Fund-Supported Programs – Policy Issues', Prepared by the Policy Development and Review Department, 16 February 2001, http://www.imf.org/external/np/pdr/cond/2001/eng/policy/021601.pdf.

——, 2002a, 'The Modalities of Conditionality – Further Considerations', Prepared by the Policy Development and Review Department, 8 January 2002.

——, IMF, 2002b, 'Review of the Key Features of the Poverty Reduction and Growth Facility – Staff Analyses', Prepared by the Fiscal Affairs and Policy Development and Review Departments, Washington, D.C.: IMF.

——, 2003a, 'IMF Conditionality and Program Ownership: A Case for Streamlined Conditionality', Prepared by S. Nuri Erbas, Middle Eastern Department, http://www.imf.org/external/pubs/cat/longres.cfm?sk = 16504.0.

——, 2003b, Annex A to Letter of Intent for Turkey, http://www.imf.org/External/NP/LOI/2003/tur/01/040503.pdf.

——, 2003c, *International Financial Statistics.*

James, Harold, 1996, *International Monetary Cooperation Since Bretton Woods*, New York: Oxford University Press.

Kapur, Devesh and Richard Webb, 2000, 'Governance-Related Conditionalities of the International Financial Institutions', G-24 Discussion Paper No. 6, August 2000.

Khan, Mohsin S. and Abdelhak Senhadji, 2002, 'Inflation, Financial Deepening, and Economic Growth', Paper prepared for the Banco de Mexico Conference on Macroeconomic Stability, Financial Markets and Economic Development, Mexico City, 12–13 November 2002.

Kristof, Nicholas D. and David E. Sanger, 1999, 'How the US Wooed Asia to Let Cash Flow In', *New York Times*, 16/2/99.

Latin American Newsletters Ltd, 1996, 'Menem Faces Rebellions as Argentina Begins to Emerge from Recession', 17 October 1996.

——, 1996, 'IMF Urges Menem to Push Reforms', 18 November 1996.

Markoff, Jonathan and Verónica Montecinos, 1993, 'The Ubiquitous Rise of Economists', *Journal of Public Policy*, 13 (1), pp. 37–38.

Messinger, Sheldon, 1955, 'Organizational Transformation: A Case Study of a Declining Social Movement', *American Sociological Review*, 20, pp. 3–10.

Michels, Robert, 1959[1915], *Political Parties: A Sociological Study of the Oligarchical Tendencies of the Modern Democracy*, translated by Eden and Cedar Paul, New York: Dover.

Mikesell, Raymond F., 1994, *The Bretton Woods Debates: A Memoir*, International Finance Section, Department of Economics, Princeton, NJ, Essays in International Finance No. 192.

Mussa, Michael and Miguel Savastano, 1999, 'The IMF Approach to Economic Stabilization', IMF Working Paper 99/104.

Naím, Moisés, 1999, 'Fads and Fashion in Economic Reforms: Washington Consensus or Washington Confusion?', Draft of Working Paper for IMF Conference on the Second Generation of Reforms, Washington, D.C., 8–9 November 1999.

Payer, Cheryl, 1974, *The Debt Trap*, Middlesex, England: Penguin.

Pfeffer, Jeffrey and Gerald R. Salancik, 1977, *The External Control of Organizations: A Resource Dependence Perspective*, New York: Harper & Row.

Polak, Jacques J., 1957, 'Monetary Analysis of Income Formation and Payments Problems', *IMF Staff Papers*, 6, pp. 1–50.

——, 1991, *The Changing Nature of IMF Conditionality*, Princeton, NJ: International Finance Section, Department of Economics, Princeton University, Essays in International Finance.

——, 1998, 'The Articles of Agreement of the IMF and the Liberalization of Capital Movements', in Stanley Fischer *et al. Should the IMF Pursue Capital-Account Convertibility?* Princeton, NJ: International Finance Section, Department of Economics, Princeton University, Essays in International Finance No. 207.

Pollack, Andrew, 1997, 'Koreans Not Rushing to Shake the Hand Holding the Bailout Check', *New York Times*, D-1, December 1997.

Prasad, Eswar, Kenneth Rogoff, Shang-Jin Wei and M. Ayhan Kose, 2003, *Effects of Financial Globalization on Developing Countries: Some Empirical Evidence*, Washington, D.C.: IMF, http://www.imf.org/external/np/res/docs/2003/031703.htm.

Ruggie, John Gerald, 1983, 'International Regimes, Transactions, and Change: Embedded Liberalism in the Postwar Economic Order', in S. Krasner (ed.), *International Regimes*, Ithaca, NY: Cornell University Press, pp. 195–231.

Scott, W. Richard, 1992 [1981], *Organizations: Rational, Natural, and Open Systems*, New York: Prentice Hall.

Selowsky, Marcelo, Ali Mansoor and Ale Kayizzi Mugerwa, 2003, 'Fiscal Adjustment in IMF-Supported Programs', Washington, D.C.: IMF, Independent Evaluation Office Report.

Selznick, Philip, 1949, *TVA and the Grass Roots: A Study of Politics and Organization*, Berkeley: University of California Press.

Smith, Alastair and James Raymond Vreeland, 2003, 'The Survival of Political Leaders and IMF Programs: Testing the Scapegoat Story', Paper prepared for the Yale University Conference on the Impact of Globalization on the Nation-State from Above: The International Monetary Fund and The World Bank, http://www.yale.edu/ycias/globalization/Smith_and_Vreeland.pdf.

Southard, Frank, 1979, *The Evolution of the International Monetary Fund*, Princeton, NJ: International Finance Section, Department of Economics, Princeton University, Essays in International Finance.

Stiglitz, Joseph E., 1998, 'More Instruments and Broader Goals: Moving the Post-Washington Consensus', WIDER Economic Lectures, No. 2.

——, 2002, *Globalization and its Discontents*, New York: Norton.

Stone, Randall W., 2002, *Lending Credibility: The International Monetary Fund and the Post-Communist Transition*, Princeton, NJ: Princeton University Press.

Taylor, Lance, 1981, 'IS/LM in the Tropics: Diagrammatics of the New Structuralist Macro Critique', in William R. Cline and Sidney Weintraub (eds), *Economic Stabilization in Developing Countries*, Washington, D.C.: Brookings Institute, pp. 465–506.

Thorp, Rosemary and Laurence Whitehead, 1979, 'Introduction', in Rosemary Thorp and Laurence Whitehead (eds) *Inflation and Stabilisation in Latin America*, London: Macmillan, pp. 1–22.

Webb, Richard, 2000, 'The Influence of International Financial Institutions on ISI', in Enrique Cárdenas, José Antonio Ocampo and Rosemary Thorp (eds), New York: Palgrave.

Weber, Max, 1946, 'Bureaucracy', in H. Gerth and C. W. Mills (eds), *From Max Weber: Essays in Sociology*, New York: Oxford, pp. 196–244.

Westney, Eleanor, 1987, *Imitation and Innovation: The Transfer of Western Organizational Patterns to Meiji Japan*, Cambridge, MA: Harvard University Press.

Williamson, John, 1982, *The Lending Policies of the International Monetary Fund*, Washington, D.C.: Institute for International Economics.

——, 2003, 'From Reform Agenda to Damaged Brand Name: A Short History of the Washington Consensus and Suggestions for What to do Next', *Finance and Development*, September, pp. 10–13.

Woods, Ngaire, 2001, 'Making the IMF and the World Bank More Accountable', *International Affairs*, 77 (1), pp. 83–100.

Zald, Mayer N. and Patricia Denton, 1963, 'From Evangelism to General Service: The Transformation of the YMCA', *Administrative Science Quarterly*, 8, pp. 214–234.

Letters of Intent (available on www.imf.org):

Argentina: SBA (1976, 1977, 1983, 1984, 1987, 1989, 1991, 1996); EFF (1992)

Bolivia: SBA (1973, 1980, 1986); SAF (1986); ESAF (1988, 1992, 1994).

Brazil: SBA (1972, 1983, 1988, 1991, 1992).

Gabon: PRGF (2003).

Haiti: SBA (1972, 1973, 1974, 1975, 1976, 1977, 1982, 1983, 1989, 1995); EFF (1978); SAF (1986); ESAF (1996).

Jamaica: SBA (1973, 1977, 1984, 1985, 1987, 1988, 1990, 1991); EFF (1978, 1979, 1981, 1992).

Peru: SBA (1954, 1963, 1977, 1978, 1979, 1984); EFF (1982, 1993, 1996).

5

UP FROM SIN: A PORTFOLIO APPROACH TO SALVATION

Randall Dodd and Shari Spiegel

Financial Policy Forum   Initiative for Policy Dialogue

Abstract:

In this chapter we develop a proposal with the potential to greatly improve the ability of developing countries to reduce their exposure to other countries' interest-rate and exchange-rate volatility and to lower their cost of raising capital abroad. The key to achieving these goals is for developing countries to borrow in their own currencies and for investors to lend by creating portfolios of local-currency government debt securities that employ the risk-management technique of diversification to generate a return-to-risk that competes favourably with other major capital market security indices. We show, based on data from 1993 to 2004, that a portfolio of emerging-market local-currency debt can generate rates of return relative to risk that compete with those of major securities indices in international capital markets. It bears noting that the early 1990s witnessed several severe shocks to international capital markets, including the crises in East Asia, Russia, and Brazil, and the failure of Long-Term Capital Management. We also analyse the implications of employing such a policy for attracting capital to developing countries, the impact on the stability of their financial systems and on their costs of borrowing, and the implications for future development of local capital markets.

Introduction

The massive amount of foreign indebtedness is one of the most significant problems facing developing countries today. The majority of this debt is denominated in the major currencies,[1] and it has left developing countries with enormous exposures to foreign exchange and foreign interest-rate risk. External shocks transmitted through these exposures have proved costly to absorb. Most of the emerging-market crises over the past two decades were caused, or at least exacerbated, by foreign borrowings (although derivatives have added substantially to foreign-currency-denominated liabilities in some cases[2]). Concerns over foreign debt were raised soon after the 1973 oil price shock, and the problem became apparent in the early 1980s after Mexico announced it would be unable to meet its debt payments in August of 1982. More recently, outstanding dollar or dollar-linked obligations were one of the main triggers of the 1994 Mexican crisis and the 1997 Asian crisis, and Argentina's large issues of external debt was a primary factor in its 2001 default.

Most of the economic policy research since the developing country debt crisis broke out in 1982 has focused on solving the problem of foreign investors' managing their credit risk exposure and the problem of developing countries' adjusting to the variability of foreign capital flows and financial crises. Less attention has been given to strategies to help developing countries reduce their foreign exchange exposure. More recently, the issue of foreign-exchange risk arising from foreign indebtedness has received greater attention as a result of a new body of economic policy research around the 'original sin' hypothesis of Eichengreen and Hausmann (1999). Today there are efforts under way to move developing countries away from foreign-currency-denominated borrowing.

In this paper we build upon some experiments[3] in local currency investing in order to provide a policy analysis of what we hope will prove to be a major new innovation in financing development. It improves market efficiency by overcoming some existing market imperfections. It requires negligible statutory or regulatory changes. And it does not necessarily require the involvement of such international financial institutions as the IMF or World Bank, even though it would benefit from some official or public sector sponsorship.

Our proposal is to raise capital in international markets by forming diversified portfolios of emerging-market local-currency debt (LCD) issued by sovereign governments. We show that the returns on such a portfolio are sufficiently independent to allow a substantial reduction in portfolio variance through diversification. The portfolio produces a risk-return profile – measured in US dollars – that would be competitive with major US and European security indices.

In the following section we discuss the context of this problem and the economic literature that addresses it. Following that, we develop the financial economic basis for the LCD portfolio and analyse its financial performance relative to some familiar alternative investments. We then analyse the development and economics implications of this new financing facility for developing economies and offer concluding comments.

Overview of the Issue

One key difference between advanced and developing economies[4] is that the latter generally cannot borrow in international capital markets in their own currency.[5] While other distinguishing features include the capital-labour ratio, productivity, education levels, and sophisticated financial systems, the inability of developing countries to borrow internationally in their own local currency is a critical element affecting their financial stability.

Many developing countries need capital inflows to augment domestic savings so as to obtain a pace of investment consistent with rapidly rising growth. In addition to foreign direct investment, developing countries need capital investment in the form of credit. If they are unable to negotiate terms denominated in their own local currency, they must enter into a Faustian compact in which the joys of lower interest rates are held captive by the volatile obligation to repay in foreign-currency denominations.

Market Description: Foreign Currency Claims

Although foreign debt can play a useful economic role in development by supplementing domestic savings, its currency denomination can create unwanted exposure to exchange-rate risk. Consider the breakdown of developing country long-term external debt. The latest year for which data are available on currency composition is 2000 (from the World Bank's Global Development Finance database). The total long-term external debt that year was $2,047.7 billion (it would rise to $2,644 billion by the end of 2003). Of that, 64 per cent was denominated in US dollars, 12 per cent in yen, and 9.5 per cent in Deutschemarks, French francs and pounds sterling. The six currencies comprise at least 85.5 per cent of the long-term indebtedness of developing countries; another 7.6 per cent was debt in 'multiple currencies' (these six currencies probably make up a large share of this figure) and 7.2 per cent in all other currencies.[6]

Two particular examples, drawn from Mexico and Korea just prior to their financial crises, illustrate the predominance of major currencies, and the lack of their own local currencies, in denominating their foreign debts. In December 1994, 61 per cent of Mexico's long-term foreign debt was denominated in US dollars, 21 percent in 'multiple currency' formulas, and 9 per cent in Japanese yen. Measured at year-end 1996 – the last data point prior to the financial crisis – the dollar composition of Korea's long-term debt was

79 per cent, while that in yen and multiple currencies stood at 13 per cent and 5 per cent respectively. Thus, 92 per cent of Korea's foreign debt was in two major currencies: the US dollar and the Japanese yen.

The Consequences of Foreign Currency Borrowing

The consequences of foreign-currency-denominated indebtedness are a major source of developing countries' exposure to international disruptions and disturbances, as well as their vulnerability to domestic fiscal solvencies and exchange-rate systems. This makes the more fragile economies of developing countries subject to monetary policy changes in the country (or countries) whose currency denominates their international debt. If foreign central banks tighten monetary policy and raise interest rates, this will increases foreign-currency interest payments for the developing countries on both variable-rate debt and new issuances while they will also see the market value of their foreign currency assets reduced. For example, in the 10 months prior to the financial crisis in Mexico in December 1994, the US central bank raised short-term interest rates six times, from 3 per cent to 5.5 per cent, and the dollar rose by more than 7 per cent against other Group of Ten (G-10) currencies. This put enormous external pressure on the peso while diminishing the Mexican central bank's capacity to defend it. Similarly, it was the rapid rise in US interest rates in response to the oil price hike in the late 1970s that precipitated the Latin American debt crises of the 1980s.[7]

An appreciation in the value of the foreign currency of denomination would also raise the cost of servicing foreign debt and put pressure on the international value of the local currency. In the months preceding the first East Asian crisis, the US dollar appreciated substantially against the Japanese yen. Starting in August 1996, the dollar rose 8.2 per cent by January 1997; it was up 19 per cent by May 1997 when the Thai baht was hit by speculative attacks; by December 1997, the dollar had risen 25.5 per cent over the previous 14 months. This had the effect of substantially raising the value of Thailand's dollar-denominated debt, and in comparison lowering the value of its yen-denominated exports.

The accumulation of international debt denominated in foreign currency poses a danger to more fragile financial systems, which often have dollar-denominated liabilities and local currency assets. Borrowing in foreign currency causes a 'currency mismatch' that exposes the developing country to devaluation or some other international disruptions; and borrowing short-term causes 'maturity mismatch' that exposes the country to other volatile economic sources that contribute to creating a fragile financial system. It creates a economic precipice by dramatically raising the cost of devaluation, and it makes policymakers more reluctant to let the currency devalue even when it becomes overvalued.[8]

Foreign-currency borrowing also reduces a country's ability to pursue independent monetary and fiscal policy. The country's monetary policy is constrained through its impact on exchange rates and, in turn, its impact on the local-currency cost of servicing foreign debt. Thus, a central bank that would otherwise respond to a contractionary shock by easing credit conditions would be hampered from doing so for fear of reducing its currency value and thereby raising the cost of servicing its foreign debt.

Foreign-currency borrowing also undermines the credibility of central banks in developing countries because their foreign reserves, which might amount to a significant proportion of their imports and trade balances, can be dwarfed by their foreign-currency debt obligations. Foreign-currency indebtedness therefore necessitates increased holdings of foreign reserve, which can be quite expensive.[9]

The ability of foreign-currency borrowers to engage in fiscal policy is also affected. It is constrained because any increase in the fiscal deficit will widen a country's credit spread and further push up the cost of borrowing. High foreign indebtedness forces countries to follow pro-cyclical macroeconomic policies, raising interest rates and tightening fiscal policy during a recession.[10] Foreign-currency borrowing also undermines the fiscal credibility of developing countries because so much of their sovereign debt is known to be denominated in foreign currency.

On the other hand, borrowing in local currency adds to the tax base for seigniorage revenue in the home country owing to the increase in demand for the local currency for the purpose of trading in the local currency instrument, as well as in the process of making and receiving payments on those securities.

Yet another benefit is that the development and growth in the market for the local currency government securities play a critical role – as a foundation or skeletal structure – in promoting more 'mature' domestic securities markets.

The danger in amassing foreign-currency debt is so great that it calls into doubt the efficiency of international capital markets in distributing risk. Why is the foreign-exchange risk so disproportionately held by those least able to bear it? If this distribution of risk signals a market imperfection, then it highlights the need for an innovation or new public policy to rectify it.

Recognition of a Problem

The recognition of the problem of borrowing in foreign currency is not new. Soon after developing countries' indebtedness began to rise rapidly following the 1973 oil price hike, and well before Mexico's payment crisis erupted in August 1982, there were public policy discussions of this concern. One notable contribution to the debate came from Gerald Pollack (1974), an Exxon Corporation executive writing in *Foreign Affairs*, who offered an early warning of the consequences of large dollar-denominated borrowing by developing countries. He stated that 'the Eurocurrency market has several defects for present purposes', and particularly that 'the Eurocurrency market is not well suited to resource-poor or politically unstable developing countries with low credit standing.' He warned, 'This question of financial instability may turn out to be the biggest of the threats posed by the energy crisis.'

Commenting upon the build-up of large foreign debts after the first and second oil price hike, Walter J. Levy (1980) stated, 'The debt problem could, of course, be solved if the values of the currencies in which the debts are incurred decline... [which] in fact did occur between 1974 and 1978 ... But it seems now that the jig is up.'

Writing just prior to the 1982 payments crisis, Bacha and Diaz-Alejandro (1982) expressed concerns about prospective borrowing conditions in the 1980s that were 'moderately pessimistic relative to repeating the favourable performance of the 1970s'. With regard to dollar-denominated debt, they stated, 'A major uncertainty for LDC [less developed countries] borrowers looking at the 1980s is whether the low or even negative real rates of interest prevailing during the 1970s will return.' In particular they cited the risk of tightening monetary policy in the United States as a factor leading to higher interest rates and a higher US dollar.

Much of the academic economics literature is focused on the issue of the credit risk faced by the international banks acting as intermediaries in this recycling process. Two noteworthy contributions came from Laurie Goodman (1980 and 1981). In a 1980 study for the New York Federal Reserve Bank, she provided an exemplary descriptive analysis of the financial instruments used for recycling petrodollars, and she then analysed the pricing of these syndicated, dollar-denominated, variable-rate bank loans. The principal concern at the time was whether the loans – which were priced as a spread above London Inter-Bank Offered Rates (LIBOR) – generated sufficient returns to banks' portfolios in proportion to their credit risk for the banks.

In a follow-up study, Goodman (1981) analysed the possible problems of credit risk from the point of view of lenders. She empirically tested a model of diversification to show that banks could gain by diversifying their credit risks across countries. Although only limited data were available at that time, Goodman showed that the country risks associated with lending to various developing countries were more different than similar – that is, the *unique* risk is greater than the *common* or *systematic* risk. Since it is the unique risk that can be reduced through diversification, Goodman suggested that international banks could successfully manage the risk on their loans to developing countries through diversification.

One of the first articles in the economics literature to discuss the market risk associated with foreign-currency borrowing (as opposed to credit risk) in the context of international lending to developing countries was written by Lessard (1983). Writing in the wake of Mexico's debt crisis in August 1982, Lessard pointed out that the form of debt issued to developing countries was 'unsound', that criticism had been too focused on the quantity of foreign borrowing, and that not sufficient attention was being paid to the fact that '[foreign lending] is structurally unsound and is likely to result in misjudgements and misbehaviour on the part of lenders and borrowers.' He went on to clarify what he meant by 'structurally unsound', stating that 'a financial system that relies overwhelmingly on bank credit is unlikely to be an ideal system in terms of world welfare. ... It involves debt service patterns that vary perversely with LDCs' net foreign exchange earnings ... [and] it shifts risks from LDCs to world capital markets only through default [i.e. bankruptcy].'

While drawing needed attention to key features of foreign debt, such as the problems caused by their variable interest-rate structure, Lessard failed to strictly identify foreign-exchange risk as a major source of the 'perverse variability of debt service obligations'. Perhaps he took it for granted that foreign debt would be denominated in foreign currency. Lessard did, however, foresee the more recent trend in development finance research, discussed below, by recommending that debt service be stabilized through the use of price-level index-linked loans.

Contemporary Insights into Foreign-Exchange Risk

Whereas the problems associated with developing countries' exposure to foreign exchange risk have been recognized by some people for quite a while, they have attracted greater attention in recent years. This can be attributed to the research and provocative title – the 'original sin' hypothesis[11] – developed by Hausmann, Eichengreen and others. Their work in Hausmann et al. (2001 and 2002) and Eichengreen et al. (2002 and 2003) has made a significant contribution to the study of development economics and sparked a much-needed debate on exposure to foreign-exchange risk. It has also contributed to the policies designed to raise living standards in the developing world by focusing attention squarely on the risks associated with the investment vehicles that conducted capital to developing countries. (A summary of their Emerging Market Index, as well as a discussion of its shortcomings, is included below in Appendix 2.)

Simply put, Hausmann and his colleagues argue that the principal problem facing development finance is that developing countries cannot borrow in their own currency. Instead they have borrowed in 'hard' currencies such as the dollar, euro (and its predecessors), sterling, and yen, and this has exposed them to foreign exchange-rate fluctuations not entirely within their control.[12] Had these countries been able to borrow in their own currency, Hausmann et al. conclude, they would have been better able to handle shocks and other policy errors.

Dodd (2001) identifies currency mismatches as a major source of vulnerability affecting financial sector stability in developing countries, and analyses the role of derivatives in increasing the magnitude of the mismatch. Developing country financial institutions were able to resort to derivatives, often unregulated or under-regulated as off-balance-sheet items, to achieve greater leverage and circumvent restrictions on their balance sheet's currency mismatches. The result was that they did not hedge their short dollar and long local currency mismatch, but rather took larger short dollar positions in order to capture the gains from the substantial interest-rate differential between the US dollar and their local currency. Dodd pointed out the difficulty for governments, as well as for private sector investors, in monitoring the volume of open interest and trading volume in a market that has no regulation to require reporting and disclosure.

Expanding on a problem they identified in 1996,[13] Goldstein and Tucker (2004) provide a comprehensive policy analysis that addresses the issue of currency risk head-on – that is, that the exposure to foreign-currency mismatches leaves developing countries vulnerable to financial shocks, deepens the impact of a shock, and hampers the use of monetary policy in preventing a contraction or crisis. The Goldstein and Tucker thesis – although largely distracted by its authors' effort to refute the original sin hypothesis that bad things happen to good countries – does provide a useful explanation for why currency mismatches are important, and how best to measure them. Unfortunately, the book's policy recommendations are little different from the advice offered before these insights were established. Instead of trying to address the problem directly, the authors advocate inflation targeting, floating instead of fixed-exchange-rates regimes, and fiscal rectitude in government budgets.

Allen et al. (2002), of the IMF's Policy Development and Review Department, provide an authoritative and comprehensive analysis of the balance-sheet aspects of developing country financial crises. They identify the major types of risk that characterize a nation's balance-sheet vulnerability and cite foreign currency mismatch as a major factor, saying that 'Almost all recent crisis episodes were marked by currency mismatch exposures.' One of their key conclusions is that 'The currency and maturity structure of the outstanding debt stock is almost as important as the total size of the debt stock.' Another is that

'A currency mismatch anywhere in the economy constrains the government's capacity to act as a lender of last resort in domestic currency.'

The policy recommendations of Allen *et al.* include the need to develop local currency equity and debt (especially long-term debt) markets in order to raise capital while limiting financial vulnerability. This includes developing derivatives markets – although they recommend that 'attention must be paid to the risks incurred by those who are supplying the hedging instruments' (Allen 2002). Allen *et al.* also cite the need to hold larger foreign reserves and the need for great external official lending (i.e. IMF, World Bank, and bilateral lending).

However, as discussed earlier, holding foreign reserves can be expensive for developing countries. Furthermore, additional external borrowing in foreign currencies – whether by the IMF, by the World Bank, or by the private sector – will only the exacerbate the problem of currency mismatch associated with external debt. The international financial institutions must look instead towards the more radical approach of lending in local currencies. In the following sections of this paper we analyse this possibility in more detail, and show why lending in local currencies is *not* a high-risk strategy for foreign creditors.

Salvation Through Diversification: A Policy Remedy

We believe that there is a better way to finance development. In this section we develop a policy remedy that is both economically more efficient and, if politics is truly 'the art of the possible', more politically feasible. One important testament to its viability is that, as described below, it has already been successfully pursued by at least one major asset manager.

We will call this approach the 'emerging-market local-currency debt portfolio' (or LCD). The original idea for this portfolio-based approach draws heavily on the work of Shari Spiegel, based on her experience in creating and managing a diversified, local-currency developing country debt portfolio for Lazard Freres (from May 1995 to January 2003).[14] The fund was operated with the goal of capturing high rates of return paid on local-currency securities while reducing risk through diversification.

The LCD proposal does not require that international financial institutions such as the IMF or World Bank play a pivotal role in its success. These official financial institutions could, however, make highly productive contributions (see below).

Although the LCD policy is low-cost and feasible, its potential benefits are substantial. It is capable of offering direct help to countries to enable them to borrow in their own currencies – both at home and abroad – in what could become a seamless market.[15] The gains from this alone are potentially enormous. Developing economies would benefit also from greater stability as a result of their reduced exposure to changes in foreign exchange rates and interest rates, which are all the greater because of their correlation with the US dollar and other major currencies. They would also gain from increased seigniorage and from the potentially lower costs of borrowing in their own currency.

Staying with the theme of Christian theology inspired by Hausmann's work, the LCD portfolio will lead – if not to outright redemption of 'original sin' – to absolution of worldly sins so as to facilitate progressive steps towards financial salvation.

The Portfolio Approach

The core idea of the LCD approach is to apply the insights of portfolio theory[16] – part of the discipline of financial economics – towards enabling developing countries to borrow in their own currencies. The insight offered by portfolio theory is that a portfolio consisting of different securities whose returns are sufficiently independent (and especially so if they are negatively correlated) can yield risk-adjusted rates of returns superior to those of the individual securities. In other words, the volatility of the whole is less than that of the sum of its parts.

The LCD portfolio would work by buying local-currency government debt[17] instruments from many different developing countries and combining them so as to produce a portfolio whose return and variance would be competitive in international capital markets. The market risk, which consists of the uncertainty of domestic interest rates (i.e. interest rates in local currency assets) and exchange rates of each local-currency security, is often significant. From 1994 to 2003, the average volatility of individual country returns on local-currency debt instruments was nearly 16 per cent.[18] At the same time, yields on local-currency debt were also high, at 13.7 per cent on average, but not high enough to compensate for the risk. Hence, investing in any one local-currency market was not attractive.

Combining the returns on individual country securities into a portfolio, however, does produce desirable results. As we will show below, returns on a diversified portfolio range from 8 to 10 per cent annually, while the risk of a diversified portfolio drops substantially to approximately 5.5 per cent (which is in line with US investment-grade bonds).

Note that this approach does not involve hedging the currency risk. It is very expensive to reduce this market risk by hedging with derivatives because the cost of hedging is equivalent to the differential between foreign and local interest rates and, as discussed above, local interest rates tend to be very high. Another reason why hedging costs may be expensive is that the derivatives markets are characterized by a disproportionate amount of short-hedgers relative to long speculators willing to take long speculative positions in local currencies.[19]

In other words, the costs of the hedge overwhelm the benefit of cross-border borrowing or investing. In this context, the most cost-effective method for mitigating risk exposure is achieved through diversification across different countries' local-currency debt. It is the *unique* aspect of this risk that can be substantially reduced through diversification. The reason for this is that, historically, currency devaluations have had extremely low correlations.

We began our analysis by examining the exchange rates of 46 developing countries (leaving out Latvia from Table 1). The countries were selected primarily on the basis of the availability of monthly data since 1980. We then eliminated some countries that had extraordinarily stable exchange rates, such as Saudi Arabia and Oman, and we dropped Zimbabwe for the opposite reason. The annual rate of change in all of these countries' exchange rates between January 1995 and March 2004 was 9.8 per cent; and of the 37 countries that had data doing back to January 1990, the average rate of change was 10.2 per cent over the longer 14-year period (with highs reaching –78.4 per cent and –43 per cent annually for Brazil and Romania respectively).

We then analysed the monthly rates of change for 47 developing country currencies from January 1980 to March 2004. The average correlation between the rates of change for those 47 countries during that time period was 0.0713 – in other words, not a high degree of correlation on average. The average correlation coefficients for the individual countries are listed in Table 1.

Diversification is also a means of reducing credit risk. For most local currency securities, however, credit risk is not the primary risk. Most developing countries are rated more highly for debt obligations in their own currencies than in foreign currencies. Table 2 shows several recent examples – Brazil is the only exception – of how local-currency credit ratings are usually two notches above that on foreign-currency debts. The differences would be larger if not for the methodologies employed by credit rating agencies in which they evaluate a country's creditworthiness on its foreign-currency-denominated debt and then make some adjustments for local-currency debt. With the exception of Russia, default on local-currency government debt has been extremely rare. The primary risk to investing in local-currency government debt is the domestic market risk (interest-rate and exchange-rate uncertainty) – and that is the type of risk that can be more easily diversified.

From an investor's perspective, credit risk is the primary risk on external debt, such as long-term Eurobonds, issued by developing countries. Consider the comparison of credit risk on dollar-denominated securities versus market risk on local-currency-denominated securities. These are captured by the average correlation coefficients for the ELMI+ and EMBI+ indices calculated by JP Morgan. The ELMI+ index measures the rates of return (change in price plus interest payments) on local-currency debt securities in each of the

Table 1. Average correlation coefficients for 47 developing economy exchange rates (1980 to 2004)

Argentina	0.013	Lithuania	0.060
Bangladesh	0.040	Malaysia	0.073
Botswana	0.123	Mauritius	0.144
Brazil	0.059	Mexico	−0.020
Bulgaria	0.025	Morocco	0.190
Chile	0.033	Namibia	0.109
Colombia	0.040	Nigeria	0.022
Côte d'Ivoire	0.087	Pakistan	0.061
Croatia	0.150	Peru	0.042
Czech Republic	0.180	Philippines	0.045
Ecuador	0.022	Poland	0.082
Egypt	−0.012	Romania	0.041
Estonia	0.217	Russia	0.021
Ghana	0.042	Slovak Republic	0.205
Hungary	0.153	Slovenia	0.206
India	0.063	South Africa	0.110
Indonesia	0.038	Sri Lanka	−0.017
Israel	0.085	Thailand	0.086
Jamaica	0.027	Trinidad and Tobago	0.008
Jordan	0.097	Tunisia	0.169
Kenya	0.077	Turkey	0.054
Korea	0.028	Ukraine	0.006
Latvia	0.078	Venezuela	−0.014
Lebanon	0.003		

Data source: IMF, *International Financial Statistics.*

Table 2. Debt ratings: long-term maturities

	Foreign currency	Local currency
Brazil	B+	B+
Chile	A−	A+
Colombia	BB	BBB−
Costa Rica	BB	BB+
Egypt	BB+	BBB
Estonia	A−	A+
Korea	A	AA−
Malaysia	BBB+	A
Mexico	BBB−	BBB
Mozambique	B	B+
Peru	BB−	BB+
Philippines	BB	BB+
Poland	BBB+	A+
South Africa	BBB	A−
Thailand	BBB	A−

Data source: Fitch ratings, February 2004.

25 listed countries. The EMBI+ index measures the rate of return on US-dollar-denominated debt securities in the 20 countries listed. There are 13 countries for which there are both ELMI+ and EMBI+ data.[20]

The correlation coefficients are presented in Table 3. Some of the correlation coefficients have high p-values which suggests that there are some periods of time in which the correlations are higher (as well as lower) than the coefficients would indicate.

Table 3. Average correlation coefficients for ELMI+/EMBI+ (May 1993–May 2004, monthly)

	ELMI+	EMBI+	Difference
Argentina	−0.011	0.396	0.407
Brazil	0.115	0.495	0.380
Bulgaria		0.469	
Chile	0.165		
China	0.129		
Colombia	0.059	0.419	0.360
Czech Rep.	0.103		
Ecuador		0.454	
Egypt	0.044	0.487	0.444
Hong Kong SAR	0.110		
Hungary	0.092		
India	0.170		
Indonesia	0.131		
Israel	0.002		
Malaysia	0.151	0.390	0.239
Mexico	0.135	0.553	0.418
Morocco		0.533	
Nigeria		0.525	
Panama		0.539	
Peru		0.533	
Philippines	0.133	0.466	0.333
Poland	0.174	0.514	0.339
Russia	0.202	0.431	0.228
Slovak Rep.	0.078		
Singapore	0.187		
South Africa	0.065	0.126	0.061
South Korea	0.159	0.405	0.246
Taiwan Province	0.186		
Thailand	0.230		
Turkey	0.074	0.334	0.260
Ukraine		0.360	
Venezuela	0.121	0.465	0.344
Average	*0.120*	0.445	0.312

[1]ELMI+ adjusted for euro/dollar rates for Central Europe.

The correlation coefficients under the column ELMI+ measure the average correlation between the country (in the column to the immediate left) and the other 24 countries for which there are data (empty rows indicate that there are no data for a country in either ELMI+ or EMBI+). The average correlation is pretty low, and is negative for Argentina.

The coefficients under the EMBI+ column are the same measures but for dollar-denominated foreign debt. Note that they are, on average, substantially higher than for local-currency debt securities. For the 13 countries for which there are common data, the average correlation coefficient is 0.312 higher for the credit risk reflected in the EMBI+ in comparison to market risk reflected in the ELMI+ series.

The financial economic lesson to be drawn from this comparison is that there are greater potential reductions in market risk through diversification than reductions in credit risk through diversification.

Principles of Financial Economics Applied to Constructing an LCD Portfolio

Given these properties of exchange rates and market returns, a portfolio of local-currency debt securities can be constructed so as to provide foreign investors with an attractive investment vehicle.

There are basically four interrelated decisions to be made in choosing the securities to be included in the portfolio: the number (n) of securities, which countries to include among the n in the portfolio, which securities in each country to include, and the weight of each security in the portfolio.

The decision to choose certain securities for inclusion in the portfolio will depend upon their returns, the distribution of those returns, and the correlation with other securities in the portfolio. If the distributions of returns on the n securities have sufficient independence, then their combined yield and variance will produces a portfolio return and variance that competes with benchmark fixed-income portfolios from the advanced capital markets in the major currency economies – e.g. US Corporate bonds – and have substantially less volatility than such equity indices as the S&P 500, DAX, FTSE 100, and the Nikkei 225 stock indexes.

An expression for the country returns – which are comprised of changes in the exchange rate, interest payments, and the change in price of the local debt instrument – can be derived from the following equation for interest-rate parity, where r is the US dollar or major currency rate of return (coupon payments plus change in market price), r^* is the local current rate of return, and e is the exchange rate in consecutive periods.[21]

$$1 + r = [(1 + r^*)e_t/e_{t-1}]$$
(1)

Equation (2) represents the portfolio rate of return (r_p) from period t to period $t + 1$ from investing in n countries' local-currency securities, where each country is weighted by a factor x in the portfolio.

$$r_p = \sum_{i=1}^{n} x_i (1 + r_i^*) e_t/e_{t-1} - 1 \qquad (2)$$

The role of diversification in forming the portfolio is critical. The LCD portfolio would consist of a sufficient number of different securities from different countries so as to reach acceptable levels of market and credit risk.

The variance of the portfolio (σ_p) is determined according to the following equation (3), where x corresponds to the weights of the securities in the portfolio, ρ is the correlation coefficient, σ is the standard deviation, the subscript p denotes portfolio, and the securities in the portfolio are represented by i and j.

$$\sigma_p^2 = \sum_{i=1}^{n} \sum_{j=1}^{n} x_i x_j \sigma_i \sigma_j \rho_{ij} \qquad (3)$$

The equation expresses how securities with different distributions can be combined so that the variance of the whole combination is potentially less than the particular securities. If the securities have a negative correlation, the variance of the combination – that is, the portfolio – can be very small. If they are not negatively correlated but nonetheless have low correlations, then the portfolio variance can still be greatly reduced. This reverses the old saw, so that we can now say that the variance of the whole is less than that of the sum of the parts.

The decision of the optimal number of securities to include in a portfolio depends on the marginal benefit of the nth security to the portfolio variance. There are perhaps 40 or more countries whose local currency securities are suitable for inclusion in an LCD portfolio. Both theoretical reasoning and empirical testing support the case that the marginal benefit to diversification declines as the number of securities is increased. The rate at which the benefits diminish will depend on the degree of independence of the returns so that a portfolio of completely independent securities will quickly overwhelm the benefits of diversification by eliminating all 'unique' risk and leave only 'systematic' or common risk. In actual markets there are degrees of independence and interdependence. As the marginal benefit diminishes, the transactions costs and portfolio management costs rise with the number of securities.

Empirical studies of the US equity markets, as discussed in Sharpe (1970), estimate that a portfolio with 10 securities will have 7 per cent more risk than the minimum (i.e. that of the market portfolio without diversifiable risk) and a portfolio of 20 securities will have only 3 per cent more than the minimum. The actual determination of the optimal number of securities will depend on the correlations and the transactions costs required to obtain and manage such a portfolio.

Our preliminary analysis of data from emerging markets in the 1990s indicates that the benefits to diversification flatten off after the nineteenth security. Thus, a portfolio of 20 securities would serve as a good estimate of the minimum number of securities necessary for diversification to be fully effective.

The decision on the weighting of securities in the portfolio can be driven by different motivations. One approach would be to treat the portfolio as if it were an index in which country weights replicated the share of the respective economy or the market size of the security's issuance relative to the others represented in the portfolio.[22] Most, but not all, security indices in advanced capital markets are based on weights that reflect the market capitalization of the security. However, the size of local-currency debt markets is generally quite difficult to measure. Most securities are traded over the counter and include bank paper and even derivative products that are not easy to quantify. In addition, government securities markets can be extremely illiquid, with a proportion of the securities held by the central bank or the Treasury, so that the number of outstanding issuances is not a good indicator of the tradable size of the market.

Another approach, followed by the JP Morgan ELMI/ELMI+, is to weight countries by the size of their foreign-exchange markets, as measured by total exports and imports. This approach avoids the problems in trying to estimate the size of the local-currency markets. But it ignores the fact that liquidity in the local securities market has very little to do with the size of foreign-exchange trading. The ELMI+ attempts to address this by including measures of liquidity in the index.

One of the results of this formulation is that countries in Asia represent nearly 40 per cent of the index, since they have the largest share of trade of countries in the investment universe. Yet from a policy perspective, countries in Asia have the least need for foreign capital because of their high savings rates and because they have the least amount of sovereign debt denominated in foreign currency. This would reduce the effect of the proposal in solving the problem of original sin. From an investment perspective, yields in most countries in Asia tend to be low. Asian currencies also tend to be highly correlated owing to their high regional trade links. Thus, a portfolio based on this approach will tend to be a higher risk/lower return portfolio. The ELMI+ approach is consistent from the perspective of building a publishable index, but it is not the foundation of an optimal portfolio.

The optimal approach would be to choose weights that produce the desired return-to-risk trade-off in the portfolio. Under this approach, securities with high yields per unit of risk, or with low covariance with the portfolio, would be weighted more heavily than those with lower returns or higher covariance. This might result in a portfolio that contains relatively more securities from a small country or a country that exhibits greater volatility but whose returns are substantially uncorrelated with those of other countries. One important implication of this last point is that it has the positive effect of rewarding countries that successfully pursue independent policies and achieve independent results.

The complicating issue with this approach is the difficulty in estimating future returns, volatility, and correlations since the historical figures are not always good predictors of future returns.[23] This is especially problematic for currencies that have had fixed-exchange-rate systems, because the past correlations and volatility do not convey the full risk inherent in the positions. The volatility of a fixed-exchange-rate currency is historically zero, even if the risk of devaluation is significant. There are several ways to address this mathematically, and there are market indicators that can also be used to assess volatility and expected returns.[24]

Even if, for simplicity, the securities were equally weighted – that is, with weights of 5 per cent for a portfolio with 20 securities – a set of sufficiently independent security returns can outperform the return-to-risk of major security indexes. This is shown below.

Track Record

Experiments with Investment in Local-Currency Debt

The potential gains from investing in local-currency debt securities were apparent by the mid-1990s and at least some parts of the private sector were aware of them. From 1993 to just prior to the Russian crisis in July 1998, short-term yields on local-currency debt averaged nearly 27 per cent. The primary risk when investing in local-currency debt is currency volatility, and so yields were high to compensate investors for the risk of devaluation. Yet the actual average currency devaluation over the same period turned out to be only 14.5 per cent (authors' calculations using list of 46 countries, as shown in Appendix 1).

Whether it was a fundamental market failure or a matter of incomplete markets giving rise to arbitrage opportunities, there were cases of private sector investors attempting to take advantage of it. Many broker-dealers set up local-currency trading desks, and several asset management financial institutions – that is, 'buy-side firms' – launched local-currency funds.[25] In the summer of 1996, JP Morgan introduced the Emerging Local Market Index (ELMI).[26]

Yet the ELMI, and later the ELMI+, never became a widely followed index. By the end of 1998 many of the new local-market funds had shut down. Most had taken large and concentrated positions in a few developing countries – notably some large long positions in Russia – and when Russia defaulted, the local-market funds came to an end.

In contrast to the funds that made concentrated bets in a few countries, those that were constructed from a risk-control perspective survived the crisis relatively unscathed, with positive returns and low volatility.[27] The successful strategy lay in recognizing that despite much of the popular discussion about currency contagion, correlations across emerging-market currencies had been actually quite low. For example, returns from investing in local-currency debt of 25 countries from JP Morgan's ELMI+ index returned an averaged 3.03 per cent monthly or 43 per cent annual rate of return over the five months from August to December 1998.[28]

Highly diversified portfolios that were constructed to take advantage of the low correlations across emerging-market currencies produced strong results, relatively high yields and low variance, throughout the various emerging-market crises.

LCD Track Record

In order to better illustrate the market risk of investing in local markets, we have created a sample LCD portfolio using JP Morgan ELMI+ data. For simplicity, our sample portfolio equally weights the countries in the index. We did not use the ELMI+ weights because, as we explained earlier, the ELMI+ is highly concentrated in Asia and thus is not optimal diversification. In addition, the ELMI+ includes major currency risks implicit in emerging-market currencies tied to the euro and yen currencies. For example, the local-currency securities in Poland, Hungary and the Czech Republic embody exchange-rate risk – when measured in US dollars – that is closely tied to the value of the euro. As a result they are more highly correlated with each other than is desirable for the purpose of diversification.

The ELMI+ dataset starts in 1994, so we begin our analysis in that year. The first striking result of our LCD portfolio is that there is only one calendar year in which returns were negative. That year is 1997, the timing of the East Asian crisis, when the LCD portfolio was down –0.78 per cent. In 1994 (the year of the Mexican crisis), 1998 (the year of the Russian crisis), and 2001 (the year of the Argentinian crisis) returns are all *positive*, at 3.2 per cent, 17.8 per cent, and 5.3 per cent. In contrast, the EMBI+ generated *negative* returns for those years of –18.9 per cent, –14.4 per cent, and –0.8 per cent.

The second striking result is that the average risk of the LCD portfolio was only 5.5 per cent from 1994 to 2003, significantly lower than the EMBI+ risk of 19.3 per cent over the same period. For comparison we have also listed the risk/return profile of the ELMI+, S&P 500, and MSCI Emerging-Market Free Index of equities. The results are listed in Table 4 and plotted in Table 5.

It is important to note that the start date of 1994 has a significant effect on measured returns on all asset classes. If the data were to start a year earlier, or a year later, returns would be higher for all emerging market indices. The results are stated in Table 6.

Another important point that is not shown in Table 6 is that the volatility of the LCD portfolio is remarkably consistent over time. We tested the data for different start dates and found that the volatility of the LCD portfolio never

Table 4. 1993–2004

Index	LCD	ELMI+	EMBI+	S&P500	MSCI EM-Free
Risk	5.5%	7.6%	19.3%	21.4%	27.6%
Return	8.7%	8.1%	9.6%	7.3%	-6.6%

Table 5. 1993–2004

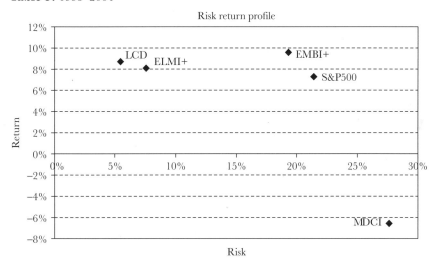

Table 6. 1994–2004

Index	LCD	ELMI+	EMBI+
Risk	5.5%	8.0%	16.8%
Return	9.3%	8.3%	13.9%

goes above 6 per cent. This further exemplifies the power of diversification at lowering risk in this asset class. In contrast, the volatility of the EMBI+ jumps from slightly over 9 per cent to nearly 20 per cent, depending on whether the start date is before or after a crisis year.

Another comparison – and indeed contrast – that illustrates this point is one with the dollar returns on the FTSE – a sterling-denominated equity index. This portfolio is diversified across the 100 securities that make up the FTSE index, but it is not diversified with regard to foreign currencies because the US dollar exchange rate with UK sterling introduces additional risk to the FTSE equity index. The average annual returns over the same period (January 1995 to January 2003) were 7.52 per cent and the standard deviation was 17.73 per cent. This represents a lower yield and higher risk than the LCD portfolio, and a lower yield for about the same level of risk for the S&P500 – or alternatively about the same yield but much higher risk than a portfolio of US Aaa corporate bonds.

Why the Private Sector Has Been Slow to Implement this Strategy

If the LCD policy is such a good idea, why has the private sector been so slow to implement it? There are several answers. One is the disappointing history of local-currency funds in the mid- to late 1990s, which led investors to be wary of this asset class. Most of that disappointment can be attributed to funds that took large concentrated bets in a few countries, especially Russia, and thus did not maintain a diversified portfolio. Nonetheless, these have served as a bad example of local-currency portfolios.

Another reason is that the one local-currency index, the JP Morgan ELMI+, did not perform as well as a more diversified portfolio.

More recently, local-currency capital markets in some countries have grown, spurring new investor interest in the asset class. A recent study by the IMF (2004b) documents several positive developments in the issuance and trading in local-currency securities in developing countries. The study cites improvements in clearing trades in local-currency securities and the settlement of payments for such trades. It also describes expanding liquidity in secondary markets for these securities, and it identifies the development of inter-dealer markets as a sign of great liquidity.

Another IMF report (2004a) describes a new initiative in Asia, called the Asian Bond Market Initiative. This initiative includes settlement and exchange regulation, a credit guarantee mechanism, issuance of local-currency bonds by non-domestic issuers, and local rating agencies. Similarly, Mexico has begun to develop a liquid local-currency bond market. The development of local pension funds in several Latin American countries, such as Chile, has also stimulated the development of domestic markets.

As local-currency bond markets have continued to develop, there has been more interest in local-currency investments. This was apparent at the December 2003 Emerging-Market Traders Association meeting at which there was a significant amount of discussion about the asset class. It is unclear, however, how much of any increased investment will go into diversified funds and how much will go into concentrated positions in the few large markets that are easily accessible to foreign investors.

Two of the biggest complaints by foreign investors are the difficulty of accessing some developing countries' local-currency securities markets and the high transaction costs in those markets. Several countries have complicated tax structures, inefficient settlement mechanisms, high custodial costs, and outright restrictions on foreign investment. Foreign investors have pressured developing countries to reduce these transaction costs, but the countries have resisted doing so. Brazil, for example, has one of the largest domestic securities markets, but it is also a market where foreign investors find access cumbersome.

So we need to ask the flip-side of the question: if local debt is so good for developing countries, why have they sometimes been slow to respond to foreign interest?

We believe that there are two main answers to this question. First, because foreign-currency financing is often cheaper than domestic financing, the risks inherent in foreign-currency financing are ignored. Second, it is possible that countries are wary of international institutional investors. These investors are seen as myopic, bringing in short-term hot money, overwhelming small capital markets in the good times and pulling out in the bad times, leading to boom-bust scenarios or currency crises. Such flows can add volatility to a local financial markets and disrupt, if not destabilize, the economy. In fact, the problems associated with short-term capital flows has been the focus of much economic policy literature in recent years.[29] Similar to concerns that excessive dollar debt is linked to crises, so too may open capital markets be.[30]

In this light, market regulations and local security market inefficiencies can be viewed as a means of restricting capital flows. For example, in the early 1990s foreigners were not allowed to purchase Hungarian government debt. Later, as the country moved towards joining the European Union, the restrictions were eased so that foreigners could buy debt securities with remaining maturities of more than one year.[31] Thus was Hungary able to use controls on its local bond market to regulate short-term capital inflows.

One implication of this insight is that 'original sin' is in some cases the result of policy decisions. Faced with a choice between two evils, opening their domestic markets to the vicissitudes of short-term capital flows or borrowing from abroad in foreign currency, developing countries have often chosen the latter.

The question then becomes: is it possible to structure local currency portfolios to keep funds in a country long-term? Can we construct the portfolio in a way that still gives policymakers the option to continue to selectively use capital account regulations to limit short-term inflows? The example of Hungary gives us a hint of how this can be done. Even when foreigners were not allowed to access the local bond market directly, they were given permission to buy into long-term closed-end funds.[32]

Alternative Ownership Structures

Another virtue of the LCD portfolio approach to financing development is its flexibility and ability to take on many different structures to the ownership of the portfolio. The minimum size for an economically viable portfolio is not very large, so this would not sharply constrain its use by a variety of financial institutions. For example, a portfolio consisting of $2 million in securities from each of 20 countries would amount to a $40 million portfolio.

There are many financial institutions in advanced economies that are large enough to purchase and manage a portfolio such as the LCD portfolio, and most of these have the regulatory authority for cross-border and foreign-currency investments. These institutions could construct such a portfolio and hold it as an asset on their balance sheets. Pension funds and insurance companies could also operate such a portfolio as a portion of these assets. Similarly, mutual funds and hedge funds could offer more direct ownership of such portfolios. In all these cases, the most important point is that managers should stick to a diversified approach, and this feature could be enforced by including diversification as a requirement in the managed fund prospectus or pension fund investment guidelines.

Multilateral development banks such as the World Bank could employ this approach to manage the risk of lending to its developing country borrowers. The Bank's portfolio is already diversified across lenders, and so this analysis shows how it could safely lend in local currency instead of its existing policy of lending in major currencies. Had the Bank been pursuing this approach all along, it would have played a much more stabilizing role in development finance than it has.

Yet another approach to ownership structure would be to securitize the LCD portfolio in a manner similar to that successfully pursued by US mortgage lending titans Fannie Mae, Freddie Mac, and Ginnie Mae. They collect together financial assets into a pool that is held by a trust; the trust then issues securities known as mortgage-backed securities that represent ownership shares of the pool of assets. These shares can then be traded in a liquid and transparent secondary market so that the process results in price discovery of the return and risk of the underlying mortgage investments. This attracts additional capital to the market, provides investors with greater diversification, and, most of all, helps the development of good standard market practices that are often lacking in the market for the underlying assets or securities.

A similar security that would be backed by local-currency debt securities – call it an 'LCDBS' – could be denominated in US dollars or any currency. The trust could be structured to reinvest all proceeds in local-currency debt and then authorized and empowered to convert the various local-currency proceeds into the currency of denomination (e.g. US dollars) in order to coupon payments on each scheduled payment date plus the payment of principal at maturity.[33] The choice of reinvestment versus regular coupon payments could vary so as to suit the preferences of the investors. Some investors, such as pension funds and insurance companies, want the regular payments for cash flow or tax purposes, while other investors might prefer reinvestment at the internal rate of return of the portfolio.

As the great wit and sage Yogi Berra warned, 'If you can't copy them, don't imitate them.' In this case, however, the application of this experience with mortgage-backed securities to local-currency developing country debt is fairly straightforward and thus lends itself to imitation.

The high performance of the LCD portfolio, which compares favourably with the dollar return on major US equity indices, US corporate bond returns, and sterling-denominated FTSE returns, will attract portfolio capital from individual investors, managed funds, and financial institutions.

Of course, the LCD portfolio might attract additional investor interest if shares were sold on different classes of the portfolio. This is a common practice in the securitization of debt through structured securities, known as collateral debt obligations, where different tranches of the pool – based on the priority in which debt service payments fulfil debt obligation – are sold separately. This generates different classes of shares based on creditworthiness, such as a class AAA, a class BB, and junk class (i.e. speculative grade debt). However, since this LCD portfolio would not be burdened with very much credit risk – most developing countries enjoy high ratings for debt payments in their own currency – the different classes of shares would be differentiated in terms of market risk. Thus, Class A might offer a very high likelihood of providing an 8 per cent return in US dollars, while Class B might offer a strong likelihood of 10 per cent and Class C might offer a speculative return of 14 per cent. Such structures have proved time and again in other areas of advanced financial markets to add significant value to the portfolio by tailoring the risk-return profile of the instrument.

Economic and Development Consequences

The primary goal of helping developing countries borrow in their own currency is to reduce their exposure to foreign-exchange risk, which has helped trigger many financial crises in recent decades. But apart from this, there are additional important economic benefits of a widespread adoption of LCD portfolios and more local-currency (and less foreign-currency) debt issuance.

The macroeconomic benefits include:

- enabling developing countries to attract more foreign capital, and to do so in more steady volumes because the returns and risks will be more akin to those found elsewhere in advanced economies' capital markets;
- raising the demand for local currency government securities, and by association other local-currency securities, so as to lower the cost of capital in those markets;
- promoting improvements in local financial markets in the areas of clearing, settlements, and secondary market trading;
- stimulating investment and growth by lowering local-currency interest rates and increasing the maturity and depth of local credit markets; and
- increasing the government's revenue from seigniorage by increasing the use of local currency for trading and servicing local-currency-denominated assets; this together with lower borrowing costs, will improve the fiscal position of developing country governments.

The microeconomic benefits of the LCD portfolio include:

- It will create a new benchmark in international financial markets.
- The portfolio, by eliminating most if not all 'unique' risk from each security, will establish the price of 'common' or 'systematic' risk in developing country debt markets.
- The new benchmark would 'price' the 'market risk' – inflation, nominal interest rates and exchange-rate risk – of investing in developing country debt instead of the credit risk.
- This benchmark rate of return will have the effect of sharpening competitive pressures on international investors by identifying where local-currency rates of return exceed that justified by the benchmark.
- The local currency interest rates and exchange rates will have the *excess* risk premiums priced out of them.

This new power to borrow abroad must come, however, with a strong warning. Some developing economies in the recent past have suffered because of their governments' fiscal imbalances – whereby large and persistent deficits were financed by borrowing that was subsequently monetized as part of monetary policy. The consequences for inflation, output and growth were sometimes dire. In this context, relaxing the constraints on developing country governments' ability to borrow in their own currency is expected to raise concerns about the possible hazard of eliminating the usual discipline of foreign borrowing.

While expanding the market for local-currency financial instruments, the LCD policy will not necessarily reward any particular country for pursuing reckless fiscal or monetary policies, as it does not guarantee any particular country the right to sell its local-currency securities abroad. It does, though, offer a reward for being able to do so, and the magnitude of the reward will be proportional to the country's ability to produce a stable economic environment with lower interest rates and low rates of currency depreciation. In this regard the policy does not eliminate any disciplinary 'stick' but rather it adds 'carrots'.

Conclusion

In this study, we describe how to construct a portfolio of emerging market local-currency-denominated debt. This portfolio can generate US dollar rates of risk-adjusted return that are competitive with familiar financial market benchmarks such as the S&P500 and FTSE indexes.

This is a feasible proposal that can be readily adopted by private financial markets for its profitable opportunities, and yet it can also be promoted at negligible expense through public policies by G-7 governments, the Finance for Development process at the UN and international financial institutions such as the World Bank. The latter could play a helpful role in establishing a demonstration project that would produce market information on prices, returns and risk that could stimulate others to follow. In addition, the project could help develop structures that would be valuable long-term investments.

By comparison to Hausmann's plan for an EM Index, this proposal stands as a simple and more straightforward policy, in that it does not require the approval and active participation of major currency governments or international financial institutions such as the World Bank and IMF. It is also more flexible in that the portfolio approach can be used to construct a variety of types of portfolios that can be directly owned or securitized and can be sold off in uniform shares or in risk-related tranches.

This proposal stands as an implicit criticism of official financial institutions that for decades have failed to identify such a policy opportunity that would allow them to use their already country-diversified portfolio to lend in local currencies. Instead, they have continued to practise a policy of lending in major currencies that has led to financial crises which have resulted in more debt in major currencies, and they have failed to help developing countries adjust to shocks from changes in foreign exchange and interest rates.

Private financial markets too have for the most part overlooked this investment opportunity. In an industry that prides itself on its innovation and its top-flight financial analysis of arbitrage opportunities, this is a large, squandered opportunity. It is an example of the proverbial $20 bill on the ground, which theoretical economists believe cannot exist.

This LCD portfolio approach has enormous potential to promote the maturation of local financial markets as a development policy. It has the capacity not only to reduce developing countries' vulnerability to financial crises, but also to foster greater stability and sustained development.

Appendix 1

List of 46 developing countries included in foreign-exchange-rate analysis:

Argentina	Bangladesh	Botswana	Brazil	Bulgaria	Chile
Colombia	Côte d'Ivoire	Croatia	Czech Rep.	Ecuador	Egypt
Estonia	Ghana	Hungary	India	Indonesia	Israel
Jamaica	Jordan	Kenya	Korea	Lebanon	Lithuania
Malaysia	Mauritius	Mexico	Morocco	Namibia	Nigeria
Pakistan	Peru	Philippines	Poland	Romania	Russia
Slovak	Slovenia	South Africa	Sri Lanka	Thailand	
Trinidad & Tobago		Tunisia	Turkey	Ukraine	Venezuela

Appendix 2

A Summary of the EM Index Proposal

The recent literature on the causes, costs, and dangers of foreign-currency borrowing – that is, the 'original sin' literature – develops a policy proposal for redemption. The proposal in Hausmann *et al.* (2002) consists of three steps. First, construct an index (called an 'EM Index') to determine the rate of return on index-linked financial instruments (bank loans, bonds, and interest-rate derivatives). The index is calculated using the changes in each country's exchange rate and inflation rate and by weighting each currency in the index by the real output of the respective country.[34] The proposal calls for the World Bank to calculate the official index.

Second, the IFIs (official international financial institutions such as the World Bank and Inter-American Development Bank) would issue at least some of their debt denominated in the EM Index. This would enable those IFIs to lend in local emerging-market currencies while maintaining a match between the currency denomination of the assets match and that of their liabilities. Similarly, the G-10 countries would be called on to issue some of their debt in the EM Index.

The IFIs and G-10 borrowers, it is argued, would be motivated by the advantages of diversifying their liabilities or alternatively capturing savings after swapping their EM Index obligations back into their respective C-5 currency (US dollars, euros, pounds sterling, yen or Swiss francs). This would have the desirable consequence of creating an otherwise rare short position in the local currency. The third step would thus consist of having the developed countries swap out of C-5-currency-denominated debt back into their own local currency.

Problems with the EM Proposal

The following are some limitations of the EM proposal, as we see them:

1. The proposal is overly complicated relative to the problem it seeks to solve. It requires industrial country governments to change their debt management policies to include the use of EM-Index-linked securities, foreign currencies, foreign-currency swap transactions, and add exposure to swap-related credit risk from counterparties. While the government of Sweden has already been successfully developing more sophisticated debt management policies, these policy recommendations stand in stark contrast to the debt management policies in such countries as the United States. Such a change in policy might not prove to be directly beneficial to the United States, Japan, and euro-zone governments. For example, the policy change would disrupt, and thereby diminish the benefits from, regularly scheduled debt auctions. Also, the proposal would require the G-10 governments to borrow in a foreign currency and swap back into their own currency at time when it might – as well as when it might not – be cheaper to borrow in their own currency.
2. Individual developing countries would still not be borrowing directly in their own currency.
3. The most immediate benefit to developing currencies from the emergence of the EM Index would be more (long positions in) foreign-currency swaps that would enable them to swap out of their hard-currency foreign debts and other obligations.
4. The EM Index proposal does not clarify how the index-linked debt and securities are to be bought, sold, or in general traded. The transaction must be denominated in some single currency unless the proposal's proponents

want the entire basket of currencies to be used. It would be impractical to buy and sell securities that require multiple currencies for engaging in price quotes, negotiations, and settlement. If the EM Index is comprised of 22 currencies, as language in the literature suggests, it will require a basket of 22 currencies to buy or sell. Otherwise, if it is traded in dollars then it will not *directly* help emerging market countries borrow in their own currency or reduce their foreign currency exposure – although it would give them a more diversified exposure.

Notes

Randall Dodd would like to thank the G-24 and the Ford Foundation for support, and for the invitation to present the paper before the XVIII G-24 Technical Group Meeting, 8 March 2004, in Geneva. Shari Spiegel would like to thank Stephany Griffith Jones and the Ford Foundation for support. She would also like to thank Ira Handler for his help in developing the EM LCD local-currency portfolio in 1995. They both would like to thank Claire Husson for research assistance.

 1 The term 'major currency' refers to the C-5 – that is, the countries of the five major currencies – US dollar, euro, yen, pound sterling and Swiss franc.
 2 See Dodd (2001) for an analysis of this dimension of the problem.
 3 One of the authors of this paper, Shari Spiegel, developed and managed a successful risk-controlled diversified local-currency debt portfolio in 1995 at Lazard Asset Management.
 4 The chapter uses IMF definitions for terms such as 'advanced economies' and 'emerging market economies', but uses the term 'developing countries' to refer to both emerging and developing countries.
 5 This is also true for most other emerging market economies and some newly industrialized economies.
 6 The numbers add to slightly more than 100 per cent due to rounding.
 7 Stiglitz (2003).
 8 For a more thorough discussion of these points see Dodd (1989), Allen *et al.* (2002), and Goldstein and Tucker (2004).
 9 Funds that could be used for development are instead held as reserves. For example, a country might borrow at 10 per cent, but then need to hold reserves against this debt in US Treasuries at, say, 3 per cent. For more on this, see the upcoming Initiative for Policy Dialogue Overview book on Macroeconomics and Capital Markets Liberalization, forthcoming from Oxford University Press.
10 For a detailed discussion of this, see the upcoming Overview Volume on Macroeconomics and Capital Markets Liberalization by the Initiative for Policy Dialogue by Ricardo Ffrench Davis, Deepak Nayyar, Jose Antonio Ocampo, Shari Spiegel and Joseph Stiglitz, forthcoming from Oxford University Press.
11 The term was coined in Eichengreen and Hausmann (1999).
12 Eichengreen and Hausmann show econometrically that a weak policy framework is not the primary reason countries have been unable to issue debt in domestic currencies; hence the term 'original sin'.
13 Goldstein and Tucker (1996).

14 The Lazard Strategic Yield Fund, May 1995 to April 1997. The Lazard Emerging Income Fund 1, from April 1997. The strategy was developed to maintain exposure to local emerging market currencies, and minimise the currency risk through diversification.

15 Chile, Colombia and Mexico have recently issued local-currency debt successfully in international markets.

16 The foundation of portfolio theory, in the words of one of the great contributors to the theory, is Sharpe (1970).

17 The term 'security' will be used to describe government debt instruments, although the portfolio could potentially contain government loans.

18 Yield and volatility data are taken from average yields published by JP Morgan as part of the ELMI+ index, from 1994 to 2003.

19 The term 'short-hedger' refers to an investor whose business normally involves a long position in the local currency and needs to hedge that exposure by taking a short position in the derivatives market.

20 Our data for these series were monthly, starting in January 1994 and ending in May 2004, although some countries do not have observations for the entire period.

21 The US dollar is chosen as an example. The same would be true for other currencies. The rate of return refers to the sum of interest payments and any change in price of the security. This equation yields a continuous time version: $r = r* + \dot{e} + r*\dot{e}$.

22 This approach to weights is in contrast to that of Hausmann *et al.* and their EM index approach (see Appendix 2), in which the index weights are decided by GDP. That would result in the largest countries having the largest impact on the index and their currencies being in greater demand in subsequent transactions. This would replicate and reinforce one of the causes of original sin – namely, the size of the economy.

23 A succinct warning could be drawn from Yogi Berra's observation that 'the future is not what it used to be.'

24 One tested method is to use a jump diffusion model instead of a normal distribution. Although this approach is useful in determining optimal weights, the results do not alter the general portfolio thesis.

25 To name a few: Lazard Asset Management launched a Local Currency Trust in 1995, ANZ Asset Management and Morgan Stanley Asset Management launched funds soon thereafter, and other asset managers launched regional funds.

26 The ELMI was later supplemented by the ELMI+. The new index includes more countries and uses currency forwards to estimate local yields.

27 The Lazard Asset Management Local Currency Trust and affiliated funds is the one fund the authors know of that maintained a diversified investment strategy, based on a risk-management perspective.

28 The countries were: Argentina, Brazil, Chile, China, the Czech Republic, Egypt, Hong Kong, Hungary, India, Indonesia, Israel, Mexico, the Philippines, Poland, South Africa, South Korea, Taiwan, Thailand, Turkey and Venezuela.

29 See Rodrik, Dani and Andrés Velasco (2000).

30 See World Bank (2000) and Demirguc-Kunt, A. and E. Detragiache (2001).

31 Eventually the market was made fully open.

32 One of the authors, Shari Spiegel, also managed one of the first local-currency fixed-income closed-end funds in the Hungarian domestic market in the early 1990s. One tranche of the fund was open to foreign investors.

33 Note that mortgage-backed securities involve a similar process of collecting receipts from the many mortgages in the portfolio, whose payments fall across many different

dates, and then efficiently managing these cash flows until they are paid out on regularly scheduled payment dates.

34 Real output is measured by the purchasing power parity (PPP) value of the gross domestic product (GDP), and inflation is measured by the consumer price index (CPI).

Bibliography

Allen, Mark, Christoph Rosenberg, Christian Keller, Brad Setser and Nouriel Roubini, 2002, 'A Balance Sheet Approach to Financial Crisis', IMF Working Paper (Policy Development and Review Department) WP/02/210, Washington, D.C.

Bacha, E. and Carlos Diaz-Alejandro, 1982, 'International Financial Intermediation: A Long and Tropical View', Essays in International Finance, #147, Princeton: Princeton University.

Demirguc-Kunt, A. and E. Detragiache, 2001, 'CML is correlated with banking crises', 'Financial Liberalization and Financial Fragility', in Gerard Caprio, Patrick Honohan and Joseph E. Stiglitz (eds) *Financial Liberalization: How Far, How Fast?*, Cambridge University Press.

Dodd, Randall, 2001, 'The Role of Derivatives in the East Asian Financial Crisis', in Lance Taylor and John Eatwell (editors), *International Capital Markets: Systems in Transition.* Oxford University Press (2002), also published in *The Financier*, Vol.7, Issue 4, 2001.

Dodd, Randall, 1989, 'Risky Foundations of Development Finance', manuscript presented at the Eastern Economics Associations conference in Baltimore, MD, in March 1989 (available at www.financialpolicy.org/dscwriting.htm).

Eichengreen, Barry and Ricardo Hausmann, 2003, 'Original Sin: The Road to Redemption', unpublished manuscript, available at http://ksghome.harvard.edu/~.rhausma.cid.ksg/Original%20Sin/roadtoredemption2003.pdf

Eichengreen, Barry and Ricardo Hausmann, 1999, 'Exchange Rates and Financial Fragility', Paper presented at symposium, New Challenges for Monetary Policy, hosted by Kansas City Federal Reserve Bank.

Eichengreen, Barry, Ricardo Hausmann and Ugo Panizza, 2002, 'Original Sin: The Pain, the Mystery, and the Road to Redemption', unpublished manuscript, November 2002, available at http://ksghome.harvard.edu/~.rhausma.cid.ksg/.

Goldstein, Morris and Phillip Tucker, 2004, *Controlling Currency Mismatches in Emerging Markets*, Washington, D.C., Institute of International Economics.

Goldstein, Morris and Phillip Tucker, 1996, 'Banking Crises in Emerging Economies: Origins and Policy Options', BIS Economic Papers, No. 26 (October).

Goodman, Laurie, 1980, 'The Pricing of Syndicated Eurocurrency Credits', *Quarterly Review*, Federal Reserve Bank of New York (Summer).

Goodman, Laurie, 1981, 'Bank Lending to Non-OPEC LDCs: Are Risks Diversifiable?' *Quarterly Review*, Federal Reserve Bank of New York (Summer).

Hausmann, Ricardo, 2002, 'Good Credit Rations, Bad Credit Ratings: The Role of Debt Denomination', unpublished manuscript, Harvard University, available at http://ksghome.harvard.edu/~.rhausma.cid.ksg/.

Hausmann, Ricardo, Ugo Panizza and Ernesto Stein, 2001, 'Why Do Countries Float the Way They Float?' *Journal of Development Economics*, 66: 387–414. Also, Inter-American Development Bank Working Paper #148, May 2000, available at http://ksghome.harvard.edu/~.rhausma.cid.ksg/WP/pubWP-418.pdf

International Monetary Fund, 2004a, Global Financial Stability Report: Market Developments and Issues, Washington, D.C.

International Monetary Fund, 2004b, Emerging Local Securities and Derivatives Markets, World Economic and Financial Surveys (from the Global Financial Stability Report), Washington, D.C.

Lessard, Donald, 1983, 'The Implications for Multinational Banking', *Journal of Banking and Finance*, 7, pp.521–536.

Levy, Walter, 1980, 'Oil and the Decline of the West', *Foreign Affairs* (Summer).

Pollack, Gerald, 1974, 'The Economic Consequences of the Energy Crisis', *Foreign Affairs* (April).

Rodrik, Dani and Andrés Velasco, 2000, 'Short-Term Capital Flows', in Boris Pleskovic and Joseph Stiglitz (eds) *Annual World Bank Conference on Development Economics, World Bank 1999*, Washington: World Bank.

Sharpe, William, 1970, *Portfolio Theory and Capital Markets*, New York: McGraw-Hill Book Company.

Stiglitz, Joseph E., 2003, 'Whither Reform? Towards a New Agenda for Latin America', the 2003 ECLA Prebisch Lecture, published in *Revista de la CEPAL*, 80, August, pp.7–40.

World Bank, 2000, 'Short-term flows and vulnerability', *Global Development Finance 2000*, Washington: World Bank.

6

TRIP WIRES AND SPEED BUMPS: MANAGING FINANCIAL RISKS AND REDUCING THE POTENTIAL FOR FINANCIAL CRISES IN DEVELOPING ECONOMIES

Ilene Grabel[1]

Abstract:

In this paper, we investigate the shortcomings of the 'early warning systems' (EWS) that are currently being promoted with such vigour in the international academic financial community. We advocate an integrated 'trip wire–speed bump' regime to reduce financial risk and, as a consequence, to reduce the frequency and depth of financial crises in developing countries.

We begin by demonstrating that efforts to develop EWS for banking, currency, and generalized financial crises in developing countries have largely failed. The paper argues that the EWS have failed because the whole idea is based on faulty theoretical assumptions, not least that the mere provision of information can reduce financial turbulence in developing countries.

We then advance an approach to managing financial risks through trip wires and speed bumps. Trip wires are indicators of vulnerability that can illuminate the specific risks to which developing economies are exposed. Among the most significant of these vulnerabilities are the risks of: large-scale currency depreciations – that domestic and foreign investors and lenders may suddenly withdraw capital, that locational and/or maturity mismatches will induce debt distress, that non-transparent financial transactions will induce financial fragility, and that a country will suffer the contagion effects of financial crises that originate elsewhere in the world, or within particular sectors of its own economy. We argue that trip wires must be linked to policy responses that alter the context in which investors operate. In this connection, policymakers should link specific speed bumps – that is, targeted and gradual changes in policies and regulations – that change behaviours in response to each type of trip wire.

Our proposal for a trip wire–speed bump regime is not intended as a means to prevent all financial instability and crises in developing countries. Indeed, such a goal is fanciful. But insofar as developing countries remain highly vulnerable to financial instability, policymakers must vigorously pursue avenues for reducing the financial risks to which their economies are exposed and curtail the destabilizing effects of unpredictable changes in international private capital flows.

We also address likely concerns about the response of investors, the International Monetary Fund (IMF) and powerful governments to the trip wire–speed bump approach. We consider as well the issue of technical and institutional capacity to pursue this approach to policy. We conclude by arguing that the obstacles confronting the trip wire–speed bump approach are not insurmountable.

Introduction

Developing countries have an interest in acting to curtail the financial risks to which they are exposed because these risks often culminate in costly and painful financial crises. Toward this end, 'trip wires and speed bumps' can be useful. We argue that the trip wire–speed bump approach presented here has a far greater ability to reduce financial risks (including the potential of these risks to induce crises) than do the 'early warning systems' (hereafter, EWS) that are currently being promoted with such vigour in the international and academic financial community (Goldstein, Kaminsky, and Reinhart 2000; and see below for further references).

The financial turbulence of the past three decades has stimulated a great deal of research into both the etiology and the prevention of financial crises. Unlike in the 1970s and early 1980s, recent research has not been stimulated by the collapse of currency pegs or by efforts to predict exchange-rate changes in wealthy countries. The chief catalyst for recent research has been recurrent, severe, costly, and contagious financial crises in the developing world.[2] The first of these recent crises occurred in Mexico in 1994–95, with contagion spread to several countries in South America. Next came the crisis in East Asia in 1997–98. This crisis began in Thailand in the summer of 1997 and quickly engulfed the economies of the Philippines, Indonesia and Malaysia. Within months the crisis spread to South Korea, Russia and Brazil.

Turkey experienced a financial crisis in early 2001, and Argentina has experienced several rounds of crisis since then. With only the exception of Malaysia during the East Asian crisis, these crises were followed by large bailouts from the IMF, painful programmes of economic reform, and severe economic and social dislocation.

In large measure, the financial crises mentioned above resulted from the decision to liberalize external and internal financial flows in the developing world from the 1980s onward. For the purposes of this study, the link between financial crisis and financial liberalization in the developing world will be assumed rather than demonstrated. This is because the link between financial liberalization and financial crisis has been explored convincingly in numerous recent works, such as Arestis and Demetriades (1997), Arestis and Glickman (2002), papers in Chang, Palma, and Whittaker (2001), Crotty and Lee (2001), Eatwell and Taylor (2000), Grabel (2003a, 2003b, 2003e, 1996), Singh and Weisse (1998), Weller (2001), Williamson and Mahar (1998), and Wyplosz (2001).[3]

The significant economic and social costs associated with recurrent financial crises has stimulated a large volume of research (and associated policy advocacy) into the matter of whether financial crises in developing countries can be prevented or mitigated through models that predict currency, banking, and generalized financial difficulties. The most important of these efforts involves the development of early warning systems. The work of Goldstein, Kaminsky, and Reinhart (2000) is the gold standard of such efforts (also see Berg and Patillo 1998; Edison 2000; Frankel and Rose 1996; Goldstein 1997a; Hardy and Pazarbasioglu 1998; IMF 2001; Kamin and Babson 1999; Kaminsky, Lizondo and Reinhart 1997; Kaminsky and Reinhart 2000; and Sachs, Tornell and Velasco 1996).

The financial turbulence of the last decade has also reinvigorated the study of certain types of capital controls as a tool for reducing the likelihood of and/or mitigating the effect of financial crises on developing economies (Epstein, Grabel and Jomo 2003). In this connection, recent discussions of capital controls in Chile, Colombia, Malaysia, China, India, Singapore, and Taiwan Province of China are quite relevant to the discussion of trip wires and speed bumps.

This study has several objectives:

1 It will establish that efforts to develop EWS for banking, currency, and generalized financial crises in developing countries have not met with success. This failure mirrors the failure of similar efforts to predict currency turbulence in the 1970s and 1980s. We argue that recent efforts to predict crisis through EWS have failed because they are based on faulty theoretical

assumptions and on the incorrect view that the mere provision of information can reduce financial turbulence in developing countries.

2 Against the current crop of proposals for EWS, this paper will advance an approach to managing financial risks (including the risk of financial crisis) through 'trip wires and speed bumps'. The trip wire–speed bump approach is initially developed in Grabel (1999, 2003a, 2003b) and is elaborated further in Chang and Grabel (2004).[4] In this paper the approach is developed more fully than in any of these works.

Trip wires are indicators of vulnerability that can illuminate the specific risks to which developing economies are exposed. Among the most significant of these vulnerabilities are:

- the risk of large-scale currency depreciations;
- the risk that domestic and foreign investors and lenders may suddenly withdraw capital;
- the risk that locational and/or maturity mismatches will induce debt distress;
- the risk that non-transparent financial transactions will induce financial fragility; and
- the risk that a country will suffer the contagion effects of financial crises that originate elsewhere in the world or within particular sectors of its own economy.

We will argue that trip wires are a necessary tool for determining the unique vulnerability (or combination of vulnerabilities) of individual developing economies. Furthermore, we will argue that trip wires must be linked to policy responses that alter the context in which investors operate. In this connection, we recommend that policymakers should link specific speed bumps that change behaviours to each type of trip wire.

3 We will argue that the proposal for a trip wire–speed bump regime is not intended to prevent *all* financial instability and crises in developing countries. Indeed, such a goal is fanciful at best. But insofar as developing countries remain highly vulnerable to financial instability, policymakers must vigorously pursue avenues for reducing the financial risks to which their economies are exposed and for curtailing the destabilizing effects of unpredictable changes in international private capital flows. It is in this context that we present the trip wire–speed bump approach.

4 We address the likely concerns about the response of investors, the IMF, and powerful governments (namely, that of the United States) to the

trip wire–speed bump approach. We also consider the issue of technical/institutional capacity to pursue this approach to policy. We conclude by arguing that the concerns anticipated are not insurmountable obstacles to adopting the trip wire–speed bump approach.

Previous Efforts to Predict Financial Turbulence

The current project to predict financial crises in developing countries through EWS has its roots in two previous research agendas. These earlier projects are etiological studies of the currency crises that followed the collapse of the Bretton-Woods-era pegged exchange-rate system and the crisis in European currency markets in 1992. In what follows we focus on the current EWS project. But before moving to the EWS models, we reflect briefly on the EWS's intellectual antecedents.

Intellectual Prehistory of EWS Models

Theoretical and empirical treatments of the etiology of currency crises is not a new area of research in macroeconomics. The starting point for theoretical treatments of the subject is Paul Krugman's seminal 1979 work on the circumstances that led to the collapse of fixed/pegged exchange-rate regimes (Krugman 1979). Krugman maintains that such regimes collapse under the pressure of weak fundamentals – to wit: excessively expansionary monetary and/or fiscal policies or persistent balance of payments deficits render fixed/pegged currency regimes untenable. Extensions of Krugman are legion; in these elaborations, weak fundamentals play a central role in triggering currency crises. The earliest extensions of Krugman (termed first-generation models) focus on the role of monetary and/or fiscal imbalances in speculative attacks against a multiplicity of exchange-rate regimes; later extensions (termed second-generation models) centre on the possibility of multiple equilibria and self-fulfilling attacks on a currency following the deterioration of fundamentals.[5]

The European currency crisis of 1992 reinvigorated efforts to understand the causes of currency crises; important work in this regard was done by Eichengreen and Wyplosz (1993), Eichengreen, Rose and Wyplosz (1995) and Rose and Svensson (1994). Neither the work in the post-Krugman tradition nor the work of the Europeanists attempted to develop explicit predictors of financial crisis.

From Etiology to Crisis Prediction: The Mexican Crisis of 1994–95 to the Current EWS Models

It was not until the Mexican crisis of 1994–95 that orthodox economists moved beyond the project of uncovering the causes of crisis and began to elaborate predictors of financial crisis in developing economies. Official efforts to understand the Mexican crisis were largely guided by the view that crises could be prevented through the provision of accurate and timely information about conditions in developing economies. The central role of information in crisis prevention was indeed the main message of the June 1995 Group of Seven Summit held in Halifax in the wake of the Mexican crisis. At Halifax, the IMF was urged to encourage the prompt publication of economic and financial statistics and to identify regularly countries that did not comply with the institution's new information standards (data standards that eventually became known as the IMF's Special Data Dissemination Standard).[6] The current project by orthodox economists to develop EWS builds directly on the IMF's failed efforts to prevent crises in East Asia through the provision of information through the Special Data Dissemination Standard.

The Underlying, General Logic of EWS

The underlying, general logic of EWS is rather straightforward. Crisis prevention requires two things:

- good predictors (embodied in EWS) that fill information gaps; and
- an open, liberalized regime in which agents are free to reallocate or liquidate their portfolios in response to problems made apparent by EWS.

In this way, the self-regulating actions that rational agents take in response to EWS will prevent the predicted event from coming to fruition (or at least will mitigate its severity). The underlying logic of the EWS is summarized in Figure 1.

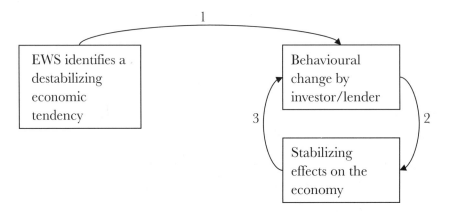

Figure 1. The underlying general economic logic of early warning systems (EWS)

The EWS approach assumes that once a dangerous economic tendency is revealed, rational private economic actors will change their behaviour in a manner that ultimately stabilizes markets.

A Brief Review of EWS Models

Economists that develop predictors of crisis propose two broad types of predictors – the 'regression' or 'probit' approach, associated with Frankel and Rose (1996), and the more frequently discussed EWS (often termed the 'signal extraction') approach, associated with Goldstein, Kaminsky and Reinhart (2000).[7]

The regression approach estimates the probability of a currency or a banking crisis and identifies the variables that are statistically correlated with crisis. Econometric work by Frankel and Rose (1996) exemplifies this approach to crisis prediction (Sachs, Tornell and Velasco 1996). For example, Frankel and Rose (1996) conclude that currency crashes occur when foreign direct investment dries up, when currency reserves are low and falling, when domestic credit growth is high, when Northern nominal interest rates rise, and when the real exchange rate is overvalued by 10 per cent.

The EWS approach compares the behaviour of a variable before a crisis with its behaviour during normal times. A variable is then assumed to be useful if it displays anomalous behaviour before a crisis but does not provide false signals of an impending crisis in normal times. When a variable exceeds or falls below a certain threshold, it is said to signal that a crisis may occur.

Goldstein, Kaminsky and Reinhart (2000) is the point of departure for all efforts to develop EWS (reviews and extensions appear in Abiad 2003; Berg and Patillo 1998, 2000; Edison 2000; Hardy and Pazarbasioglu 1998; Hardy 1998; Hawkins and Klau 2000; IMF 1998; Kamin and Babson 1999).[8] Goldstein, Kaminsky and Reinhart (2000) find that there is a systemic pattern of empirical abnormalities leading up to most currency and banking crises in developing economies over a sample period ranging from 1970 to 1995. For currency crises, they find that the best predictors using monthly data are appreciation of the real exchange rate (relative to trend), a banking crisis, a decline in stock prices, a fall in exports, a high ratio of broad money (M2) to international reserves, and a recession. Among the annual predictors of currency crises, the two most reliable predictors are a large current account deficit relative to both GDP and investment. For banking crises, they find that using monthly data the most reliable predictors of crisis (in descending order of importance) are appreciation of the real exchange rate (relative to trend), a decline in stock prices, a rise in the M2 money multiplier, a decline in real output, a fall in exports, and a rise in the real interest rate.[9] Among the annual predictors of banking crises, the most reliable are a high ratio of short-term capital inflows to GDP and a large current account deficit relative to investment. They find that in most banking and currency crises, a high proportion of the monthly leading indicators – of the order of 50–75 per cent – reach their signalling threshold. In other words, when a developing economy is moving toward a financial crisis, many of the leading indicators signal a crisis.

Goldstein, Kaminsky and Reinhart (2000) show that there is a wide divergence in the performance across leading indicators; warnings usually appear 10 to 18 months prior to the onset of crisis. The authors remain firm in their view that the EWS can make apparent an economy's vulnerability to crisis. They do make clear, however, that the system does not speak to the timing of a crisis.

The Bank for International Settlements currently uses an EWS model. The IMF employs two EWS models and also monitors the EWS used by numerous private firms (such as the Credit Suisse First Boston Emerging Markets Risk Indicator, Deutsche Bank Alarm Clock, and Goldman Sachs GS-Watch) (IMF 2001). Much mention is made in the business press of the Damocles model developed by economists at Lehman Brothers-Asia (Subbaraman, Jones and Shiraishi 2003). The Damocles model relies on 10 predictors of financial crises (many of which figure in the Goldstein, Kaminsky and Reinhart model). Indeed, all of the new EWS are very close cousins of the model developed by Goldstein, Kaminsky and Reinhart (2000).

The Empirical Performance of EWS (and Other Predictive) Models

The empirical performance of crisis predictors (both of the EWS and the less frequently discussed regression/probit models) is rather dismal. Numerous empirical tests (many indeed conducted by proponents) conclude that predictive models would not have provided *ex ante* signals of the events in Mexico or East Asia.

For example, Flood and Marion (1999), Hawkins and Klau (2000), and the IMF (1998) conclude that all predictive models have a mixed record of success. Goldfajn and Valdes (1997) and Hardy and Pazarbasioglu (1998) are less ambiguous: the former study concludes that exchange-rate crises are largely unpredictable events, a result they demonstrate in the case of the currency crises in Mexico and Thailand; the study by Hardy and Pazarbasioglu (1998) concludes that the East Asian banking crises would not have been predicted by the usual macroeconomic predictors. Eichengreen's (1999) survey of predictive models concludes that they have remarkably poor power (IMF 2001;

Eichengreen, Rose and Wyplosz 1995). Eichengreen's assessment is worth quoting at length:

> If investors, with so much at stake, cannot reliably forecast crises, then it is hard to see why bureaucrats should do better ... Their [predictors'] track record is not good. Models built to explain the 1992–93 European exchange rate mechanism (ERM) crisis did not predict the 1994–95 Mexican crisis. Models built to explain the Mexican crisis did not predict the Asian crisis.

Several studies test a comprehensive battery of crisis predictors; these studies, also, fail to offer empirical support to the predictors project. In a test of nearly all existing predictors (both of the regression and the EWS variety), Berg and Patillo (1998) find that some models perform better than guesswork in predicting the East Asian crisis. But they find that none of these models reliably predicts the timing of the crisis (that is, whether there would be a crisis in 1997). This is because false alarms, in almost all cases, always outnumber appropriate warnings. Edison (2000) also concludes that predictive models issue many false alarms and miss important crises. Sharma's (1999) review of the empirical performance of predictive models concludes that they would not have predicted the events in East Asia (a conclusion echoed by Corbett and Vines (1998). Sharma sums up the matter definitively: 'the holy grail of crisis prediction may be intrinsically unattainable.'

The most prominent advocates of predictors remain unshaken by the weight of discouraging empirical evidence. Goldstein (1997a), for example, concludes that preliminary tests of the predictors he develops indicate that they would have predicted the Thai crisis. Goldstein, Kaminsky and Reinhart (2000) conclude that their EWS model performs quite well, not only in tracking currency and banking crises in developing economies during the 1970–95 sample period, but also in anticipating most of the countries affected by the East Asian crisis (particularly as regards currency crises in the region).[10] To their credit, the authors clearly acknowledge that their EWS is prone to many false alarms and would have missed some important crises: the best indicators send a significant share of false alarms on the order of one false alarm for every two–five true signals.

With respect to the recent difficulties of Argentina, there is no evidence that EWS models would have predicted the collapse of the currency peg. Indeed, the general bullishness of the international investment and policy community on the Argentine economy from the inception of its currency board in 1991 and up until a few months before its collapse in 2002 suggests that EWS were not providing indications that the country was heading toward crisis.[11]

The empirical shortcomings of the EWS project are clear, even to some of its most ardent proponents. What is not clear is why efforts to refine existing predictors and to develop new ones proceed despite the resounding empirical failure of this enterprise. This failing suggests the need to develop other strategies for reducing financial risks in general, and for reducing the risk of financial crisis in particular. The discussion below presents one such approach.

Why have Existing Predictive Models Failed to Predict and Curtail the Risk of Financial Crises?

We argue that the failings of existing predictive models stem from the fact that they are based on six misguided initial assumptions. Recall that the general economic logic of EWS models begins from the presumption that the provision of accurate and timely information about an economy's vulnerability is ultimately market stabilizing, provided that investors are able to adopt appropriate defensive postures in response to this information (see Figure 1). In our opinion, this view is indefensible on several grounds.

- *The informational prerequisites for EWS are simply unreasonable in the developing economy context.* The success of EWS depends very much on the accuracy and availability of information about a range of economic conditions. But these informational prerequisites cannot be accommodated in the developing economy context. Problems of data inaccuracy are to be expected. Indeed, identification of precisely this problem motivated the IMF's creation of the Special Data Dissemination Standard. But identification of the problem has not solved it.

  False and missed alarms are likely as long as the integrity of data are compromised. And false alarms are obviously no small matter insofar as they can trigger real crises by causing an investor panic. Moreover, governments have a strong 'incentive to deceive' (i.e. to misreport data) once EWS are in place, and this incentive deepens as a country enters crisis territory. Paradoxically, then, the introduction of predictors is likely to reduce the quality of reported data.[12]

  We know that the quality of economic data is far from ideal, even in such industrial countries as the United States. The Federal Reserve and various departments of the US government issue *ex post* adjustments of data as a matter of course. For example, the dating of business cycles is always subject to *ex post* adjustment; the accuracy of data on US productivity has been the subject of much discussion over the last few years. The need for *ex post* revision (and/or disputes about methodology) may cause little problem when the matter at stake is the dating of recessions (or calculating productivity growth), since this news is unlikely to affect behaviour in consequential ways. But inaccurate data reporting in the context of predicting crisis is another matter entirely. In this context, inaccuracies are not benign.

- *The interpretation of predictors is endogenous to the economic environment.* The EWS model presumes that the interpretation of predictors is a science rather than an art. The former implies that the determination as to what constitutes a 'dangerous reading' is independent of the economic climate and the state of expectations. In contrast, we argue that the interpretation of predictors is far more art than science. The determination as to what constitutes a dangerous level for some set of predictive variables is endogenous to the economic environment. The interpretation of the consequences of a rising current account deficit is an example of the endogeneity of the interpretation of crisis predictors. A rising current account deficit may be taken as a sign of an impending crisis and a reflection of underlying economic fragility, or may be seen as a reflection of a country's strength and desirability to investors.

- *EWS models are predicated on the false notion that crises in developing countries have the same etiology.* This is simply not the case. The etiology of every crisis is at least slightly different. Thus, we have no reason to expect that a standard EWS model based on a static set of crisis predictors would be appropriate for the job. For example, the root causes of the European, Mexican, East Asian, and Argentinian crises remain distinct. Therefore, it comes as no surprise that predictors developed after each crisis failed to predict the next one (Corbett and Vines 1998).

- *Refining existing EWS models will not end the pattern of recurrent crisis in developing economies. The problem lies with the creation of highly liberalized, internationally integrated financial markets that render developing countries particularly vulnerable to crises.* The refinement of EWS models assumes that crises are a consequence of informational inadequacy rather than a fundamental, structural feature of the liberalized financial and regulatory environment that has been promoted in developing countries over the last two decades. Economies with internationally integrated, liquid, liberalized financial systems are inherently crisis-prone, as recent events have well shown. Several empirical studies show that financial liberalization in developing countries is a strong (and, in some cases, the best) predictor of banking, currency, and/or generalized financial crises (Corbett and Vines [quoting Wyplosz] 1998; Demirgüç-Kunt and Detragiache 1998; Weller 2001). Empirical evidence that links financial liberalization and financial crisis is also reviewed in Arestis and Demetriades (1997), Arestis and Glickman (2002), Brownbridge and Kirkpatrick (2000), papers in Chang, Palma and Whittaker (2001), Crotty and Lee (2001), Grabel (2003a, 2003e), Palma (1998), Singh and Weisse (1998), and Williamson and Mahar (1998).[13]

- *Economists have never succeeded in predicting economic turning points.* Efforts at divining market swings have never met with much success. The spectacular failure of the hedge fund, Long-Term Capital Management, a fund managed by Nobel Laureates and other distinguished economists, demonstrates that even pioneers of elaborate risk-management models cannot anticipate market shifts with great accuracy.[14] Developing economies simply cannot afford to bear the costs of failed efforts at crisis prediction through EWS (namely, false signals that trigger investor panics or missed signals).
- *We know that investors can respond to new information in a manner that is either market stabilizing* or *market destabilizing.* By making agents aware of fragilities in the economy, predictors of crisis may induce market-stabilizing or desta- bilizing changes in behaviour. Given the herd-like behaviour of investors and the inherent instability of liquid, liberalized, internationally integrated financial markets, rational economic actors are just as likely to engage in destabilizing behaviour in response to information on problems in the economy as they are to engage in market-stabilizing behaviour. In the game of musical chairs, no one wants to be the last one left standing, as John Maynard Keynes noted long ago. We simply cannot predict with certainty whether agents will respond to the information provided by predictors in a market-destabilizing or market-stabilizing manner. Indeed, investor panic seems a likely response to warnings of dire circumstances ahead.

The general, underlying logic of this critical view of predictive efforts is summarized in Figure 2.

At best, predictors of crisis have indeterminate effects on macroeconomic stability in the context of the current environment – one of liberalized, internationally integrated financial markets in which investors are free to take defensive actions in response to new information (such as changes in market sentiment).

Ironically, there is reason to expect that the presence of EWS might promote higher levels of financial instability in developing countries. This may be

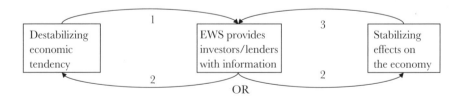

Figure 2. The indeterminate effect of early warning system (EWS) models in the current environment of liberalized, internationally integrated financial markets

termed the 'predictor credibility paradox'. The paradox may be introduced if the presence of EWS induce a heightened level of confidence among economic actors, such that they may be apt to engage in riskier financial arrangements, provided that the EWS do not provide an indication of looming difficulties.

A Proposal for Trip Wires and Speed Bumps

This paper responds to the failure of current efforts to reduce the likelihood of financial crises by predicting them through EWS. We maintain that the trip wire–speed bump approach has the potential to reduce the specific financial risks that national policymakers deem most important to their own economies.

Contrasting Trip Wires–Speed Bumps and EWS

The trip wire–speed bump approach differs from EWS in several critical ways:

Trip wires are diagnostic tools only. In contrast to the EWS approach, the information provided by trip wires is understood to have a rather narrow value as a diagnostic tool. Thus, unlike predictors in the EWS models, trip wires themselves are not expected to curtail financial risks and stabilize markets. Trip wires are necessary – but not sufficient – for the task of curtailing financial risks.

The trip wire–speed bump approach rests on the idea that specific, targeted changes in policy and/or behaviour are necessary to curtail particular financial risks as soon as they are identified. In contrast to the EWS, trip wires and speed bumps do not assume that the self-correcting actions of private actors or private rating agencies will prevent identified financial risks from culminating in a financial crisis. Indeed, the trip wire–speed bump approach begins from the assumption that the actions of private actors in response to information about financial vulnerabilities can trigger additional financial instability (for instance, as investors run for the exits at the first sign of trouble; see Figure 2).

The trip wire–speed bump approach calls upon regulators to activate gradual speed bumps at the first signs of vulnerability. It is these behavioural and/or regulatory changes that can reduce financial risks and prevent them from culminating in financial crises. Thus, and unlike EWS, the warning signalled by a trip wire does not itself carry the full weight of crisis prevention. Instead, it triggers a series of regulatory actions that alter investor behaviour in ways that avert crisis.

Note that there is precedent for the trip wire–speed bump approach in US stock markets and futures exchanges. Within these markets, automatic circuit-breakers and price limits are used to dampen market volatility and stabilize extreme market swings. Regulatory authorities also have discretionary authority to stop trading or temporarily close an exchange or the trading in one particular security or derivative.[15] We return to this point later on.

Problems of informational inadequacy are not nearly as damaging to the success of trip wires and speed bumps as they are to EWS. The adequacy of the information used in trip wires is quite obviously an important matter. But it is not nearly as significant a concern as it is for EWS. This is because the goal of a trip wire is not to *predict crisis*, but to identify a risk of looming difficulty that warrants regulatory response. In this approach, the regulatory response bears the principal weight of ensuring stability, while under the EWS approach, information must do the full job.

In a trip wire–speed bump approach, regulators monitor trip wires constantly. So close to the ground, regulators are well positioned to monitor the quality of the information they gather – indeed, they are in a far better position to do so than distant market actors or rating agencies (who must rely in part on the reporting of these regulators). Moreover, the gradual, early activation of speed bumps can reduce the cost of regulatory error associated with incorrect information. Under this approach, it is true that incorrect information may induce over- or under-regulation; but under the EWS, incorrect information is apt to induce sudden, dramatic reactions of private actors that precipitate economic instability and crisis.

A government's incentive to deceive under an EWS evaporates under a trip wire–speed bump approach. Under the EWS, the government has an incentive to misreport the value of important economic variables and to exaggerate the quality of the government's data collection (so as to achieve and maintain credibility). Under the trip wire–speed bump approach, the officials who monitor the trip wires have no such incentive, since they are themselves the agents who will use the information they produce. Moreover, they now have an incentive to assess carefully the quality of the data they report and to take account of this quality when activating and calibrating speed bumps. For instance, where data quality is known (or suspected) to be poor, speed bumps would be imposed earlier than otherwise.

Trip Wires

One may envision a variety of trip wires that measure the types of financial risks that confront individual economies. Before proceeding, we note two caveats about the trip wires presented below.

First, the trip wires proposed here are illustrative only. They are neither exhaustive nor definitive. Our hope is that this paper will stimulate discussion of how these trip wires can be refined by national or regional policymakers (or by the Group of Twenty-Four countries).

Second, the financial risks identified below are of differential relevance to particular developing countries. National policymakers are best equipped to design specific trip wires that speak to their own economy's unique vulnerabilities. For example, many developing countries do not confront the risk of portfolio investment flight because they receive very little (or no) international portfolio investment. Indeed, over the last 13 years, eight middle-income countries have accounted for 84 per cent of total net flows of portfolio investment to the developing world; and 10 large, middle-income countries received 70 per cent of the FDI flows that went to the developing world in 2002 (World Bank 2003). But the risk of flight is highly consequential for the small number of developing countries that receive the majority of these flows. Other developing countries are far more vulnerable to sudden, significant declines in inflows of bilateral or multilateral loans or private remittances. These risks require a different set of trip wires.

In what follows, we suggest trip wires that focus on particular financial risks. Among the most significant of these risks are the risk of large-scale currency depreciations, the risk that investors and lenders may suddenly withdraw capital, the risk that locational and/or maturity mismatches will induce debt distress, the risk that non-transparent financial transactions and other financing strategies will induce financial fragility and inter-sectoral contagion, and the risk that a country will experience cross-border contagion.

Trip wires for currency risk. Currency risk refers to the possibility that a country's currency may experience a sudden and significant depreciation.[16] Currency risk can be evidenced by the ratio of official reserves to total short-term external obligations (the sum of accumulated foreign portfolio investment and short-term hard-currency-denominated foreign borrowing), and by the ratio of official reserves to the current account deficit.

Trip wires for fragility risk. Fragility risk refers to the vulnerability of an economy's private and public borrowers to internal or external shocks that jeopardize their ability to meet current obligations. Fragility risk arises in a number of ways. Borrowers finance long-term obligations with short-term credit, causing maturity mismatch. This leaves borrowers vulnerable to changes in the supply of credit, and thereby exacerbates the ambient risk level in the economy. A proxy for maturity mismatch could be given by the ratio of short-term debt to long-term debt (with foreign-currency-denominated obligations receiving a greater weight in the calculation).

Fragility risk also arises when borrowers contract debts that are repayable in foreign currency, causing locational mismatch. This leaves borrowers vulnerable to currency depreciation/devaluation that may frustrate debt repayment. Locational mismatch that induces fragility risk could be evidenced by the ratio of foreign-currency-denominated debt (with short-term obligations receiving a greater weight in the calculation) to domestic-currency-denominated debt. In general, we might think of the dangerous interactions between currency and debt market conditions as introducing the possibility of inter-sectoral contagion risk.

Fragility risk is also introduced whenever economic actors finance private investment with capital that is either highly subject to reversal, is highly vulnerable to changes in the price at which additional funds are forthcoming, or is highly vulnerable to changes in the value of the underlying collateral that supports the investment. For instance, commercial real estate often serves as collateral for bank loans. A decline in real estate prices can then undermine bank balance sheets. This type of fragility risk raises the spectre of inter-sectoral contagion. Trip wires that illuminate the fragility risk associated with particular financing strategies are discussed below in the context of flight risk.

Finally, fragility risk is introduced whenever economic actors finance their projects with highly risky non-transparent financial instruments, such as derivatives or off-balance-sheet activities more generally. For example, in the case of derivatives the sudden necessity to meet collateral requirements often requires the selling of some other securities (often in an area not yet hit by turmoil).[17] This forced selling spreads turmoil to other sectors of the financial system and can ultimately create difficulties in the economy as a whole.

The risk that arises from such off-balance-sheet activities as derivatives is not amenable to trip wires precisely because data on these activities are not readily available. For this reason, it is our view that these activities have no place in developing economies because they introduce far too much financial risk (e.g. foreign exchange exposure) to financial systems that are already quite vulnerable. Indeed, research on the East Asian crisis illuminates the important role that off-balance-sheet activities played in the crisis (Dodd 2001; Neftci 1998; Kregel 1998). Thus financial regulators in developing countries might consider banning the use of these activities altogether. An alternative direction for policy toward derivatives is to mandate their transparency, such that these transactions appear on firm balance sheets. See Dodd (2002) for a discussion of transparency and other aspects of prudential financial regulation vis-à-vis derivatives in developing economies. With transparency, it would be reasonable to think about the development of appropriate trip wires (and speed bumps) for derivatives.

Trip wires for flight risk. Lender flight risk refers to the possibility that private, bilateral or multilateral lenders will call in loans or cease making new loans in the face of perceived difficulty. An indicator of lender flight risk is the ratio of official reserves to private and bilateral and multilateral foreign-currency-denominated debt (with short-term obligations receiving a greater weight in the calculation).

Portfolio investment flight risk refers to the possibility that portfolio investors will sell off the assets in their portfolio, causing a reduction in asset prices and increasing the cost of raising new sources of finance. Vulnerability to the flight of portfolio investment can be measured by the ratio of total accumulated foreign portfolio investment to gross equity market capitalization or gross domestic capital formation.

Lender and portfolio investment flight risk often creates a self-fulfilling prophecy that deflates asset and loan collateral values, induces bank distress, and elevates ambient economic risk. In addition, lender and/or portfolio investment flight risk can interact with currency risk to render the economy vulnerable to financial crisis (causing inter-sectoral contagion).

Trip wires for cross-border contagion risk. Cross-border contagion risk refers to the threat that a country will fall victim to financial and macroeconomic instability that originates elsewhere. This threat has of course been amply demonstrated in recent years. It would seem that a trip wire–speed bump approach must take account of this risk. Fortunately, this mechanism is well suited to the task: a trip wire may be activated in Country A whenever crisis conditions emerge in Country B, or whenever speed bumps are implemented in Country B, assuming that policymakers in Country A have reason to expect that investors would view countries A and B in a similar light (correctly or incorrectly).

Speed Bumps

Speed bumps are narrowly targeted and gradual changes in policies and regulations that are activated whenever trip wires reveal particular vulnerabilities in the economy (Table 1).

The trip wire–speed bump strategy is straightforward. It would be the task of policymakers within their own countries to establish appropriate thresholds for each trip wire, taking into account the country's particular characteristics (e.g. size, level of financial development, regulatory capacity) and its unique vulnerabilities (e.g. existing conditions in the domestic banking system, stock market and corporate sector). Critical values for trip wires and the calibration of speed bumps would be revised over time in light of experience, changes in the economy, and improvements in institutional and regulatory capacity.

Table 1. Key financial risks confronting developing countries and examples of associated trip wires and speed bumps

Key financial risks	Examples of trip wires	Examples of speed bumps
	Trip wires measure the types of financial risks that confront individual economies.	Speed bumps are narrowly-targeted gradual changes in policies and regulations that are activated whenever trip wires reveal particular vulnerabilities in the economy.
Currency risk Investors flee currency, inducing sudden, dramatic depreciation.	Ratio of official reserves to total short-term external obligations (the sum of accumulated foreign portfolio investment and short-term hard-currency-denominated foreign borrowing), *or* Ratio of official reserves to the current account deficit.	Limit the fluctuation of the domestic currency value, *or* Restrict currency convertibility in various ways (e.g. foreign exchange licensing, selective currency convertibility, controls over non-resident access to the domestic currency).
Flight risks *Portfolio investment* Portfolio investors sell off a country's assets, causing a reduction in asset prices and increasing the cost of raising new sources of finance.	Ratio of total accumulated foreign portfolio investment to gross equity market capitalization or gross domestic capital formation.	Graduated series of speed bumps would slow the entrance of new inflows until the ratio falls either because domestic capital formation or gross equity market capitalization increased sufficiently or because foreign portfolio investment falls, *or* Outflow controls can be employed.
Lender Private, bilateral or multilateral lenders call in loans or cease making new loans in the face of	Ratio of official reserves to private, bilateral and multilateral foreign-currency-denominated debt (with short-term obligations	Preclude new inflows of foreign loans (particularly those with a dangerous maturity and/or locational profile) until circumstances

Table 1. Continued

Key financial risks	Examples of trip wires	Examples of speed bumps
perceived difficulty.	receiving a greater weight in the calculation).	improved, *or* Use the tax system to discourage domestic borrowers from incurring new foreign debt obligations (e.g. surcharges based on maturity/locational structure of loans, level of indebtedness of particular borrowers, or type of activity financed by foreign loan).
Fragility risks Shocks that jeopardize the ability of private and public borrowers to meet current obligations.		
Locational mismatch Proliferation of debts that are repayable in foreign currency.	Ratio of foreign-currency-denominated debt (with short-term obligations receiving a greater weight in the calculation) to domestic-currency-denominated debt.	Locational and/or maturity mismatch could be mitigated by a graduated series of speed bumps that require borrowers to reduce their extent of locational or maturity mismatch, *or* Impose surcharges or ceilings on financing strategies that involve locational maturity mismatch whenever trip wires reveal the early emergence of these vulnerabilities.
Maturity mismatch Proliferation of long-term debts financed with short-term credit.	Ratio of short-term debt to long-term debt (with foreign-currency-denominated obligations receiving a greater weight in the calculation).	See speed bump for locational mismatch above.
Off-balance-sheet Proliferation of	This type of fragility risk is	Policy options: Ban the use of

Table 1. Continued

Key financial risks	Examples of trip wires	Examples of speed bumps
financing strategies that involve risky non-transparent financial instruments.	is not amenable to trip wires precisely because data on these activities are not readily available.	non-transparent instruments in developing countries, *or* Mandate the transparency of these instruments so that trip wires and speed bumps can be devised.
Cross-border contagion risk Guilt by association: threat induced by crisis abroad.	Trip wire is activated in Country A whenever crisis conditions emerge in Country B, or whenever speed bumps are implemented in Country B, assuming that policymakers in Country A have reason to expect (correctly or incorrectly) that investors would view Countries A and B in a similar light.	See discussion of trip wire for cross-border contagion risk (left column). Note: Well-functioning trip wires and speed bumps would reduce levels of financial risk in the economy, and as a consequence, mollify anxious investors. Moreover, trip wires and speed bumps would increase the resilience of an economy to a speculative attack were it nevertheless to materialize

Sensitive trip wires would allow policymakers to activate graduated speed bumps at the earliest sign of heightened risk, well before conditions for investor panic had materialized (cf. Neftci 1998; Taylor 1998). When a trip wire indicates that a country is approaching trouble in some particular domain (such as new short-term external debt to GDP has increased over a short period of time), policymakers could then immediately take steps to prevent crisis by activating speed bumps. Speed bumps would target the type of risk that is developing with a graduated series of mitigation measures that compel changes in financing and investment strategies and/or dampen market liquidity.

Trip wires could indicate to policymakers and investors whether a country approached high levels of currency risk or particular types of fragility or flight risk. The speed bump mechanism provides policymakers with a means to manage measurable risks, and in doing so, reduces the possibility that these risks will culminate in a national financial crisis. Speed bumps affect investor behavior *directly* (e.g. by forcing them to unwind risky positions, by providing them with incentives to adopt prudent financing strategies, etc.) and *indirectly* (by reducing their anxiety about the future). Together, their effects mitigate the likelihood of crisis. Those countries that have trip wires and speed bumps in place would also be less vulnerable to cross-country contagion because they would face lower levels of risk themselves.

Specific speed bumps for the risks revealed by trip wires. Speed bumps can take many forms. The range of possible speed bumps that correspond to the specific financial risks illuminated by trip wires might include:

- *Speed bumps for currency risk.* Currency risk can be managed by the activation of speed bumps that limit the fluctuation of the domestic currency value or that restrict currency convertibility in a variety of ways. The fluctuation of the domestic currency might be managed through a short-term programme of sterilized intervention.

  Historical and contemporary experience demonstrates that there are a variety of means by which currency convertibility can be managed. For instance, the government can manage convertibility by requiring that those seeking access to the currency apply for a foreign exchange licence. This method allows the authorities to influence the pace of currency exchanges and distinguish among transactions based on the degree of currency and financial risk associated with the transaction. The government can suspend or ease foreign exchange licensing as a type of speed bump whenever trip wires indicate the early emergence of currency risk.

  The government can also activate a policy of selective currency convertibility, if trip wires illuminated the emergence of currency risk. Specifically, a speed bump might allow the currency to be convertible for current account transactions only. The IMF's Articles of Agreement (specifically, Article 8) provide for this type of selective convertibility.

  Another type of speed bump might allow the government to curtail (but not eliminate) the possibility that non-residents will speculate against the domestic currency by controlling their access to it. This can be accomplished by preventing domestic banks from lending to non-residents and/or by preventing non-residents from maintaining bank accounts in the country. The Malaysian government took precisely these steps in the aftermath of the Asian financial crisis. It restricted foreigners' access to the domestic currency via restrictions on bank lending and bank account maintenance and by declaring currency held outside the country inconvertible.
- *Speed bumps for lender flight risk.* Policymakers would monitor a trip wire that measures the economy's vulnerability to the cessation of foreign lending. If the trip wire approached an announced threshold, policymakers could then

activate a graduated speed bump that precluded new inflows of foreign loans (particularly those with a dangerous maturity and/or locational profile) until circumstances improved.

Alternatively, a speed bump might rely on the tax system to discourage domestic borrowers from incurring new foreign debt obligations whenever trip wires indicated it would be desirable to slow the pace of new foreign borrowing.[18] In this scenario, domestic borrowers might pay a fee to the government or the central bank equal to a certain percentage of any foreign loan undertaken. This surcharge might vary based on the structure of the loan, such that loans that involve a locational or maturity mismatch incur a higher surcharge. Surcharges might also vary based on the level of indebtedness of the particular borrower involved, such that borrowers who already hold large foreign debt obligations face higher surcharges than do less-indebted borrowers. This tax-based approach would encourage borrowers to use (untaxed) domestic sources of finance. Surcharges might also vary according to the type of activity that was being financed by foreign loans. For instance, borrowers might be eligible for a partial rebate on foreign loan surcharges when loans are used to finance export-oriented production.

Note that policymakers in Chile and Colombia employed several types of tax-based policies to discourage foreign borrowing during much of the 1990s. Consistent with the trip wire–speed bump approach, the level and scope of these taxes were adjusted as domestic and international economic conditions changed. For instance, in Chile, foreign loans faced a tax of 1.2 per cent a year (payable by the borrower), and all foreign debts and indeed all foreign financial investments in the country faced a non-interest-bearing reserve requirement tax during this time. In Colombia, foreign loans with relatively short maturities faced a reserve requirement tax of 47 per cent, and foreign borrowing related to real estate transactions was simply prohibited.[19]

- *Speed bumps for portfolio investment flight risk.* If a trip wire revealed that a country was particularly vulnerable to the reversal of portfolio investment inflows, a graduated series of speed bumps would slow the entrance of new inflows until the ratio falls either because domestic capital formation or gross equity market capitalization increased sufficiently or because foreign portfolio investment falls. Thus, a speed bump on portfolio investment would slow unsustainable financing patterns until a larger proportion of any increase in investment could be financed domestically. *We emphasize the importance of speed bumps governing inflows of portfolio investment because they exert their effects at times when the economy is attractive to foreign investors, and so are not as likely as outflow restrictions to trigger investor panic.* Though not a substitute for outflow controls, inflow restrictions also reduce the frequency with which outflow controls must be used, as well as their magnitude.[20]

Consistent with the trip wire–speed bump approach, the Malaysian authorities twice imposed temporary, stringent restrictions over portfolio investment in the 1990s. The first such effort was in early 1994. At that time, the Malaysian economy saw dramatic increases in the volume of private capital inflows (including, but not limited to, portfolio investment). Policymakers were concerned that these inflows were feeding an unsustainable speculative boom in real estate and stock prices and creating pressures on the domestic currency. In this context, policymakers implemented stringent, temporary inflow controls. These measures included restrictions on the maintenance of domestic-currency-denominated deposits and borrowing by foreign banks, controls on the foreign exchange exposure of domestic banks and large firms, and prohibitions on the sale to foreigners of domestic money market securities (with a maturity of less than one year). Reaction to these measures was rapid and dramatic – so much so that authorities were able to dismantle them as planned in less than a year (as they achieved their goals during this time). The immediate, powerful reaction to these temporary controls underscores the potential of speed bumps to stem successfully incipient difficulties.

The Malaysian government again implemented stringent controls over capital inflows and outflows in 1998 during the East Asian crisis. These took the form of restrictions on foreign access to the domestic currency, on international transfer and trading of the currency, and on the convertibility of currency held outside of the country. The government also established a fixed value for the domestic currency, closed the secondary market in equities, and prohibited non-residents from selling local equities held for less than one year. By many accounts, these rather stringent measures prevented the further financial implosion of the country – a notable achievement since the country was also then gripped by a severe political and social crisis. Comparing Malaysia to other countries affected by the East Asian crisis, studies find that the country's capital controls were responsible for the faster recovery of its economy and stock market as well as its smaller reductions in employment and wages (Kaplan and Rodrik 2002). The latter achievements were possible because capital controls allowed the Malaysian government to implement reflationary economic and social policies uninhibited by the threat of additional capital flight or IMF disapproval.

As discussed in the context of speed bumps on foreign borrowing, policymakers in Chile and Colombia adjusted restrictions on portfolio investment during much of the 1990s as domestic and international circumstances warranted. Consistent with the trip wire–speed bump approach, many other developing countries (such as China and India) have adjusted their restrictions on portfolio investment as circumstances warranted (Grabel 2003b; Epstein, Grabel and Jomo 2003; and Chang and Grabel 2004).

- *Speed bumps for fragility risks.* The fragility risk that stems from excessive reliance on inflows of international portfolio investment or foreign loans can be curtailed by the speed bumps that focus on these types of flight risks (see above). The fragility risk from locational and/or maturity mismatch could be mitigated by a graduated series of speed bumps that require borrowers to reduce their extent of locational or maturity mismatch by unwinding these activities, or by imposing surcharges or ceilings on them whenever trip wires revealed the early emergence of these vulnerabilities. Recall that speed bumps for off-balance-sheet activities necessitate legislating their transparency.

- *Speed bumps for cross-border contagion risks.* A trip wire–speed bump programme that reduces currency, flight, and fragility risks would render an individual economy far less vulnerable to cross-border contagion. This is because well-functioning trip wires and speed bumps would reduce levels of financial risk in the economy and thereby mollify anxious investors. Moreover, trip wires and speed bumps would increase the resilience of an economy to a speculative attack were it nevertheless to materialize.[21] This certainly helps to account for the resiliency of the Chilean, Malaysian and other economies during recent financial crises.

- *Considerations in the design of speed bumps.* Several guidelines might guide the design of speed bumps in particular countries:

  1 Speed bumps that govern *inflows* are preferable to those that govern outflows because measures that target outflows are more apt to trigger and exacerbate panic than to prevent it.[22] This does not mean that outflow controls are not useful during times of heightened vulnerability, especially if the government uses the 'breathing room' garnered by temporary outflow controls to make changes in economic policy or to provide time for an investor panic to subside. Indeed, Malaysia's successful use of temporary controls on outflows in 1994 and again in 1998 shows that temporary outflow controls can protect the economy from cross-border contagion risk in a time of heightened financial risks.

  2 Graduated, modest, and transparent speed bumps can address a financial risk before it is too late for regulators to take action. Such speed bumps are also less likely to cause an investor panic.

  3 Should speed bumps be automatic (i.e. rule-based) or subject to policymaker discretion? Automatic speed bumps have the advantage of transparency and certainty, attributes that may be particularly important to

investors. They also have lower administrative costs. But discretionary speed bumps have advantages too. They provide regulators with the opportunity to respond to subtle and unique changes in the international and domestic environment. Discretionary speed bumps, however, have higher administrative costs and require a greater level of policymaking capacity.

The most prudent answer to the question of discretion is that there is no single, ideal framework for speed bumps in all developing countries. In general, the best that can be said is that speed bumps should be largely automatic and transparent in their operation, though this does *not* mean that regulators could or even should be expected to eliminate all discretion in the activation of speed bumps. It is the task of national policymakers to determine the appropriate balance between automatic and discretionary speed bumps, particularly in light of their assessment of immediate technical capacities.

The Feasibility of the Trip Wire–Speed Bump Approach

We now anticipate and respond to a number of likely concerns raised by sceptics of the trip wire–speed bump approach.

Concern No.1. A trip wire–speed bump programme cannot reduce the unpredictability and volatility of cross-border and/or cross-currency capital flows. Therefore the utility of this approach is questionable. This approach to policy responds precisely to the volatility and lack of predictability of cross-border capital and currency flows in largely unregulated global financial markets. Rather than trying to do a better job of predicting what cannot be predicted (i.e. financial flows in unregulated global financial markets), this approach *manages and 'domesticates' otherwise unruly flows.*

Concern No. 2. The activation of trip wires and speed bumps might trigger the very instability that they are designed to prevent. This is usually referred to as the 'Lucas critique'. However, the Lucas critique does not take account of the possibility that if an economy is less financially fragile by virtue of a trip wire–speed bump programme, then investors and lenders will not be so likely to rush to the exits at the first sign of difficulty. Moreover, an economy in which financial risks are curtailed (by trip wires and speed bumps) will be more resilient in the face of investor/lender flight risk.

Early warning systems magnify the problem highlighted by Lucas because they are crude and blunt. The trip wire–speed bump approach entails moderate and graduated responses to small changes in conditions. The activation of speed bumps is therefore not apt to trigger market anxiety in the same way as an EWS announcement of pending crisis.

Concern No. 3. The trip wire–speed bump proposal is unnecessary because private investors and credit rating agencies can do a better job of identifying financial vulnerabilities than can governments. There is no reason to expect that private investors will identify financial risks as they emerge, and engage in behaviours that curtail these risks. Moreover, the panicked responses of private foreign and domestic investors to identified risks can actually aggravate – rather than ameliorate – financial instability. Indeed, we saw precisely this dynamic unfold in all of the recent financial crises in developing countries.

The experience of the East Asian crisis provides no basis to expect that trip wires and speed bumps are unnecessary since private credit-rating agencies provide useful diagnostics on emerging financial vulnerabilities. Indeed, evidence shows that assessments by private credit-rating agencies failed to highlight emerging problems in Argentina, East Asia and Turkey (Reisen 2002, and Goldstein, Kaminsky and Reinhart 2000).

By contrast, there is ample evidence that policymakers in a large number of developing countries have effectively curtailed particular financial risks in their own economies by modifying existing financial regulations and even implementing new ones as circumstances warranted. Indeed, Epstein, Grabel and Jomo (2003) show that from the 1990s to early 2003 policymakers in Chile, Colombia, Taiwan Province of China, India, Singapore and Malaysia tightened existing regulations and implemented new ones when financial vulnerabilities were identified. The success of these strategies illustrates the broader potential of a trip wire–speed bump approach.

Concern No. 4. Trip wires and speed bumps will not achieve their objectives because economic actors will evade them. Policy evasion (in any domain of policy) cannot be ignored. In the case of trip wires and speed bumps, financial innovation may provide a means for some economic agents to evade these polices. However, the middle-income countries that have the most to gain from trip wires and speed bumps are also in the best position to enforce them. Also, a degree of policy evasion does not imply policy failure (Grabel 2003b). This is clearly illustrated by the achievements of numerous financial controls in South Korea, Chile, Colombia, Malaysia, Taiwan, province of China and Singapore. It is imperative that the particular speed bumps adopted be consistent with national conditions, including state/regulator capacity.

Concern No.5. Many developing countries do not have the technical policymaking capacity that is necessary for the success of trip wires and speed bumps. It is certainly true that policymaking capacity differs dramatically across developing countries. Those developing countries (generally speaking, middle-income countries) that have the highest levels of policymaking capacity are certainly in the best position to adopt trip wires and speed bumps. This is, in some sense, a happy coincidence because policymakers in these same countries have the most to gain by curtailing many of the financial risks that are targeted by trip wires and speed bumps.

In addition, the technical prerequisites for operating trip wires and speed bumps are no greater than those demanded of policymakers that operate in an environment of liberalized, internationally integrated financial markets. Moreover, technical capacity can be acquired. Support for increased education and technical training of financial policymakers by the Bretton Woods institutions could be fruitful, particularly in smaller, low-income countries where financial policymakers may have had less opportunity to develop high levels of capacity. Regional cooperation among developing countries and/or the leadership of middle-income countries is another avenue for increasing the capacity of smaller, low-income countries to design and use trip wires and speed bumps that are best suited to their economies.

Concern No.6. The negative reaction of the Bretton Woods institutions, the US government and/or international investors is an obstacle to the implementation of trip wires and speed bumps. These actors have certainly been – individually and collectively – quite corrosive of policy autonomy in developing countries over the last two decades. But there are several reasons to be cautiously optimistic about the political feasibility of a trip wire–speed bump programme.

First, recent studies (by academics, policymakers, and even by the IMF) have concluded that certain types of financial controls in developing countries have enabled developing countries to manage the challenges and opportunities associated with global financial integration (Grabel 2003b; Grabel 2003e; Epstein, Grabel and Jomo 2003; Prasad, Rogoff, Wei and Kose 2003; Ariyoshi *et al.* 2000).

Second, the position of negotiators for Chile and Singapore in their individual discussions with the Unites States on bilateral free trade agreements is heartening. In these negotiations, representatives for Chile and Singapore vigorously defended their countries' right to activate temporary financial controls during times of financial crisis. Although the US administration steadily refuted this right, the final agreements reached did incorporate the right, but in attenuated form (e.g. under certain circumstances, US investors have the right to sue either country for losses incurred as a consequence of the capital controls).[23] On a related note, the assertiveness and the expression of solidarity among many developing countries at the World Trade Organization talks in Cancun in September 2003 may signal a greater resolve to press the case that new types of trade and financial policies are now needed.

Third, there may be reason to expect that foreign investors value financial stability in developing countries. Indeed, there is no empirical evidence that foreign investors shun developing countries that have well functioning financial controls in place, provided that they also offer investors attractive opportunities and an environment of economic growth. It may be that in the post-Asian, post-Argentinian crisis environment, developing countries with well-functioning and transparent financial controls might have a comparative advantage in attracting international private capital inflows.

Fourth, as noted earlier, circuit-breakers and price limits in US stock markets and futures exchanges are used effectively by regulators. This suggests that the broader trip wire–speed bump approach presented here may ultimately be accepted as a necessary evil even by advocates of liberalized markets, since it appears they play an important, beneficial role even in the most advanced financial markets in the world.

Concern No. 7. Countries that implement trip wires and speed bumps will face increased capital costs and lower rates of economic growth.[24] Contrary to the predictions of orthodox economic theory, there is no unambiguous empirical evidence of a trade-off between speed bumps and increased capital costs or reduced economic growth.[25] This may be because although foreign investors value the liquidity associated with unregulated financial markets, they may come to favour economies that give them less reason to fear financial crisis (since during sudden crises liquidity is jeopardized). For this reason, developing economies as a whole might find it substantially easier and less costly to attract private capital flows if they reduce their vulnerability to crisis through collective implementation of trip wire–speed bump policies. In short, and contrary to orthodox economic predictions, the 'hurdle rate' (the anticipated return sufficient to induce investment) might actually decline following the imposition of regulations that, in the first instance, reduce investor freedoms to liquidate their holdings.

Summary

Critics are likely to advance many arguments against the feasibility and utility of a trip wire–speed bump approach. Upon examination we find these arguments unconvincing.

Trip wires and speed bumps represent one new direction for managing the financial risks that are identified by national policymakers. The chief advantages of this approach are that it can target only those risks that policymakers deem most important, it can be implemented gradually, it is transparent, and it provides a way for developing countries to pursue international financial integration without increasing the likelihood of financial crises.

Notes

1 I am grateful to George DeMartino, Randall Dodd, Guillaume Arias and K. Kanagasabapathy for critical reactions to this paper, and to Rob Parenteau and Jamie Galbraith for reactions to related work. I thank Vladimir Zhapov for excellent research assistance.

2 The European currency crisis of 1992–93 is a notable exception in the recent literature as it involved wealthy countries. Like the financial crises in the developing world over the last decade, the European currency crisis stimulated a rather large body of etiological research.

3 Certainly, other analysts present alternative views on the etiology of financial crises in developing countries. For instance, some explain it as the product of widespread cronyism and corruption in developing countries, others as the outcome of policy mistakes (such as the mistaken decision to maintain a soft or a hard currency peg), and others as the outcome of a rational self-fulfilling prophecy. Concise and somewhat critical reviews of this literature appear in Eichengreen (1999:Appendix B) and Arias (2003). More extensive critiques appear in the studies of the link between financial crisis and financial liberalization (see above for citations), and also in Chang (1998) and Grabel (1999).

4 Accordingly, parts of the discussion in the following sections draw heavily on Grabel (1999, 2003a, 2003b). The discussion on our proposal for trip wires and speed bumps draws modestly on Chang and Grabel (2004).

5 The vast theoretical literature on currency crises is reviewed in Arias (2003), Eichengreen (1999, Appendix B), Goldfajn and Valdés (1997), and Kaminsky, Lizondo and Reinhart (1997). Many reviews of the literature correctly point out that the differences between the first- and second-generation models of crises are far less important than their architects suggest (see Eichengreen (1999) and Arias (2003)).

6 See Eichengreen and Portes (1997) and the papers collected in Kenen (1996) for a summary and evaluation of the decisions taken at the Halifax Summit. These works also discuss the recommendations of the Rey Committee (formed at Halifax) and the decisions taken at the 1996 G-7 Summit (in Lyons) on crisis prevention and the need for information dissemination.

7 General descriptions of these two approaches draw on Edison (2000), Goldstein, Kaminsky and Reinhart (2000), and Sharma (1999).

8 Goldstein, Kaminsky and Reinhart (2000) draw on the 'signals methodology' elaborated in Kaminsky and Reinhart (1999) and other related work by these authors – e.g. Goldstein (1997a), Kaminsky, Lizondo and Reinhart (1997), and Kaminsky and Reinhart (2000). The description of the authors' empirical findings is taken from Goldstein, Kaminsky and Reinhart (2000).

9 Note that they find that banking crises in developing economies are harder to predict using monthly data than are currency crises.

10 They acknowledge that their EWS would neither have predicted difficulties in Indonesia during the Asian crisis, nor Argentina's difficulties following the Mexican crisis.

11 Indeed, numerous IMF reports on Argentina during the 1990s extolled the virtues of the country's currency board and made a case for its export to other developing countries (Grabel 2000, 2003c).

12 We discuss the relevance of this issue in the context of the trip wire–speed bump approach in the next section.

13 Financial liberalization is a variable that rarely figures in EWS models. Kaminsky and Reinhart (1999) are an exception among orthodox economists in this regard.

14 I thank James Crotty for bringing this point to our attention. See Lowenstein (2000) on the failure of Long-Term Capital Management.
15 We thank Randall Dodd for raising this point.
16 Of course, rapid currency appreciation can also cause problems from the perspective of export performance. Although this is beyond the scope of this paper, the trip wire–speed bump approach could also address this 'trade risk'.
17 We thank Randall Dodd for raising this point.
18 Tax-based speed bumps on foreign borrowing are discussed in Chang and Grabel (2004).
19 See Grabel (2003b, 2003d) for further details on tax-based policies in Chile and Colombia; and see Epstein, Grabel and Jomo (2003) and Chang and Grabel (2004) for details on policies toward foreign borrowing in other developing countries.
20 Outflow controls can play a useful role in some circumstances, as suggested by Malaysia's experience in 1998.
21 The reduction in financial risks associated with trip wires and speed bumps would also increase the economy's resilience in the face of external shocks.
22 The same argument regarding inflow versus outflow controls pertains to speed bumps that compel investors to unwind risky positions. Speed bumps that provide incentives to change new financing behaviour are preferable to those that force investors to unwind existing positions (because the latter can trigger a crisis in other sectors).
23 For instance, investors can sue for losses only when restrictions on the sale of bonds and FDI extends beyond six months. For other financial assets, the 'cooling-off period' is 12 months.
24 Discussion in this subsection borrows heavily from Grabel (2003b).
25 See Edwards (1999) for a dissenting view on capital costs in Chile during its financial controls of the 1990s. See Epstein, Grabel and Jomo (2003) for a critical response to Edwards.

References

Abiad, A., 2003, 'Early-Warning Systems: A Survey and Regime-Switching Approach', IMF Working Paper 32, IMF, Washington, D.C.

Arestis, P. and P. Demetriades, 1997, 'Financial Development and Economic Growth: Assessing the Evidence', *Economic Journal*, May, pp. 783–799.

Arestis, P. and M. Glickman, 2002, 'Financial Crisis in Southeast Asia: Dispelling Illusion the Minskyian Way', *Cambridge Journal of Economics*, pp. 237–260.

Arias, G., 2003, 'Currency Crises: What We Know and What We Still Need to Know', C.E.F.I. Working Paper, 13 November.

Akira Ariyoshi, Karl Habermeier, Bernard Laurens, Inci Otker-Robe, Jorge Iván Canales-Kriljenko and Andrei Kirilenko, 2000, 'Country Experiences with the Use and Liberalization of Capital Controls', IMF Occasional Paper No. 190.

Berg, A. and C. Pattillo, 1998, 'Are Currency Crises Predictable? A Test', IMF Working Paper, November.

Berg, A. and C. Pattillo, 2000, 'The Challenges of Predicting Economic Crisis', *IMF Economic Issues*, 22.

Brownbridge, M. and Kirkpatrick, C., 2000, 'Financial Regulation in Developing Countries,' *Journal of Development Studies*, October: pp. 1–24.

Chang, H. J. and I. Grabel, 2004, *Reclaiming Development: An Alternative Economic Policy Manual*, London: Zed Press.

Chang, H. J., G. Palma and H. Whittaker (eds) 2001, *Financial Liberalization and the Asian Financial Crisis*, Basingstoke, Hampshire: Palgrave.

Corbett, J. and D. Vines, 1998, 'The Asian Crisis: Competing Explanations', Working Paper Series III, July, Center for Economic Policy Analysis.

Crotty, J. and K. Lee, 2001, 'Neoliberal Restructuring in Korea: "Miracle" or Disaster?', Paper presented at the conference on Financialization of the world economy, University of Massachusetts and Political Economy Research Institute, December.

Demirgüc-Kunt, A. and E. Detragiache, 1998, 'Financial Liberalization and Financial Fragility', IMF Working Paper 83, IMF, Washington, D.C.

Dodd, R., 2002, 'Derivatives, the Shape of International Capital Flows and the Virtues of Prudential Regulation', WIDER Discussion Paper 93.

Dodd, R., 2001, 'The Role of Derivatives in the East Asian Financial Crisis', Derivatives Study Center/Financial Policy Forum, Special Policy Report 1, 14 August, available at www.financialpolicy.org.

Eatwell, J. and L. Taylor, 2000, *Global Finance at Risk*, W. W. Norton & Co.

Edison, H., 2000, 'Do Indicators of Financial Crises Work? An Evaluation of an Early Warning System', Board of Governors of the Federal Reserve System, International Finance Discussion Papers, July.

Edwards, S., 1999, 'How Effective are Capital Controls?', *Journal of Economic Perspectives*, 13 (4).

Eichengreen, B. and R. Portes, 1997, *Managing Financial Crises in Emerging Markets, in Maintaining Financial Stability in a Global Economy*, A Symposium sponsored by the Federal Reserve Bank of Kansas City, August: pp. 193–225.

Eichengreen, B. and C. Wyplosz, 1993, 'The Unstable EMS', *Brookings Papers on Economic Activity*, pp. 51–124.

Eichengreen, B., R. Rose and C. Wyplosz, 1995, 'Exchange Market Mayhem: The Antecedents and Aftermath of Speculative Attacks', *Economic Policy*, October, pp. 249–312.

Eichengreen, B., and A. Toward, 1999, *New International Financial Architecture: A Practical Post-Asia Agenda*, Washington, D.C.: Institute for International Economics.

Epstein, G., I. Grabel and K. S. Jomo, 2003, 'Capital Management Techniques in Developing Countries: An Assessment of Experiences From the 1990s and Lessons for the Future', Paper prepared for the XVI Technical Group Meeting of the Group of Twenty-Four, Port of Spain, Trinidad and Tobago, February, pp. 13–14.

Flood, R. and N. Marion, 1999, 'Perspectives on the Recent Currency Crisis Literature', *International Journal of Finance and Economics*, pp. 1–26.

Frankel, J. and A. Rose, 1996, 'Currency Crashes in Emerging Markets: An Empirical Treatment', *Journal of International Economics*, November, pp. 351–368.

Goldfajn, I. and R. Valdés, 1997, 'Are Currency Crises Predictable?', IMF Working Paper, WP/97/159, December.

Goldstein, M., 1997a, 'Presumptive indicators of vulnerability to financial crises in emerging Economies', in P. Basu (ed.), *Creating Resilient Financial Regimes in Asia: Challenges and Policy Options*, Oxford University Press, pp. 79–132.

Goldstein, M., G. Kaminsky and C. Reinhart, 2000, *Assessing Financial Vulnerability: An Early Warning System for Emerging Markets*, Washington, D.C.: Institute for International Economics.

Grabel, I., 1996, 'Marketing the Third World: The Contradictions of Portfolio Investment in the Global Economy', *World Development*, Vol. 24 (11): 1761–1776.

Grabel, I., 1999, 'Rejecting Exceptionalism: Reinterpreting the Asian Financial Crises', in J. Michie and J. Smith (eds), *Global Instability: The Political Economy of World Economic Governance*, London: Routledge: pp. 37–67.

Grabel, I., 2000, 'The Political Economy of "Policy Credibility": The New-Classical Macroeconomics and the Remaking of Emerging Economies', *Cambridge Journal of Economics*, Vol. 24 (1): 1–19.

Grabel, I., 2003a, 'Predicting Financial Crisis in Developing Economies: Astronomy or Astrology?', *Eastern Economics Journal*, Vol. 29 (2): 245–260.

Grabel, I., 2003b, 'Averting Crisis: Assessing Measures to Manage Financial Integration in Emerging Economies', *Cambridge Journal of Economics*, Vol. 27 (3): 317–336.

Grabel, I., 2003c, 'Ideology, Power and the Rise of Independent Monetary Institutions in Emerging Economies', in J. Kirshner (ed.), *Monetary Orders: Ambiguous Economics, Ubiquitous Politics*, Ithaca: Cornell University Press, pp. 25–52.

Grabel, I., 2003d, 'The Revenue and Double Dividend Potential of Taxes on International Private Capital Flows and Securities Transactions', World Institute for Development Economics Research (WIDER)/United Nations University, Helsinki, Finland, WIDER Discussion Paper 83.

Grabel, I., 2003e, 'International Private Capital Flows and Developing Countries', in H. J. Chang (ed.), *Rethinking Development Economics*, London: Anthem Press, pp. 325–345.

Hardy, D., 1998, 'Are Banking Crises Predictable?', *Finance and Development*, December, pp. 32–35.

Hardy, D. and C. Pazarbasioglu, 1998, 'Leading Indicators of Banking Crises: Was Asia Different?', IMF Working Paper, June.

Hawkins, J. and M. Klau, 2000, 'Measuring Potential Vulnerabilities in Emerging Market Economies', Bank for International Settlements Working Papers, October.

IMF, 2001, 'Anticipating Crises: Model Behavior or Stampeding Herds', *IMF Economic Forum*, November.

IMF, 1998, 'Financial Crises: Characteristics and Indicators of Vulnerability', *World Economic Outlook*, May, pp. 74–97.

Kamin, S. and O. Babson, 1999, 'The Contributions of Domestic and External Factors to Latin American Devaluation Crisis: An Early Warning Systems Approach', Board of Governors of the Federal Reserve System, International Finance Discussion Papers, September.

Kaminsky, G. and C. Reinhart, 1999, 'The Twin Crises: The Causes of Banking and Balance-of-Payments Problems', *The American Economic Review*, June, pp. 473–500.

Kaminsky, G. and C. Reinhart, 2000, 'On Crises, Contagion and Confusion', *Journal of International Economics*, pp. 145–168.

Kaminsky, G., S. Lizondo and C. Reinhart, 1997, 'Leading Indicators of Currency Crises', IMF Working Paper 79, July.

Kaplan, E. and D. Rodrik, 2002, 'Did the Malaysian Capital Controls Work?', in S. Edwards and J. Frankel (eds), *Preventing Currency Crises in Emerging Markets*, Chicago: University of Chicago Press, pp. 393–441.

Kenen, P. (ed.), 1996, 'From Halifax to Lyons: What Has Been Done About Crisis Management?', *Princeton Essays in International Finance*, Princeton University: Department of Economics, October.

Kregel, J., 1998, 'Derivatives and Global Capital Flows: Applications to Asia', *Cambridge Journal of Economics*, pp. 677–692.

Krugman, P., 1979, 'A Model of Balance-of-Payments Crises', *Journal of Money, Credit, and Banking*, November, pp. 311–325.

Lowenstein, R., 2000, *When Genius Failed: The Rise and Fall of Long-Term Capital Management*, NY: Random House.

Neftci, S., 1998, 'FX Short Positions, Balance Sheets and Financial Turbulence: An Interpretation of the Asian Financial Crisis', Working Paper, Center for Economic Policy Analysis, New School University.

Prasad, Eswar, Kenneth Rogoff, Shang-Jin Wei and M. Ayan Kose, 2003, *Effects of Financial Globalization on Developing Countries: Some Empirical Evidence*, IMF, 17 March, available at http://www.imf.org/external/np/res/docs/2003/031703.htm.

Reisen, H., 2002, 'Ratings Since the Asian Crisis', WIDER Discussion Paper 2.

Rose, A. and L. Svensson, 1994, 'European Exchange Rate Credibility Before the Fall', *European Economic Review*, May, pp. 1185–1216.

Sachs, J., A. Tornell and A. Velasco, 1996, 'Financial Crises in Emerging Markets: The Lessons From 1995', *Brookings Papers on Economic Activity*, pp. 147–215.

Sharma, S., 1999, 'The Challenge of Predicting Economic Crises', *Finance and Development*, IMF, June, pp. 40–42.

Singh, A. and B. Weisse, 1998, 'Emerging Stock Markets, Portfolio Capital Flows and Long-Term Economic Growth: Micro and Macroeconomic Perspectives', *World Development*, Vol. 26 (4): 607–622.

Subbaraman, R., R. Jones and H. Shiraishi, 2003, 'Financial Crisis: An Early Warning System', Lehman Brothers Asia, available at ascorpcomm@lehman.com.

Taylor, L., 1998, 'Capital Market Crises: Liberalization, Fixed Exchange Rates and Market-Driven Destabilization', *Cambridge Journal of Economics*.

Weller, C., 2001, 'Financial Crises after Financial Liberalization: Exceptional Circumstances or Structural Weakness?', *Journal of Development Studies*, Vol. 38 (1): 98–127.

Williamson, J. and M. Mahar, 1998, 'A Survey of Financial Liberalization', *Essays in International Finance*, Princeton University: Department of Economics, November.

World Bank, 2003, *Global Development Finance 2003*, Washington, D.C.

Wyplosz, C., 2000, 'How Risky is Financial Liberalization in the Developing Countries?', Paper presented at the Technical Group Meeting of the Group of Twenty-Four and the UNCTAD, Geneva, Switzerland, 14–15 September.

7

A FISCAL INSURANCE SCHEME FOR THE EASTERN CARIBBEAN CURRENCY UNION

Laura dos Reis

Abstract:

A fiscal insurance mechanism for the member countries of the Organization of Eastern Caribbean States (OECS) would be important for cushioning OECS members against transitory shocks and also reinforce the monetary union's long-term viability. These countries are already linked together through a common currency, administered by the Eastern Caribbean Central Bank (ECCB) under a currency board arrangement. This paper shows that volatility in fiscal accounts would be reduced if OECS countries joined a fiscal insurance arrangement that would provide for cross-compensations under a risk-sharing scheme. Moreover, as regional fluctuations of output and government revenues are not significantly correlated, a fiscal insurance mechanism would take advantage of these asymmetries and lead to welfare gains for all members. This paper presents numerical simulations for partial and full insurance schemes and quantifies the required size of the initial buffer fund. It also simulates the potential welfare gains in terms of lower initial buffer funds relative to self-insurance.

Introduction

This paper provides empirical evidence to support the creation of a fiscal insurance mechanism for member countries of the Organization of the Eastern Caribbean States (OECS) monetary union.[1] Fiscal insurance refers to a system of intra-country compensating payments undertaken to smooth cyclical fluctuations in fiscal expenditures. Member countries would agree to contribute to a buffer fund administered by a supra-national institution or a centralized fiscal authority. The risk-sharing scheme would consist of a set of rules that determine the amounts of net transfers according to permanent and cyclical components of government revenues.

In a monetary union of countries subject to large exogenous shocks, such as the OECS, a fiscal insurance mechanism can be of great value for coordinating fiscal policy and for strengthening the commitment to participate in the monetary union. For example, during recessions, members lacking financing could opt to leave the union in order to pursue monetary financing or to use monetary policy to accommodate relative prices. The incentive for such action, which undermines the union, can be reduced if members are able to receive transfers from a common pool of funds.

The literature on monetary unions recognizes that fiscal insurance constitutes an important instrument for currency unions to respond to asymmetric shocks whenever there is a market failure in the provision of insurance.[2] Fiscal deterioration in the OECS, as reflected by recent high fiscal deficits and indebtedness, has given union members less scope for further access to outside credit markets and debt rollovers. In addition, there are very limited market-based insurance mechanisms to accommodate transitory shocks, such as hurricanes and terms-of-trade shocks.[3] Fiscal insurance is therefore important not only to cushion against transitory shocks but also to reinforce the union's long-term viability.

This paper begins by presenting data on the economic characteristics of the region with particular attention to the sources of volatility. It then discusses the trade-off between efficiency gains and the incentive costs of a fiscal insurance scheme. It provides empirical evidence showing that volatility in fiscal accounts would be reduced if countries were to join a fiscal insurance arrangement, since fiscal accounts are not significantly correlated across countries. It then presents a basic framework to analyse the proposed policy, and suggests the optimal characteristics of the contract, given the incentives problems explained earlier. It also presents a Monte Carlo simulation to quantify the required initial buffer funds for full and partial insurance cases, and an assessment of the risk-sharing gains of the group as opposed to self-insurance. Finally, it discusses further steps needed to implement the proposed scheme and offers concluding comments.

Background

This section presents data on the economic characteristic of the region. It considers the sources of volatility in the OECS region given that member countries are small open economies. The sources of volatility have undermined the OECS's growth performance and have posed problems for the management of government finances.

The volatility in economic performance in the region is the result of multiple factors, including natural disasters, terms-of-trade shocks and fluctuations in the demand for export services – in particular, financial services and tourism. Recent shocks hurt regional growth performance, which fell from an average rate of 6 per cent in the 1980s to 3 per cent in the 1990s (Figure 1).

Natural disasters such as hurricanes and flooding frequently hit the region. Table 1 shows the frequency and average cost of natural disasters, in terms of GDP, during 1970–2000. In that period St Lucia was the worst affected, with an average cost of 143 per cent of GDP, while the least affected was Grenada, with an average cost of 4 per cent of GDP. The same results hold if the cost is weighted by frequency. As shown in Table 1, the cost as well as the frequency varies across members.

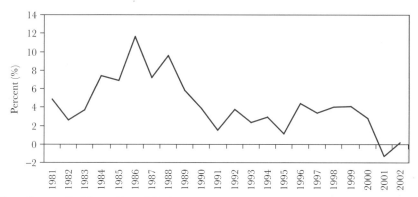

Source: Eastern Caribbean Central Bank

Figure 1. OECS real growth GDP

Table 1. Frequency and cost of natural disasters in OECS 1970–2000

Country	Frequency	Average cost/GDP (per cent)
Antigua and Barbuda	6	10.76
Dominica	6	29.40
Grenada	4	3.93
St Kitts and Nevis	7	32.94
St Lucia[*]	8	143.93
St Vincent and the Grenadines	8	17.13

[*] In 1988, Hurricane Gilbert caused an estimated $1 billion damage.
Source: World Bank (2002a).

In addition, Table 2 shows which countries were affected by shocks in terms of persons and total costs for different periods. It shows that natural disasters have hit different countries in different years – with the exception of 2000, when most of the countries were affected.

The high degree of openness – about 60 per cent – makes OECS members highly vulnerable to terms-of-trade shocks. Figure 2 shows the volatility of terms-of-trade shocks where price volatility is weighted by openness. Note that OECS terms-of-trade volatility is fairly high relative to other regions.

Table 2. Main natural disasters in OECS 1979–2000

Year	Country (hurricane[s] name[s])	Persons affected	Damage in US $000s*
1979	Dominica (David and Frederick)	72,100	44,650
1980	St Lucia (Allen)	80,000	87,990
1989	Montserrat (Hugo)	12,040	240,000
1989	Antigua, St Kitts and Nevis, Montserrat (Luis)	33,790	3,579,000
1995	St Kitts and Nevis (Luis)	1,800	197,000
1999–2000	Antigua, Dominica, Grenada, St Lucia (Lenny)	—	268,000

* Damage is valued as at the year of the event.
Source: World Bank (2002c).

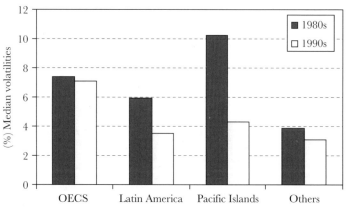

* Terms-of-trade shocks are defined as (Trade/GDP) (change in terms of trade)
Source: World Bank based on *World Development Indicators* 2003 and *Global Development Finance* 2003. Terms-of-trade data is from the IMF.

Figure 2. Volatility of terms-of-trade shocks*

This vulnerability is aggravated by the fact that the OECS countries have a high export concentration in few commodities – that is, tobacco, bananas, cocoa, beverages and sugar – and especially by high dependence on tourism. Exports of such services as tourism constitute one of the main sources of income. When tourism is added to the calculation of export concentration in the first four commodities, the average share over total exports for the region is about 60 per cent.[4] However, if only the first four commodities are considered, export concentration is only 10 per cent.

The different shocks described above have affected OECS countries' growth volatility in different ways depending on their economic structure and on the particular contribution to GDP growth made by each sector of each member country.

The economic structure of the OECS is such that it is concentrated in services related to tourism and financial services. While the agricultural sector has been shrinking, the manufacturing sector has been growing over time. Some countries are more agriculturally oriented (such as Dominica) whereas others have a larger manufacturing sector (such as St Kitts and Nevis) (Table 3). Hurricanes and flooding typically have a greater impact on primary producers since agricultural producers find it hard to insure their production against natural disasters.[5] On the other hand, fluctuations in tourism and financial services have a greater impact in countries with a larger services sector, which in contrast to agriculture, have better access to insurance.[6]

Table 3. OECS economic structure (% of GDP)

	1982	1992	2001
Antigua and Barbuda			
Agriculture	6.2	4.2	4.0
Industry	14.6	19.4	21.1
Manufacturing	5.3	2.8	2.3
Services	79.2	76.4	74.9
Dominica			
Agriculture	30.4	22.4	17.5
Industry	20.5	20.3	23.2
Manufacturing	8.2	8.2	8.0
Services	49.1	57.3	59.3
Grenada			
Agriculture	21.6	11.2	8.2
Industry	17.8	19.8	23.2
Manufacturing	5.5	7.0	8.4
Services	60.6	68.9	68.6

Table 3. (Continued)

	1982	1992	2001
St Kitts and Nevis			
Agriculture	14.4	7.0	2.9
Industry	24.1	26.2	29.2
Manufacturing	13.2	12.1	10.2
Services	61.5	66.9	68.0
St Lucia			
Agriculture	13.9	13.4	6.6
Industry	20.8	20.0	18.2
Manufacturing	9.1	7.5	4.4
Services	65.3	66.7	75.2
St Vincent and the Grenadines			
Agriculture	16.5	19.4	10.3
Industry	25.3	24.3	24.4
Manufacturing	10.9	9.5	5.4
Services	58.2	56.3	65.3

Source: World Bank.

Figure 3 shows each sector's contribution to growth in each OECS country. The poor growth performance in agriculture in St Kitts and Nevis, St Lucia, St Vincent and the Grenadines and Dominica reflects the fact that these countries were the most affected by hurricanes during the 1990s and that some of them have agricultural sectors with higher shares in overall GDP – on which natural disasters have greater impact. In addition, Dominica's zero and negative growth rates during 2000 and 2001 respectively result from a decline in export earnings in the banana industry.[7]

These sources of volatility have not only affected economic growth but have also complicated the management of government finances. The authorities have had to resort to fiscal expenditures to respond to large shocks which affected countries' compliance with the fiscal guidelines set by the Eastern Caribbean Central Bank (ECCB). Currently, the ECCB sets fiscal guidelines without any enforcement mechanism, resulting in a lower rate of compliance by its members. Moreover, the external debt of these countries has grown substantially in the late 1990s as well as central government's overall deficit (Table 4).

The current policy of the ECCB is to issue recommendations about the desired level of fiscal savings in order to reduce expenditures or increase revenues. Most countries, however, do not comply with the fiscal targets set by the central bank. This complicates the overall fiscal outlook and affects the institutional stability of the union, which has sought to maintain an environment of growth and price stability since its creation in 1981.[8]

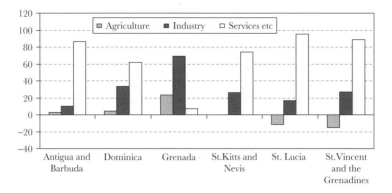

Source: World Bank (2002a)

Figure 3. Sectoral contributions to growth in OECS (1990–2000)

Table 4. OECS selected economic indicators (percentage of GDP)

	GDP growth (% change)	Central government deficit (% GDP)	Current account deficit (% GDP)	Public external debt (% GDP)
1998	4.0	−1.5	−14.2	42.7
1999	4.1	−2.9	−16.1	45.8
2000	2.8	−4.4	−14.8	46.4
2001	−1.3	−6.4	−14.7	52.7
2002	0.2	−6.8	−16.5	62.7

Source: Eastern Caribbean Central Bank (ECCB).

The Benefits and Limitations of Fiscal Insurance

Benefits

The literature on monetary unions[9] suggests that fiscal insurance mechanisms may be important for making a union's operation smoother because of their potential ability to buffer transitory shocks and thereby reinforce the sustainability of the union.

In a currency union, member states cannot pursue independent monetary policy to smooth business cycle fluctuations. This increases the importance of a fiscal insurance policy, which could help to accommodate asymmetric and country-specific shocks that are not addressed by the centralized monetary authority. If members of the union coordinate their fiscal policies in such a way that asymmetries in cyclical fluctuations of economic activity or tax revenues are smoothed out by transfers from a buffer fund as part of a fiscal insurance scheme, potential conflicts in the pursuit of the desired short-run monetary policy can be reduced.

In addition, the ability to conduct countercyclical fiscal policy in bad times through a risk-sharing scheme could bring about better access to financial markets and lower debt levels. Aggregate public debt may be lower under a fiscal insurance scheme, as the system of internal cross-compensations may substitute for the current problem of liquidity constraints that make debt rollover costs higher. This would improve the markets' perceptions about a country's fiscal sustainability, leading to more favourable access to international credit markets. In addition, under this scheme the central bank may be able to issue debt with the buffer fund as collateral, thereby lowering the actual borrowing cost.

Another source of welfare gains would be a reduction in volatility from government responses to accommodate shocks as the fiscal insurance system of cross-compensation payments would make the union's output and fiscal accounts less volatile than that of its individual members.[10]

Finally, a fiscal insurance scheme can also contribute to more efficient outcomes, assuming that financial markets cannot provide insurance. Market failure in the provision of insurance can arise in the form of negative externalities, among other things. In the case of the OECS, negative externalities can take the form of financial instability being transmitted to all members – that is, when local governments cannot service their debt – thus affecting the union's financial stability. In such a case, the central bank would have to intervene and could then impose debt and fiscal deficit targets. Such targets, however, would constitute a burden during a recession. In such a case, fiscal insurance would help OECS countries comply with the fiscal targets through better fiscal coordination from the system of fiscal transfers.

Limitations

A fiscal insurance proposal, however, has several incentive problems. First, moral hazard problems may arise if countries are guaranteed a certain level of revenues. In that event, countries might have low incentives to collect tax revenues as they can benefit from insured revenues levels. In addition, free-rider problems can arise from government's incentives to tax at lower rates and access resources collected from other members.

Second, common-pool problems arise when each country has an incentive to abuse the insurance mechanism since its cost is fully financed by the union's taxpayers, not just domestic contributors. This can result in reduced willingness to participate as countries may not want to end up transferring resources to others. Finally, rent-seeking behaviour by politicians may be exacerbated with a pooling of reserves or centralized buffer mechanisms.[11]

In the case of the OECS, moral hazard problems can be considered moderate. Moral hazard, by definition, arises under asymmetric information and unobservable actions that affect outcomes – but in the case of the OECS, member countries are affected mostly by exogenous shocks which are observable, such as terms-of-trade shocks, hurricanes and floods. This is not to imply that perverse incentives under full insurance do not exist, but rather that they are tempered, since the main source of risk cannot be affected by governments' actions.

Preliminary Evidence for the OECS

The empirical results presented in this section suggest that fiscal insurance may be highly beneficial and feasible to implement among OECS countries. We document two stylized facts:

- Aggregate volatility in growth and in fiscal accounts is lower than that of individual members; and
- Cyclical asymmetries in fiscal accounts could be a source of possible cross-compensations at the aggregate level.

The volatility of GDP growth for OECS as a whole has been lower than that of each individual member (Table 5). The data in Table 5 are divided into two 10-year periods, 1980–90 and 1991–2001, because growth performance slowed down during the 1990s.

Moreover, Table 6 shows that volatility in growth for each individual country is higher than that for the OECS as a whole. Also, the growth volatility of each of the six members is higher than that of the other five members together (that is, the first column in Table 6, individual country, is always higher than the second and third column). This implies that no single member seems to be overwhelmingly more stable than its partners. As a result, the likelihood of

Table 5. GDP growth and volatility in OECS (as a percentage)

Countries	Growth (%)		Standard dev (%)	
	1980–90	1991–01	1980–90	1991–01
Antigua and Barbuda	6.1	3.4	3.7	3.3
Dominica	5.4	0.8	3.6	3.3
Grenada	6.2	3.8	3.2	3.4
St Kitts and Nevis	6.6	4.4	4.4	2.3
St Lucia	7.3	2.0	4.8	2.8
St Vincent and the Grenadines	6.1	3.4	3.2	2.6
OECS	6.4	2.9	2.8	1.4

Source: statistical data from the Eastern Caribbean Central Bank (ECCB).

countries' deciding not to participate to avoid importing volatility from very unstable partners does not appear very high.

These results support the conclusion that countries will have an incentive to participate because they will end up reducing volatility as a group as compared with individual experiences.

An analysis of volatility in government fiscal accounts shows evidence supporting the same conclusions shown with respect to volatility in GDP growth. Figure 4 presents what has been the volatility in the real growth of public

Table 6. Growth volatility in the OECS region 1990–2001 (as a percentage)

Countries	Individual country	All six countries	Five countries*
	Std dev (%)	Std dev (%)	Std dev (%)
Antigua and Barbuda	3.3	1.4	1.7
Dominica	3.3	1.4	1.3
Grenada	3.4	1.4	1.3
St Kitts and Nevis	2.3	1.4	1.5
St Lucia	2.8	1.4	1.4
St Vincent and the Grenadines	2.6	1.4	1.6

* 'Five countries' calculates the standard deviation in growth for the five *other* countries listed.
Source: statistical data from the Eastern Caribbean Central Bank (ECCB).

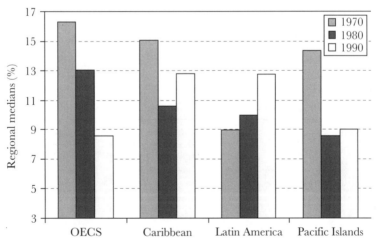

Source: World Bank estimates, World Bank (2002a)

Figure 4. Volatility in real growth of public consumption (standard deviation, in percentage points)

consumption relative to other regions. In addition, Figures 5 and 6 compare the volatility of expenditures and revenues across individual countries in the region. Volatility in real growth of public consumption has been high compared with other regions, but it has been lower than at times in the past (Figure 4).

A more detailed picture of the volatility of regional revenues and expenditures is presented in Figures 5 and 6, which show the standard deviation for different sample periods and countries (depending on data availability).

The volatility in the case of revenues (Figure 5) shows that the aggregate for the OECS is consistently lower than that for all other individual members with the exception of St Vincent and the Grenadines for more recent periods.

In the case of expenditures (Figure 6), volatility was consistently lower for the aggregate in both of the periods considered. Furthermore, volatility in expenditures and in revenues was decreasing over time.

In particular, for the period 1984–92, volatility in expenditures for each country was on average higher than volatility in revenues, on average 14 per cent

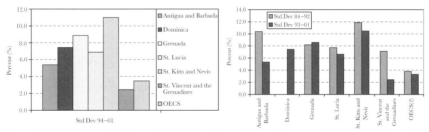

Figure 5b includes no initial quantity for Dominica owing to data unavailability for the period 1984–92.

Source: statistical data from the Eastern Caribbean Central Bank

Figure 5. Volatility in OECS revenues

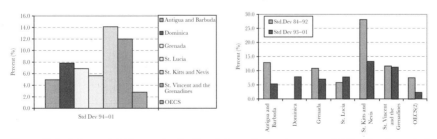

Figure 6b includes no initial quantity for Dominica owing to data unavailability for the period 1984–92.

Source: statistical data from the Eastern Caribbean Central Bank

Figure 6. Volatility in OECS expenditures

and 9 per cent respectively. This is also reflected in the average for the aggregate for expenditures (7.5 per cent) and for revenues (3.8 per cent).

In contrast, more recently (1993–2001), volatility in expenditures and in revenues has been closer across countries and to the regional aggregate. It has been on average 9 per cent in the case of expenditures and 7 per cent in the case of revenues, and 3 per cent and 3.3 per cent respectively, for the regional aggregate.

The fact that aggregate volatility for the OECS region has been lower than that for individual countries provides an important incentive to join a fiscal insurance mechanism. In addition, the convergence in the volatility between expenditures and revenues might facilitate the operation of an insurance scheme since the centralized fiscal authority would have to guarantee a certain level of expenditures that would have to be attained with revenue resources.

To evaluate the gains in term of reduced volatility and inter-temporal smoothing, we also look at the volatility in cyclical revenues for the period 1983–2001, since the objective of the buffer fund is to stabilize cyclical revenues. The results shown in Table 7 serve as an indication of what the gains would have been if countries had been benefiting from a risk-sharing scheme, and thus reducing the overall volatility by smoothing all cyclical fluctuations in revenues by receiving transfers from a buffer fund.

Appendix 2 shows the cyclical fluctuations around the revenue trend for the OECS as a whole and for individual countries from 1983 until 2001. Fluctuations of revenues around the revenue trend for the OECS are smoother than are those of individual members, meaning that when some countries have cyclical revenues that are above the revenue trend, others' are below, thus allowing for country cross-compensations and resulting in lower volatility in the OECS aggregate. In fact, for the period analysed, individual

Table 7. Cyclical revenue volatility in OECS (1983–2001)(as a percentage)

Countries	Std dev (%)
Antigua and Barbuda	10.7
Grenada	5.6
St Lucia	13.6
St Kitts and Nevis	13.6
St Vincent and the Grenadines	8.8
OECS	6.8

Source: Own calculations based on ECCB data.

members' volatility in cyclical revenues would have been higher than regional fluctuations around the revenue trend (Table 7) for all members except Grenada.

Cross-compensation under a risk-sharing mechanism implies that cyclical fluctuations should ideally be negatively correlated if the proposed policy is to yield maximum potential benefits (see Table 8 for correlations of revenues and expenditures with regional GDP).

As can be seen when the union as a whole is in a boom or a bust, there is no clear pattern of behaviour in the individual fiscal accounts. While some countries' fiscal accounts move pro-cyclically relative to the union cycle – for example, Antigua, St Lucia and St Vincent and the Grenadines – others seem to move in the opposite direction.

In addition, Table 9 shows how the cyclical fluctuations in revenues are correlated across members. As can be seen, correlation coefficients can be negative, positive, or near zero, but in most cases they are not significant at the 5 per cent level.

We can conclude from Tables 8 and 9 that for this particular period of time, and taking into account the limitation of having a small sample, there is not a perfect correlation in the cyclical component of revenues among member countries and with regional GDP.

Table 8. Correlation of regional GDP with OECS countries' revenues and expenditures (1981–2001)

Countries	Correlation coefficient Revenues-GDP[*]	Correlation coefficient Expenditures-GDP[*]
Antigua and Barbuda	0.89(**)	0.79(**)
	(0.00)	(0.00)
Dominica	0.06	0.24
	(0.88)	(0.53)
Grenada	0.27	−0.39
	(0.27)	(0.10)
St Kitts and Nevis	−0.11	−0.28
	(0.64)	(0.21)
St Lucia	0.94(**)	0.74(**)
	(0.00)	(0.00)
St Vincent and the Grenadines	0.62(**)	0.34
	(0.00)	(0.12)

[*] Correlation of the cyclical component of revenues and expenditures with OECS cyclical output.
(**) 5 per cent statistical significance. Standard errors in parenthesis.
Source: Eastern Caribbean Central Bank (ECCB).

Table 9. Correlation matrix of cyclical revenues (1981–2001)

	Antigua and Barbuda	Dominica	Grenada	St. Kitts and Nevis	St. Lucia	St. Vincent and the Grenadines
Antigua and Barbuda	1					
Dominica	0.3315 (0.3835)	1				
Grenada	−0.0526 (0.8306)	−0.0538 (0.8907)	1			
St Kitts and Nevis	0.8027(*) (0.0000)	0.1219 (0.7548)	0.3469 (0.1456)	1		
St Lucia	−0.129 (0.5673)	0.7495(*) (0.0201)	−0.1803 (0.4600)	−0.1669 (0.4580)	1	
St Vincent and the Grenadines	0.7124(*) (0.0002)	0.5250 (0.1467)	0.1343 (0.5837)	0.5940(*) (0.0036)	−0.5646(*) (0.0062)	1

(*) 5 per cent statistical significance level. Standard error in parenthesis.
Source: based on ECCB fiscal data. Correlations are calculated with the cyclical revenues in logarithms.

A Fiscal Insurance Scheme for the OECS

We now consider what the optimal contract under the proposed fiscal insurance policy could be, given the incentives problems described earlier. We calculate the initial buffer size requirements alternatively for full and partial insurance contracts, and we provide quantitative measurements of how the savings of the proposed scheme might turn out be in relation to self-insurance.

Possible Contracts

We consider two alternatives: full insurance and partial insurance. The types of contract will depend on the degree of the incentive problems – i.e. moral hazard and free-rider problems.

If the incentives problems referred to earlier are not a concern, then full insurance will be optimal. The fact that most of the shocks are exogenous and observable may reduce the moral hazard problems since countries are not able to affect revenue outcomes, making full insurance a case worth analysing. However, it will be very difficult to apply in practice since it will only work under completely asymmetric shocks. As a result, the simulation exercise for full fiscal insurance serves as a benchmark of the maximum amount of initial buffer funds required to implement the policy.

On the other hand, if countries can affect revenue outcomes, if incentive problems are a concern, a contract that provides full insurance will have to deal with moral hazard and free-rider problems. In that case, partial insurance would be useful, not only to reduce the incentives problems but also for making a fiscal insurance proposal more feasible to implement since access to the buffer will be possible under extraordinary outcomes. However, partial coverage will be costly in terms of countries' welfare because it will only permit partial smoothing of expenditures. The optimal contract will trade off the benefit of additional coverage against the incentive cost of moral hazard. As a result, countries will have to internalize a part of the risk in order to moderate incentive problems.

The simulation for full coverage below shows the maximum amount of initial buffer funds needed to put this policy in place. Member countries will be assured of a certain level of revenues that guarantees a target level of expenditures; resources will be transferred if revenues are above or below that target, smoothing cyclical fluctuations. This kind of arrangement will result in the buffer fund's receiving positive transfers from countries whose revenues are above the insured level of expenditures and experiencing negative transfers from countries below that level. The buffer fund will in this way close the gap between insured expenditure levels and observed fiscal revenues. This is equivalent to a contract in which the buffer fund charges an actuarially fair premium[12] at the beginning of each period, and transfers resources to each country in accordance with the *ex post* realization of shocks.

The simulation in the case of partial insurance shows the range of buffer fund requirements depending on the desired coverage levels, ranging from 90 per cent to 50 per cent. This is equivalent to a contract that includes a deductible *d* in order to limit coverage. The buffer fund will disburse resources to ensure expenditures that fall below some threshold level as determined by the deductible *d*. This means that governments will have to issue debt or rely on their own savings to prevent expenditures from falling within some limited range. If the optimal deductible over cyclical revenues were *d*, payments from the buffer would only be liable after *d* occurs and will only cover cyclical revenues that fall to a predetermined value N – for example, two standard deviations below the trend. Thus, from zero to *d* and above N the country will have to cover the risk.[13] In this way, the fiscal authority would transfer N – *d* resources partially covering the revenue shocks.

Simulation for Full- and Partial-coverage Contracts

Appendix 1 describes the simulation exercise and assumptions for the Monte Carlo simulation for full and partial insurance coverage to obtain the amount of resources needed to launch a fiscal insurance scheme. The percentage of coverage will be the number of histories that the buffer fund is not depleted out of 100 50-year histories of simulated revenues.

Simulation for full coverage. The simulation exercise for full coverage gives the maximum cost of the proposed policy – that is, a Monte Carlo simulation for full insurance is run provided that the initial buffer fund is never depleted or that in none of the 100 simulations does the buffer turn negative. As a result, the fiscal authority managing the buffer fund will completely cover expenditure fluctuations from falling revenues owing to transitory shocks.

Table 10 presents the equilibrium buffer fund required as a share of regional GDP in the case of full insurance. It also shows robustness for different periods relative to the baseline case of 100 50-year histories. The equilibrium buffer fund required to implement the fiscal insurance policy will be equivalent to 12.3 per cent of GDP.

It is interesting to compare this result with the OECS countries' international reserve assets at the ECCB (Table 11), which has been between 13 per cent and 17 per cent of GDP in recent years. In particular, in 2002 Grenada and Antigua registered the maximum and minimum share, respectively, with reserves of 21.2 per cent and 12.2 per cent relative to GDP. As can be seen, these countries have been holding reserves as buffer funds at the ECCB in magnitudes comparable to those implied in the simulation exercise above, with the caveat that they are not exercising risk-sharing with these resources. In fact, the ECCB can lend up

Table 10. Initial OECS buffer fund: simulation for full insurance

Periods	Bo/GDP (%)
50 years (baseline)	12.339
100 years	12.339
30 years	12.264

Note: 'Bo/GDP' is the share of the initial period buffer fund over GDP trend.

Table 11. OECS international reserves assets minus gold (percentage of GDP)

	1999	2000	2001	2002
Antigua and Barbuda	10.7	9.6	11.4	12.2
Dominica	11.8	11.0	11.9	17.9
Grenada	13.4	14.2	16.1	21.2
St Kitts and Nevis	16.3	13.7	16.4	18.5
St Lucia	11.2	11.5	13.7	14.2
St Vincent and the Grenadines	12.9	16.4	17.6	14.7
Average	**12.7**	**12.7**	**14.5**	**16.5**

Source: IMF, *International Financial Statistics* (IFS) and *World Economic Outlook* (WEO) April 2004.

Table 12. Initial OECS buffer fund: simulation for partial insurance, baseline case (100 50-year histories)

Coverage*	Bo/GDP (%)
100%	12.3
90%	6.2
80%	4.6
70%	3.4
60%	2.2
50%	1.7

* The percentage of coverage is the number of histories the buffer fund is depleted out of a total of 100 histories.

Note: 'Bo/GDP' is the share of the initial period buffer fund over GDP trend.

to only 40 per cent of these reserves under very strict conditions. As a result, countries cannot fully tap these reserves amounts as a buffer against transitory shocks.

Simulation for partial coverage. Partial fiscal insurance contracts would be more appropriate to apply if we assume that individual members may affect outcomes – that is, the level of revenues they can collect. As a result, we run a Monte Carlo simulation provided that countries will have to bear a share of the costs in the case of low revenue levels, alleviating the incentives problems. Sometimes, therefore, the buffer is depleted ('bust') and the fiscal authority then covers only a portion of the shocks.

Table 12 shows the initial buffer requirements for a Monte Carlo simulation assuming coverage between 90 per cent and 50 per cent as compared with full coverage (100 per cent). One interesting result of the simulation is that for coverage of 90 per cent, the regional initial buffer needed would be 6.2 per cent of the regional GDP, representing half of the buffer requirement in the case of full insurance (12.3 per cent). For coverage between 80 per cent and 70 per cent, the initial buffer needed would be about 3.4–4.6 per cent of GDP, and for coverage between 60 per cent and 50 per cent, about 1.7–2.2 per cent.[14]

Welfare Gains

This section presents quantitative measures of the risk-sharing gains of the proposed fiscal insurance policy for full and partial insurance contracts. We demonstrate that the buffer fund relative to GDP for the aggregate OECS will be lower than the individual buffer funds required under self-insurance for all members.

Table 13. Self-insurance and risk-sharing: simulation for full insurance, baseline case (100 50-year histories)

	Bo/GDP (%)
Self-insurance	
Antigua and Barbuda	16.3
Grenada	12.6
St Lucia	28.4
St Kitts and Nevis	61.8
St Vincent and the Grenadines	11.2
OECS (1)	24.1
Risk-sharing	
OECS (2)	12.3
Difference (OECS (2)–(1))	*–11.8*

Note: 'Bo/GDP' is the share of the initial period buffer fund over GDP trend. 'OECS(1)' is the weighted aggregate by countries' GDP. 'OECS(2)' is the buffer fund under pooling of revenues.

Given that the centralized fiscal authority is pooling risk under an actuarially fair scheme, risk-averse countries will benefit in expected value terms from participation – that is, self-insurance will be more costly than union insurance. The welfare gains of a risk-sharing mechanism for the group, as opposed to individual cases, are shown in Table 13 for the baseline simulation of 100 50-year histories.

As Table 13 shows, the buffer fund for the aggregate in the case of risk-sharing (OECS(2)) is lower by 11.8 percentage points than the weighted aggregate of individual cases under self-insurance (OECS(1)). In fact, the initial buffer fund required under self-insurance for each country would have been higher than the buffer required under risk-sharing (12.3 per cent), except in the case of St Vincent and the Grenadines. The countries benefiting from this risk-sharing mechanism are Antigua and Barbuda, St Lucia, St Kitts and Nevis, and Grenada, and they would have to start with a higher initial buffer fund to provide coverage for all shocks in cyclical revenues. In particular, St Kitts and Nevis and St Lucia benefit the most. Considering that cyclical revenues during 1981–2001 were between –9 per cent and 7.5 per cent of GDP, achieving a level of savings equivalent to 12.3 per cent of GDP to launch this policy (as shown in Table 13) would have been costly for the region. The previous simulation only shows the maximum cost of the proposed policy.

Table 14 shows the results for partial insurance. Depending on the desired coverage, countries will not only need lower initial resources for the aggregate as compared to individual cases but also lower than the full coverage. This can make the risk-sharing mechanism easier to implement. For coverage cases

Table 14. Self-insurance and risk-sharing: simulation for partial insurance, baseline case (100 50-year histories)

Countries	100%	90%	80%	70%	60%	50%
	Bo/GDP (%)	Bo/GDP (%)	Bo/GDP (%)	Bo/GDP (%)	Bo/GDP (%)	Bo/GDP (%)
1: Self-insurance						
Antigua and Barbuda	16.3	8.2	5.6	3.3	2.3	1.3
Grenada	12.6	9.8	7.0	5.5	4.6	3.3
St Lucia	28.4	14.8	11.9	8.6	7.0	4.3
St Kitts and Nevis	61.8	38.0	31.1	25.6	21.9	16.1
St Vincent and the Grenadines	11.2	4.7	3.1	1.8	0.7	0.4
OECS(1)	24.1	13.6	10.5	7.7	6.2	4.2
2: Risk-sharing						
OECS (2)	12.3	6.2	4.6	3.4	2.2	1.7
Difference						
(OECS (2)–(1))	*–11.8*	*–7.3*	*–5.8*	*–4.3*	*–4.0*	*–2.6*

Note: 'Bo/GDP' is the share of the initial period buffer fund over GDP trend. 'OECS(1)' is the weighted aggregate by countries' GDP. 'OECS(2)' is the buffer fund under pooling revenues.

ranging from 90 per cent to 50 per cent, the regional requirements of fund resources under risk-sharing will be lower than the sum of individual cases under self insurance.

The difference in the required initial buffer funds show the overall gains of the proposed policy, from a 11.8 percentage-point difference under full insurance to between 7.3 and 2.6 percentage points under partial insurance. In particular, the regional fund requirements under risk-sharing (OECS(2)) will be lower than that of individual members under self-insurance, except for St Vincent and the Grenadines in all cases, and Antigua and Barbuda for a lower level of coverage.

Further Steps on Implementation

The previous sections have presented a framework on the type of fiscal insurance contracts, the possible size of the initial buffer, and the degree of coverage. For the insurance scheme to be implemented, however, further work would be needed on the institutional characteristics of the central fiscal authority and on the initial buffer financing.

The initial buffer financing would depend on international market conditions at the time the buffer is established, together with countries' initial conditions. In particular, a study of regional fiscal savings would be important for determining whether countries can rely on regional savings or whether additional resources from financial markets would be needed.

In terms of market access, if when the policy is implemented interest rates are low and access to international financial markets is not restricted for government bonds, this would help add to government savings; in this case, governments could issue a bond using the buffer fund as a guarantee. In contrast, if interest rates were very high and the debt level reaches an upper limit, countries would have to rely on their own resources. International organizations could be a source of additional funds at the beginning, depending on the coverage provided (full or partial insurance). This could be particularly important in the case of full insurance, since it would require a larger buffer fund.

The fact that managing the buffer would require coordination at the regional level may argue for a supra-national organization. The Eastern Caribbean Central Bank, which is currently coordinating the monetary policy and establishing fiscal targets guidelines, may be one good candidate to operate this policy. In addition, the Organization of the Eastern Caribbean States, which decides on economic and development issues at the union level, may be important for political coordination among member countries. Although fiscal insurance may require coordination with a centralized authority, the fact that fiscal policy is currently run at the country level may require at the first stage a certain degree of decentralization to help countries build institutional as well as technical knowledge to support the work of the centralized fiscal authority.

Individual countries should discuss this policy within their parliaments and in close contact with the ECCB, so that they can determine the potential welfare gains of a fiscal insurance policy. Such an information campaign would be critical since countries would want to keep control of the fiscal policy at the country level and could oppose the policy for political reasons. If the source and magnitude of gains for each OECS member country is not clearly established, it will be difficult to gain support for the policy.

Conclusions and Suggestions for Future Research

This paper has provided empirical evidence to support the establishment of a fiscal insurance mechanism in the OECS monetary union. A fiscal insurance mechanism would help cushion transitory shocks and reinforce the monetary union's long-term viability. Fiscal deterioration, as reflected by members' indebtedness problems, has given union members limited scope for further market access and debt rollover. The fact that there are limited insurance mechanisms provided by the market to accommodate for transitory shocks underscores the need to consider fiscal insurance at the regional level.

We have shown that volatility in fiscal accounts would be reduced if countries joined a fiscal insurance arrangement because of the possibility of cross-compensations under a risk-sharing scheme. Moreover, since the regional fluctuations in output and government revenues are not highly correlated, a fiscal insurance mechanism can also exploit these asymmetries and achieve welfare gains for all members. Also, a fiscal insurance scheme would reinforce the OECS countries' commitment to their monetary union. Fiscal insurance would therefore be important not only to cushion its members against transitory shocks but also to reinforce the union's long-term viability.

The simulation exercise with full coverage showed that an initial buffer of 12.3 per cent of regional GDP would be required. But the fact that these countries are very open economies indicates that full coverage may be difficult to implement and risky – especially if moral hazard problems are a concern. In contrast, the simulation with partial coverage shows that for lower coverage the amount of resources required might be halved: 6.3 per cent in the case of 90 per cent coverage or lower.

Finally, we have shown that a risk-sharing mechanism can exert clear welfare gains in terms of lower aggregate volatility and a lower buffer fund requirement, as opposed to self-insurance. The regional buffer requirements (12.3 per cent) are substantially smaller than the buffer requirements under self insurance, reducing the cost relative to self-coverage cases by 11 percentage points on average in the case of full insurance, and between 7 and 3 percentage points on average in the case of lower coverages.

Further research in this area, in particular on the type of contracts and possible premiums for a fiscal insurance scheme, would be useful not only for the OECS but for other monetary unions suffering a lack of fiscal coordination and similar shocks.[15]

Appendix 1

Monte Carlo Simulation

This appendix explains in detail the Monte Carlo simulation used to estimate the initial buffer size for both full and partial insurance. To measure the size of the required buffer, 100 50-year histories of revenues were generated for the five member countries: Antigua and Barbuda, Grenada, St Lucia, St Kitts and Nevis and St Vincent and the Grenadines.[16]

First, to estimate the relationship among member countries' fiscal revenues, a first-order vector auto-regression (VAR) was run with the original cyclical revenues for the period 1983–2001, as follows:

$$R_{t,i} = \alpha + \beta R_{t-1,i} + \varepsilon_{t,i} \qquad \text{where } i = 1\ldots5 \text{ economies} \qquad (1)$$

The coefficients α and β capture the relationship among the five member countries and ε is the observed or reduced form residual. Following Sims (1980) equation (1) can be re-expressed as a reduced form equation that comes from a structural VAR:

$$R_{t,i} = B^{-1}\Gamma_0 + B^{-1}\Gamma_1 R_{t-1,i} + B^{-1}\mu_{t,i} \tag{2}$$

where,

$$\mu \sim N(0, 1)$$
$$B^{-1}\Gamma_0 = \alpha$$
$$B^{-1}\Gamma_1 = \beta$$
$$B^{-1}\mu_{t,i} = \varepsilon_{t,i}$$

Matrix B^{-1} is the Cholesky factorization matrix

From equations (1) and (2), note that ε is the observed or reduced form residual and μ is the unobserved structural innovation.

Second, to generate five thousand new revenue variables the estimated coefficients (α and β) from (1) are used in periods of 50 years and it is assumed that the initial period revenues are zero ($R_0 = 0$). In addition, five thousand new random variables ε are needed to get the new revenues variables recursively from (1). In order to get ε, five thousand random numbers μ are generated for each of the economies.[17] Using the Cholesky factorization matrix (B^{-1}), the observed errors (ε) are recovered as follows:

$$\varepsilon_{t,i} = B^{-1}\mu_{t,i} \tag{3}$$

Finally, using the 100 50-year histories of revenues and the buffer accumulation identity (see below), the initial buffer depends on what type of insurance is provided. Two options are considered:

Full insurance: B_0 is such that in every period $B_t > 0$ for 100 50-year histories and for all t.

Partial insurance: B_0 is such that for specific t and depending on the level of coverage it becomes $B_t < 0$. That is, sometimes the buffer is depleted ('bust'), provided that there is no full insurance. Thus, the buffer coverage will be equal to:

$$\% \text{ Coverage} = \frac{\# number\_of\_histories\_whereB_t > 0}{\# of\_histories(100)} * 100$$

Simulation Exercise, Assumptions and Methodology[18]

1 We assume that the economies are in a balanced growth path with constant long-term real growth rates of GDP; fiscal revenues and expenditures are assumed over the long run.

2 The centralized fiscal authority will only cover for transitory shocks; only cyclical changes in revenues will be considered.

3 To determine permanent and transitory components in revenues and expenditures we compute a linear trend on the logarithm of real revenues and expenditures.[19] The trend in revenues sets the basis for the calculation of the permanent sustainable path of expenditures for each country, which is the path of the expenditures that the centralized fiscal authority guarantees to each member considering all expenditure targets for the following period as the position of the revenue trend.

4 A Monte Carlo simulation of 100 50-year histories of fiscal revenues observations is generated to test the performance of the insurance scheme for different random shocks and assuming full insurance and partial insurance.

5 Rules for net transfers: total fiscal revenues in excess of the expenditure trend target are transferred to the centralized fiscal authority. If revenues are below the expenditure target, financing is provided by the fiscal authority.

6 The initial buffer fund level is determined as a percentage of revenue trend and also as a percentage of GDP trend. In the case of full insurance, it is calculated by iterations as the minimum initial buffer level such that it is never depleted in the 100 histories. In the case of partial insurance, the buffer remains positive all times between 90 and 50 of the simulated revenue trajectories out of 100 histories, which represent 90 per cent and 50 per cent coverage, respectively.

7 The Law for the dynamic evolution of the buffer stock in real terms as share of the aggregate (OECS) revenue trend:

$$B_{t+1} = (1+r)B_t + Cyc\,RevOECS \qquad (1)$$

Rewriting (1) we obtain the following identities,

$$\frac{B_{t+1}}{Rev\,TrendOECS_t} = (1+r)\frac{B_t}{Rev\,TrendOECS_t} + \frac{Cyc\,RevOECS}{Rev\,TrendOECS_t} : \tag{1.b}$$

$$b_{t+1}(1+g) = b_t(1+i) + cycrev_t \qquad t = 0, \ldots, 50 \text{ (100 histories)} \tag{1.c}$$

where,

b_t is the share of the buffer stock over OECS revenue trend.

$cycrev_t$ is the share of the OECS revenues over OECS revenue trend. This variable has mean zero.

$(1+i)$ real interest rate (3%).

$(1+g)$ real growth in OECS revenue trend.

Solving (2) forward for T iterations,

$$b_T = \left(\frac{1+r}{1+g}\right)^T b_0 + \left(\frac{1}{1+g}\right)\sum_{t=0}^{T-1}\left(\frac{1+r}{1+g}\right)^{T-t-1} cycrev_t \tag{2}$$

And multiplying (2) by $\left(\dfrac{1+r}{1+g}\right)^{-T}$, taking the limit as $T \to \infty$, and imposing

the transversality condition: $Lim_{T\to\infty} b_T \left(\dfrac{1+r}{1+g}\right)^{-T} = 0$

The initial buffer (b_0) as share of revenue trend converges to:

$$b_0 = -\left(\frac{1}{1+g}\right)\sum_{t=0}^{\infty}\left(\frac{1+g}{1+r}\right)^{t+1} cyrev_t \tag{3}$$

Appendix 2

OECS Cyclical Revenue and Revenue Trend (1983–2001)

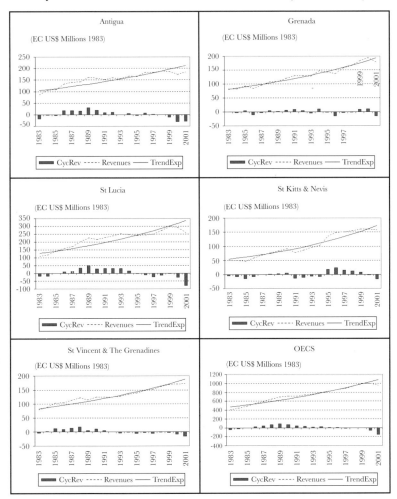

Source: own calculations based on Eastern Caribbean Central Bank (ECCB)

Appendix 3

OECS compliance with ECCB fiscal benchmarks and guidelines as of 2002

Benchmarks

Central Government savings of 4–6% of GDP

Do not comply (Savings, percent of GDP)		Comply (Savings, percent of GDP)	
ECCU	-3.8	St Vincent	1.4
Antigua & Barbuda	-11.8		
Dominica	-6.8		
Grenada	-1.9		
St Kitts and Nevis	-3.0		
St Lucia	-0.9		

Overall Central Government Deficit not greater than 3% of GDP

Do not comply (Deficit, percent of GDP)		Comply (Deficit, percent of GDP)	
ECCU	9.6	St Vincent	3.6
Antigua & Barbuda	13.2		
Dominica	11.0		
Grenada	8.1		
St Kitts and Nevis	13.4		
St Lucia	7.4		

Central Government Debt of not greater than 60% of GDP

Do not comply (Debt, as percent of GDP)		Comply (Debt, as percent of GDP)	
ECCU	92.5	St Lucia	56.6
Antigua & Barbuda	102.3		
Dominica	105.8		
Grenada	103.7		
St Kitts and Nevis	137.2		
St Vincent	74.1		

Guidelines

Public Sector Savings 7–8% of GDP

Do not comply (Savings, percent of GDP)		Comply (Savings, percent of GDP)	
ECCU	-1.4	St Lucia	7.5
Antigua and Barbuda	-11.8		
Dominica	-6.8		
St Kitts and Nevis	-3.0		
Grenada	2.1		
St Vincent	4.3		

Public Sector Investment 12% of GDP

Do not comply (Investment, percent of GDP)		Comply (Investment, percent of GDP)	
ECCU	8.8	Grenda	13.2
Antigua and Barbuda	1.5	St Kitts and Nevis	14.4
Dominica	5.4	St Vincent	12.1
St Lucia	10.4		

Public Sector Primary Balance

Do not Comply (Primary Balance, percent of GDP)		Compy (Primary Balance, percent of GDP)	
ECCU	-3.2	St Lucia	4.0
Antigua & Barbuda	-7.8		
Dominica	-5.7		
Grenada	-3.8		
St Kitts and Nevis	-6.1		
St Vincent	-2.1		

Source: based on Kufa, Pellechio and Rizavi (2003) and IMF staff estimates.

Notes

I would like to thank Ricardo Hausmann and Roberto Rigobon for valuable comments and technical advice. Also, I extend my thanks to participants at the XVIII G-24 Technical Group Meeting in Geneva, in particular to Ariel Buira, Chandra Hardy and Aziz Ali Mohammed. The views expressed in this paper are mine, and do not necessarily reflect those of the G-24 Secretariat.

1 The Eastern Caribbean countries are institutionally organized following the establishment in 1981 of the OECS. It includes six independent states: Antigua and Barbuda, Dominica, Grenada, St Kitts and Nevis, St Lucia, and St Vincent and the Grenadines. The OECS also includes three additional members that are overseas territories of the United Kingdom: Montserrat, Anguilla and the British Virgin Islands. Montserrat is a full member, whereas Anguilla and the British Virgin Islands are associate members. This paper will consider only the six independent states mentioned above. Although the monetary union was consolidated in 1981, the OECS member countries have had a common currency since they were British colonies. The common currency – the Eastern Caribbean dollar (EC$) – is issued by the Eastern Caribbean Central Bank (ECCB) and it has been pegged to the US dollar since 1976 at the rate of EC $2.70 = US $1.

2 For an example of fiscal insurance and the European monetary union, see Eichengreen (1997), and for an example of fiscal insurance in United States, see Sala-i-Martin and Sachs (1992).

3 In the case of terms-of-trade shocks, not all shocks are transitory as there can be permanent change in terms of trade prices. For example, the fact that the OECS is going to lose preferential market access to the European Union in certain products would imply a permanent change in commodity export prices. In addition, it is sometimes more difficult to disentangle the transitory from the permanent component in the case of terms-of-trade shocks – e.g. changes in oil prices.

4 Export concentration (the first four commodities plus tourism, over total exports) in 1998 was approximately 58 per cent in the case of Antigua and Barbuda, 38 per cent Dominica, 48 per cent Grenada, 86 per cent St Lucia, 60 per cent St Kitts and Nevis, and 57 per cent St Vincent and the Grenadines (World Bank staff calculations based on *Global Development Finance 2003* (GDF) and *World Development Indicators 2003* (WDI)).

5 'The average farmer in these countries is particularly vulnerable to catastrophes because he is unlikely to have any form of crop insurance coverage,' World Bank (2002b).

6 In general the assets that are insured are the ones where financial institutions have interests like utilities, heavy manufacturing, medium- and high-income households, and medium-sized and large commercial business (World Bank 2002b).

7 The fall in export earnings is mainly due to the change in the European Union banana regime in 1993 and to the WTO's ruling against the preferential market access that Dominica had enjoyed with the EU. This sector's value-added was around 20 per cent of GDP during the 1990s.

8 See Appendix 3 for information on ECCB quantitative guidelines and country compliance.

9 See Alesina (2001, 2002), Bayoumi and Masson (1997), Blejer, Frankel, Leiderman and Cheney (1997), Eichengreen (1997), De Grauwe (2001), Masson and Patillo (2001), Sala-i-Martin and Sachs (1992), and Wyplosz (2001).

10 Ahmad and Singh (2003) emphasize that 'even in the absence of a negative correlation between regional shocks, a region with a volatile income, such as an oil producer, would still have an incentive to form a federation with regions with more stable incomes.'

11 In the case of common-pool problems, constitutional rules that restrain the discretionary power of politicians could resolve this problem (Brennan and Buchanan 1977). Alternatively, as suggested by Rogoff (1985), competition for resources among regional governments could solve the rent-extraction problem. In the case of free-rider nations, an alternative to consider in this regard is that countries can be extended a bond to account for the value of their net asset position with the buffer fund if fiscal insurance is implemented. The buffer would issue a bond in exchange for each country's contribution (that is, every time each member pays a premium) and would have to redeem bonds to the centralized fiscal authority every time it qualifies to withdraw resources. In this way, countries would feel ownership of 'their share' of the buffer fund, and their own net asset position in the buffer would reflect their own past fiscal behaviour.

12 This assumes zero profits, such that the expected losses equal the expected rev-enues, and that the fiscal authority would be risk-neutral while member countries are risk-averse.

13 This is one possible contract with partial coverage. An alternative feature could be a falling coverage after the upward threshold is reached. That is, when revenues fall below two standard deviations, the buffer would only pay two standard deviations for additional falling revenues beyond the threshold.

14 Further research on the optimal contract is needed to take into account countries' preferences for risk.

15 The Communauté Financière Africaine (CFA) franc zone countries in West Africa is a possible candidate.

16 Dominica was not included owing to data unavailability for 1983–2001.

17 These random numbers are drawn from a standard normal cumulative distribution. In order to obtain the original values, we calculate the inverse of the cumulative distribution.

18 Dominica is not included due to data unavailability.

19 An alternative method would be to filter the data using the Hodrik-Prescott (H-P) filter. But the H-P filter has two limitations that make it difficult to apply. First, the position of the trend in the last portion of the sample changes as the sample size grows over time, which implies a large degree of uncertainty in the last points of the trend estimate. Second, the trend estimate is very sensitive to the weight parameter. A linear trend is more stable since all the observations in the sample have equal weight whereas H-P gives a relatively larger weight to the last observation.

References

Alesina, Alberto, Roberto J. Barro and Silvana Tenreyro, 2002, *Optimal Currency Areas*, Harvard University.

Alsina, Alberto, Ignazio Angeloni and Federico Etro, 2001, 'The Political Economy of International Unions', Working Paper 8645, NBER, Cambridge, MA.

Ahmad, Ehtisham and Raju J. Singh, 2003, 'Political Economy of Oil-Revenue Sharing in a Developing Country: Illustration from Nigeria', IMF Working Paper 03/16, Washington D.C.

Bandt, Olivier and Paolo Mongelli, 2000, 'Convergence of Fiscal Policies in the Euro Area', European Central Bank, Working Paper No. 20.

Bayoumi, Tamim and Paul Masson, 1997, 'Debt-Creating Versus Non-Debt-Creating Fiscal Stabilization Policies: Ricardian Equivalence, Fiscal Stabilization, and EMU', in M. Blejer, J.A. Frenkel, L. Leiderman and A. Razin, *Optimum Currency Areas: New Analytical and Policy Developments*, pp. 97–100.

Blejer, Mario, Jacob Frankel, Leo Leiderman, Assaf Razzin and David Cheney (eds) 1997, *Optimum Currency Areas: New Analytical and Policy Developments*, Washington D.C.: IMF.

Brennan, G. and J.M. Buchanan, 1977, 'Towards a Tax Constitution for Leviathan', *Journal of Public Economics*, Vol. 8, 255–273.

De Grauwe, Paul, 2001, *The Political Economy of Monetary Union*, The International Library of Critical Writing in Economics, p. 134.

Ehrlich, Isaac and Gary S. Becker, 1972, 'Market Insurance, Self-Insurance and Self-Protection', *Journal of Political Economy*, Vol. 80 (4), 623–648.

Easterly, William and Aart Kraay, 2000, 'Small States, Small Problems? Income, Growth, and Volatility in Small States', *World Development*, Vol. 28, No. 11, 2013–2027.

Eastern Caribbean Central Bank, Annual Report 2003, available at http://www.eccb-centralbank.org/.

Eichengreen, Barry, 1997, *European Monetary Unification*, Massachusetts and London, England: MIT Press.

Eichengreen, Barry, Jeffrey Frieden and Jürgen von Hagen (eds) 1995, *Monetary and Fiscal Policy in an Integrated Europe*, Spring.

Ericsson, Neil and J. Halket, 2002, 'Convergence of Output in the G-7 Countries', Washington, D.C.: Federal Reserve System.

Engel, Eduardo and Patricio Meller, 1993, *External Shocks and Stabilization Mechanisms*, Washington, D.C.: Inter-American Development Bank.

Hausmann, Ricardo and Helmut Reisen, 1996, *Securing Stability and Growth in Latin America*, Paris: OECD.

Inman, Roberto and Daniel Rubinfeld, 1998, 'Subsidiarity and the European Union', Working Paper 6556, NBER, Cambridge, MA.

Juan-Ramon, V. Hugo, Ruby Randall and Oral Williams, 2001, 'A Statistical Analysis of Banking Performance in the Eastern Caribbean Currency Union in the 1990s', IMF Working Paper 01/105, Washington, D.C.

Phebby, Kufa, Anthony Pellechio and Saqib Rizavi, 2003, 'Fiscal Sustainability and Policy Issues in the Eastern Caribbean Currency Union', IMF Working Paper 03/162, Washington, D.C.

Kletzer, Kenneth M., 1998, 'Monetary Union, Asymmetric Productivity Shocks and Fiscal insurance: An Analytical Discussion of Welfare Issues', Working Paper 419, University of California, Santa Cruz.

Ligon, Ethan, Jonathan P. Thomas and Tim Worrall, 1998, 'Mutual Insurance, Individual Savings and Limited Commitment', mimeo, University of California at Berkeley.

Masson, Paul and Catherine Pattillo, 2001, 'Monetary Union in West Africa: An Agency of Restraint for Fiscal Policies?', IMF Working Paper 01/34, Washington, D.C.

Masson, Paul and M. Taylor, 1993, *Policy Issues in the Operation of Currency Unions*, Cambridge University Press.

Mossin, Jan, 1968, 'Aspects of Rational Insurance Purchasing', *The Journal of Political Economy*, Vol. 76, Part 1.

Olson, Mancur, 1971, *The Logic of Collective Action*, Cambridge, MA: Harvard University Press.

Rogoff, Kenneth, 1985, 'Can International Monetary Policy Coordination Be Counterproductive?', *Journal of International Economics*, Vol. 8, 199–217.

Sala-i-Martin, Xavier D. and Jeffrey Sachs, 1992, 'Federal Fiscal Policy and Optimum Currency Areas', in M. Canzonery, V. Grilli and P. Masson (eds), *Establishing a Central Bank: Issues in Europe and Lessons from the U.S.*, Cambridge: Cambridge University Press, pp. 195–220.

Sims, Christopher A., 1980, 'Macroeconomics and Reality', *Econometrica*, Vol. 48 (1), 1–48, Econometric Society.

Williams, Oral, Tracy Polius and Selvon Hazel, 2001, 'Reserve Pooling in the Eastern Caribbean Currency Union and the CFA Franc Zone: A Comparative Analysis', IMF Working Paper 01/104, Washington, D.C.

World Bank, 2002a, 'Macroeconomic Volatility, Household Vulnerability, and Institutional and Policy Responses', Private Sector and Infrastructure Department, Latin America and the Caribbean Region, The World Bank, Washington, D.C.

World Bank, 2002b, 'Caribbean Region Catastrophic Insurance', Poverty Reduction and Economic Management Unit, Latin America and the Caribbean Region, The World Bank, Washington, D.C.

World Bank, 2002c, 'Natural Risk Management in the Caribbean: Revisiting the Challenge', Private Sector and Infrastructure Department, Latin America and the Caribbean Region, The World Bank, Washington, D.C.

Wyplosz, Charles, 2001, 'Fiscal Policy: Institutions vs. Rules', Geneva: Graduate Institute for International Studies.

8

WHO PAYS FOR THE WORLD BANK?

Aziz Ali Mohammed

Abstract:

The allocation of IBRD net income is the lens through which this paper considers the burden-sharing issue in the World Bank Group. The paper concludes that (1) the distribution of voting power in the Bank does not reflect the contribution to IBRD equity made by its borrowing members as the share of retained earnings has risen while the share of paid-in capital has declined over the years; (2) the major shareholders have used their control rights to allocate portions of IBRD net income to serve their interests in ways that have been at the expense of the borrowing members; and (3) the continuation of a stagnating loan portfolio in nominal terms, and a declining one in inflation-adjusted terms, is likely to constrain the Bank's net income from lending operations and to render it increasingly dependent for its continuing profitability on its role as a financial trader and arbitrageur. To regain its competitiveness as an international development lending intermediary, it is important to review the pricing of loans and the conditions attached to them, as well as the constraints on the purposes for which the Bank lends.

Introduction

This paper looks at one aspect of the financial governance of the World Bank Group through the lens of the net income earned by the International Bank for Reconstruction and Development (IBRD), the principal income earning unit of the World Bank Group[1] (WBG), as defined in this paper. We first look at the growing divergence between voting rights and the contributions made to IBRD equity by shareholders and borrowers as the share of retained earnings has risen while the share of paid-in capital has declined over the years. We then explain the framework established to guide the allocation of net income and review the equity implications of the actual distribution of net income in recent years (fiscal years 1999–2003). We argue that the Bank's net income from its lending operations is becoming increasingly constrained by a stagnant loan portfolio in nominal terms, and a declining one in inflation-adjusted terms, and suggest that the IBRD risks becoming increasingly dependent for its continuing profitability on its financial trading and arbitrage operations. We conclude by recommending a review of the pricing of loans and the conditions attached to them as well the restraints that have applied on the purposes for which the Bank lends. The objective is to reverse the trend of declining net disbursements, which have actually turned negative in the last two years, and to have the Bank regain its competitiveness as an international development lending intermediary.

Evolution of IBRD Equity

The IBRD was established in 1946 – with an authorized capital of US $10 billion – to lend to its member governments to finance reconstruction and development.[2] Members were required to pay in 2 per cent of their subscribed capital shares in gold and another 18 per cent in their own currencies. The remaining 80 per cent constituted 'callable' capital that was available to guarantee the Bank's borrowings. In accordance with the weighted voting principle applied in the Bretton Woods Institutions (BWIs), voting shares were aligned with contributions to Bank capital, the United States receiving 23 per cent of the total. Subsequently, there have been three general capital increases (GCIs) – in 1959, 1979, and 1988 – and one special capital increase in 1976 to modify relative rankings. The last GCI required only 3 per cent to be paid in, and there has been no general increase since 1988.

A large influx of new members (e.g. former Soviet Union countries and Switzerland) in the 1990s was accommodated through selective additions to authorized capital. At the end of fiscal year 2003, the authorized capital was $190.8 billion, of which $189.6 billion was subscribed. Of the subscribed capital, $11.5 billion had been paid in, the rest being 'callable'. However, a portion of the paid-in subscriptions of members has remained restricted so that only $ 8,581 million of the paid-in capital was available for lending (designated as 'usable' capital). The Bank's equity base has been built up over the years by expanding reserves through retained earnings, which in turn, are based on decisions on the allocation of IBRD net income.

What are the burden-sharing implications of the rising share of retained earnings contributing to IBRD equity? Table 1 sheds light on the answer.

The table shows that the Bank's equity is built up from two sources: paid-in capital subscriptions available for lending and retained earnings. Whereas the

Table 1. IBRD: equity and reserves 1955–2003

Years	Equity (US $ billion)	Reserves and surplus (as % of equity)	Usable capital (as % of equity)
1955–56	1.1	19	81
1968–69	3.2	44	56
1981–82	6.3	58	42
1994–95	25.5	69	31
2002–03	32.8[a]	74[b]	26

[a] Excluding Financial Accounting Standards (FAS) 133 adjustments for comparability with earlier periods.
[b] Reserves carried at 'fair value'.
Source: The World Bank: Its First Half Century, Volume 1, Table 16-9, and World Bank Annual Report, 2003, Volume 2, table on p. 61.

initial and selective capital subscriptions and the first two GCIs required members to pay in 20 per cent of their subscribed capital shares, the last general increase required only 3 per cent of the capital increase to be paid in, not all of which was immediately available for lending. The continuous decline in the ratio of usable capital to equity has meant that the percentage contribution made by Part I countries[3] to reducing the cost of Bank funding has declined steadily. The failure to inject new capital through a GCI after 1988 has meant that additions to usable equity have come mainly from retained earnings; these derive largely from loan charges paid by IBRD borrowers, and to a lesser extent, from income generated by the Bank's investments, designated as its liquid assets portfolio.

It has been argued that even though paid-in capital has been only a small proportion of the Bank's subscribed capital, the unpaid portion constitutes callable capital that is available to meet obligations of the IBRD for funds borrowed or loans guaranteed by it. Thus member countries of the Development Assistance Committee (DAC) have subscribed $110.5 billion of IBRD capital, of which $103.6 billion constitutes the uncalled portion, an amount that slightly exceeds IBRD outstanding borrowings (including swaps) as of 30 June 2003. This is said to enable the Bank to raise capital on the world's financial markets at the finest rates on offer to an AAA-rated borrower; the Bank can then pass through to countries that borrow from it at lending rates that, it is contended, provide an implicit subsidy over what they would have had to otherwise pay.

No call has ever been made on the Bank's callable capital, however, and the financial and risk-planning scenarios of the Bank are explicitly based on an assumption that precludes having to make such a call. The fact that transfers from net income have built up reserves that exceed 20 per cent of the Bank's outstanding borrowings[4] has created a substantial cushion. Moreover, the repayment record of Bank clients has been exemplary. At the end of FY2003, the total amount of principal and interest overdue was only $629 million against a total loan portfolio exceeding $116 billion. The Bank is a 'preferred creditor'[5] and the vast majority of members have been punctilious in meeting their repayment obligations – a fact well known to capital market participants. Hence, the subsidy element could just as well be attributed to the low debt default rates experienced on IBRD loans – reflecting borrower debt-servicing discipline – rather than to the existence of untouched (and presumably untouchable) callable capital.

Nor does the 'subsidy' argument take into account several indirect costs of those IBRD transactions involved in satisfying a variety of safeguards whose objective is 'ring-fencing' the Bank from risk (Kapur 2003).[6] The additional administrative costs of these new safeguard/fiduciary policies were estimated at about $81 million in FY2001. Borrower costs in meeting these requirements were estimated in the range of $118–215 million by Devesh Kapur, a member of the team that produced a massive two-volume history of the Bank under the auspices of the Brookings Institution in 1997 (Kapur, Lewis and Webb 1997). Kapur goes on to argue that 'the[se] multiple safeguards have turned the Bank into a high-cost operation whose administrative costs have little to do with lending and a lot to do with the bells and whistles that keep many other constituencies satisfied' (ibid.).

In sum, even if the implicit subsidy associated with callable capital is considered ambiguous in its impact, the direct contribution made by Part I countries to reducing borrower costs is basically restricted to their steadily declining percentage share in IBRD equity, namely, their share in the Bank's paid-in capital (approximately $7 billion).[7] What is especially important to note is that despite the changing pattern of burden-sharing, the historical control rights deriving from weighted voting based on capital shares have remained unchanged.

The Allocation of Net Income and Associated Issues

The sense of inequity in the allocation of voting shares intensifies as one looks at decisions on the allocation of net income for purposes additional to the building up of reserves. Table 2 provides data on the derivation of net income on a reported basis for FY2001–03 (see explanatory notes for the table in the Appendix).

The net income concept (Table 3) pertains to 'allocable net income' – that is, it excludes the component deriving from the adjustments owing to the application of Financial Accounting Standards (FAS) 133. This narrower concept has the

Table 2. IBRD net income[a] (in US $ millions)

	FY2003	FY2002	FY2001
Sources			
1 Income from loans	5,742	6,861	8,143
2 Income from investments	418	734	1,540
3 Service fee revenues	178	155	146
4 Income from staff retirement plans, etc.		93	155
5 Other net income	15	21	16
6 Sub-total: Gross income (1 through 5)	6,353	7,864	10,000
Offsets			
7 Borrowing expenses	3,594	4,903	7,152
8 Administrative expenses[b]	1,038	1,052	1,028
9 Sub-total: Gross income after offsets (6–7–8)	1,721	1,909	1,820
10 Provision for losses on loans and guarantees	+1,300	+15	−676
11 Operating income (9+10)	3,021	1,924	1,114
12 Effect of FAS 133	2,323	854	345
13 Net income (11+12) on reported basis	5,344	2,778	1,489
14 Allocable net income[c]	3,050	1,924	1,144
Memorandum items			
Loans outstanding	116,240	121,589	118,866
Borrowings outstanding	108,554	110,263	106,757
Cash and liquid investments	26,620	25,056	24,407

[a] On reported basis in accordance with Financial Reporting Standards (FAS 133 and IAS 39).
[b] This figure includes 'Contributions to Special Programmes', averaging $160 million a year for certain high-priority development purposes. Excluding these grants, the net administrative expenses attributed to IBRD average $850 million a year. However, this is roughly one half of the World Bank's administrative budget, the rest being allocated to the IDA on the basis of an agreed cost-sharing formula that reflects the administrative costs of service delivery to countries eligible for lending from the IBRD and IDA.
[c] Excluding FAS 133 adjustments.
Source: Box 1: Selected Financial Data (on reported Basis), Vol. 2, FY2003 World Bank Annual Report.

advantage of providing comparable figures with the net income of years earlier than FY2001 when no such accounting adjustments were made; it also permits our analysis to cover the debates that have revolved around the allocation decision over the years. The debates have been contentious. In some cases, differences among the Bank's shareholders run along the North-South fault line, while some other decisions on the use of net income have had a more complicated line-up. This is because the decisions have generated conflicts of interests within the developing country membership, specifically between those eligible to borrow from the IBRD and those depending exclusively on the concessionary lending window provided by the International Development Association (IDA).

Table 3. Allocation of IBRD net income (in US $ millions)

Fiscal year	Allocable net income[a]	Transfers to			
		Reserves	IDA	HIPC Trust	Other
1999	1,518	976	352	100	90 [b]
2000	1,991	1,318	348	200	125 [c]
2001	1,144	647	302	250	95 [d]
2002	1,924	1,291	300	240	93 [e]
2003	3,050	2,410	300	240	100 [f]

[a] Excluding effects of FAS 133 adjustments.
[b] Trust Funds for Gaza and the West Bank.
[c] Trust Funds for Gaza and the West Bank (60), East Timor (10), Kosovo (25), and Capacity Building in Africa (30).
[d] Trust Fund for Kosovo (35), Former Republic of Yugoslavia (30), and capacity-building in Africa (30).
[e] Transfer to staff retirement funds.
[f] Transfer to 'surplus account'.
Source: World Bank Annual Reports (FY1999–2003).

The allocation decision on IBRD net income has two components: one that the Executive Board is authorized to make, specifically, transfers to IBRD general reserves and the grant of interest waivers (refunds) to borrowers. A second set of decisions can only be made by the Board of Governors (on the recommendation of the Executive Board) for other developmental purposes. The two-step procedure means that decisions on the allocation of net income for a given year are made in the following fiscal year.

Under the framework agreed in 1991 to guide the annual process of net income allocation, first priority is accorded to achieving a targeted 'reserves-to-loan ratio' (later broadened to an equity-to-loan ratio). Next in priority is reducing borrower costs by pre-funding waivers of loan interest charges for the following fiscal year (up to 25 basis points) to all borrowers who serviced their loans within 30 days of their due dates during the previous six months. In addition, the IBRD waives a portion of the commitment charge on undisbursed balances on all loans (except for one category of special structural and sector adjustment loans).

Two other uses for the residual net income were identified in the 1991 framework: to support high-priority development activities that could be characterized as 'global public goods' (UNCTAD 2003; Kaul *et al.* 2003), and to temporarily accumulate funds in a 'surplus account', pending future decisions on their use. The initial rationale for creating this account was as a compromise between highly divergent views on the appropriate level of reserves. The account (with a movable cap) was meant to be a device that could be added to equity if additional paid-in capital was required but could not be raised through a general capital increase.

In the event, no GCI has been approved since 1988 owing to strong resistance from the Bank's principal shareholders, despite the fact that they did not have to contribute more than 3 per cent of the 1988 GCI as paid-in capital. Ironically, practically the same shareholders proceeded, at roughly the same time, to establish a new institution, the London-based European Bank for Reconstruction and Development Bank (EBRD), and to pay 30 per cent as paid-in capital to perform many of the same functions that the IBRD was fully competent to discharge.[8]

The Bank's borrowers have recognized that building up the Bank's equity through large transfers from net income has the advantage of reducing the Bank's funding costs, but they are also aware that this does not result automatically in a reduction in their borrowing costs. They accept that such a reduction depends on a number of offsetting cost entries, of which the largest is the IBRD administrative budget, which was already approaching $1 billion (see Appendix table). Instead of questioning some of these offset elements that affect the level of net income, borrowers chose instead to focus on the allocation of net income, specifically its use for prefunding the waiver of interest charges and commitment fees.

The issue of the allocation of net income came to a head in 1997–98. Confronted with a widening gap between the Bank's net income and the demands being placed upon it, the Bank's management proposed an increase in the contractual loan spread (over the Bank's borrowing cost) from 50 to 80 basis points; charging borrowers a 1 per cent front-end fee; maintaining the commitment fee at 75 basis points; and eliminating – for the next two fiscal years – the interest-rate waiver of 25 basis points on loans that are serviced on time. The strong resistance of borrowing countries resulted in a slight modification of the management proposal – that is, the interest rate waiver on new loans (which attracted the 75 basis points contractual lending spread) was maintained while it was reduced to 5 basis points on old loans (on which the spread remained at 50 basis points). The rest of the management proposal was adopted, but the vote 'was the closest in the World Bank's history'(Kapur 2000)[9] – a dramatic example of a contention running largely along North-South lines.

A more contentious strand in the debate was the decision to begin transferring a portion of IBRD net income to fund IDA, the World Bank Group's concessionary lending window for countries with per capita incomes below $450 (later raised to $750). As indicated in Table 3, these transfers have averaged $320 million annually in the last five years, although in some earlier years the amounts have been much higher (for example, in 1997, $600 million was transferred to IDA). These transfers have divided developing country members, with IBRD borrowers – such as Brazil and other Latin American countries, joined by some other developing and transition countries that were not IDA-eligible – 'insisting that net income be used to lower loan charges rather than supplement IDA' (Kapur, Lewis and Webb 1997).

A second priority has been transfers in support of the Heavily Indebted Poor Countries (HIPC) Initiative, launched by the major shareholder countries in 1996 and greatly expanded in 1999 to help the poorest countries achieve sustainable debt positions by writing down their sovereign debts to the multilateral financial institutions (in addition to their bilateral official debts). The Bretton Woods Institutions were chosen as the principal instruments for implementing the Initiative,[10] with the World Bank Group taking responsibility, through its HIPC Trust Fund, for helping some of the regional development banks (notably the African Development Bank) meet their share of HIPC debt-reduction claims, in addition to its own.

The use by the major shareholders of the Bank's net income to fund an Initiative entirely of their own design is only the latest instance of a number of other causes that have been funded with IBRD net income (see footnotes to Table 3). In three instances, the funds were used to provide technical assistance to countries that were not members at the time the allocations were authorized.[11] To the extent that net income was attributable to the excess of income from loans over IBRD borrowing costs, its use for purposes, however worthy, could be seen as a transfer from one set of developing countries to another. It could also be seen as a 'substitute for declining donor contributions to IDA' while enabling them to maintain their voting power in that institution and to extend decisions made by the IDA Deputies (representing *only* donor countries) to the World Bank Group as a whole.[12]

The IBRD as Financial Arbitrageur[13]

Our analysis has thus far focused on the burden-sharing issues associated with the contribution to its net income of the industrial non-borrowers and the IBRD borrowers. An aspect that needs exploration is the role that the Bank's own Treasury operations have played in contributing to the IBRD's net income. This operation is based on the Bank's liquid assets portfolio and its liquidity and risk-management arrangements.

Under the IBRD's liquidity-management policy, aggregate liquid asset holdings should be kept at or above a specified prudential minimum in order to deal with two sets of risks:

- the risk of being unable to fund its portfolio of assets at appropriate maturities and rates;

and

- the risk of being unable to liquidate a position in a timely manner at a reasonable price.

To this end, the portfolio's objective is to ensure the availability of sufficient cash flows to meet all IBRD financial commitments (note the reference to *financial* and not only its *lending* commitments). The prudential minimum is currently set as equal to the highest consecutive six months of expected debt service obligations for the fiscal year plus one-half of net approved loan disbursements as projected for the fiscal year. The 2004 prudential minimum is set at $18 billion, unchanged from that set for FY2003. Yet at the end of 2003, the 'carrying value' of the investment portfolio (trading and other liquid portfolio instruments) was more than $26.4 billion, or almost 50 per cent above the specified prudential minimum.

Under normal circumstances, there should be a net cost for carrying liquidity, for as the Bank history points out (Kapur, Lewis and Webb 1997), the Bank's borrowings are primarily medium- and long-term while its liquidity investments are short-term and yield curves typically are upward-sloping. Yet the Bank carries excess liquidity well above its own prudential minimum, indicating a judgement that the management of the liquid assets portfolio is in fact viewed as a net 'profit centre' for the Bank.[14] Income from the investment portfolio was as high as $1.54 billion in FY2001, and although it declined successively in the following two years (because of lower interest earnings in a period of falling interest rates) it was still positive, at $418 million in FY2003 (Table 2). It appears, however, that this figure for investment income is gross of the 'cost-of-carry', and that this cost is included in the overall figure for 'borrowing expenses'. Support for this view is to be found in the Annual Report for 2003; the report shows that investment income, net of funding costs, amounted to $36 million in FY2003 as against $140 million in FY2001.[15] This indicates that the IBRD was able to extract a modicum of net income even in the face of the steep yield curve of recent years.

A net return of $36 million on a portfolio in the range of $26–27 billion must appear trivial and suggests the existence of some additional benefit that the Bank is obtaining from holding such a large liquid assets portfolio. Clearly, this portfolio makes the IBRD an important player in financial markets. According to the Bank's history, by the mid-1980s, the liquid portfolio had increased to about $20 billion and the Bank was turning it over on average 'every two days: this amounts to more than $3 trillion a year' (op. cit.). As noted above, by the end of FY2003, the Bank was managing a liquid assets portfolio exceeding $26.4 billion, and if the transaction volume is anywhere comparable to that obtaining in the mid-1980s, the Bank's Treasury operations could be exceeding several trillions of dollars a year and the Bank must have become a highly significant operator in the explosively growing derivatives markets on its own account.

IBRD officials contend that the purpose of these Treasury transactions is essentially to obtain lower cost (below-Libor) funding in its own borrowing operations in international capital markets. Since the IBRD functions as a 'cost-plus' lender, IBRD officials note, the benefit is reflected in the Bank's lower lending rates to its borrowers. However, the savings on this account, it is argued, are not quantifiable because of contrafactual element involved – namely, that it is not possible to know what IBRD funding costs would have been if it did not have at its disposal a substantial portfolio of liquid assets that could be continuously deployed in financial markets to garner opportunities for funding bargains.

It appears difficult to accept this argument as the *sole* justification for employing such a large investment portfolio to extract savings of unquantifiable magnitude. The membership should expect to see some demonstration of the putative savings that IBRD borrowers enjoy from the deployment of funds in Treasury operations. That this is a truly massive involvement is illustrated by the fact that on top of its loan assets of $116 billion and its own borrowing liabilities of $110 billion, the IBRD has erected a superstructure of swaps and other assets and liabilities of almost equivalent magnitude to reach total asset/liability figures of $230 billion in its balance sheet at the end of FY2003.

In the absence of any other satisfactory explanation, one is led to ask whether the results of the accounting change made in FY2001 of adopting FAS 133 provide any insight into the non-interest income benefit being obtained from Treasury operations. While the results for the first year are distorted by the one-time costs of shifting from one set of accounting protocols to another, there has been a sharp rise in gains attributed to marking-to-market all derivative instruments, as defined by FAS 133. From $345 million in the transition year, the effect has been to raise net income by $854 million in FY2002 and by $2.3 billion in FY2003. Profits of this magnitude – exceeding loan interest income, net of funding costs, in FY2003[16] – raise the question of whether the Bank has morphed into a very different institution from that envisaged by its founders.[17]

This issue becomes especially pertinent in light of the fact that the level of outstanding IBRD loans has stayed in the range of $116–121 billion during the past five years,[18] while annual commitments have remained in the range of $10.5–11.5 billion in the past four. Equally troubling is the fact that while gross disbursements have stayed in the $11–12 billion range over the past three years, net disbursements have turned negative – owing to large pre-payments – in the past two. What has caused members to make such large pre-payments – which reached almost $7 billion in FY2003 – is important to consider if it suggests that the Bank has lost some competitiveness as a preferred development lender.[19]

Even more troubling, if one takes a longer-term view, is the contrast between rising administrative costs (ignoring the rather artificial division of costs between the IBRD and IDA) and the negative trend of IBRD net transfers (net disbursements minus debt service payments by borrowers)(see Appendix table).

Concluding Remarks

If current trends continue – that is, if the IBRD continues to record a stagnant loan portfolio in nominal terms and a declining one in inflation-adjusted terms – the IBRD would forfeit its traditional role as the world's premier development lender by a growing loss of competitiveness. It would mean that perhaps the finest international lending intermediary created in the postwar period is likely to become overly dependent for its continuing profitability – and for its AAA credit-rating in capital markets – on its role as a financial trader and arbitrageur. To reclaim its role as a preferred development lender, it is essential for the IBRD's membership – especially the developing country groupings – to consider whether the pricing of loans and the conditions attached to them have discouraged creditworthy borrowers from using the IBRD. The membership must also review the restrictions that have been applied on the purposes for which the IBRD lends.

The Bank has been essentially a 'cost-plus' lender. As noted earlier, it charges a contractual spread of 75 basis points over its borrowing cost on its 'new' loans (that is, loans signed after 1 July 1998) to cover its overhead and it refunds 25 basis points through interest waivers (in the following fiscal year) to borrowers who have serviced their loans within 30 days of their due dates (during the prior six months). Loans made earlier carry a contractual spread of 50 basis points but the interest rate waiver on these is only 5 basis points. Moreover, the IBRD charges a commitment fee of 75 basis points (where there is a partial refund), plus a front-end fee of 100 basis points, on the entire amount of each loan, and these fees are never refunded. A reduction in the front-end fee would provide an immediate cost saving for new loans, as would a reversion to the contractual spread of 50 basis points in effect prior to mid-1998, together with a reduction in the time-lag between an adjustment of interest charges on variable-rate loans and the borrowing costs of funding them. Similarly, the complex body of safeguard and fiduciary policies that have accumulated over the years for 'ring-fencing' the Bank from risk need to be re-examined.

A significant change in the composition of Bank lending is also required if the Bank is to fulfil its core mission at a time when public-sector development needs are enormous and growing. Bank lending for infrastructure has declined sharply in the past few years – for electric power and energy, for example, from $2 billion to $0.75 billion; for transportation by 28 per cent over the same period; and for water and sanitation by 25 per cent.[20] Additional non-quantifiable costs are associated with the Bank's retreat from these sectors that arise from the fact that 'Bank involvement in infrastructure projects, more often than not, reduces both the scope for corruption and inappropriate policies, which can result in substantial costs on a country.'

In sum, it is essential that the IBRD's membership review, on an urgent basis, the working of the IBRD in a number of areas, including among other things:

- the factors behind the recent stagnation of the loan portfolio, such that the Bank is operating at roughly one half of its statutory lending capacity;
- the reasons for the trend of declining net disbursements – which have actually turned negative in the last two years under review owing to large prepayments by members;
- the rationale for the deployment of a 50 per cent excess over the statutory minimum requirement for its liquid assets portfolio;
- whether the policy conditionalities and ring-fencing stipulations attached to loans are eroding the Bank's competitiveness as a commercial lender;
- whether instead of continuing to add to its retained earnings, IBRD net income could be applied to lowering its lending rates, especially for poverty alleviation projects in countries not eligible for IDA funding; and
- whether the Bank should significantly expand its lending for infrastructure projects.

Appendix 1

What Constitutes IBRD Net Income?

This Appendix sets out the elements that enter into the determination of the World Bank's net income. The Bank has two principal income streams and several subsidiary ones. The first principal stream derives from its lending operations and the second from its investments. The former covers interest earnings and other charges on loans. In FY2003, the gross income on the loan portfolio amounted to $5.7 billion, as against $6.9 billion in FY2002 and $8.1 billion in FY2001.

The second stream results from the income on investments, largely comprised of a liquid assets portfolio that is maintained to ensure sufficient cash flow to meet IBRD obligations. At the end of FY2003, this portfolio of cash and liquid investments was valued at $26.4 billion and yielded an income of $418 million, as compared with $734 million earned from a portfolio of $25.1 billion in FY2002 and $1.5 billion from a portfolio of $24.4 billion in FY2001. The reduction in contractual yield on the portfolio over the three-year period is attributed primarily to the lower interest rate environment in the later years.

Among the subsidiary income streams, two are identifiable: 'service fee revenues' earned by the Bank from non-lending operations and 'income from the Staff Retirement Plan and other post retirement benefit plans'. Finally, there is a non-identifiable category of 'net other income'.

Against these sources of income are two principal offsets: the Bank's borrowing costs and its administrative expenses. The former have fallen sharply from a peak of $7.2 billion in FY2001 to $4.9 billion in FY2002 and to $3.6 billion in FY2003. The decline reflects primarily a lower cost of borrowing and a reduction in the level of outstanding borrowings over the three-year period (see Memorandum items in Table 2).

The second offset is administrative expenses attributable to the IBRD, which have been roughly stable over the period under review, at an average level of $1.04 billion a year. However, this item includes 'Contributions to Special Programmes' that average $160 million annually. These contributions consist of grants made by the IBRD for certain high-priority developmental purposes, such as funding for the Consultative Group for International Agriculture (CGIAR) for agricultural research, the Global Development Network (for knowledge creation and dissemination), the Global Alliance for Vaccines and Immunization (preventive health services), the Global Environment Facility (environment protection), and the Global Water Partnership. Two additional grant-like programmes were added in the late 1990s: the Institutional Development Fund (IDF) and the Consultative Group to Aid the Poorest (CGAP). Excluding these special grant programmes, IBRD administrative expenditure (net) has averaged $850 million a year.

An adjustment is made to the income remaining after offsetting the two major categories of expense to arrive at the Bank's 'operating income'. This adjustment arises from changes in the accumulated provision for losses on income and guarantees. Management judgements are made as to the appropriate level of provision for each borrower based on the probability of default, the total size of outstanding loans extended to the borrower, and the assumed severity of loss in the event of default. These judgements are based on many factors, including an assessment of a borrower's past and prospective economic performance and its economic policy framework. The IBRD periodically reviews these risk factors and reassesses the adequacy of the accumulated provision for losses. A decision to increase the accumulated loan-loss provision becomes a charge on operating income while a decrease in the outstanding provision adds to operating income. Thus a sharp increase in operating income in FY2003 of $1.1 billion (relative to the previous year) resulted from two sources:

(1) a reduction of $709 million in the accumulated provision requirement due to a net improvement in borrowers' risk ratings and a large decrease in loans outstanding, attributable to substantial negative net disbursements, including $7.0 billion in loan prepayments; and
(2) the decision to reclassify loans to the former Socialist Federal Republic of Yugoslavia when its successor states undertook responsibility for servicing them, resulting in an additional $591 million being taken into income.

Finally, one moves from operating income to net income on a reported basis by taking into account the effects of applying Financial Accounting Standard (FAS) 133 and International Accounting Standard (IAS) 39, which require that derivative instruments be reported at fair value, with changes in fair value being recognized immediately in earnings. During FY2003, the effects of applying FAS 133 added as much as $2.3 billion to operating income of $3.0 billion compared with additions of $854 million in FY2002 and $345 million in FY2001.

Notes

1 The 'World Bank Group' consists, in addition to the IBRD, of the following institutions: the International Development Association (IDA), the International Finance Corporation (IFC), the Multilateral Investment Guarantee Agency (MIGA), and the International Centre for Settlement of Investment Disputes. For the purposes of this paper, the IFC and the MIGA are treated as separate, autonomous institutions. References in the paper to 'the Bank' are meant to apply to the IBRD unless specifically indicated otherwise.

2 The US dollar was defined as the 'dollar of the weight and fineness of 1 July 1944'. This unit of value was the basis for the determination of the amounts payable by members and for determining the obligations of members to the Bank on account of the maintenance of value with respect to their subscription to the capital stock after the initial payment for it. The unit of value was redefined in 1973 as equivalent to 1.20635 current US dollars, and it has been applied thereafter for the valuation of the Bank's capital for meeting the maintenance of value obligation by members.

3 Member countries choose whether they are Part I or Part II based primarily on their economic standing. Thus, the 27 countries currently identified as Part I are almost all donors to the concessionary IDA and they pay their contributions in freely convertible currencies. While mainly industrial countries, the list includes two OPEC members (Kuwait and the United Arab Emirates) and one developing country (South Africa).

4 Note also that the Bank employs another $26–27 billion of its borrowings for its liquid assets portfolio.

5 It also requires borrowers to adhere to a 'negative pledge' to assure the Bank equality of treatment with other creditors and to require them to obtain specific waivers for any deviation.

6 Kapur has argued that 'the increasingly stringent compliance standards of the World Bank … are imposing high financial and opportunity costs on the Bank's borrowers … It is trivially easy for the major shareholders to insist on standards whose costs they do not bear.'

7 It has been argued that the contribution of Part I countries is greater than the amount paid in because they have not received dividends on their contributions. On the other hand, the same countries have been major beneficiaries of procurement contracts emanating from IBRD loans in the amount of $333.5 billion over the years.

8 It also raised, for the authors of the Bank's history (Kapur, Lewis and Webb 1997), 'interesting questions on the relative priorities of the Bank's major shareholders, as well as the perceptions of the European shareholders, concerning the Bank's relative effectiveness and governance'.

9 The paper notes that 'the resolutions were approved by just nine of the 24 Executive Directors (representing 51.7 per cent of the votes) while 12 Executive Directors (representing 36 per cent) voted against the resolutions and an additional three Executive Directors (representing 12.3 per cent) abstained.'

10 For an explanation of how the IMF met its share of HIPC claims, see Mohammed (2003) 'Who Pays for the IMF?', in *Challenges to the World Bank and IMF: Developing Countries Descriptions*, London: Anthem Press, pp. 37–54 (edited by Ariel Buira for the G-24 Research Programme).

11 'Several of these cases represent foreign policy interests of some of the Bank's largest shareholders, rather than intrinsic merits of the benefits to the institution's membership as a whole. Traditionally, the large shareholders would have funded their interests through direct claims on their budgetary resources, but in the strained financial environment of the 1990s the cost would be borne by all of the Bank's members'(Kapur, Lewis and Webb 1997, p. 1085).

12 This has been characterized as a 'creeping constitutional coup that has fundamentally subverted the role of the Executive Board in the institution's governance' (ibid.).

13 This section draws on material in recent World Bank Annual Reports, Volume 2.

14 *The World Bank Annual Report 2003*: Volume 2 (p. 15) explains that the holding of liquid assets over the specified minimum was required 'to provide flexibility in timing its borrowing transactions and to meet working capital needs'.

15 World Bank 2003, Table 15, Volume 2.

16 Income from loans has fallen from $8.1 billion in FY2001 to $6.8 billion in FY2002 and $5.7 billion in FY2003; while this has been offset by a decline in borrowing costs, the net income from the loan portfolio at $2.1 billion in FY2003 falls below the addition to net income attributable to FAS 133.

17 It is contended that FAS 133 profits are not genuine profits *over time* but simply a snapshot of a particular profit/loss position *at a point of time*, and that the 'unrealized' gains and losses from swap operations get cancelled when specific swap contracts are closed out. For this reason, the Bank does not take FAS 133 profits into its 'allocable net income', which, rather than 'reported net income', serves as the basis for allocations shown in Table 3. Reporting on the basis of the FAS 133 accounting standard became applicable from FY2001 and the Bank has had to adopt it for reporting its results. However, 'because of the extent of IBRD's long-dated funding, the reported volatility under FAS 133 may be more pronounced than for many other financial

institutions ... IBRD believes that its funding and asset/liability management strategies achieve its objectives of protection from market risk and provision of lower cost funding', and that its current value basis provides estimates of the economic value of its financial assets and liabilities, 'after considering interest-rate, currency and credit risks', that are more meaningful 'for risk management and management reporting' (Vol. 2 , Annual Report 2003, p. 5).

18 A stagnating outstanding loan volume also begins to constrain the ability to increase lending because of risk-dictated ceilings on commitments to a single borrower; this is already affecting China's access.

19 The large prepayments in FY2003 are attributed to two factors: (1) a one-off repayment of $2 billion from an emergency credit extended to Korea at the time of the Asian payments crisis, and (2) a strong incentive on the part of borrowers in the single-currency fixed-interest-rate pool to pay off loans that carry much higher interest rates than are available on variable-rate loans or when compared with the very low returns earned on their holdings of foreign exchange reserves. With borrowers no longer willing to enter the single-currency pool, these prepayments are expected to taper off sharply in the next few years.

20 Op.cit., footnote 6.

References

Kapur, Devesh, J. Lewis and Richard Webb, 1997, *The World Bank: Its First Half Century*, Washington D.C.: Brookings Institution Press.

Kapur, Devesh, 2002, 'The Common Pool Dilemma of Global Public goods: Lessons from the World Bank's Net Income and Reserves', *World Development*, Vol. 30, 30: 337–354.

Kaul, Inge, P. Conceicão, K. Le Goulven, R. Mendoza, 2003, *Providing Global Public Goods: Managing Globalization*, New York: Oxford University Press.

Mohammed, Aziz Ali, 2003, 'Who Pays for the IMF?', in *Challenges to the World Bank and IMF: Developing Countries Descriptions*, London: Anthem Press: 37–54.

UNCTAD, 2003, Kapur, Devesh, 'Do as I Say, Not as I Do: A Critique of G-7 Proposals on Reforming the Multilateral Development Banks', G-24 Discussion Paper Series, United Nations Publications, New York and Geneva.

World Bank, 1999–2000, *World Bank Annual Reports 1999–2000*, Washington, D.C.

World Bank, 2001–03, *World Bank Annual Reports 2001–03*: Volume 1–2, Washington, D.C.

9

REINVENTING INDUSTRIAL STRATEGY: THE ROLE OF GOVERNMENT POLICY IN BUILDING INDUSTRIAL COMPETITIVENESS

Sanjaya Lall

Abstract:

As liberalization and globalization gather momentum, some developing countries are coping well, but the majority are not. Among the various reasons for growing economic divergence, differences in industrial competitiveness are one important factor. This paper examines two approaches to the problem of growing differences in competitiveness: neoliberal and structuralist. The neoliberal approach is that the best strategy for all countries and in all situations is to liberalize. Integration into the international economy, with resource allocation driven by free markets, will let them realize their natural comparative advantage. No government intervention can improve upon this. The structuralist approach puts less faith in free markets and more in the ability of governments to mount interventions effectively.

The paper reviews the growing divergence in industrial performance in developing countries, considers the case for industrial policy, and argues that interventions are necessary to overcome market failures in industrial development. It draws on evolutionary theories of technical change as manifested in the 'technological capability' approach. It describes the strategies of the Asian Tigers to build industrial competitiveness, noting the pervasiveness of selective interventions and strategic differences between them. It concludes with lessons for other developing countries.

Introduction

As liberalization and globalization gather momentum, concern with industrial competitiveness is growing, in industrial as well as in developing countries. But developing countries face the most intense competitive pressures: many find that their enterprises are unable to cope with the rigours of open markets both in exporting and in competing with imports, as they open their economies. Some countries are doing very well, but many are not. Diverging industrial competitiveness among developing countries is one of the basic causes of the growing disparities in income that are now a pervasive feature of the global economy. The immense potential that globalization offers for industrial growth is being tapped by a relatively small number of countries, and liberalization is driving the wedge deeper.

Much of this is well known. The Millennium Development Goals of the United Nations were conceived to deal with just such concerns. However, there is little consensus yet on what can be done to deal with lagging growth in developing countries, particularly in the industrial sphere. What *can* poor countries do to strengthen their industrial competitiveness in the current international economic setting? Should they persist with liberalization and hope that free market forces will stimulate growth and bring about greater convergence? Or should they look again at national and international policy? What, specifically, is the correct role for government in stimulating industrial-ization as an engine for growth and structural transformation?

Two approaches to the issue of industrial policy can be identified: *neoliberal* and *structuralist*. The *neoliberal* approach holds that the best strategy for all countries and in all situations is to liberalize – and not do much else. Integration into the international economy, with resource allocation driven by market forces, will allow them realize their 'natural' comparative advantage. This will in turn optimize a country's dynamic advantage and so yield maxi-mum sustainable growth. No government intervention can improve upon this outcome and will only serve to reduce economic welfare. With the neoliberal approach, the only legitimate role for the state is to provide a stable macro-economy with clear rules of the game, open the economy fully to international product and factor flows, give a lead role to private enterprise, and furnish essential public goods like skilled human capital and infrastructure. This approach has the backing of the industrial countries and the Bretton Woods institutions (which is why it is also referred to as the 'Washington consensus'). It has become enshrined in the new rules of the game being formulated and implemented by the World Trade Organization (WTO).

The neoliberal approach has strong theoretical premises: markets are 'efficient', the institutions needed to make markets work exist and are effective, and if there are deviations from optimality they cannot be remedied effectively by governments. The premises are a mixture of theoretical, empirical and political assumptions. Their theoretical core relies, among other things, on a narrow view of the technological basis of competitiveness. The empirical assumption relies on a particular interpretation of the experience of the most successful industrializing economies, the 'Tigers' of East Asia. The political assumption that governments are necessarily and universally less efficient than markets has less to do with economics than with ideology.

The *structuralist* view puts less faith in free markets as the driver of dynamic competitiveness and more in the ability of governments to mount interventions effectively. It questions the theoretical and empirical basis for the argument that untrammelled market forces account for the industrial success of the East Asian Tigers (or, indeed, of the earlier industrialization of the now rich countries). Acknowledging the mistakes of past industrialization strategies and the need for greater openness, structuralist advocates argue that greater reliance on markets does not pre-empt a proactive role for the government. Markets are powerful forces but they are not perfect; the institutions needed to make them work efficiently are often weak or absent. Government interventions by well-functioning institutions are thus able to improve on market outcomes.

Structuralists accept that some industrialization policies have not worked well in the past. To the neoliberals this justifies denying any role for proactive policy both in past success and in future strategy: if there are market failures, the costs are always less than those of government failures. The structuralists, on the other hand, see a vital role for policy in industrial success. For them, therefore, past policy failure is not a reason for passive reliance on deficient markets but for improving government policymaking capabilities. The structuralists note that many poor regions that have implemented neoliberal policies recently have not experienced the industrial growth or export success that characterized more interventionist economies. To structuralists, a projection of current trends suggests that persisting passively with liberalization in the context of globalization will worsen rather than reverse worldwide divergence in industrial competitiveness.

The growing unease with the consequences of neoliberalism led the Zedillo Commission, in its Report of the High-Level Panel on Financing for Development to the Monterrey Conference on Financing for Development in 2002, to phrase the issue in diplomatic terms. Noting that 'Sadly, increasing polarization between the haves and have-nots has become a feature of our world,' the Report goes on to say the following on infant industry protection (a policy tool banned under the new rules): 'However misguided the old model of blanket protection intended to nurture import substitute industries, it would be a mistake to go to the other extreme and deny developing countries the opportunity of actively nurturing the development of an industrial sector' (Zedillo Commission, 2001, Executive Summary, pp. 9–10).[1]

The controversy over industrial policy is, of course, not new; it goes back decades and, in earlier guises, centuries (Reinert 1995; Chang 2002). Despite the frequent assertion that the debate is now dead and the efficacy of free markets established beyond doubt, this is not the case. This paper suggests that the case for industrial policy remains strong, and is in fact becoming stronger with technical change and globalization. However, the kinds of intervention needed are changing; as a structural force, globalization reduces the feasibility of some strategies while increasing that of others.

Structural changes are supported by new 'rules of the game' on participation in the international system. Some rules are necessary to facilitate the changes, but they must take account of the fact that the field has players of very different strengths. Imposing a level playing field can lead to an uneven distribution of benefits between the strong and the weak. It can constrain the ability of poorer countries to build the capabilities they need for industrialization by banning policies used with spectacular success by several countries, including advanced ones. Before discussing the new rules and the legitimate role of policy, let us review briefly the main features of the recent industrialization.

The New Dimensions of Industrial Competitiveness

Structural Features

Competitiveness has always mattered for industrial growth, but its nature has changed. Rapid technological change, shrinking economic distance, new forms of industrial organization, tighter links between national value chains and widespread liberalization have altered radically the environment facing enterprises. Competition now arises with great intensity from across the world, using a bewildering array of new technologies. To survive it, all producers must use new technologies at or near 'best practice'. The production system spans many countries, tapping differences in costs, skills and resources to optimize efficiency (Radosevic, 1999).

Technological change is shifting industrial and trade structures towards more complex, technology-based activities. Table 1 shows the growth of manufacturing value-added (MVA) for three technological sets of activities: resource-based (RB), low-technology (LT) and medium- and high-technology (MHT).[2] For exports the data allow us to show high-technology products separately. Over the past two decades exports have grown faster than production, and complex activities have grown faster than other branches of manufacturing. Developing countries have done better in all branches than industrialized economies.

Organizational structures and the location of production are changing in response to technological change. Industrial firms are becoming less vertically integrated and more specialized by technology, scouring the world for more economical locations. Shrinking economic space allows them to locate functions in far-flung corners of the globe. Some facilities are under the control of

Table 1. Growth of manufacturing value-added and manufactured exports by technology (annual percentage 1980–2000)

Activity	World	Industrialized countries	Developing countries
Manufacturing value-added			
Total MVA	2.6%	2.3%	5.4%
RB MVA	2.3%	1.8%	4.5%
LT MVA	1.7%	1.4%	3.5%
MHT MVA	3.1%	2.6%	6.8%
Manufactured exports			
Total manufactured exports	7.6%	6.6%	12.0%
RB manufactured exports	5.6%	5.2%	6.7%
LT manufactured exports	7.4%	8.4%	11.4%
MHT manufactured exports	8.4%	7.3%	16.5%
o/w Hi-tech exports	11.5%	9.9%	20.2%

Source: Calculated from UNIDO and Comtrade data.

transnationals from the industrialized countries but others are independent, interwoven with the leaders in intricate contractual and non-contractual relations. This 'fragmentation' is rewriting the geography of industrial activity.[3]

New technologies change the institutional and policy structures needed for competitiveness. Countries require new skills to manage technical change and so the institutional ability to upgrade skills (Narula 2003). They need technical support agencies in standards, metrology, quality, testing, R&D, productivity and SME extension. They need advanced infrastructure in information and communication technologies (ICTs) and they need to cushion the impact of new technologies on declining activities and disadvantaged groups.

Globalization also transfers productive factors across economies more rapidly. However, capital, technology, information and skills do not spread evenly. They go only to places where competitive production is possible, where there are inputs and institutions to complement the mobile factors. It requires, in brief, new industrial capabilities (Best 2001). Cheap unskilled labour or raw natural resources are no longer sufficient to sustain industrial growth: strong local capabilities determine competitive success. However, industrial capabilities develop slowly, in a cumulative and path-dependent manner subject to agglomeration economies. Economies that enter a virtuous circle of growth, competitiveness and new capabilities can carry on doing better than those that are stuck in a 'low-level equilibrium' and cannot muster the resources to break out. Industrial performance can continue diverging over time, with no inbuilt forces towards convergence.

Rules of the Game

Liberalization in the developing world has been partly voluntary, partly driven by external pressures and partly enforced by the rules of international economic relations. Some changes were initiated by developing countries disillusioned with earlier strategies, some by developed countries, the Bretton Woods agencies, and bilateral or regional agreements, and some by international agreements. One effect has been to constrict the scope for industrial policies. The most affected are: *protection of infant industries,*[4] *performance requirements on foreign investors, export targeting and incentives and other subsidies affecting trade,*[5] *slack IPRs (intellectual property rights) protection to promote copying and reverse engineering,* and *local content rules.*[6]

The rules cannot be analysed here, but some points may be noted. First, rules on trade allow for exceptions, particularly for the least developed countries (although many exceptions are coming to an end). Second, rules now carry the threat of sanctions: trading partners can impose compensatory tariffs or other measures. Third, most important is the underlying *trend towards greater liberalization.* The scope and coverage of the rules are steadily increasing, and pressures are coming in many forms. The trade regime in developing countries is likely to become very similar to that in the OECD.

Policies on FDI and technology imports have undergone rapid liberalization, to a greater extent than those on trade and domestic credit. Most liberalization has occurred over the past decade or so, with the pace accelerating in the 1990s. There are practically no policy controls left on technology transfer, in contrast to the 1970s when there were extensive interventions by governments on licensing.

Some of the main issues in the multilateral agreements are:[7]

- *Services:* The General Agreement on Trade in Services (GATS) covers the supply of markets by foreign firms present in those markets under WTO. The GATS allows a 'positive list' of permitted investments, allowing host countries freedom to exclude activities not in the list.
- *Performance requirements on TNCs:* This is treated under the Agreement on Trade-Related Investment Measures (TRIMs). TRIMs affect trade in goods and are important in that they prohibit tools traditionally widely used to extract greater benefits from FDI: local content requirements, trade balancing, technology transfer, local employment and R&D, and so on.
- *Intellectual property rights (IPRs):* The protection of IPRs has moved in effect from the World Intellectual Property Organisation to WTO under the TRIPS (Trade-Related Aspects of Intellectual Property Rights) Agreement. The most important point about this shift is that trade sanctions can be applied to countries deemed deficient protecting IPRs.[8] The implications

for developing countries are worrying (Lall 2003). While stronger IPRs may benefit innovators in the developed countries, they can inhibit technological development in developing ones. They raise the cost of formal technology transfers by allowing technology sellers to impose stricter restrictions and by preventing copying and 'reverse engineering', the source of much technological learning in newly industrialising countries.

Trends in Industrial Competitiveness in the Developing World

This section uses two indicators: world market shares in *manufacturing value-added* (MVA) and in *manufactured exports*. Developing regions are: 'East Asia', in which EA includes China and all countries in the South-East Asian region apart from Japan, whereas EA2 excludes China. 'LAC' (Latin America and the Caribbean) includes Mexico, but LAC2 excludes it. South Asia includes the five main countries in that region. 'MENA' (Middle East and North Africa) includes Turkey but not Israel (an industrialized country). 'SSA' (Sub-Saharan Africa) includes South Africa, but not SSA2.

MVA: The developing world performed well in 1980–2000. Its share of global MVA rose by 10 percentage points (from 14 per cent to 24 per cent) and its annual rate of growth (5.4 per cent) was over twice the 2.3 per cent recorded by the industrialized world. Does this mean that globalisation and liberalization were conducive to development? Unfortunately not: success in the developing world was very concentrated (Figure 1). East Asia dominated, raising its world share from around 4 per cent to nearly 14 per cent – exactly the 10-point rise for the developing world as a whole (Figure 2). EA, while strongly export-oriented, was not 'liberal' in the Washington consensus sense.[9] LAC, the region that liberalized the most, the earliest and the fastest, was the worst performer.

LAC and East Asia illustrate the central issues nicely. The regions had different approaches to industrialization, initially to develop industry[10] and later to liberalize[11] – EA has had much more strategic industrial policy than LAC. The resulting differences in outcomes are intriguing, as the next two charts show. They separate China in EA and Mexico in LAC, both regional outliers. Both did well in FDI-based manufactured exports, but their differences are of interest. The link between export and MVA growth is stronger in China than in Mexico: China is less exposed to import competition and has used industrial policy to induce greater local content in export activity. Figure 3 shows MVA market shares *within the developing world* for EA without China, China, LAC without Mexico, and Mexico.

Figure 4 shows changes in market shares over 1980–90 and 1990–2000. In 1980, LAC accounted for 47 per cent of developing world MVA and East Asia for 29 per cent; two decades later, the shares were 22 per cent and

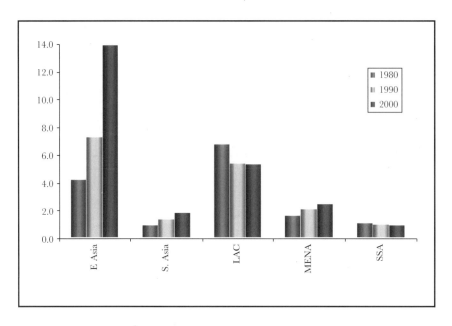

Figure 1. Developing regions' shares of global MVA (per cent)

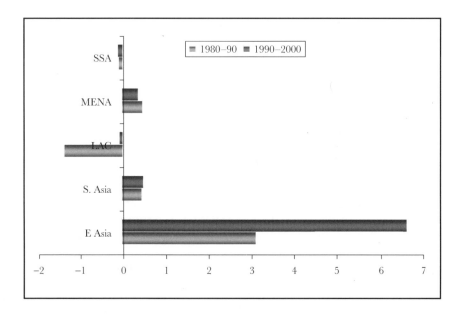

Figure 2. Changes in shares of global MVA (percentage points)

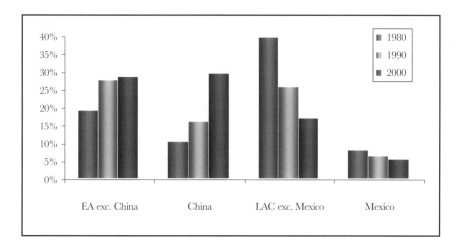

Figure 3. East Asia and LAC, shares of developing world MVA (percentage)

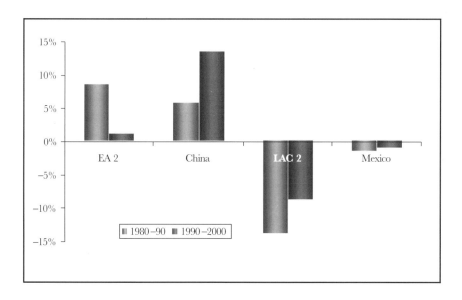

Figure 4. East Asia and LAC, changes in shares of developing world MVA (percentage)

58 per cent respectively. The main surge in MVA in EA2 was in the 1980s, with a slowing down in the 1990s because of financial crisis and global recession. In China the trends are reversed, with the more rapid growth in the 1990s, making its share of developing world MVA higher than the rest of East Asia. LAC2, excluding Mexico, loses MVA shares more rapidly than

Mexico, the 1980s (the 'lost decade' after the debt crisis) being much worse than the 1990s.

LAC started the 1990s with considerable slack engendered by the 'lost decade', which better macro policy and liberalization should have allowed it to exploit for rapid production and export growth. However, the region continued to perform poorly: LAC2 had MVA growth of only 1.9 per cent per annum., much lower than developing countries as a whole (6.4 per cent) or East Asia (9.5 per cent). It underperformed relative to South Asia and MENA, both highly interventionist regions. Mexico's more robust growth of 4.4 per cent was largely a consequence of trade privileges over other developing regions under NAFTA – hardly a neoliberal recipe. In any case it did not match EA2 (6.7 per cent) or China (13.1 per cent), and this despite the fact that the 1990s were a bad period for EA2, reeling from the effects of the 1997 financial crisis.

Export performance: Figure 5 shows world market shares for manufactured exports for 1981–2000 and the value of such exports in 2000, separating China from East Asia 2 and Mexico from LAC2. East Asia as a whole accounted for 18.4 per cent of world manufactured exports in 2000, up from 6.8 per cent in 1981. Within it, EA2 raised its share from 5.8 per cent to 12.0 per cent and China from 1.0 per cent to 6.5 per cent. China has a much

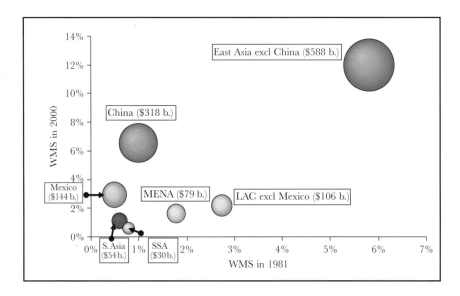

Figure 5. World market shares for manufactured products in 1981 and 2000, and the values of manufactured exports in 2000 ($ billion)

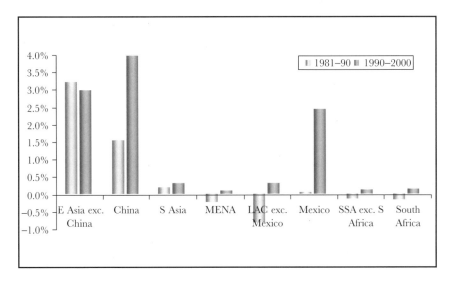

Figure 6. Changes in world market shares for manufactures (percentage points)

higher share of regional MVA than exports – its industry, perhaps not surprisingly in view of the size of the economy and its late entry to export markets, is less export-oriented than its neighbours'. LAC lost world market share in 1981–90 (from 3.2 per cent to 2.4 per cent) then raised it over the next decade to 5.1 per cent (see Figure 6). The initial fall was due entirely to LAC2 (from 2.7 per cent to 1.9 per cent), Mexico holding steady at a 0.5 per cent share. Other regions were relatively stagnant, though each did better in the 1990s than the 1980s. Thus:

- MVA performance is broadly correlated with manufactured export perfor-mance, although the fit is not perfect. EA2 and Mexico fare better in exports than in MVA in the 1990s, while the opposite is true of South Asia and MENA.
- Neither MVA nor export growth is strongly related to liberalization in the Washington consensus sense.
- Industrial success remains concentrated. Liberalization is not leading to convergence, contradicting the neoliberal premise that liberalization *per se* would promote industrial growth and competitiveness.

Why the World Differs from the Neoliberal Ideal

The Neoclassical Approach

Neoliberal economists accept a role for the state to provide basic public goods, law and order and sound macro management. Selectivity (the support of particular activities, firms or technologies, or 'picking winners') is taboo, and became the arena for the industrial policy debate in the 1990s. The early neoliberal interpretation of East Asian success – that it was due to non-interventionist policies – was subjected to intense criticism. It was noted that most successful countries had been very interventionist in trade, FDI, technology and domestic resource allocation.[12] The neoliberals responded with a '*moderate neoclassical*' stance that devoted enormous effort to explaining why selectivity, while it existed, was redundant and unnecessary (World Bank 1993).[13] They admitted *some* market failures and *some* role for the state, but only as long as interventions were functional – there was no role for policy in influencing allocation at the activity, firm or technological level. This 'market-friendly' approach segmented market failures not according to whether market failures existed but according to the level at which policies affected investment decisions.

Neoclassical theory provides no reason for such a distinction; it arises instead from a *political economy premise* that it is impossible for governments to mount effective selective interventions. The World Bank (1993) admitted that some selectivity might have worked in East Asia, but the circumstances were unique; other governments did not and *could not* have the capabilities needed. The moderate position, later called the 'Washington consensus', coincided with the World Bank's operations (in health, education and infrastructure), policy advice (greater liberalization) and structural adjustment programmes (stabilization, liberalization and privatization).

The moderate position retained the simplifying assumptions of the strong position on technology. Both assumed that markets affecting technology were 'efficient'. In the theoretical sense, efficiency has stringent requirements: product markets give the correct signals for investment and factor markets respond to these signals. At the firm level there are no scale economies or externalities. Firms have perfect information and foresight and full knowledge of all available technologies. They choose the right technology if faced with free market prices. Having selected the right technology they use it instantaneously as 'best practice'. There are no significant learning processes, no risks, no externalities and no deficiencies in the skills, finance, information and infrastructure available to them.

In this model, any policy intervention in prices facing enterprises is by definition distorting.[14] The critical assumption concerns *learning and capability-building*, and changing it yields very different conclusions for policy (below). But showing that there may be market failures in technology markets does not establish the case for selectivity. It is also necessary to show that such failures are important in practice and not theoretical curiosities, and that governments can effectively remedy them in real life. Both *can* be shown, and the transition from an admittedly simplified neoclassical model to a universal, timeless neoliberal policy *diktat* is not justified in theory, history or practice.[15] To do this we turn to the structuralist approach to technology in developing countries.

The Technological Capability Approach

How enterprises in developing countries actually use technology is analysed by a large recent literature on technological capabilities.[16] The literature is mainly empirical but has its theoretical roots in the evolutionary approach of Nelson and Winter (1982) and the modern information theory of Stiglitz.[17] It argues that industrial success in developing countries depends essentially on how enterprises manage the process of mastering, adapting and improving upon existing technologies. The process is difficult and prone to widespread and diffuse market failures, which have important implications for policy (Box 1).

Box 1

Ten features of technological learning in developing countries

1 Technological learning is a real and significant process. It is vital to industrial development, and is primarily conscious and purposive rather than automatic and passive. Firms using a given technology for similar periods need not be equally proficient: each will be at the point given by the intensity of its capability-building efforts.

2 Firms do not have full information on technical alternatives. They function with imperfect, variable and rather hazy knowledge of technologies they are using. There is no uniform, predictable learning curve for a given technology. Each faces risk, uncertainty and cost. Differences in learning are larger between countries at differing levels of development.

3 Firms may not know how to build up the necessary capabilities – learning itself often has to be learned. In a developing country, knowledge of traditional technologies may not be a good base on which to know how to master modern technologies. For a latecomer to a technology, the fact that others have already undergone the learning process is both a benefit and a cost. It is a benefit in that they can borrow from the others' experience (to the extent this is accessible). It is a cost in that they are relatively inefficient during the process (and so have to bear a loss if they compete on open markets). The cost and risk depend on how new the technology is relative to the entrant's base of knowledge, how developed factor markets are, and how fast the technology is changing.

4 Firms cope with these uncertain conditions not by maximising a well-defined function but by developing organisational and managerial routines (Nelson and Winter 1982). These are adapted as firms collect new information, learn from experience and imitate other firms. Learning is path-dependent and cumulative.

5 The learning process is highly technology-specific, since technologies differ in their learning requirements. Some technologies are more embodied in

equipment while others have greater tacit elements. Process technologies (like chemicals) are more embodied than engineering technologies (machinery or automobiles), and demand different (often less) effort. Capabilities built up in one activity are not easily transferable to another. Different technologies involve different breadth of skills and knowledge, some needing a narrow range of specialization and others a wide range.

6 Different technologies have different degrees of dependence on outside sources of knowledge or information, such as other firms, consultants, capital goods suppliers or technology institutions.

7 Capability building occurs at all levels – shopfloor, process or product engineering, quality management, maintenance, procurement, inventory control, outbound logistics and relations with other firms and institutions. Innovation in the conventional sense of formal R&D is at one end of the spectrum of technological activity; it does not exhaust it. However, R&D does become important as more complex technologies are used; R&D is needed just for efficient absorption.

8 Technological development can take place to different depths. The attainment of a minimum level of operational capability (know-how) is essential to all activity. This may not lead to the development of deeper capabilities, an understanding of the principles of the technology (know-why): this requires a discrete strategy to invest in deepening. The deeper the levels of technological capabilities aimed at, the higher the cost, risk and duration involved. It is possible for an enterprise to become efficient at the know-how level and stay there, but this is not optimal for its long-term capability development. It will remain dependent on other firms for all major improvements to its technologies, and con-strained in what it can obtain and use. The development of know-why allows firms to select better the technologies they need, lower the costs of buying those technologies, realize more value by adding their own knowledge, and develop autonomous innovative capabilities.

9 Technological learning is rife with externalities and inter-linkages. It is driven by direct interactions with suppliers of inputs or capital goods, com-petitors, customers, consultants, and technology suppliers. Others are with firms in unrelated industries, technology institutes, extension services, uni-versities, industry associations and training institutions. Where information and skill flows are particularly dense in a set of related activities, clusters of industries emerge, with collective learning for the group as a whole.

10 Technological interactions occur within a country and abroad. Imported technology provides the most important input into technological learning in developing countries. Since technologies change constantly, more-over, access to foreign sources of innovation is vital to continued tech-nological progress. Technology import is not, however, a substitute for indigenous capability development – the efficacy with which imported technologies are used depends on local efforts. Similarly, not all modes of technology import are equally conducive to indigenous learning. Much depends on how the technology is packaged with complementary fac-tors, whether or not it is available from other sources, how fast it is changing, how developed local capabilities are, and the policies adopted to stimulate transfer and deepening.

Source: Lall (2001).

Technology has 'tacit' elements that need the user to invest in new skills, routines, and technical and organizational information. Such investment faces market and institutional failures whose remedies require intervention. Many interventions *have* to be selective because technologies differ inherently in their tacit features and externalities. Industrial success in the developing world – and indeed in the presently developed world in its early phases of industrialization – is thus traceable to how effectively governments overcome these market and institutional failures.

Capability development can face market failures in building *initial capacity* and in *subsequent deepening*. Both need support, functional and selective. Support entails a mixture of policies apart from infant industry protection.[18] Take building initial capacity in new industrial activities. Free markets may not give correct signals for investment in new technologies when there are high, unpredictable learning costs and widespread externalities. This is, in modern garb, the classic case for infant industry protection: classical economists clearly recognized that in the presence of such costs, an industrial latecomer faced an inherent disadvantage compared to those that had undergone the learning process.[19] Add to this the extra costs and disadvantages faced by firms in developing countries – unpredictability, lack of information, weak capital markets, absence of suppliers, poor support institutions, and so on – exposure to full import competition is likely to prevent entry into activities with relatively difficult technologies. Yet these are the technologies that are likely to carry the burden of industrial development and future competitiveness.

Why do interventions have to be *selective*? Offering uniform protection to all activities makes little sense when learning processes and externalities differ by technology, as they inevitably do. In some activities the need for protection is low because the learning period is brief, information easy to get, and externalities limited. In complex activities or those with widespread externalities, newcomers may never enter unless measures are undertaken to promote the activity. The only complex activities where investments may take place without promotion are those based on local natural resources, if the resource advantage is sufficient to offset the learning costs. However, the processing of many resources now calls for strong capabilities; both Africa and Latin America have large resource bases but advanced processing has only taken root in the latter, based on decades of capability-building under import-substitution.

Infant *industry protection is only one part of industrial policy*, and *by itself can be harmful and ineffective*. First, protection cannot succeed if not offset by competitive pressures on firms to invest in capability-building: cushioning the costs of capability-building can remove the incentive for undertaking it. One reason why industrial policy failed in most countries is precisely that this dilemma was not overcome. But it is possible to do so by strengthening domestic competition, setting performance targets and, most effectively, by forcing firms into export markets. Many such measures also have to be *selective*, since the costs of entering export markets differ by product. Thus, differentiated export targets, credits and subsidies were often used in East Asia.

The second reason why industrial policy involves more than protection is the need for *coordination with factor markets*. Firms need new inputs for learning: new skills, technical and market information, risk finance, or infrastructure. Unless factor markets respond to these needs, protection cannot allow firms to reach competitive levels. Factor market interventions also *have to be selective as well as functional*, for three reasons. First, several factor needs are specific to particular activities; if they lack the coordination to meet these needs, interventions are needed to remedy the deficiencies. For instance, the skill needs of electronics may not be fully foreseen by education markets,[20] or the financial needs of emerging new technologies may not be addressed by capital markets. Second, government resources for supporting factor markets are limited, and allocating them among competing uses entails selectivity at a high level (say, between education and other uses). Third, where the government is already targeting particular sectors in product markets, factor markets have to be geared to those activities if the strategy is to succeed.

The *deepening* of capabilities suffers similar problems. The more complex the functions to be undertaken, the higher the costs involved and the greater the coordination required. Getting into production may be easy compared to design, development and innovation. Neoclassical theory accepts that free markets fail to ensure optimal private innovative activity because of imperfect appropriability of information. However, developing countries face an additional problem. It is generally easier to import foreign technologies fully packaged than to develop an understanding of the basic principles involved – the basis of local design and development. 'Internalized' technology transfer takes the form of wholly foreign-owned direct investment. This is an effective and rapid way to access new technology, but it may result in little capability acquisition in the host country apart from production skills.[21] The move from production to innovative activity involves a strategic decision that foreign investors tend to be unwilling to take in developing countries. While some relocation of innovative activity *is* taking place (UNCTAD 2002), it is largely in advanced countries and a few newly-industrializing economies.

Over history most countries that have built strong local innovative capabilities have done it in local firms, often by restricting FDI selectively. Some have done it by stimulating foreign investors to invest in R&D, but this also involved selective intervention. Thus, complete openness to internalized technology imports may not be a good thing if it truncates the process of technological deepening and internalized transfers may have to be subjected to interventions to extract greater technological benefits.

Industrialization Strategies in the Mature East Asian Tigers

There was no generic 'East Asian model'. Each country had a different model within the common context of export orientation, sound macro management and a good base of skills. Each model reflected different objectives and used different interventions. As a result, each had a different pattern of industrial and export growth, reliance on FDI, technological capability and enterprise structure. However, for none was 'getting prices right' sufficient for industrial success. The different objectives are shown in Table 2.

Figure 7 shows recent MVA growth for these four countries, China and industrialized and developing countries for 1980 to 2000. Figure 8 shows manufactured export growth from 1981 to 2000, with very similar patterns except that Singapore marginally outperforms Korea in the 1990s.

Hong Kong was nearest to the neoliberal ideal, combining free trade with an open door policy to FDI. However, its success does not provide many lessons in the virtues of free markets to other countries. Hong Kong had unique initial conditions and its industrial performance, after the initial spurt, was weak. Its initial conditions included a long *entrepôt* tradition, global trading links, established infrastructure of trade and finance, the presence of large British companies (the 'Hongs') with immense spillovers in skills and information, and an influx of entrepreneurs, engineers and technicians (with developed capabilities) from the mainland. This allowed it to launch into light export-based manufacturing: other *entrepôt* economies in the developing world have provided similar environments but not enjoyed similar success. Moreover, the colonial government did intervene to help industry, allocating land to manufacturers and setting up strong support institutions like the Hong Kong Productivity Council, an export promotion agency, a textile design centre and a technical university.

The absence of industrial policy constrained industrial development as capabilities were 'used up'. Hong Kong *started with and stayed with* light activities where learning costs were low. There was progress in terms of product quality and diversification, but little technological deepening, in contrast to Singapore, a smaller *entrepôt* economy with strong industrial policy. Hong Kong de-industrialized as costs rose; manufacturing is now less than 5 per cent of GDP compared to over 25 per cent at the peak. Its manufacturers shifted to other countries, mainly China, and its own exports went into decline in the 1990s. The economy grew slower than the other Tigers, and its main competitive advantage – financial and other services to the mainland – is under threat as China builds its own capabilities.

Table 2. Industrial policy objectives of NIEs

	Deepening industrial structure	Raising local content	FDI strategy	Raising technological effort	Promotion of large local enterprises
Hong Kong	None	None	Passive 'open door'	None except technology support for SMEs	None
Singapore	Very strong push into specialized high skill/tech industry, without protection	None, but subcontracting promotion now started for SMEs	Aggressive targeting and screening of TNCs, direction into high value-added activities	None for local firms, but TNCs targeted to increase R&D	None, but some public sector enterprises enter targeted areas
Taiwan	Strong push into capital, skill- and technology-intensive industry	Strong pressures for raising local content and subcontracting	Screening FDI, entry discouraged where local firms strong. Local technology diffusion pushed	Strong technology support for local R&D and upgrading by SMEs. Government orchestrated high-tech development	Sporadic: to enter heavy industry, mainly by public sector
Korea	Strong push into capital, skill- and technology-intensive industry, especially heavy intermediates and capital goods	Stringent local content rules, creating support industries, protection of local suppliers, subcontracting promotion	FDI kept out unless necessary for technology access or exports, joint ventures and licensing encouraged	Ambitious local R&D in advanced industry, heavy investment in technology infrastructure. Targeting of strategic technologies	Sustained drive to create giant private conglomerates to internalize markets, lead heavy industry, create export brands

Note on abbreviations: SMEs refers to small and medium enterprises, FDI to foreign direct investment, TNCs to multinational corporations, R&D to research and development.

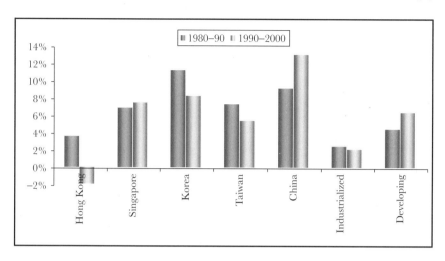

Figure 7. Growth rates of MVA (percentage per year)

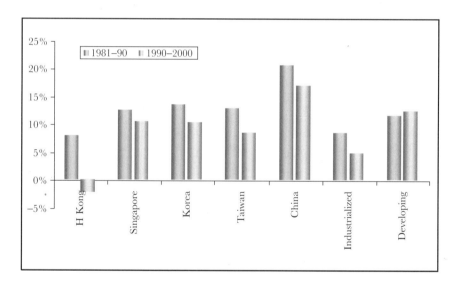

Figure 8. Growth rates of manufactured exports (percentage per year)

Singapore used interventionist policies to promote and deepen industry in a free trade setting, showing how industrial policy takes many forms apart from import protection. With half the population of Hong Kong, even higher wages and a thriving service sector, Singapore did not suffer a similar industrial 'hollowing out'. Its industrial structure deepened steadily over time, allowing it to sustain rapid industrial growth. It relied heavily on TNCs but, unlike Hong Kong, the government targeted activities for promotion and aggressively sought and used FDI as the tool to achieve its objectives (Wong 2003).

Singapore started with a base of capabilities in *entrepôt* trading, ship servicing and petroleum refining. After a decade or so of light industrial activity, the government acted firmly to upgrade the industrial structure. It guided TNCs to higher value-added activities, narrowly specialized and integrated into their global operations. It intervened extensively to create the specific skills needed (Ashton *et al.* 1999), and set up public enterprises to undertake strategic activities where foreign investment was unfeasible or undesirable.

Box 2
Singapore's use of FDI

The Singapore philosophy on foreign investment is that multinationals are to be 'tapped' for the competitive assets they bring to the country. The government's goal is to maximize learning, technological acquisition, rapid movement up the industrial ladder, and the skills and incomes of its working population. To this end it is willing to contribute capital, tax concessions, infrastructure, education and skills training, and a stable and friendly business environment. While the country is well integrated into international production networks in certain sectors, its fortunes are not tied to those of particular multinational companies, which (like local companies) the government refuses to help if they are unable to compete in the rapidly changing local environment and the world market. Thus over time many multinational factories in Singapore have closed their doors – particularly in low-value labour-intensive product lines and processes like simple electronic components and consumer goods – and shut down completely or relocated to neighbouring countries, with the Singapore government's blessing.

The decisions of MNCs about what new technologies to bring into Singapore are strongly influenced by the incentives and direction offered by the government. The Singapore government is the only one in the region which, like many governments in Western countries, gives grants to firms for complying with specified requirements. These are often to do with entering particular (advanced) technologies. The government supports these incentives, acting in consultation with MNCs (or anticipating through proactive planning) by providing the necessary skilled manpower.

In many instances, it is the *speed and flexibility* of government response that gives Singapore the competitive edge compared with other competing host countries. In particular, the boom in investment in offshore production by MNCs in the electronics industry in the 1970s and the early 1980s created a major opportunity. The government responded by ensuring that all supporting industries, transport and communication infrastructure, as well as the relevant skill development programmes, were in place to attract these industries to Singapore.

This concentration of resources helps Singapore to achieve significant *agglomeration economies* and hence first-mover advantages, and has allowed it to set up many advanced electronics-related industries. An example is the disk-drive industry, where all the major US disk-drive-makers have located their assembly plants in Singapore. These industries demanded not only electronics components and PCB assembly support, but also various precision-engineering-related supporting industries such as tool and die, plastic injection moulding, electroplating and others. These supporting industries have been actively promoted by the government as part of a 'clustering' approach to ensure the competitiveness of the downstream industries.

As labour and land costs have risen, the Singapore government has encouraged MNCs to reconfigure their operations on a regional basis, relocating the lower-end operations in other countries and making Singapore their regional headquarters to undertake the higher-end manufacturing and other functions. This has often led MNCs to set up regional marketing, distribution, service and R&D centres to service the ASEAN and Asia-Pacific region. To promote such reconfiguration, various incentives have been offered under the regional headquarters scheme, the international procurement office scheme, the international logistics centre scheme, and the approved trader scheme. There are now some 4,000 foreign firms located in Singapore, about half of them in regional headquarters. Some 80 of these regional headquarters have an average expenditure in Singapore of around US $18 million per year

The management of industrial policy and FDI targeting has been centralized in the Economic Development Board (EDB), part of the Ministry of Trade and Industry (MTI) that gave overall strategic direction. EDB was endowed with the authority to coordinate all activities relating to industrial competitiveness and FDI, and given the resources to hire qualified and well-paid professional staff (essential to manage discretionary policy efficiently and honestly). Over time the agency has become the global benchmark for FDI promotion and approval procedures. Its ability to coordinate the needs of foreign investors with measures to raise local skills and capabilities has also been critical – and a feature that many other FDI agencies lack. The government conducts periodic strategic and competitiveness studies to chart the industrial evolution and upgrading of the economy: the latest was published in 1998 (Ministry of Trade and Industry). Unlike many other countries, MNC leaders are actively involved in the strategy formulation process and are given a strong stake in the development of the economy.

Since its 1991 Strategic Economic Plan, the government has focused its strategy around *industrial clusters*. The term 'cluster' was not used to denote geographical agglomerations (though in view of the tiny size of the economy all industry is in fact very tightly concentrated) but inter-linked activities in a value chain. In the manufacturing sector the cluster programme (called 'Manufacturing 2000'), the government analyses the strengths and weaknesses of leading industrial clusters, and undertakes FDI promotion and local capability/institution building to promote their future competitiveness. One explicit objective of the programme is to avoid the kind of industrial 'hollowing out' experienced by Hong Kong (and many other industrial countries).

This strategy has allowed it, for instance, to become the leading centre for hard-disk-drive production in the world, with considerable local links with advanced suppliers and R&D institutions. In 1994, the government set up an S $1 billion Cluster Development Fund (expanded to S $2 billion later) to support specific clusters like a new wafer fabrication park. It also launched a Co-Investment Programme to provide official equity financing for joint ventures and for strategic ventures, not just in Singapore but also overseas (as long as this serves its competitive interests). The EDB can take equity stakes to support cluster development by addressing critical gaps and improving local enterprises.

Such heavy reliance on FDI reduced the initial need for local technological effort. Over time, however, the government induced TNCs to establish R&D and foster innovation in local enterprises (Wong 2003). This strategy worked well, and Singapore now has the third-highest ratio in the developing world of enterprise-financed R&D in GDP, after Korea and Taiwan (UNIDO 2002).

The two larger Tigers, *Korea* and *Taiwan*, adopted the most interventionist strategies, spanning product markets (trade and domestic competition) and factor markets (skills, finance, FDI, technology transfer, infrastructure and support institutions). Their export drive was led by local firms, backed by a host of policies, including FDI restrictions, that allowed them to develop impressive technological capabilities. The domestic market was not exposed to free trade; quantitative and tariff measures were used to give infant industries 'space' to develop capabilities. The deleterious effects of protection were offset by strong export incentives.

Korea went much further in building heavy industry than Taiwan. To compress its entry into complex, scale and technology-intensive activities, its interventions were far more detailed and pervasive. Korea relied primarily on capital goods imports, technology licensing and OEM agreements to acquire technology. It used reverse engineering, adaptation and product development to build upon these arm's length technology imports and develop its own capabilities (Amsden 1989; Westphal 1990). Its R&D expenditures are now the highest in the developing world, and ahead of all but a handful of leading OECD countries. Korea accounts for some 53 per cent of the developing world's total enterprise-financed R&D (UNIDO 2002).

One of the pillars of Korean strategy, and one that marks it off from the other Tigers (but mirrors Japan), was the deliberate creation of large private conglomerates, the *chaebol*. The *chaebol* were hand-picked from successful exporters and were given various subsidies and privileges, including the restriction of TNC entry, in return for furthering a strategy of setting up capital and technology-intensive activities geared to export markets. The rationale for fostering size was obvious: in view of deficient markets for capital, skills, technology and even infrastructure, large and diversified firms could internalize many of their functions. They could undertake the cost and risk of absorbing very complex technologies (without a heavy reliance on FDI), further develop it by their own R&D, set up world-scale facilities and create their own brand names and distribution networks.

This was a costly and high-risk strategy. The risks were contained by the strict discipline imposed by the government: export performance, vigorous domestic competition and deliberate interventions to rationalize the industrial structure. The government also undertook various measures to encourage the diffusion of technology, putting pressures on the *chaebol* to establish supplier

Box 3
Managing Korean industrial strategy

Korean industrial targeting and promotion was pragmatic and flexible, and developed in concert with private industry. Moreover, only a relatively small number of activities were supported at a given time, and the effects of protection were offset by strong export orientation (below). These features strongly differentiate its interventions from those in typical import substituting countries, where infant industry protection was sweeping and open-ended, non-selective, inflexible and designed without consultation with industry.

One of the leading authorities on Korean industrial policy, Larry Westphal (1997) describes it thus: 'Since the economy's take-off in the early 1960s, the hallmark of the government's approach to developing the business sector has been its pragmatic flexibility in responding in an appropriate manner to changing circumstances. Several instances demonstrate this well: the means used at the outset to abolish the pervasive rent-seeking mentality that had been engendered by a decade of dependence on US foreign assistance; and the way that rampant pessimism about its growth prospects was overcome through sensible planning between government and business, the success of which soon created conditions that stimulated radical changes in the mode of economic planning.

'Another central feature has been the government's ability to adapt policy approaches borrowed from other countries. Here notable examples include the placement of the budget authority in the planning ministry and the entire apparatus of export promotion. But the most important characteristic of the government's approach has undoubtedly been its generally non-restrictive stance. More important, where many other governments have constrained business activities not in line with their development priorities, the government has practised 'benign neglect' rather than repression. As a result, entrepreneurial initiatives have identified significant business areas that were later incorporated into the government's priorities.'

Export promotion was a compelling system to force firms into export activity. Korea's export targeting system is well known. Targeting was practised at the industry, product and firm levels, with the targets set by the firms and industry associations in concert with the government. There were monthly meetings between top government officials (chaired by the President himself) and leading exporters.[22] These targets were also enforced by several punitive measures: access to subsidised credit and import licences; income tax audits; and a number of other measures of suasion, publicity and prizes. On a long-term basis, moreover, bureaucrats were held responsible for meeting export targets in their respective industries, and had to keep in close touch with enterprises and markets. These measures were supported by regular studies of each major export industry, with information on competitors, technological trends, market conditions, and so on.

networks. Apart from the direct interventions to support local enterprises, the government provided selective and functional support by building a massive technology infrastructure and creating general and technical skills. Korea today has the highest rate of university enrolment in the world, and produces more engineers each year than the whole of India. Its enrolments in technical subjects at the tertiary level come to an appreciable percentage of its total population, over twice the ratio in the OECD.

Even more striking than its creation of high-level skills was its promotion of industrial R&D. Enterprise-financed R&D in Korea as a percentage of GDP is the second-highest in the world, after Sweden, and exceeds such technological giants as the USA, Japan and Germany. Such R&D has grown dramatically in the past two and a half decades as a result of the promotion of the *chaebol*, export orientation, incentives, skill availability and government collaboration. *All this was an integral part of its selective industrial policy.*

Taiwan's industrial policy encompassed import protection, directed credit, selectivity on FDI, support for indigenous skill and technology development and strong export promotion (Wade 2000). While this resembles Korean strategy in many ways, there were important differences. Taiwan did not promote giant private conglomerates, nor did it attempt a similar drive into heavy industry. Taiwanese industry remained largely composed of SMEs, and, given the disadvantages to technological activity inherent in small size, it supported industry by a variety of R&D collaboration, innovation inducements and extension assistance. Taiwan has probably the developing world's most advanced system of technology support for SMEs, and one of the best anywhere. But it also built a large public sector in manufacturing, to set up facilities where private firms were unwilling or unable to do so.

In the early years of industrialisation, the Taiwanese government attracted FDI into activities in which domestic industry was weak, and used a variety of means to ensure that TNCs transferred their technology to local suppliers. Like Korea, Taiwan directed FDI into areas where local firms lacked world-class capabilities. The government played a very active role in helping SMEs to locate, purchase, diffuse and adapt new foreign technologies. Where necessary, the government itself entered into joint ventures – for instance, to get into technologically very difficult areas such as semiconductors and aerospace (Mathews and Cho 1999).

The contrast between the success of industrial policy in the Tigers and its failures elsewhere suggests that there is no justification for the general neoliberal case against selective interventions. It shows that the outcome depends not on *whether* but *how* governments intervene. On 'how to intervene', the differences between import-substituting strategies and those used in the Tigers lay in:

- Selectivity (picking a few activities at a time) rather than promoting all industrial activities indiscriminately and in an open-ended way;
- Picking activities and functions that offered significant technological benefits and linkages;

Box 4
Taiwanese industrial targeting

In Taiwan early trade policies had 'extensive quantitative restrictions and high tariff rates [that] shielded domestic consumer goods from foreign competition. To take advantage of abundant labour, the government subsidized light industries, particularly textiles' (World Bank 1993, pp.131–133). As import substitution started to run out of steam, by 1960 'a multiple exchange-rate system was replaced with a unitary rate, and appreciation was avoided. Tariffs and import controls were gradually reduced, especially for inputs to export. In addition, the Bank of Taiwan offered low-interest loans to exporters. The government also hired the Stanford Research Institute to identify promising industries for export promotion and development. On the basis of Taiwan's comparative advantage in low-cost labour and existing technical capabilities, the institute chose plastics, synthetic fibres and electronic components. Other industries subsequently promoted included apparel, consumer electronics, home appliances, watches and clocks' (ibid.).

In the 1970s the Taiwanese government again drew upon foreign advice, now from consultants Arthur D. Little, to upgrade the industrial structure and enter into secondary import substitution. These interventions included the setting up of 'capital-intensive, heavy and petrochemical industries to increase production of raw materials and intermediates for the use of export industries'. In the 1980s, as its light exports lost competitiveness, Taiwan's government 'again moved to restructure the economy. After extensive consultation with domestic and foreign advisers, the government decided to focus on high-technology industries: information, bio-technology, electro-optics, machinery and precision instruments, and environmental technology industries.'

The shift to a high-technology economy necessitated the close coordination of industrial, financial, science and technology, and human resource policies. 'Individual tariff rates still varied widely, with widespread quantitative restrictions in use: the use of these protective instruments was made conditional on prices moving towards international levels in 2–5 years. The average legal tariff rate in 1984 was as high as 31 per cent, higher if additional charges are added; this is higher than the 34 per cent prevalent in the developing world' (Wade 1990, p.127).

Mathews (2001) describes one of the most successful and distinctive recent tools of industrial policy used in Taiwan, *R&D consortia*. 'Unlike the case of many of the collaborative arrangements between established firms in the USA, Europe or Japan, where mutual risk reduction is frequently the driving influence, in the case of Taiwan it is technological learning, upgrading and catch-up industry creation that is the object of the collaborative exercises. Taiwan's R&D consortia were formed hesitantly in the 1980s, but flourished in the 1990s as institutional forms were found which encourage firms to cooperate in raising their technological levels to the point where they can compete successfully in advanced technology industries. Many of these alliances or consortia are in the information technology sectors, covering personal computers, work stations, multiprocessors and multimedia, as well as a range of consumer products and telecommunications and data-switching systems and products. But they have also emerged in other sectors such as automotive engines, motor cycles, electric vehicles, and now in the services and financial sector as well. Several such alliances could be counted in Taiwan in the late 1990s, bringing together firms and public sector research institutes, with the added organizational input of trade associations, and catalytic financial assistance from the government. The alliances form an essential component of Taiwan's national system of innovation.

'Taiwan's high technology industrial success rests on a capacity to leverage resources and pursue a strategy of rapid catch-up. Its firms tap into advanced markets through various forms of contract manufacturing, and are able to leverage new levels of technological capability from these arrangements. This is an advanced form of "technological learning", in which the most significant players have not been giant firms (as in Japan or Korea), but small and medium-sized enterprises whose entrepreneurial flexibility and adaptability have been the key to their success. Underpinning this success are the efforts of public sector research and development institutes, such as Taiwan's Industrial Technology Research Institute (ITRI). Since its founding in 1973 ITRI and its laboratories have acted as a prime vehicle for the leveraging of advanced technologies from abroad, and for their rapid diffusion or dissemination to Taiwan's firms ... This cooperation between public and private sectors, to overcome the scale disadvantages of Taiwan's small firms, is a characteristic feature of the country's technological upgrading strategies, and the creation of new high technology sectors such as semiconductors.

'It is Taiwan's distinctive R&D consortia that demonstrate most clearly the power of this public-private cooperation, in one successful industry intervention after another. Taiwan's current dominance of mobile (laptop) PCs, for example, rests at least in part on a public-private-sector-led consortium that rushed a product to world markets in 1991. Taiwan's strong performance in communications products such as data switches, which are used in PC networks, similarly rests on a consortium which worked with Taiwan's public sector industry research organization, ITRI, to produce a switch to match the Ethernet standard, in 1992–93. When IBM introduced a new PC based on its PowerPC microprocessor in June 1995, Taiwan firms exhibited a range of computing products based on the same processor just one day later. Again this achievement rested on a carefully nurtured R&D consortium involving both IBM and Motorola, joint developers of the PowerPC microprocessor, as external parties. Taiwan is emerging as a player in the automotive industry, particularly in the expanding China market, driven by its development of a 1.2-litre 4-valve engine. Again, this is the product of a public-private collaborative research endeavour involving three companies, which have now jointly created the Taiwan Engine Company to produce the product. Thus, the R&D consortium is an inter-firm organizational form that Taiwan has adapted to its own purposes as a vehicle for catch-up industry creation and technological upgrading. The micro-dynamics of the operation of these alliances or consortia is therefore a matter of some substantial interest.'

Sources: Lall (1996), Mathews (2001), World Bank (1993).

- Forcing early entry into world markets, using exports to discipline bureaucrats and enterprises;
- Giving the lead role in productive activity to private enterprises but using public enterprises as needed to fill gaps and enter exceptionally risky areas;

- Investing massively in skill creation, infrastructure and support institutions, all carefully coordinated with interventions in product markets;
- Using selectivity in FDI to help build local capabilities (by restricting FDI or imposing conditions on it) or to tap into dynamic high-technology value chains;
- Centralizing strategic decision-making in competent authorities who could take an economy-wide view and enforce policies on different ministries;
- Improving the quality of bureaucracy and governance, collecting huge amounts of relevant information and learning lessons from technological leaders;
- Ensuring policy flexibility and learning, so that mistakes could be corrected *en route*, and involving the private sector in strategy formulation and implementation (Lall and Teubal 1998).

The list could be longer but it suffices to show that there are *many ways to design and implement* industrial policy. The analysis offers important lessons on what to do now. There are also *many levels* of selectivity, and adopting 'industrial policy' does not mean that the country has to copy the comprehensive and detailed interventions used in Korea or Singapore. In fact, the new setting may provide a case for lower degrees of selectivity in some areas. At the same time, the rigours imposed by globalization and technical change may well strengthen the case for more intervention in others.

Industrial Policy for the New Era

What difference do technical change and globalization make to the policies that developing countries need to promote industrialization?

Technical change: the rapid spread of information technology, the shrinking of economic distance and the skill and institutional needs of new technologies have made the competitive environment more demanding. Minimum entry levels in terms of skill, competence, infrastructure and 'connectivity' are higher. All these raise the need for support of learning by local enterprises. Low wages matter for unskilled labour, but they matter less. Only natural resources give an independent competitive advantage, but only for extraction; subsequent processing needs competitive capabilities.

The policy needs of capability-building have not changed much. They are *direct* – the infant industry case to provide 'space' for enterprises to master new technologies without incurring enormous and unpredictable losses – and *indirect*, to ensure that skill, capital, technology and infrastructure markets meet their needs. There is also a need to *coordinate learning* across enterprises and activities, when these are linked in the production chain and imports cannot substitute effectively for local inputs. At the same time, technical change makes it necessary to *provide more access to international technology markets*; it also makes it more *difficult to anticipate which activities are likely to succeed*. The information needs of industrial policy rise in tandem with technological change and complexity. The greater complexity of technology does not make selectivity unfeasible. Detailed targeting of technologies, products or enterprises may be more difficult because of the pace of change, but targeting at higher levels is feasible and more necessary. Technological progress may actually make industrial policy easier in some respects: information on technological trends and markets is more readily available, more is known about the policies in successful countries, and benchmarking is easier.

The *neoliberal alternative*, leaving capability development to free market forces, is hardly more promising. It can result in slow and truncated technological development, with gaps between countries rising. Some upgrading does take place, but is slower and more limited than with promotion. Given the speed at which technologies are changing and path-dependence and cumulativeness in capability-building are increasing, it can lead to latecomers being mired in low growth traps.

With weak local capabilities, industrialization has to be more dependent on FDI. But FDI cannot drive industrial growth without local capabilities, for several reasons:

- FDI concentrates in technology and marketing intensive activities and does not cover large areas of manufacturing with mundane skill, branding and technological requirements (the heartland of industrial growth in latecomers). If local enterprises are not capable, the industrial sector cannot sustain lopsided growth in the long term.
- Attracting manufacturing FDI into complex activities needs strong local capabilities, without which TNCs cannot launch efficient operations.
- Retaining an industrial base with a strong foreign presence needs rapidly rising capabilities as wages rise and skill demands change.
- FDI is attracted increasingly to efficient agglomerations or clusters of industrial activity, again calling for strong local capabilities.
- The cumulative nature of capabilities means that once FDI takes root in particular locations, it becomes difficult to newcomers to break in, particularly in the more complex activities and functions. First-mover advantages mean that late-latecomers face increasing entry costs – without strong local capabilities they will find it difficult to overcome these costs.

It is also difficult to see how host countries that have FDI can tap its potential fully without such strategies as local content rules, incentives for deepening technologies and functions, inducements to export, and so on. Performance requirements have been deployed inefficiently in many countries, but, as with protection, they have also been used very effectively.

Globalization: The spread of integrated production systems makes it *more difficult and risky* to take the autonomous route of Korea or Taiwan. It is much easier for countries to attract segments of TNC activity and build upon these rather than to develop local capabilities. In any case, local firms today would find it extremely hard to enter export markets emulating the OEM contractors from Korea and Taiwan. All the later entrants into globalized systems, from Malaysia to Mexico and Costa Rica, have gone the FDI route. As FDI regimes are more liberal, TNCs are also less willing to part with valuable technologies to independent firms.

Thus, *globalization does not do away with the need for all selective industrial policies*; it only reduces the scope and raises the potential cost of some. FDI is complementary to local enterprises and capabilities after a certain level of development. Strong local capabilities raise the possibility of attracting high-value systems and of capturing skill and technology spillovers from them; these capabilities need selective policies. Moreover, attracting export-oriented FDI increasingly requires selective promotion and targeting; the most effective targeting is undertaken by advanced economies (Loewendahl 2001).

There is a more fundamental issue: how far *can* globalized production systems spread across the developing world? Fragmentation is feasible only when production processes can be separated in technological and geographical terms and where differences in labour cost affect the location of each process. In low-technology activities, it is strong in clothing, footwear, sports goods and toys; in high-technology, it is strong in electronics; in medium-technology industry, it is strong in automobiles (but the weight of the product and its high capability requirements mean that it only goes to a few proximate, relatively industrialized locations). This leaves a broad range of industries in which FDI and exports are not driven by global production systems.

Where such systems exist, they are likely to continue relocating to lower-wage countries in only some activities. Low-technology industries are the best candidates because of low entry requirements, but here the abolition of the Agreement on Textiles and Clothing (formerly MFA) next year raises the risk that garment production will shift back to East Asia. It is indicative that other labour-intensive systems that do not have trade quotas driving location – footwear, toys, and the like – have not looked for production bases in these regions.

In high-technology systems like electronics the picture is different. Entry levels are higher than in the late 1960s when the industry first moved to South-East Asia. Production techniques have advanced and manufacturing systems have 'settled down' in their new locations, with established facilities, logistics, infrastructure and support institutions. If these systems grow, they are likely to cluster around established sites rather than spread to new, less-developed ones. Entry by newcomers *is* possible, of course: China is the obvious case – but most poor countries lack the industrial capability, size, location and other advantages of China. And most cannot use selective industrial policy to attract hi-tech FDI and induce it to source local inputs in the way that China does (and is likely to continue after WTO rules come into play). The prospects of complex global production systems spreading to most of Africa, LAC, South Asia or MENA are fairly dim.

New systems may emerge to catalyse the growth of FDI-driven production in new sites but they may not transform competitiveness in poorer economies. Those in resource-based activities are likely to be demanding in skills, technology and infrastructure. Industrialization in the developing world thus continues to face many of the same constraints that it did before integrated systems. The need to foster the development of local capabilities remains the bottom line, and globalization offers an alternative route only in some activities, to some countries, and even to these only for some time.

The Desirable, the Practical and the Permissible

WTO rules do not prohibit all selective interventions, only those that affect trade. However, other forces making for liberalization are less formal and rule-based (structural adjustment programmes, bilateral trade and investment agreements and pressures by rich countries) and they are as powerful. Together they constitute a formidable web of constraints on governments mounting industrial policy. Some constraints may be useful and may prevent the more egregious forms of intervention that have led to inefficiency, rent-seeking and technological sloth. They are also beneficial to countries with strong capabilities developed behind protective barriers: India, Brazil or China should accelerate liberalization if they can combine this with a strategy to restructure activities and enter promising new activities.

At this time, it is possible to selectively promote skill formation, technology support, innovation financing, FDI promotion and targeting, infrastructure development and other general subsidies that do not affect trade. These tools – and some not in line with the spirit of the rules (US tariff protection on steel) – are used vigorously by industrialized countries. Most semi-industrial countries also use them, but the less-developed countries generally do not (on weaknesses in technology support in Africa, see Lall and Pietrobelli 2002). The critical issues facing the development community in industrialization are: *Is the degree of policy freedom left to developing countries sufficient to promote healthy industrial development?*

If East Asia offers lessons for industrial policy, will the new environment allow them to be implemented? Without strong policy intervention, will persistence with liberalization suffice to drive industrialization?

The answer is 'probably not'. The permissible tools are probably not enough to foster the rapid development of technological capabilities. They may force poor countries with weak industrial bases to become over-dependent on FDI to drive industrial development. This cannot meet a major part of industrialization needs. Even countries able to plug into global production systems can only do so as providers of the low-level labour services; subsequent deepening may be held back by constrictions on capability development. For developing countries with a capability base the rules can deter diversification into new technologies and activities. In general, the rules threaten to *freeze comparative advantage* in areas where capabilities exist at the time of liberalization, yielding a relatively short period of competitive growth before the stock is 'used up'. Subsequent upgrading of competitiveness is likely to be slower than if governments had the tools to intervene selectively.

While local capabilities matter more than ever in an era of globalization, this does *not* mean that all developing countries can replicate the selective policies of Singapore, Korea or Taiwan. What it means is drawing appropriate lessons from their experience and adapting them to local circumstances.

- The *first* stage of a desirable international policy regime would be to provide policymakers with an objective and detailed analysis of what successful countries did to build industrial capabilities.
- The *second* would be to create greater 'policy space' for industrial policy.
- The *third* stage would be to help develop the capability to mount industrial policy. An integral part of industrial policy must be the building of the administrative competence, information and insulation that governments need.
- The *fourth* stage would be to help devise strategies appropriate to each country. Creating more policy space and strengthening government capabilities should not mean returning to the 'bad old days' of import substitution. It should be used for careful and flexible policymaking, with clear targets and checks aimed at specific forms of technology development.

If this seems a forlorn hope, consider the alternative of continued wholesale liberalization, which would support the strong and penalize the weak. Globalization by itself will not be able to catalyse industrial development. There is enough evidence that well-designed industrial policy can transform economic prospects. The development community should accept this, provide the 'space' for policy and help countries to mount it – not deny its usefulness and practicability.

Notes

I am grateful to Larry Westphal for discussions and detailed comments on an earlier draft, to Robert Wade for sending me pre-publication copies of papers on the issues addressed here, and to Manuel Albaladejo for help in collecting the data.

1 For an interchange based on this recommendation, see Wood (ed.) 2003. Rodrik (2001) raises similar issues.
2 For a description of the categories and the rationale behind the classification see Lall (2001a).
3 The international fragmentation of value chains has, for economic reasons, gone furthest in activities with discrete and separable production processes and high-value products. Electronics is the best example, placing production in several countries, each site specializing in a process or function according to its labour costs, skills, logistics, and so on (Sturgeon 2002). The segmentation of software, business process services and other IT-based activities like call centres is another manifestation of this phenomenon outside manufacturing. Fragmentation goes beyond the spread of transnational companies (TNCs). It encompasses the closer integration of national value chains under several governance systems, with direct ownership by TNCs being at one end and loose buying relationships at the other (Gereffi et al. 2001; Humphrey and Schmitz 2001).
4 No new protection can be offered to products for which members have 'bound' their tariffs, although if actual tariffs are lower than bound tariffs they can be raised. Export processing zones may come under the purview of the subsidies ban in the future (LDCs are exempt so far).
5 General subsidies that do not create a cost advantage for identifiable activities may not be actionable. Only subsidies given to particular activities or locations that create such an advantage are subject to potential sanctions.
6 Local content rules are actionable if there are specific subsidies or incentives linked to achieving the prescribed levels. All countries, regardless of income levels, are now subject to this restriction.
7 For a comprehensive analysis, see UNCTAD (2003).
8 The WTO Agreement on Subsidies and Countervailing Duties may also affect traditional means of supporting technological activity by subsidies. Although the Agreement excludes 'fundamental research' from its actionable provisions (i.e. governments may still subsidize research), the text leaves scope for interpreting what the limits of this are. In any case, R&D now comes under WTO scrutiny, and subsidies for research deemed non-fundamental could be limited in the future.
9 Most East Asian economies used infant industry protection, export subsidies and targets, credit allocation, local content rules and so on to build their industrial capabilities, disciplining the process by strong export orientation (Amsden 1989; Stiglitz 1996; Wade 1990; Westphal 2002; World Bank 1993). There were strategic differences. Singapore, the Republic of Korea and Taiwan Province of China invested massively in human capital (particularly technical skills), fostered local R&D and built strong support institutions (Lall 1996 and 2001a). They tapped FDI in different ways, Singapore by plugging into global production systems and the other two by drawing on its technologies via arm's length means like licensing, copying and original equipment manufacturing. The second-tier Tigers like Malaysia, Thailand, Indonesia and the Philippines relied more

heavily on FDI in export processing enclaves and less on indigenous capabilities; their export success was driven by global value chains, particularly in electronics. China combined different strategies, some similar to its neighbours and others, like public enterprise restructuring, uniquely its own (Lall and Albaladejo 2003). The region as a whole liberalized cautiously and has retained a significant role for the state. As Stiglitz says in the new Human Development Report, 'China and other East Asian economies have not followed the Washington consensus. They were slow to remove tariff barriers, and China still has not fully liberalised its capital account. Though the countries of East Asia "globalized", they used industrial and trade policies to promote exports and global technology transfers, against the advice of the international economic institutions' (UNDP 2003, p. 80).

10 In the first phase, LAC, in common with other developing regions, relied heavily on protected import-substitution, sheltering enterprises from international competition but failing to offset this with incentives or pressures to export. It did little to attract export-oriented FDI (in EPZs) and so missed the surge in global production systems in electronics. It did not deepen local technological activity (by encouraging R&D) or develop the new skills needed for emerging technologies. In concert with widespread macroeconomic (and in some cases political) turbulence, this meant that LAC failed to develop a broad base of industrial capabilities that would drive competitiveness as it liberalized. As a high-wage region, LAC needed competitive advantages in complex activities to offset wage disadvantage vis-à-vis Asia. Despite its tradition of entrepreneurship and base of skills, it failed to foster the necessary capabilities. There were exceptions, such as the automotive industry in the larger economies and resource-based activities more generally, but many such activities are not growing rapidly in world trade. LAC failed to raise export market shares rapidly, the exception being Mexico, due to NAFTA than to strategy.

11 In the second (liberalization) phase, policy reform in LAC was rapid and sweeping, with no strategy to foster competitive capabilities and target promising activities. Again, there were exceptions, including the auto industry (restructured with the help of complementation programmes, banned under new WTO rules), agro-based exports in Chile or national 'champions' like Embraer in Brazil, but the lack of industrial strategy meant that the region failed to catalyse export dynamism. Its main growth was in resource-based sectors where it largely exploited static advantages Some other developing regions that also used import substitution strategies liberalized more slowly and carefully – India is a good example – and did better in terms of MVA growth (but almost as poorly in terms of export competitiveness).

12 The objections to the strong neoliberal position came from such authors as Amsden (1989), Lall (1992), Pack and Westphal (1986), Wade (1990) and Westphal (1982 and 1990).

13 The strong neoliberal stance was that *no* markets failed and that there was no role for the government apart from providing basic public goods and a stable setting for market-driven activity. For a critique of the World Bank (1993) publication, see Lall (1996), and for a recent restatement of the moderate neoclassical position, see Noland and Pack (2003).

14 Neoclassical economists admit the possibility of market failure arising from such textbook cases as monopoly, public goods and some externalities, although they tend to treat failures as special cases rather than the rule. The market failures that may call for selective interventions are capital market deficiencies, scale economies and externalities arising

from the imperfect appropriability of investments in knowledge, technology, and skills. However, the admission that these theoretical possibilities exist does not translate into recommendations that government actually mount selective policies to overcome them (as in the World Bank, 1993). Moreover, the neglect of firm-level learning processes (below) means that the list of market failures remains incomplete – the most critical ones for developing countries are ignored. For a longer discussion, see Lall and Teubal (1998).

15 Wade, in the introduction to the forthcoming new edition of his path-breaking book of industrial policy in Taiwan, *Governing the Market*, says: 'The remarkable thing about the core Washington Consensus package is the gulf between the confidence with which it is promulgated and the strength of supporting evidence, historical or contemporary. There is virtually no good evidence that the creation of efficient, rent-free markets coupled with efficient, corruption-free public sectors is even close to being a necessary or sufficient condition for a dynamic capitalist economy. Almost all now-developed countries went through stages of industrial assistance policy before the capabilities of their firms reached the point where a policy of (more or less) free trade was declared to be in the national interest. Britain was protectionist when it was trying to catch up with Holland. Germany was protectionist when trying to catch up with Britain. The United States was protectionist when trying to catch up with Britain and Germany, right up to the end of the World War II. Japan was protectionist for most of the twentieth century up to the 1970s, Korea and Taiwan to the 1990s. Hong Kong and Singapore are the great exceptions on the trade front, in that they did have free trade and they did catch up – but they are city-states and not to be treated as economic countries. In Europe some countries abutting fast-growing centres of accumulation were also exceptions, thanks to the "ink-blot" effect. But by and large, countries that have caught up with the club of wealthy industrial countries have tended to follow the prescription of Friedrich List, the German catch-up theorist writing in the 1840s: "In order to allow freedom of trade to operate naturally, the less advanced nation [read: Germany] must first be raised by artificial measures to that stage of cultivation to which the English nation has been artificially elevated"' (Wade 2003). For a longer historical perspective, see Reinert (1995).

16 See Lall (1992, 1996, 2001), Westphal (2002), UNIDO (2002).

17 In his analysis of East Asian success Stiglitz (1996) argues that '... whenever information was imperfect or markets were incomplete, government could devise interventions that filled in for these interventions and that could make everyone better off. *Because information was never perfect and markets never complete, these results completely undermined the standard theoretical basis for relying on the market mechanism.* Similarly the standard models ignored changes in technology; for a variety of reasons markets may under-invest in research and development ... Because developing economies have underdeveloped (missing) markets and imperfect information and because the development process is associated with acquiring new technology (new information), these reservations about the adequacy of market mechanisms may be particularly relevant to developing countries' (Stiglitz 1996, p. 156, emphasis added).

18 See the contributions by Wade and Lall in Wood (ed.) (2003).

19 On the case for infant industry protection John Stuart Mill, the most powerful advocate of free trade in classical economic thought, says: 'The only case in which, on mere principles of political economy, protecting duties can be defensible, is when they are imposed temporarily (especially in a young and rising nation) in the hopes of naturalising a foreign industry, in itself perfectly suitable to the circumstances of the country. The superiority of one country over another in a branch of production often arises only from having begun

it sooner. There may be no inherent advantage on one part, or disadvantage in another, but only a *present superiority of acquired skill and experience* … But it cannot be expected that individuals should, at their own risk, or rather to their certain loss, introduce a new manufacture, and bear the burden of carrying on until the producers have been educated to the level of those with whom the processes are traditional. *A protective duty, continued for a reasonable time, might sometimes be the least inconvenient mode in which the nation can tax itself for the support of such an experiment.* But it is essential that the protection should be confined to cases in which there is good ground for assurance that the industry which it fosters will after a time be able to dispense with it; nor should the domestic producers ever be allowed to expect that it will be continued to them beyond the time necessary for a fair trial of what they are capable of accomplishing' (Mill 1940, p. 922, italics added). The nineteenth century saw intense debates, particularly in the USA, on the need for infant industry protection, and most early industrializing countries used the tool extensively.

20 On the selectivity of education and training policies in East Asia, and their intimate relationship to industrial policy more narrowly defined, see Ashton *et al.* (1999). Also see Narula (2003).

21 TNCs also have to undergo costly capability development in new locations but the costs are generally lower for them. They know how to go about building capabilities, have 'deeper pockets', more information and better training resources. If a developing host country engages only in simple assembly operations, TNCs may be able to achieve competitive production without protection because the learning period is short and relatively predictable. However, deepening and diversification into more advanced activities or functions may need government support to improve the quality of local factors and suppliers and to induce TNCs to transfer these activities and functions. This may not involve protection if the local workforce is sufficiently skilled – the Singapore story. However, Singapore had to use a battery of selective interventions to attract and target TNCs and provide them with the factor inputs, infrastructure and incentives needed to force the pace of upgrading. FDI may reduce the need for interventions for capability-building but cannot remove it altogether. Once countries move beyond simple processing, they have to provide the factors that allow TNCs to undertake complex functions efficiently.

22 According to Rhee *et al.* (1984), 'The export targets and monthly meetings provide some of the most important information needed to administer the Korean export drive. Perhaps the most important is the up-to-date information on export performance by firm, product, and market and on reasons for discrepancy between target and performance. The government also gets much solid information on what is going on in the world. (The firms, meanwhile, get much solid information about the priorities and undertakings by government). But the government has not only acquired this information. The ministries, in concert with the firms, have sought first to identify the problems and opportunities and to determine appropriate actions. These actions have been characterized by pragmatism … speed … flexibility. … This willingness to implement new policies without careful, deliberate planning was generally a virtue for export policymaking – primarily because the test of those policies was success in the international marketplace. Firms thus saw the flexibility and frequent adjustments in the incentive system not as characteristics that would create uncertainty about the automaticity and stability of that system. They saw them as part of the government's long-term commitment to keep exports profitable – a commitment made possible by the continuity of the government. Without such commitment, firms would have faced much more uncertainty in their export production, and exports would have suffered as a result' (pp. 35–36).

References

Amsden, A., 1989, *Asia's Next Giant*, Oxford: Oxford University Press.

Ashton, D., F. Green, D. James and J. Sung, 1999, *Education and Training for Development in East Asia*, London: Routledge.

Best, M., 2001, *The New Competitive Advantage*, Oxford: Oxford University Press.

Chang, Ha-Joon, 2002, *Kicking Away the Ladder*, London: Anthem Press.

Cheng, T-J, S. Haggard and D. Kang, 1998, 'Institutions and Growth in Korea and Taiwan: the Bureaucracy', *Journal of Development Studies*, 34 (6), 87–111.

Economist, The, 2003, 'Mexico's Economy: The Sucking Sound from the East', London, 24 July.

Evans, P., 1998, 'Transferable Lessons? Re-examining the Institutional Prerequisites of East Asian Economic Policies', *Journal of Development Studies*, 34 (6), 66–86.

Gereffi, G., J. Humphrey, R. Kaplinsky and T. J. Sturgeon, 2001, 'Introduction: Globalisation, Value Chains and Development', *IDS Bulletin*, Institute of Development Studies, Sussex, 32 (2), 1–8.

International Herald Tribune, 2003, 'Mexico Manufacturers Lose Business to China', Paris, 3 September.

Lall, S., 1992, 'Technological capabilities and industrialization', *World Development*, 20 (2), 165–186.

Lall, S., 1996, *Learning from the Asian Tigers*, London: Macmillan.

Lall, S., 2001a, *Competitiveness, Technology and Skills*, Cheltenham: Edward Elgar.

Lall, S., 2001b, 'Competitiveness Indices and Developing Countries: an Economic Evaluation of the Global Competitiveness Report', *World Development*, 29 (9), 1501–1525.

Lall, S., 2003, 'Indicators of the Relative Importance of IPRs in Developing Countries', *Research Policy*, p. 32.

Lall, S. and M. Albaladejo, 2003, 'China's Export Surge: The Competitive Implications for Southeast Asia', Oxford: Queen Elizabeth House, Report for the World Bank East Asia Department.

Lall, S. and C. Pietrobelli, 2002, *Failing to Compete: Technology Development and Technology Systems in Africa*, Cheltenham: Edward Elgar.

Lall, S. and M. Teubal, 1998, '"Market Stimulating" Technology Policies in Developing Countries: A Framework with Examples from East Asia', *World Development*, 26 (8), 1369–1385.

Loewendahl, H., 2001, 'A framework for FDI promotion', *Transnational Corporations*, 10 (1), 1–42.

Mathews, J. A., 2001, 'The Origins and Dynamics of Taiwan's R&D Consortia', *Research Policy*, 30.

Mathews, J. A. and D. S. Cho, 1999, *Tiger Technology: The Creation of a Semiconductor Industry in East Asia*, Cambridge: Cambridge University Press.

Mill, J. S., 1940, *Principles of Political Economy* (first published 1848), London: Longmans Green.

Narula, R., 2003, *Globalization and Technology*, Cambridge: Polity Press.

Nelson, R. R. and S. J. Winter, 1982, *An Evolutionary Theory of Economic Change*, Cambridge (MA): Harvard University Press.

Noland, M. and H. Pack, 2003, *Industrial Policy in an Era of Globalization: Lessons from Asia*, Washington, DC: Institute for International Economics.

Pack, H. and L. E. Westphal, 1986, 'Industrial Strategy and Technological Change: Theory versus Reality,' *Journal of Development Economics*, 22(1), pp. 87–128.

Radosevic, S., 1999, *International Technology Transfer and Catch-Up in Economic Development*, Cheltenham: Edward Elgar.

Reinert, E., 1995, 'Competitiveness and its Predecessors – A 500-Year Cross-National Perspective', *Structural Change and Economics Dynamics*, 6, 23–42.

Rhee, Y., B. Ross-Larson and G. Pursell, 1984, *Korea's Competitive Edge*, Baltimore: Johns Hopkins.

Rodrik, D., 2001, 'The Global Governance of Trade as if Development Really Mattered', April, Background paper for UNDP, available at http://ksghome.harvard.edu/~.drodrik.academic.ksg/papers.html.

Stiglitz, J. E., 1996, 'Some Lessons from the East Asian Miracle', *The World Bank Research Observer*, 11 (2), 151–177.

Sturgeon, T. J., 2002, 'Modular Production Networks: A New American Model of Industrial Organization?', *Industrial and Corporate Change*, 11 (3).

UNCTAD, 1996, *The TRIPS Agreement and Developing Countries*, Geneva: United Nations.

UNCTAD, 1999, *World Investment Report 1999*, Geneva: United Nations.

UNCTAD, 2002, *World Investment Report 2002*, Geneva: United Nations.

UNCTAD, 2003, *World Investment Report 2003*, Geneva: United Nations.

UNDP, 2003, *Human Development Report 2003*, New York: United Nations.

UNIDO, 2002, *Industrial Development Report 2002/2003*, Vienna: United Nations.

Wade, R. H., 1990, *Governing the Market*, Princeton: Princeton University Press.

Wade, R. H., 2003, 'Creating Capitalisms', Introduction to new edition of *Governing the Market*, Princeton: Princeton University Press.

Westphal, L., 2002, 'Technology Strategies for Economic Development in a Fast-Changing Global Economy', *Economics of Innovation and New Technology*, 11, 275–320.

Westphal, L. E., 1990, 'Industrial Policy in an Export-Propelled Economy: Lessons from South Korea's Experience', *Journal of Economic Perspectives*, 4 (3), 41–59.

Westphal, L. E., 1997, 'Government-Business Relations: Experience of the Republic of Korea', Background note prepared for UNCTAD Expert Group Meeting.

Westphal, L. E., 1982, 'Fostering Technological Mastery by Means of Selective Infant-Industry Protection', in M. Syrquin and S. Teitel (eds), *Trade, Stability, Technology, and Equity in Latin America*, New York: Academic Press, pp. 255–279.

Wong, P. K., 2003, 'From Using to Creating Technology: The Evolution of Singapore's National Innovation System and the Changing Role of Public Policy', in S. Lall and S. Urata (eds), *Competitiveness, FDI and Technological Activity in East Asia*, Cheltenham: Edward Elgar, pp. 191–238.

Wood, A. (ed.), 2003, 'Symposium on Infant Industries', *Oxford Development Studies*, 31 (1), 3–20, with contributions by J. Roberts, R. Wade and S. Lall.

World Bank, 1993, *The East Asian Miracle*, Oxford: Oxford University Press.

WTO, 1998, *World Trade Organization, Annual Report 1998*, Geneva: World Trade Organization.

Zedillo Commission, 2001, 'Report of the High-Level Panel on Financing for Development', for the Monterrey Conference, at www.un.org/reports/financing/full_report.pdf.

10

ASSESSING THE RISKS IN THE PRIVATE PROVISION OF ESSENTIAL SERVICES

Tim Kessler

Abstract:

Essential services, such as water and electricity, are public goods, in that their benefits extend well beyond the consumption of the individual. They are also critical for poverty reduction, and must be universally affordable and accessible in order to achieve the Millennium Development Goals. For these reasons, the standards that apply to investments in other sectors are insufficient for essential services.

Accordingly, this paper argues that private provision requires a higher burden of proof than policies reforming existing state services. It suggests that policymakers considering options for reforming essential services should look beyond the most common performance indicators, like productivity and quality. While these are clearly important, decisions about service reform should be informed by an analysis of social, fiscal and institutional issues. The evidence about the risks of private provision show that in many cases the benefits of better performance are outweighed by costs in these other areas.

The paper identifies four common rationales for private provision and provides evidence that challenges their validity in many cases.

Private provision helps balance budgets. When public subsidies are needed to make services available to poor people, private provision does not reduce the subsidy, and may complicate its allocation. In addition, governments often lure firms to poor or risky areas through government incentives such as tax breaks, grants, and guarantees, which entail serious fiscal obligations and undermine budget discipline.

The private sector invests in public services. In reality, private investment in utilities has been falling in developing countries. Moreover, private participation is often contingent on contractual terms that guarantee profits, shift financial risk onto taxpayers or consumers, or leave governments responsible for major investments.

Private providers improve service performance. The record here is mixed, for actual experiences range from improvement to disaster. Similarly, public sector corruption is matched by corporate scandals in public services. An important reason that private provision often fails to deliver is that governments with limited resources cannot design and enforce contracts.

Private provision makes reform irreversible. This is often true, but also undesirable. Policymakers lack the information and analysis to anticipate the social and economic impacts of policies that cannot be reversed, such as commitments made under the WTO's General Agreement on Trade in Services, which could permanently bind governments to commitments that undermine their ability to regulate or subsidize public services.

Introduction

Considerable scholarship has been devoted lately to researching how best to deliver essential public services, including water, sanitation, electricity and health care. The issue of the private provision of essential services[1] is explored in considerable depth in both the United Nations Development Programme's (UNDP) 2003 Human Development Report (HDR), entitled 'Millennium Development Goals: A Compact among Nations to End Poverty', and in the World Bank's 2004 World Development Report (WDR), entitled 'Making Services Work for Poor People'. Based on a reading of the preliminary WDR draft, it appears that the World Bank is considerably more sanguine about market-based approaches to the provision of essential services, especially such infrastructure services as water and electricity, than is the UNDP – or the author of this paper.

The World Bank and UNDP documents present substantially different positions on the question: *What is government for?* The HDR urges a larger role for government in the direct provision of services and is circumspect about private provision. 'The supposed benefits of privatizing social services are elusive, with inconclusive evidence on efficiency and quality standards in the private relative to the public sector. Meanwhile, examples of market failures in private provisioning abound' (p. 113). The WDR, in contrast, promotes a government role in facilitating the private provision of services, and cites a number of examples of effective private service delivery to support its case.[2]

Notwithstanding their differences, both organizations are careful to avoid categorical claims. The UNDP readily concedes that private provision can work under the right circumstances, while the World Bank both acknowledges and finances improvements in public sector delivery. However, policymakers need to undertake specific analyses to make good judgments about which kind of provision will be both feasible and effective. This paper seeks to make explicit the costs, risks and trade-offs of private provision.

Because essential services contribute directly to livelihood, health, and dignity, we argue that the decision to deliver those services through private providers should be subjected to a *threshold requirement*: the improvement of social equity and poverty reduction. Specifically, policymakers should determine if private providers are likely to deliver essential services to low-income people who cannot afford to pay commercial prices, and if so, under what conditions.

We also explore the following dimensions of private service provision:

- *Service delivery performance.* To what extent will private provision improve existing levels of quality, reliability and access?
- *Fiscal impact.* When attracting private investment requires financial incentives, guarantees or subsidies, how costly are these liabilities relative to options for reforming existing government-provided services?
- *Balance of payments impact.* What is likely to be the impact on the balance of payments of the outflow of profits and dividends to investors? This is particularly important in the case of transnational corporate acquisitions and investment.

Although operational and economic considerations are significant, achieving improvements in these areas alone should not be taken as sufficient justification for adopting or expanding private provision. Indeed, in many cases the success of the private provision model is predicated on a social bargain that excludes the poor: higher prices in exchange for better operational and financial performance. Accordingly, a normative premise of this paper is that *the standards pertaining to investments in other sectors are insufficient for essential services.* There is evidence that private provision can bring improvements in service quality for the urban middle class, profitability for companies, and fiscal discipline for governments. While these achievements, when attainable, are entirely legitimate, they have little to offer the poor given the higher cost of privately-provided services.

This paper demonstrates that improvements in any given area can be more elusive than private provision advocates admit. Although private provision often achieves real improvement in some aspect of service delivery, there is often a trade-off among the other dimensions. We argue that where private providers demand high or guaranteed returns on investment for delivering quality equitable services, governments need to balance these costs against alternative reforms. Moreover, where private providers are not concerned with delivering services to poor people and concentrate on providing services for those parts of the population that can afford to pay, governments that are left with the responsibility for serving society's most vulnerable people must frankly rethink private provision on both humanitarian and fiscal grounds.

The Privatization Paradox

The recommendation to privatize public services often makes contradictory assumptions about the capacity of governments. One assumption is that poor-quality public services –characterized by corruption, low capacity or political capture – cannot be reformed sufficiently to deliver quality services. However, another assumption is that, given the need for effective public regulation to prevent market failures, the (same dysfunctional) state will take the leading role in monitoring and disciplining private providers.

This 'privatization paradox' underlies the critical precautionary principle that informs the title of this paper: *private provision of essential services bears a heavier burden of evidence than public provision*. Given the unique social contributions of essential services and the economic challenges of providing them privately, evidence of public sector failure is not, by itself, sufficient justification to adopt private provision. Private provision advocates should therefore make an empirical case that the conditions for controlling market failure and promoting social welfare are substantially in place before adopting private provision policies. The precautionary principle is informed by three important features of essential services:

1 *Public goods.* Essential services are *public goods*. The benefits of water, sanitation, electricity and health care extend well beyond the particular individuals who consume them. Common public goods include improved public health (e.g. the absence of epidemics) and greater economic productivity. As the 2003 Human Development Report states, governments have traditionally provided public goods because 'their market value alone would not capture their intrinsic value and social benefits'.

   There is broad consensus that citizens should collectively pay for 'pure' public goods such as national and personal security (military and police) and environmental protection. One never hears complaints that such services 'run losses' – even though they are financed entirely by tax revenue – because their social benefit is so obvious. Infrastructure and social services differ from pure public goods because they can be rationed and are excludable. Virtually all wealthy countries whose governments provide essential services, however, justify the decision largely because of the economic challenges to providing collective goods privately.

As the massive August 2003 US blackout demonstrated, private providers have little incentive to make low-yield investments. In the United States, for every dollar of electricity purchased, generation is worth 70 cents, distribution brings in 20 cents, and transmission is worth only 10 cents. After the 1992 deregulation and unbundling of a vertically integrated sector (which separated the three main functions), investment in transmission facilities stalled, leaving the national energy grid vulnerable to overload.

2 *Market failure and perverse incentives.* A distinctive market logic presents serious challenges for the efficient private provision of essential services. Many argue that increased private provision in competitive sectors empowers consumers by giving them choice – primarily the option to exit. However, as will be discussed below, health care is subject to market failure related to asymmetric information: doctors can induce over-consumption of certain drugs and procedures. Unlike social services, infrastructure is not a competitive sector. In most settings there can only be one energy grid or centralized water system, making the issue of choice irrelevant. Monopoly power enables firms to extract excessive rents from consumers lacking alternative suppliers.

For both social services and 'natural monopolies', claims of superior efficiency and performance can only be realized when vigilant *public* regulators – not individual households – hold firms accountable. Most developing countries, however, have weak public institutions and any institutions can take decades to establish. Moreover, where essential services have historically been delivered by the state, sudden privatization may take place without the necessary regulatory experience and capacity to monitor and control private-sector behaviour.

3 *Poverty reduction.* The provision of essential services is a basic requirement for poverty reduction. Essential services are widely acknowledged as the principal means through which the Millennium Development Goals (MDGs) can be achieved. Without effective public intervention, however, poor people can be excluded from, or denied access to, essential services. This is especially true when private providers lack incentives to serve unprofitable populations.

Where private provision requires commercial tariff rates and precludes progressive cross-subsidy arrangements, there are two basic options for dealing with poor people. One is to let market prices ration the poor's consumption of essential services (or other consumption that is crowded out by higher prices).

Policymakers need to assess the impact of this option on livelihood and on the provision of public goods. The other is to subsidize the consumption of privately-provided services with public resources. Policymakers should weigh the real and potential financial costs of using the general budget (or foreign aid) to provide low-cost services through providers that require profit and may also seek to shift operational risks onto the state.

Trends in Resource Flows

Since 1998, the developing world has become a net capital exporter to the developed world. At the same time, growth rates are declining in many countries. In 2000, the world community committed itself to a set of eight Millennium Development Goals that would, among other things, halve by 2015 the proportion of people whose income is less than one dollar a day. In the poorest countries, the shortage of capital is compounded by a drop in official development assistance (ODA) from bilateral donors. Hence, while donors and creditors espouse the importance of meeting the MDGs, they are not providing the capital needed to raised investment levels to achieve these targets. For example:

- In 2000, donor aid for education totalled $4.1 billion, with just $1.5 billion for primary education. In the 1990s, bilateral aid for education fell from $5 billion to $3.5 billion, dropping to just 7 per cent of ODA – an all-time low (UNDP 2003).
- In 2000, the median per capita spending on public health was $1,061 in high human development countries, $194 in medium human development countries, and $38 in low human development countries.
- In the 1990s, an average of $3 billion a year in ODA was allocated to water and sanitation projects. The share of water and sanitation in total ODA remained relatively stable throughout the decade, at 6 per cent of bilateral and 4–5 per cent of multilateral aid. (Non-concessional World Bank lending adds over $1 billion a year.)
- The total share of funding from the World Bank's concessional lending arm, the International Development Association (IDA) devoted to basic social services (basic health, primary education and water and sanitation), has rarely surpassed 10 per cent. The multilateral share (UN agencies, the World Bank, and regional development banks) accounts for one third of ODA.

Even more troubling than stagnating aid levels is the recent decline in *private* investment. Indeed, the fact that foreign direct investment (FDI) levels were so much larger than official development assistance was portrayed as evidence that multilateral development banks were becoming irrelevant. Between 1988 and 1999, service-sector foreign direct investment increased at an annual rate of 28 per cent, and in 1999 it accounted for 37 per cent of the total stock of FDI in developing countries. The share of infrastructure in total FDI flows nearly doubled during 1990–98. It is thus significant that net FDI inflows to developing countries fell sharply in 2002 to an estimated $143 billion from $171 billion in 2001. FDI has dropped to Latin America, given that the region has sold most of its assets, many to foreign buyers (World Bank 2003, 2002).

While FDI is often touted as the critical resource for the entire developing world, FDI flows to developing countries remain highly concentrated. Today about three-quarters of FDI to developing countries go to just 10 countries, and most of this amount flows to China, Brazil and Mexico. All low-income countries combined received only $11 billion in FDI in 2002. Economist David Woodward divides developing countries by per capita equity inflows. He finds that the 71 countries receiving less than $1 per capita received a combined total of just 0.1 per cent of total equity flows, despite having 22.3 per cent of the population of the developing world (Woodward 2001).

Moreover, not all FDI has the same developmental potential. Increasingly, foreign investors are spending on mergers and acquisition (M&A), rather than new 'greenfield' investment in new assets and production capacity. Private provision of essential services by foreign investors, especially infrastructure, usually takes the form of sale – or long-term lease – of existing assets. According to a study by UNCTAD, the share of M&A in total FDI among developing countries – excluding China, the largest recipient of greenfield investment – grew from 22 per cent in 1988 to 72 per cent in 1997. According to Cambridge University economist Ajit Singh, 'When FDI takes the form of greenfield investment, it represents a net addition to the host country's capital stock. However, FDI entry via an acquisition may not represent any addition at all to the capital stock, output or employment' (Singh 2001).

Recent research not only questions the developmental potential of a large part of FDI but also suggests that the most common forms can actually undermine the balance of payments in recipient countries. Especially when returns on investment are very high, as they tend to be for poorer countries (reflecting the private sector's risk premium), repatriated profits can have serious implications for the management of foreign exchange (see Box 1).

If the overall FDI picture is somewhat bleaker, when it comes to investment in basic services for developing countries the situation is still worse. Many multinational firms have been scaling back such investment plans. In January 2003, as part of its efforts to restructure massive debt, Suez announced that it would pull back from new water business in developing countries and curtail investment in existing operations (Hall 2003). The investment prospects for

Box 1

Limitations of Foreign Direct Investment

Foreign Direct Investment is usually portrayed as an economic blessing that countries should strive to increase. To be sure, a drop in FDI can cause losses in capital, technology and jobs. But recent evidence reveals a number of limitations to development strategies that prioritize high levels of FDI:

- The FDI share is higher in countries with higher-quality institutions, suggesting that countries trying to expand their access to international capital markets should concentrate on developing credible enforcement mechanisms instead of trying to get more FDI (Albuquerque 2000). There is very little evidence that more open investment regimes or investment protection treaties do much to stimulate foreign direct investment. Rather, foreign corporations appear to be attracted primarily by the prospects of high profits, either from exploiting the domestic market or by achieving cost savings on export production through low-wage labour.
- FDI in some sectors can weaken governments vis-à-vis foreign corporations, which can exercise considerable influence over public policy through control of information and management decisions. The Chairman of Barclays Capital Hans Joerg Rudloff – hardly an enemy of capitalism – recently stated: 'I'm not a protectionist, but [some] countries sold their silver spoons to foreign buyers without any safeguard for their national interests. They didn't realize that by selling all of their assets like utilities and their banking industries to foreign investors they moved the entire decision-making power over their economic destiny in their own country to people in other parts of the world' (IMF and World Bank 2002). Even as the United States, Europe and Japan seek to open up developing country markets to their corporations, governments in these countries routinely limit the ability of foreign investors to control firms or sectors involved in national security, technology development, financial markets and essential services.
- FDI can adversely affect a recipient country's balance of payments. Recent research suggests that levels of FDI stock in developing countries are far higher than currently believed, and that the rates of return on these investments are extremely high. The repatriation of profits reduces net foreign exchange inflows for foreign investment in export sectors. FDI in such sectors as essential services can actually undermine the balance of payments. According to economist David Woodward, a former Executive Director to the World Bank and IMF: 'For equity investment and some types of direct investment (especially the purchase of existing productive capacity and new investment in non-tradable sectors), the net foreign exchange effect will be substantially negative'.

rural water service are particularly discouraging. As British Environment Minister Michael Meacher puts it (Meacher 2001):

Private sector finance will certainly be important but it will generally not be used for basic services. Thus the World Bank's database on Private

Participation in infrastructure, whilst it shows that private investment in water and sanitation in developing countries to date totals $25 billion, also reveals that none is in South Asia, and almost none is in Africa. Yet these are the two regions in the world without adequate water and sanitation services. This indicates that private sector investment is at present insignificant at providing basic water and sanitation services to the very people who most need it.

According to International Rivers Network, 'Water multinationals have little or no interest in rural drinking-water systems. Corporations are rarely able to profit from poor and dispersed rural populations who mainly depend on local water sources such as wells, springs and streams' (McCully 2002). Even small businesses appear hesitant to invest in the areas that need it the most. As a WaterAid study of rural water reform in Uganda explains, 'Communities that are disadvantaged by the terrain in their locality – where the more expensive technical options are required – are unlikely to benefit from [private sector] projects … Contracts to the private sector avoid expensive deep drilling operations.'

The World Panel on Financing Water Infrastructure, chaired by former International Monetary Fund (IMF) Director Michel Camdessus, which promotes private capital investment, concedes that, 'Compared with other types of infrastructure, the water sector has been the least attractive to private investors, and the sums involved have been the smallest' (Winpenny 2003). In a meeting on water policy in Uganda, staff from the French multinational Vivendi stated that the imperative of making a reasonable profit limits investment to larger cities with sufficient per capital income. Not surprisingly, Vivendi also indicated that the decision to invest in even these urban areas would depend on the certainty of revenue streams from either government or users (Bourbigot and Picaud 2001).

Similarly, in a World Bank presentation, the Chief Executive Officer of another French water multinational, Saur, articulated what he characterized as unreasonable demands on the private sector in developing countries, such as universal provision requirements. Noting a 'marked increase in risk for the private operators, particularly in developing countries', he lamented the 'emphasis on unrealistic service levels [which leads to] limited interest in the market'. He concluded that investment requirements cannot be met by the private sector and that 'Service users can't pay for the level of investments required, not for social projects … The scale of the need far outreaches the financial and risk-taking capacities of the private sector' (Talbot 2002).

Mechanisms for Promoting Private Provision of Services

Since the mid-1990s, multilateral development organizations have tended increasingly to promote private provision for utilities experiencing financial difficulties. The World Bank and regional development banks are more commonly financing a series of reforms that lead up to transferring control of public assets to private firms. Typically these include decentralization, corporatization, full cost recovery through commercial pricing, and segregating profit-making and loss-making markets ('unbundling'), so that profitable parts can be more easily privatized. In some cases, the World Bank also finances 'strategic communication campaigns' to persuade citizens in borrowing countries of the soundness of privatization (World Bank 2003). These campaigns typically contrast best examples of private provision with the worst examples of public provision.

The IMF, whose loans are widely recognized as a 'seal of approval' for developing countries, also sets important conditions for use of its financial assistance. It can require governments to take measures that severely limit the ability of local governments to deliver public services, even when decentralization reforms devolve service delivery responsibilities to lower levels of government. For instance, given its institutional priority to ensure macroeconomic stability, the IMF may pressure central governments to: reduce or eliminate budget subsidies (and domestic credit) to services, especially utilities that operate in the red; limit fiscal transfers to subnational governments; allow the creditors of local governments to 'intercept' transfers to local governments in order to collect debt-related obligations; and refrain from bailing out indebted local governments.

The multilateral development banks also appear to be a source of pressure in favour of private provisional public services. Conditions for commercialization and private provision can be found in policy 'triggers' for lending in World Bank country assistance strategies, as well as 'tranche release' criteria for structural adjustment loans. Considerable independent research confirms such conclusions. In the electricity sector, a World Resources Institute study of six developing countries found that reforms were driven by the immediate need for capital, usually the result of the withdrawal of international donor support for the power sector (WRI 2002). In Argentina, the IDB and World Bank withheld assistance to the provinces unless they agreed to conform to federal pricing requirements. In Orissa, India, donors instructed consultants to 'create a process that was irreversible' (Dubash 2002). In a study of ten cities by the Director of Water and Sanitation at the Asian Development Bank, only one (Macau) was found to have privatized of its own volition, having done so a century ago (MacIntosh 2000).

Decentralization has become an increasingly common 'first step' toward the private provision of services. When adequate revenues are not available for local government, decentralization can lead to privatization by default. When local governments face rising social demands without receiving corresponding increases in resources or capacity, they have strong incentives to unload these political liabilities onto the private sector. As the UNDP explains, 'As urban populations increase, fiscally strapped local authorities cannot expand services to cover them. As a result water services decline in quantity and quality in middle-class neighborhoods – and fail to reach new poor neighborhoods' (UNDP 2003). Unfortunately, local governments are even less prepared to negotiate and regulate private contracts than national governments, which themselves have shown serious limitations in governing private providers.

While the logic behind decentralization is to bring services closer to the people and improve accountability, in practice local governments are often given responsibility for delivering services without sufficient capacity or resources. 'Financial decentralization often renders local governments vulnerable to macroeconomic shocks and remedial measures to control public expenditures and national budget deficits ... [Amid] sharply reduced [national] spending ... the quality and reach of public services is bound to suffer in the absence of complementary measures to raise local resources' (Robinson 2003).

While local governments may not make a deliberate, premeditated decision to contract out public services, when faced with serious resource gaps they often have to choose between reducing access and quality or transferring responsibility for service delivery to a private provider. In this decentralized context, the fiscal rationale for pursuing privatization may simply be one of desperation. The IMF and World Bank have played a major role in creating fiscal constraints that undermine the local delivery of services (see Box 2).

Box 2
External pressures for local government austerity

The experience of state-owned enterprises (SOEs) suggests the need for caution when making fiscal arrangements with local governments that deliver essential services. Former World Bank economist John Nellis, now a researcher at the Center for Global Development in Washington, states that commonly: 'IMF involvement and surveillance [of the economy] led to a choking off of direct budgetary financing of SOEs ... In response, private sector management, financing or ownership was proposed. The World Bank then became more directly involved in terms of reform/privatization design, and assistance in implementation' (Nellis 2003). One way that the IMF imposes fiscal discipline on central governments in decentralized countries is to cut back fiscal transfers during periods of economic difficulty. Another is to forbid central governments from bailing out local ones that raise their own resources through borrowing.

An example from Bolivia is illustrative. To help curb instability and foster investment, the IMF and World Bank may direct governments to promote the development of a municipal credit market. In recent loans, the World Bank required that the government of Bolivia use revenue intercepts as collateral to municipal credit operations with any lender, and to require municipalities to enter into Financial Restructuring Agreements (FRAs) ensuring that they maintain hard budget ceilings (World Bank 2001 and 2002). Such steps are intended to improve the access of municipalities to international financing, by increasing confidence among investors. Seven municipalities entered into FRAs and accepted fiscal targets based on the IMF's assumption of growth of 4 per cent of GDP in 2001. The actual GDP growth rate was only 1.2 per cent. Central government revenues plunged by 26 per cent in 2001 and general transfers from the central to municipal governments were *11 per cent less than projected.* Because municipalities with FRAs were constrained from borrowing, they instituted new local taxes and user fees and cut back programmes and staffing.

When appropriate fiscal resources are not provided, decentralization can lead to local services that are segregated by income. In South Africa, after decentralization reform and re-zoning, the municipality of Nelspruit found its population multiplied by a factor of 10 in 1994, while its total revenues grew only by 38 per cent. Moreover, most of the new residents were poorer people. These challenges were increased further after the 2000 demarcation process, which doubled the municipality's population while keeping the same tax base. As a result, cash-strapped local government wanted to 'wash its hands of responsibility' for water by handing it over to a private concession (Smith, Mottiar and White 2003). In this episode, privatization of water became a convenient political exit strategy for local officials desperately lacking resources. A review of Latin American education reform in four decentralized countries (Mexico, Argentina, Chile and Colombia) revealed severe reductions in public spending (primary teachers' salaries) and a widening of the quality gap between public and private providers (Prawda 1993). In sub-Saharan Africa, where inadequate fiscal transfers restricted local revenue raising and poor planning has been the norm, decentralization has led to consistently disappointing results (Robinson 2003).

Even more important than the traditional conditions on loans is the emerging practice of *selectivity*. Through a number of new initiatives, the MDBs are beginning to use the 'carrot' more readily than the 'stick', a shift with potentially profound implications for aid allocation. The principle of selectivity may eventually obviate the need for conditions in country assistance strategies or adjustment loans. As countries and localities are rewarded for 'good policies', the World Bank increasingly focuses its resources on governments that agree to implement liberalization and privatization policies. For example, the Bank is concentrating the bulk of its lending in India to just three states that have shown a willingness to adopt policies that it supports.

The World Bank has created a number of recent initiatives to advance the agenda of service privatization. Four examples illustrate how diverse lending and non-lending instruments converge on a common policy approach.

- *Private sector development.* The World Bank's 1995 Annual Report referred to the institution's shift toward direct support of private sector investment (as opposed to direct lending to governments) as 'a dramatic departure from what had been Bank policy for half a century'. The Private Sector Development (PSD) Strategy, approved by the Bank's Board in February 2002, puts real power behind this shift (Bijlmakers and Linder 2003; Bayliss and Hall 2001; Alexander 2001–02).[3] Under the PSD strategy, the World Bank's private sector affiliate, the International Finance Corporation (IFC), is to team up with the International Development Association (IDA) to privatize services in low-income countries, including 'frontier' areas, such as social programmes and basic infrastructure. The PSD Strategy's purpose is to transform much of the World Bank Group's traditional operations into support for the role of the private sector.
- *Output-based aid.* The World Bank is scaling up the financing of infrastructure and social service projects through output-based aid (OBA) design (Marin 2002). OBA projects delegate service delivery to private 'third parties' under contracts that tie provision of financial support to the outputs or services actually delivered. (We discuss challenges to implementing so-called 'performance-based' contracts in the following section.) A Global Partnership for OBA was launched in 2003 by the World Bank Group, with support from DFID. It is now experimenting with, and scaling up, OBA schemes, some of which would provide subsidies to corporations that deliver services or meet certain performance benchmarks. Examples of pro-poor OBA payments include a one-time payment for expanding coverage (e.g. through new connections), gradually reduced financial support for phased tariff increases, and ongoing subsidies for minimum consumptions in poor households.
- *Community-driven development.* One approach to private service provision that the World Bank has embraced with particular enthusiasm is community-driven development (CDD), which currently absorbs about half of IDA credits and grants. According to the Bank's website, CDD gives control of decisions and resources to community groups, not to local governments. 'These groups often work in partnership with demand-responsive support organizations and service providers, including elected local governments, the private sector, NGOs, and central government agencies …' A common type of CDD is the Social Fund, through which the Bank has channelled $3.7 billion in 57 countries, with donor and government co-financing bringing the total to about $9 billion. Social Fund resources are distributed directly to communities, rather than to

local governments; they often contain thousands of sub-projects that are bid out to private and non-profit contractors. In light of concerns over weak local-level governance, some have expressed concerns about how effectively CDD approaches prepare local governments to facilitate transparent privatization, or manage financial resources (Tendler 2000).

- *Low-Income Countries Under Stress.* The World Bank addresses the special needs of failed states through its Low-Income Countries Under Stress (LICUS) programme. LICUS turns the idea of improving governance on its head. Rather than building the institutions of governance, an external institution – the independent service authority – simply replaces the state's essential functions entirely. Such service authorities are largely autonomous from government, with high standards and accountability directly to donors. They are wholesale institutions, contracting out services with multiple providers, including firms and NGOs, for retail services that they monitor and compare to ensure cost-effectiveness.

In addition to pressure to implement policies that may not be appropriate or feasible, borrowing countries may have other economic and operational reasons for reducing reliance on external donors. Critics of foreign aid projects have long argued that development projects create financial traps owing to *recurrent costs*, such as salaries, maintenance, fuel, and routine supply requirements. For this reason, some governments prefer to borrow only for 'one-time' capital expenditures, such as construction, and fund essential service provision only through user fees and budget outlays. Just as important as financial sustainability is *operational* sustainability, an area in which MDBs have not had a good record. In 1993, only 27 per cent of World-Bank-financed water projects had likely sustainability (defined as long-term provision of continued benefits after project completion), while today the figure stands at about 40 per cent (World Bank 2003).

Rationales for Private Provision of Essential Services

We will now evaluate four common rationales given for privatizing essential services:

- budgetary discipline,
- attracting private investment,
- improved efficiency and performance, and
- irreversibility.

We do not argue that these rationales are categorically invalid. Rather, we highlight risks that may make each rationale less compelling, or irrelevant, and we provide illustrative examples of those risks.

Rationale No. 1: Balancing Budgets

The first rationale for privatization is that it provides important benefits for budget stability. By freeing up scarce budgetary resources, governments that sell off public assets or put them under private management can dedicate those funds to other pressing social goals. Unfortunately, this rationale has been used to privatize even well-functioning services, as the sale of attractive assets generates a one-time revenue windfall. From the perspective of private sector bidders, the most attractive services are those that already perform efficiently and satisfy a broad, lucrative customer base. Thus, governments searching for large 'lump sum' revenue gains may be tempted to trade away viable and effective services. There is often an inherent tension between profitability on one hand, and competition and poverty reduction on the other. Some governments have enticed companies to make high offers by allowing arrangements that have little to do with the public interest. As several World Bank researchers explain (Estache, Foster and Wodon):

> In many countries, privatization transactions are spearheaded by the Ministry of Finance, which tends to view the process in narrow transactional terms, with the focus on maximizing the fiscal revenues from the asset sale. This is unfortunate because there are some important trade-offs between the sale value of the assets and the downstream economic and social impacts of the reform. For example, revenue considerations point toward keeping service tariffs high, minimizing rollout obligations, postponing the introduction of competition, and overlooking many of the details of regulation. However, experience shows that these are precisely the strategies that are likely to be most damaging to the poor ...

Privatization of well-functioning services that are financially viable are particularly dubious. In the mid-1990s, Gabon's water utility SEEG was doing fine before being privatized, even in the opinion of officials involved in the sale. IFC investment officer François Wohrer, just before the sale, said that SEEG was a 'relatively wealthy company ... and will make a decent profit in 1996 ... The company was a little messy before 1993 but there has been a nice cleaning process over the last three years. There is no overstaffing and the company is quite well managed' (*Financial Times* 1997).

Stopping losses by reducing subsidies. While the revenue-generating rationale has been used to justify the selling of good services, fiscal considerations have greater legitimacy for bad ones. From a fiscal perspective, getting rid of loss-making services to improve macroeconomic discipline is more justifiable than selling off profitable or budget-neutral services. Any fiscally-driven decision to privatize, however, should be informed by an analysis of the *cause of losses.*

Some advocates of privatization argue that the problem underlying loss-making government services is invariably inefficiency. In many cases, there is certainly a valid case for public service organizations using up more general tax revenues than they need to. At the same time, as argued earlier in the discussion about public goods, the mere existence of a fiscal loss is not an argument for privatization of essential services. Indeed, one of the main characteristics of public goods is that they can only be provided through collective contributions from all citizens – that is, at a loss.

Privatization inevitably commercializes prices through user fees. Without some sort of subsidy mechanism, the poor will not be able to afford essential services, which leads to both greater poverty and reduction of public goods provision. For this reason, the implementation or increase in user fees almost invariably entails a subsidy dimension. The practicality of reducing poverty through targeted subsidies has therefore received considerable attention. Unfortunately, targeted subsidies often fail to reach the intended beneficiaries. A study of Chile's private water provision demonstrates the extent of subsidy leakage in fee-based systems. This study found an 80 per cent exclusion of poor people and an 80 per cent inclusion of affluent people (Contreras 2003). The finding is particularly troubling given that Chile's institutional capacity is among the best in the developing world.

While subsidies often contribute little to poverty reduction, user fees themselves may contribute little to financial viability of essential services, especially in very poor areas. Health care cost recovery experiences in African countries shows that average fees yield only about 5 per cent of operating costs. The net yields are lower – or even negative – when collection costs are factored in. This finding is confirmed by a Harvard University study of health care in Tanzania which found that the administration of the user fee programme cost more than the user fee revenues (Arhin-Tenkorang 2003). While these may be extreme examples, the administration of subsidy systems in low-income countries inevitably creates costly bureaucratic systems for implementation. Where private provision is linked to fiscal measures that preclude progressive cross-subsidies – especially in the context of widespread poverty – then the state may have to commit to long-term transfers from the regular budget (or foreign aid).[4]

Unfortunately, *there is no evidence that subsidy systems under private provision are any more effective than those under public provision.* According to the World Bank's Operations Evaluation Department, 'getting the private sector to focus on the alleviation of poverty and to design tariffs in a way that does not discriminate against the poor has proved hard to achieve in practice …' (Pitman 2002).

Under traditional arrangements, governments typically provide a direct subsidy to means-tested households or to communities designated as poor. Under 'output-based' contracts (discussed earlier), governments could pay the private provider a fee for each low-income customer served at reduced prices (Marin 2002). Such arrangements provide a profit margin for the private provider, while requiring the government to incur substantial monitoring costs in order to ensure compliance.

Fiscal costs of attracting private capital. The more a private provider is expected to serve the interests of poor or excluded users, the less attractive will become the opportunity to invest in the sector (see earlier discussion on trends in resource flows). However, the unwillingness of private firms to invest in low-income people has led much of the development community not to re-think privatization, but rather to re-think how *to finance* privatization. The influential report *Financing Water for All* (commonly known as the Camdesssus Report) specifically recommends greater use of multilateral guarantees for private investment, as well as direct use of development assistance to 'facilitate water projects managed by private operators under public control'. The global development institutions have increasingly turned to financial incentives to attract private providers to otherwise financially unattractive investments.

The use of such mechanisms to attract private financing underscores an apparent double standard. When governments run losses to subsidize publicly delivered services, the conventional wisdom is that such arrangements are not financially sustainable. However, when funds from the same public sector (or lending institution) are used to finance private provision of the same service, the arrangement is characterized as an innovative approach to poverty reduction.

The salient point is that *governments must engage in some form of social redistribution when poor people cannot afford basic services.* From a financial perspective, the main question in considering the choice of provider is: which is likely to cost the government more money? In many cases a public service may require significant subsidies, especially if it has to reach a lot of poor people. Such 'loss-making' enterprises are one of the main justifications for bringing in private firms. But if governments have to offer major financial incentives to attract more private capital, policymakers need to ask how high that price is, and whether it justifies a major policy change.

The public sector is increasingly channelling financial support to private providers in an effort to lure new investment in services. As one labour union researcher concludes: 'Lease contracts in the water sector are designed to ensure that the risk levels that private firms face are not so high that they will put off investing. Private operators are usually invited to take over responsibility for operating and managing the network, but are not required to invest in the infrastructure' (Bayliss 2002). This finding is corroborated even by institutions that support private provision. As the World Bank explains, incentives to attract private firms include 'cash contributions during the construction period; subsidies during the operating period (e.g. in the form of non-refundable grants), and a favourable tax regime – including tax holidays, refunding of tax on construction and operating costs' (World Bank 1998).

Under World Bank tutelage, the government of Pakistan began allowing private ownership of electricity generation plants in 1992. After two years without investment, a high-level government commission produced the Policy Framework and Package of Incentives for Private Sector Power Generation Projects in Pakistan; this package included: a bulk tariff of US cents 6.5/kWh for the sale of electricity to the public utility, with indexation for fuel prices, US and Pakistani inflation, exchange-rate fluctuations, and operating and maintenance costs (see following section for more details); exemption from corporate income tax, customs duties, sales tax, and other surcharges on imported equipment; and permission for power generation companies to issue corporate bonds and shares at discounted prices (Augustus 1997).

Examples abound throughout the developing world. In 2001, the Kenyan government suspended a water contract with a subsidiary of Vivendi.

> Originally this was a $5 million billing and accounting project but there was an outcry when critics pointed out that Sereuca would not invest any money in infrastructure during the 10 years that the contract was to be in force but was to just install a new billing system at City Hall for which the company was to earn 14.9 per cent of the Ksh12.7 billion ($169 million) collected over the period. Furthermore, the city council's water and sewerage department was supposed to reimburse the cost of the computer equipment and hardware to the company at the end of the 10 years with no provision for depreciation.[5]

In South Africa, a power consortium led by the United Kingdom's BiWater provided only about a quarter of capital investment in upgrading and expanding service in the Nelspruit municipality. Most of the capital for this private venture was supplied by the South African Development Bank.[6] In Honduras, AES obtained exemptions on all taxes and charges as a condition for building an 800 MW power plant in Puerto Cortes.

On top of government incentives to attract capital are multilateral guarantees to reduce corporate risk. These instruments are usually provided by the World Bank's private sector affiliates, the International Finance Corporation (IFC) and the Multilateral Investment Guarantee Agency (MIGA), which protect against commercial and political risks, respectively. When private firms lend to or invest in a utility project in a country, the Bank's guarantee promises the private firms compensation for certain losses if, under specified conditions, the government does not meet its obligations. The borrower may be the member country or a private company.

Multilateral guarantees can dramatically increase the 'off-budget' fiscal burdens of recipient countries. Subsovereign guarantees provided to state and local governments currently require backing by the central government. However, this requirement may soon be eliminated. When that happens, if private ventures backed by a subsovereign guarantee fail, the local government is likely to assume large debt-like financial obligations without any mechanisms for restructuring or writing down the obligations. Guarantees can account for half or even more of the indebtedness in a given infrastructure service sector. (On the potential fiscal costs of guarantees, see Box 3.)

Box 3
Multilateral guarantees

Private lenders and investors in infrastructure projects seek to protect themselves from risks by obtaining commercial or political guarantees from export credit agencies, private insurers, and multilateral institutions. Such guarantees shift private sector risk onto taxpayers – precisely the reverse of what privatization proponents promise for greater private sector participation in services. When private firms lend to or invest in a water project in a borrowing country, the World Bank's guarantee promises the private firms compensation for certain losses if, under specified conditions, the borrower does not meet its obligations. The MDBs claim that guarantees are indispensable for building confidence and providing incentives for private financiers to invest in infrastructure projects. Critics argue that such guarantees distort risk calculations and foist unsustainable price, demand, and currency risks upon the government.

The multilateral development banks offer two primary types of guarantees:

- *Partial risk guarantees* cover government obligations spelled out in agreements with the project entity and ensure payment in the case of debt-service default resulting from non-performance of contractual obligations undertaken by governments or their agencies in private sector projects.
- *Partial credit guarantees* cover all events of non-payment for a specified part of financing. This helps extend maturity periods, which is often significant for obtaining longer-term financing for large construction projects.

There is no clear distinction between political and commercial realms, an ambiguity that creates its own set of problems. As a general rule, however, the commercial side refers to the risks to profits attributable to production inefficiencies or lack of demand. The political aspect risks refer to those risks over which the government has some measure of power. Mitigating political risks involves obtaining government commitments not to expropriate private holdings, to protect the investment from consequences of war and unrest. World Bank guarantees also cover local currency financing.

The World Bank is exploring arrangements to help subsovereign borrowers obtain financing without needing sovereign guarantees. The Swedish International Development Cooperation Agency (SIDA) has helped to establish GuarantCo, which will provide partial guarantees on issues of paper by private sector infrastructure service providers and possibly municipalities and/or public sector authorities.

The World Bank's issuance of guarantees can constitute a serious conflict of interest. If Bank action to address social or environmental difficulties with privately-financed projects results in the disruption of a project or an escalation of costs, the guarantee could be called. In other words, it could be in the public interest for the Bank to 'blow the whistle' on privately-financed projects. However, the Bank would be constrained from taking such action given its liability – namely, the guarantee.

Furthermore, since guarantees are provided by the private sector, it is redundant for the MDBs to offer these products. If projects are not viable, the Bank could be seriously distorting risk calculations by providing extra comfort to investors and lenders. Assuming that the institutions continue to offer guarantees, they should use investment screens to ensure that projects meet specified 'sustainable development' criteria.

Investment screens have been commonly used by private investors in the United States and other industrial nations to select the portfolios of Socially Responsible Investment (SRI) funds. An investment screen is essentially a set of non-financial (such as social or environmental) criteria that must be met by all companies in an investment portfolio. There are two kinds of investment screens: 'negative screens' which are a set of criteria delineating what characteristics companies in the portfolio cannot have (production of nuclear weapons, operations in Burma, Superfund sites, etc.), and 'positive screens', which are a set of criteria delineating what characteristics companies in the portfolio must have.

In June 2000 MIGA paid out a claim for political risk insurance for the first time (Bayliss 2002). It made a payment of $15 million to Enron when the Indonesian government cancelled a power project. The contract – to build, operate and maintain a 500-megawatt power plant near Surabaya – was one of several independent power producer (IPP) contracts signed with the dictatorship of President Suharto. The contracts were suspended in 1997 in response to the country's economic crisis and the collapse of the rupiah, the Indonesian currency. A power utility, PLN, made clear to all the independent power producers in the country that it simply could not afford to pay the prices specified in the their long-term power purchasing agreements. Moreover, PLN and other utilities nullified the contracts on the grounds that they were created in a corrupt manner.

The rationale for the cancellation and the payment of the claim were straightforward. After the payment was made, however, MIGA insisted that the Indonesian government *reimburse* it the $15 million. As an incentive,

MIGA refused to issue any more coverage for business in Indonesia until it was paid. After lengthy negotiations, the government agreed to repayment terms. Only then did MIGA consent to provide insurance coverage for investors in Indonesia once again.

This episode was remarkable because the project was recognized even by MIGA as economically and politically unsustainable. The guarantee agency actually agreed that proceeding with the project was not a viable policy option. 'While we understand the circumstances that led to [the Enron] project suspension, international law dictated that the cancellation be compensated,' said Luis Dodoro, MIGA's general counsel and World Bank Group vice-president. Thus, Indonesian taxpayers have to pay the bill for a politically corrupt and economically unviable contract signed between a dictatorship and a multinational firm. Enron, which negotiated the agreement, has received compensation, while the government of Indonesia has reimbursed MIGA.

Rationale No. 2: Attracting Investment Capital

The second rationale for private provision of essential services is that the private sector has access to far more capital resources than cash-strapped, deficit-ridden governments. Especially for sectors with high sunk costs, such as infrastructure, proponents argue that fiscal constraints (or the inability to impose higher user fees) cripple developing country governments in their quest to upgrade and expand expensive services. As we saw earlier, however, expectations about private capital have run far ahead of actual investment levels, especially in the places that need it the most.

Reducing poverty. The most explicitly 'social' rationale for private service provision is that it reduces poverty. It does so by increasing capital investment in infrastructure and social services used by poor people, improving quality or expanding access. Especially where government has failed to invest in marginalized people, because of budget constraints or lack of political priorities, many argue that private capital represents the only viable opportunity for reaching these excluded citizens. Indeed, during the booming 1990s, market reformers made a mantra of the argument that the private sector was the only viable source of capital for major public investment. Particularly in the capital-intensive utility sectors, cash-strapped governments were portrayed as unable to keep up even with basic maintenance, much less able to expand or upgrade costly infrastructure. Large corporations and nimble capital markets, however, could make large investments wherever needed.

As discussed earlier, these cheerful predictions have fallen flat. Because of the dynamic of 'cherry-picking', corporations have little incentive to invest in 'unprofitable people'. In the case of utilities, private providers like to expand household access (e.g. hook up water pipes, make connections to the electrical grid) or upgrade services in urban areas, especially where middle-class consumers demand more and better services. They are less likely to go into peri-urban, slum or rural areas, where topography is more difficult, per capita consumption is less, and most important, incomes are lower. Because the poor tend to live in outlying urban and remote rural areas, the unit costs of providing them with utility services may actually be much higher than for wealthier people living in major cities. Moreover, variation in investment location within countries is replicated on a global scale. Of total foreign investment in private infrastructure, very poor countries have received only a tiny fraction of that capital (Krina 2002).

Many examples can be cited to illustrate how capital investment fails to reach the poor. In the Indian city of Tiripur, a textile and garment centre, a consortium comprised of United Utilities (UK), Bechtel, and a local partner are working with the state government development corporation to deliver piped water to customers who now rely on tanker trucks. Under current plans, the knitwear industry would receive 115 million litres per day (mld). 'Tirupur municipality, which includes 60,000 slum dwellers, will get 26 mld, while 792 rural settlements in its neighbourhood will share the remaining 36 mld' (Ninan 2003).

After the British firm BiWater pulled out of a privatization project in Zimbabwe because local consumers could not pay high enough prices to generate a sufficient profit, the company's manager remarked: 'Investors need to be convinced that they will get reasonable returns. The issues we consider include who the end users are and whether they are able to afford the water tariffs. From a social point of view, these kinds of projects are viable but unfortunately from a private sector point of view they are not' (*Zimbabwe Independent* 1999).

Cherry-picking incentives also constrain investment in social services. In the health care sector, doctors want to serve patients with higher incomes, while insurance companies want to avoid sick customers and drop those who develop conditions requiring medical attention. Expanding direct private provision of health care affects rich and poor countries alike. Under Germany's deregulation, 'people with a sufficiently high income are allowed to opt out of the statutory health insurance funds. The private insurers can offer their services to young (and healthy) people far more cheaply. As a result, the statutory health insurance funds are retaining a larger proportion of higher-cost members' (*Social Watch Report* 2003).

An IDB paper on privatization in Chile reports how health insurers 'try to exclude beneficiaries who develop expensive illnesses'. Although government responded by requiring them to renew all policies upon request, the insurers 'have found a way around this obligation: they raise the price of the renewal plans while offering new plans with similar benefits at the original lower prices to clients that do not represent as high a risk level' (Fischer *et al.*). This finding is reinforced by the *Social Watch* country report, which states that commercially priced health insurance for women of child-bearing years is three to four times higher than for men in the same age bracket (Arteaga 2003).

Shifting risk, guaranteeing profits. The World Bank strongly promotes private participation in water and sanitation, accepting that such arrangements must ensure the profitability of firms that risk large amounts of capital. One Bank researcher calls for 'the need for realism' and warns that naïve developing country officials may openly question the need for adequate profit levels (Cowen 1997):[7]

> There is often a sharp difference between what private companies see as the minimal return necessary to go into business in a risky country and what governments view as an acceptable level of profit … (Advisers to developing country governments considering private participation in water will all be familiar with the gasps of disbelief and indignation when they first voice assumptions about expected returns on equity.) Governments that have happily (or at least blindly) tolerated high levels of rent-seeking and wasteful behaviour by public water company officials can become positively puritanical about relatively modest profit-taking by a private company. This is not to say that private companies with a monopoly to supply water services should be allowed to take any level of profit that they choose. But governments should be realistic about the profits that they should allow, recognizing the need of their private partners to earn a reasonable return and to be rewarded for the risks that they shoulder.

Needless to say, what constitutes 'minimal return' and 'relatively modest profit' is a judgement call. Governments that are admonished to be 'realistic' routinely confront private firms that have strong incentives to overstate the costs of providing services. Moreover, once private providers win a concession, they also exercise control over financial information that governments need to assess their claims.

The record of private service provision is littered with examples of contracts that guaranteed profits for firms while placing virtually all risk onto the government and consumers. The most direct way that firms avoid commercial risk is through contracts that quantify profit margins. For example, in Cochabamba, Bolivia, where civil society mobilization against water price hikes exploded into a political crisis, the public auction for the city's water system featured exactly one bid. The Bechtel-owned consortium Aguas del Tunari negotiated terms with a government lacking any real bargaining leverage and demanded exclusive rights to all local water resources, as well as a guaranteed 15 per cent profit margin, to be indexed to US inflation (Finnegan 2002). Enron's ill-fated gas-fired power plant in Dahbol was initially granted a 16 per cent guaranteed return by the Indian government, on top of a five-year tax exemption.

Some private provision arrangements create enormous contingent liabilities for governments. A good example is the so-called 'take-or-pay' contract. In the energy sector, power purchasing agreements (PPAs) commit the government to purchase a predetermined quantity of production regardless of economic conditions. Although such obligations are not technically debts, they can actually be more intractable than traditional debt because they are not subject to rescheduling and write-downs. As a survey of financially disastrous power purchasing agreements concludes: 'bankruptcy is not an option under the contract terms' Corral, Bayliss and Hall 2001). For this reason, policymakers need to assess the potential *off-budget* implications of private provision options.

In the Indian state of Maharashtra, Enron's $3 billion Dahbol power plant was touted as the country's largest foreign investment project. However, over a decade after Enron formed the Dahbol Power Corporation (in partnership with Bechtel and General Electric), the plant is dormant while a bitter legal dispute between the government and DPC continues. In the midst of allegations of government oppression against protesters, the operators have been charged with manipulating prices through a PPA. At the end of 2000, the Maharashtra State Electricity Board claimed that the DPC was charging over double the rate of comparable publicly-owned generators. The Board subsequently called a moratorium on payments to the DPC and in May 2001 cancelled the PPA, which led Enron to shut down operations (Biswas 2003). The case remains tied up in litigation in multiple venues, while the power plant physically deteriorates as it remains mothballed. (For a case study of a failed PPA in Pakistan, see Box 4.)

Box 4

Hubco: Pakistan's power dispute

In its efforts to attract foreign capital to the energy sector, Pakistan has developed a framework of financial incentives that include a long-term PPA. According to a case study published by American University, 'Investors were reassured that the Water and Power Development Authority (WAPDA) and Karachi Electric Supply Corporation (KESC) would purchase electricity for a very reasonable 6.5 cents/kWh. This guaranteed the foreign producer that, regardless of a potential drop in demand for electricity, the government would purchase the supply of electricity at a favourable price.' Pakistan's largest power plant in 1997 was Hubco, located about 40 km northwest of Karachi. 'The state-owned WAPDA will purchase power from Hubco and the power purchase agreement assures a guaranteed revenue equivalent to 60 per cent of gross capacity utilization, irrespective of the actual takeoff from the power station' (Augustus 1997).

At the time Hubco was going online, the World Bank hailed the arrival of independent power producers as a solution for Pakistan's energy shortage, as well as a way to stem subsidy outlays needed to cover loss-making public generators. Shortly after operations began, however, problems resulting from the PPA became apparent. As the Asian Development Bank's Country Director to Pakistan explained (Shah 2002):

With the commissioning of some IPP power plants in 1997, WAPDA and KESC purchased electricity from these IPPs. From 1998, Pakistan had excess capacity with the utilities contracted to purchase expensive IPP electricity while their own plants were underutilized. Faced with the problem of having to purchase power from the IPPs and the two private sector operators HUBCO and KAPCO at an expensive rate, the Government's financing of other public enterprises in the power sector was adversely affected. The Government contended that the $0.065/kWh rate of the IPPs, as per their agreement with the previous Government, is unaffordable for a country like Pakistan. In 1996 and 1997, WAPDA and KESC faced serious liquidity problems and defaulted on some of their financial commitments.

The year after, the Sharif administration accused Hubco of using deception to influence the former Bhutto government to accept an excessively-priced PPS with WAPDA. Although corruption charges were not upheld in court, tariffs were eventually reduced significantly.

The Hubco case demonstrates not only the fiscal problems that PPAs can cause, but also the difficulties associated with governments that lack experience with complex contracts. Particularly in poor countries characterized by high risk, powerful corporations are in a strong position to demand lucrative contract terms from governments lacking negotiating power and skill. The 'take it or leave it' position of a dominant firm can leave a government with no choice but to offer concessions never contemplated in textbooks on economic theory.

In Uganda, the US energy firm AES negotiated a PPA for the Bujagali hydroelectric project that was later shown to be excessively expensive. The government has little experience with such contracts and relied on World Bank advice in setting up the PPA provisions. An independent review by an Indian consulting firm concluded that not only were capital costs the same as other power plants with twice the generating capacity, but the PPA imposes excessive payment requirements and restricts the government's ability to sign other agreements that could reduce its fiscal exposure (Prayas Energy Group 2002).[8]

Long-term power contracts have generated numerous disputes with governments that accused companies of extracting excessive financial benefits through high prices or selling unneeded energy. In addition to the cases described above, such contracts have been renegotiated or cancelled in Costa Rica, Croatia, the Dominican Republic, Hungary and Indonesia.[9]

Rationale No. 3: Improved Efficiency and Performance

The third rationale for privatization of essential services is both common and compelling: superior efficiency and performance of private providers. Privatization advocates often portray public sector providers as bound by bureaucratic inertia, lacking incentives to innovate, and unresponsive to help-less consumers who have nowhere else to go. Private providers are expected to improve efficiency and expand service because of inherent incentives to cut costs and to satisfy a growing number of paying customers. The state retains the role of market regulator.

There is considerable evidence supporting claims that privatized firms have performed better than the state-run services that they replaced. Research on privatization of state-owned enterprises (SOEs) reveals overwhelming evidence of increased efficiency and profitability (Megginson and Netter 2001). Moreover, efficiency improvement in basic services has often been accompanied by improved service quality and access. A review of evidence by a former World Bank economist and IDB vice-president concluded that although privatization in developing countries was associated with worse distribution of assets, it has increased access to utilities such as electricity for poor people (Birdsall and Nellis 2002).

In addition, anecdotal evidence of improved performance makes clear that private service provision can bring significant benefits in terms of both financial sustainability and consumer welfare (World Bank 2003). For example, while the failure of the Maynilad water concession in Manila has eroded the enthusiasm over this 'model' privatization, the chief regulator of the water utility involved in the dispute has vigorously defended the policy itself. He notes that tap water is actually cheaper now than before privatization, and that the other privatized concession in Manila is performing quite well financially. 'Also, there are now 9.8 million people who have connections as compared with only 7.3 million people prior to privatization ... The water coverage was only 67 per cent then and now it is 92 per cent ...' (Santos 2003).

A review of privatization in Chile reveals significant gains in productivity for private electricity generation, though less so for distribution, indicating that competition can have powerful effects (Fischer 2003). Even more impressively, Chile's privatized water system makes safe water available to 97 per cent of its urban population and sanitation to 80 per cent. In Cartagena, Colombia, the private venture Acuacar has proved considerably more responsive to its users than the public utility and has undertaken substantial improvements in maintenance and rehabilitation – the first investments to occur after an 11-year hiatus. Water quality has also improved.

Even privatizations that have been plagued by problems have shown important improvements. In Nelspruit, South Africa, despite the threat of financial collapse attributable to rampant non-payment, the private firm BiWater has added thousands of new connections and meters and water reliability has improved significantly. In Trinidad and Tobago, despite the financial failure of an interim operating agreement with Severn Trent, the first two years saw an increase in average water production, greater distribution of potable water to the country's southern region, rehabilitation work on pipes and a rural water supply project benefiting several hundred thousand customers (Commonwealth Finance Ministers 2003).

The main indicator for performance in virtually all privatization studies is *profitability or efficiency*. However, the profitability indicator is an inappropriate measure for the performance of essential services because it reflects the satisfaction of shareholders, not consumers. The indicator of efficiency, such as labour productivity or number of outputs per cost unit, is a legitimate consideration – but it is not the only one. Essential services are expected not only to run efficiently but also to provide high-quality service and reach the poor. Equity goals in particular, however, may undermine efficiency.

Moreover, even taking efficiency on its own terms, comparative evidence does not always support private provision. A recent statistical analysis of efficiency among public and private water companies in Asia revealed that there is no significant difference (Estache and Rossi 2002). In a comparison of five countries with public (United States, Japan, and Netherlands) and private (France, England) water provision, the number of utility staff per 1,000 connections is considerably lower in countries with public than with private provision. Moreover, the level of 'unaccounted-for' water is far higher in private-provision countries (Hall 2001). And, as numerous examples show later in this section, among developing countries, there is a growing record of private firms that have failed to turn around service utilities.

The remainder of this section examines performance among competitive and monopolistic services, as well as the critical issue of corruption.

Monopoly services and regulation. When a private provider is a natural monopoly, public regulation is needed to prevent market failure. The mechanism for ensuring compliance of monopolistic private providers is the performance contract, and the government's main job is to enforce it. While private providers in these sectors may still have incentives to improve efficiency, they have no incentive – or natural pressures – to translate higher productivity into gains for consumers. For this reason, the state emerges as the unique institution to protect the public interest. As one analyst has observed, private sector participation 'may actually place more rather than less demand on effective and capable public authorities. Intervention through incentives requires more skill than intervention through investment. New regulatory capacity is required to deal with these new roles' (Thompson 2001).

Proponents of putting natural monopolies under private provision are very enthusiastic about performance-based contracts (PBCs). A considerable body of economic literature has developed concerning the ability of PBCs to improve the bottom line of firms that contract out for goods and services that they used to produce internally. Much of this literature concerns the so-called 'principal-agent' problem. When agents (subcontractors) have much more information and knowledge about a given task than the principals (contracting firms), they may be able to withhold or manipulate that information to their own advantage.

The only way for the principal to overcome this problem is through adequate monitoring and evaluation of the agent's output. However, this can be quite costly, and often forces the principal to reconsider whether the extra costs – and risks – are worth subcontracting in the first place. Generally speaking, *the easier it is to observe and measure an output, the less costly it will be to enforce* a PBC. As outputs become more complex or subjective, the likelihood of undetected non-compliance or contractual disputes grows. According to John Donahue, author of a seminal study on privatization, when outputs cannot be precisely described and measured, the case for the in-house option becomes stronger. 'The relative appeal of *employing* people, as opposed to *contracting* with them, increases ... the more the task at hand is uncertain at the outset and prone to revision' (Donahue 1989).

Notwithstanding the spotty record of PBCs in the private sector, they are now a central feature of a new development paradigm for services, commonly called 'output-based aid' (OBA). Although private provision of government services has not been subject to systematic analysis in developing countries, it has been in the North. Such studies reveal a very mixed record in the developed countries, ranging from much better than, to much worse than, to about the same performance as the public sector. According to a review of evidence from the United States conducted by Columbia University Professor Elliott Sclar, private providers tend to do a better job than government when performing simple low-skill activities, and a poorer job when performing more complex activities.[10] Indeed, privatized services often cost more than public services that were provided in-house.

Why is this the case? As two management researchers put it: 'Performance contracts are not self-administering, self-correcting, or self-improving.

Performance contracts do not quickly or automatically solve the problems of vendor performance' (Behn and Kant 1999).[11] As former World Bank senior economist David Ellerman puts it (Ellerman 2001):

> From time to time, private sector management 'discovers' the idea of paying for performance (not just for time put in), of paying for outputs (not just inputs), and of management by objectives accomplished (not just intentions). It all sounds so obvious and so sensible that one must ask 'Why didn't people think of this before?' The answer is that they did. And they discovered that it doesn't work too well – aside from fairly rude forms of labour. In areas of human effort where effort, commitment, and the application of intelligence are important, the carrots and sticks of external motivation are insufficient for sustained performance. Beyond simple and specific products, the determinants of quality are rarely susceptible to external monitoring.

In short, the main limitation of performance contracts is *transaction costs*. As services become more complex – and as the economic and social outcomes they are supposed to achieve become more difficult to measure with simple indicators – the public sector inevitably gets involved. Governments often impose strict requirements on contractors regarding production processes and outputs, as well as information and reporting requirements. These details become part of excruciatingly complex and highly legalistic contracts, and they end up raising the costs of producing the desired services.

From a developmental perspective, Sclar's study is revealing in two ways. First, it dispels the myth of the superiority of private management of public services by demonstrating just how difficult it can be to adequately specify terms in a performance contract. Even when well-paid lawyers, accountants, bureaucrats, and technicians work together to ensure that payment is based on objectively measured outputs, the record has often been disappointing. Second, Sclar's study raises serious questions about the ability of governments in poor countries to even produce, much less enforce, the complex contracts

Even specifying a seemingly simple output such as 'number of connections' in a water contract is unlikely, by itself, to achieve equitable social outcomes. That is because there is inevitable uncertainty about what kinds of goods and services are needed, where they are needed, and by whom. A World Bank research note acknowledges this constraint: 'Even if a [water] contract were bid on the basis of perfect information about the current status of the water company's assets and about new investments needed, the future would hold uncertainties that could not be handled by contract. And an initial contract is usually based on highly incomplete information' (Cowen 1997).

involved in transferring responsibility for public services to profit-motivated agents who have far more information than the principals.

Proponents of private provision are fond of pointing out that monopoly providers require regulation regardless of whether they are public or private. And there is no shortage of evidence about the failure of public regulators to discipline failing public providers. As the World Bank's 2003 World Development Report argues, there is sometimes a conflict of interest when one government entity is charged with controlling another. The poor performance of public service provision thus justifies privatization even under weak regulation. Indeed, without a private sector to monitor, how can regulators ever learn their job? While problems and setbacks may arise at the beginning, over time the necessary institutions will be created.

Although there may certainly be cases in which adequate regulation of private providers is a viable option, policymakers must base their decisions on the risks of pursuing such arrangements. At a minimum they should ask how feasible it will be to establish a functioning, independent regulator, and the time horizon for doing so. Equally important, the decision to privatize should be informed by an impact analysis of private provision under weak or non-existent regulation.

In the case of long-term contracts, the lack of adequate regulation at the beginning can result in a flawed contract and regulatory 'capture' that is difficult to overcome. Moreover, if it is possible to create effective regulators of private providers from scratch, it may also be possible to strengthen the capacity and autonomy of regulators that enforce public provision. From the perspective of the policymaker, it is important to ask which of these tasks is most feasible, and to assess the relative costs of poor regulation.

Not surprisingly, regulation in developing countries is generally weak, sometimes even non-existent. According to the World Bank publication *Privatization in Africa* (1998), 'In not one country with a privatization programme has there been an effort to develop a regulatory framework as an integral part of that programme.' Similarly, economist Manuel Angel Abdala concluded in his study of Latin American privatization: 'Widespread privatization has been encouraged all over the region. With a few exceptions, however, the transfer of ownership was hurried or performed under constraints imposed by economic and political objectives that tended to overlook the importance of regulating private monopolies' (Baer and Birch 1994, and Bangura 2000).

In the developing world there is a long and growing record of private monopoly services characterized by poor quality, financial mismanagement and unaccountably high price hikes. One of the most spectacular failures involved Maynilad Water Services, a French-Filipino consortium that began supplying drinking water to about half of Manila in 1997, and was touted by the World Bank as a showcase of successful privatization. After successfully petitioning the water regulator MWSS to grant a series of tariff hikes not formally permitted under the terms of the original contract, Maynilad angrily announced in December 2002 that it would terminate its contract. MWSS and citizens' groups argued that the company had received extraordinary leniency for raising prices and amending the contract to postpone performance targets. However, the regulator's refusal to allow yet another rate hike in late 2002 led the debt-burdened company to abandon the concession (Raquizza 2003). As of this writing, litigation for damages – the government and company both demand compensation from the other – is still pending.

In 1995, a Vivendi affiliate took full control of Puerto Rico's water utility PRASA. Four years later the Office of the Comptroller issued a scathing report, describing unsatisfactory maintenance and repair, incomplete financial disclosure, neglect of consumer enquiries, customers billed without receiving water, and financial mismanagement that required stop-gap funding from the state development bank. Not far away, in the Dominican Republic, the 1999 privatization of the electricity utility – which admittedly was in very bad shape – has been a major disappointment. By 2001 blackouts were even more frequent than under public provision. 'Business owners have refused to pay higher prices for an even worse service, with the result that whole communities are now disconnected' (Bayliss 2002).

In Orissa, India, a special government commission was appointed to review the state's energy reform programme, which included private provision of electricity from US-based AES. In May 2001, after consulting with stakeholders from the provider, government, and consumers, a state-appointed review committee comprised of retired officials and academics issued a blistering report. The report cited no progress in improving transmission losses after five years, deterioration of bill collection, higher debt, increased costs of generation, steep tariff increases with no corresponding improvement in finances, and the virtual absence of new capital investment (Prayas Energy Group).

In the 2003 *Social Watch* Report, a number of country reports describe serious performance failures under private provision.[12] Before being resold in 2002, Bulgaria's private water company routinely overcharged customers, randomly cut off services, and failed to respond to consumer complaints. Between 2000 and 2001, El Salvador's privatized electricity companies presided over 44,000 power outages and fielded complaints from half a million customers. The list of grievances from Nicaragua included incorrect (and uncorrected) billing, service paid for but not delivered for public street lighting, and voltage failures resulting in damage to small appliances and business production.

Competitive services and choice – but for whom? For services with (at least potentially) low barriers to entry, the rationale for private provision is *choice*: consumers buy services based on price and quality. Here the government's main role is to ensure adequate levels of competition that create viable choices for all citizens. Expanding private provision in competitive service sectors can certainly increase choice, but not necessarily for all consumers.

A pervasive problem associated with greater choice is the practice of cherry-picking, as noted earlier. When private providers enter the market, they have strong incentives to serve primarily people who are able to pay commercial prices and who enable firms to minimize overhead costs. Not only are poor people least able to pay, they are often the most costly to serve, living in less accessible areas and more prone to getting sick.

Especially when existing public services are of low quality, expanding the choice of providers draws better-off consumers into the private sector. However, those who are unable to afford commercially priced private services must remain with the state, thus creating a 'two-tier' system based on income. Public services that are funded through progressive cross-subsidies – or where high-use customers account for the bulk of revenues – are especially vulnerable to increased private sector participation, which reduces the public sector's revenue base.

If policymakers do not address market failures associated with natural disincentives to serve vulnerable populations, improved efficiency may go hand in hand with increased social exclusion. Policy constraints inevitably raise issues of fairness. On the one hand, neither middle-class consumers (nor any anyone else) should be forced to use low-quality services. If greater choice can improve quality and efficiency, such benefits should not be ignored. On the other hand, poor people are already marginalized politically. After addressing the interests of the more influential constituencies by increasing private provision, governments may be tempted to 'move on' and neglect complementary policies needed to serve the poor.

Multilateral lenders and borrowing governments increasingly turn to the catch-all policy of 'social safety-nets' to address equity under private provision policies. When done well, these can be effectively targeted subsidies and 'lifeline tariffs' that ensure provision for all. At worst, they can be a budgetary gesture with no programmatic features to reach intended beneficiaries.

Privatization advocates frequently cite health care as an area in which competition can generate both greater efficiency and superior service. (The argument is difficult to make for utilities, since they tend to be monopolies, making public regulation essential.) However, claims about the ability of the private sector to improve equity and choice in health care provision are contradicted by considerable evidence about imperfect information and 'market failure, such as those arising from the strong power imbalance between providers and patients' (Bijlmakers and Lindner 2003). Even for contracting out of specific services, an empirical review calls into question the private sector's management capabilities, the existence of genuine competition and the translation of competition into efficiency gains, as well as government capacity to deign and enforce appropriate contracts with private providers (Waelkens and Greindl).

Provision of health care is unusually complex. There is a vast array of public, private, and mixed systems that range from highly successful to dysfunctional. Unlike basic infrastructure, choosing health care reform is not a matter of selecting among a small number of distinct models with clear ownership arrangements, but rather shaping incentives for public and private providers. There is no 'boilerplate' health care contract that a government can easily adapt to its own circumstances.

There is growing consensus, however, on several principles about health care provision. According to an IMF researcher: 'Allocation cannot be based solely on cost-effectiveness, which focuses on efficiency, but ignores equity ... Markets alone cannot produce efficient outcome in the health care sector, which suffers serious [market] failures due to asymmetry of information, imperfect agency relationships, barriers to entry and moral hazard.' Because patients know far less than physicians about how to 'consume' health care, doctors have tremendous power to induce consumption (Hsiao 2000). In other words, because of the supply-side particularities of health care, demand can be induced with relatively little consideration for price. As a result, private provision that is not rigorously regulated is often characterized by over-supply.

Another area in which competition is supposed to demonstrate the potential of private service provision is electricity generation (as opposed to distribution, which is usually a natural monopoly.) When different energy producers are allowed to enter the market, using different kinds of fuel and production processes, customers should benefit through lower prices. Deregulated energy sectors in a number of localities in highly industrialized countries, however, have been characterized by market manipulation and spectacular price increases. The states of California, United States, and Ontario and Alberta, Canada, could not control electricity prices under a unregulated power market. Regulators in developing countries that promote private sector generation therefore face a daunting challenge.

Fighting corruption. One of the most common justifications for privatizing services is the high level of corruption often evident in government-provided services. However, if there was ever a double-edged sword in the debate over reforming services, corruption is it. Private provision proponents argue that front-line government service providers routinely engage in petty bribery and theft of supplies and portray high-ranking officials as perpetrators of massive graft. They have no shortage of evidence. Sceptics, in turn, can choose from a large and growing menu of non-transparent and criminal practices among firms that deliver essential services. Former World Bank Chief Economist Joseph Stiglitz once memorably referred to privatization as 'briberization'. This paper draws no conclusions about which is worse. Rather, it proposes that policymakers assess existing or potential accountability mechanisms as they consider which kind of provider is more likely to serve the public welfare.

Neither public officials nor private businesses are inherently honest. If not made accountable to service users, both can engage in egregious rent-seeking activities. Information disclosure and external monitoring are therefore essential for both kinds of arrangements. Corrupt governments clean up their act only when they have to answer to citizens. Where policymakers depend on rent-seeking elites for political survival, or citizens lack the information they need to evaluate the behaviour of those entrusted to serve the public, accountability is hard to deliver. By contrast, private firms refrain from corruption when they have to answer to government. Because they are directly accountable to shareholders, keeping them honest requires, above all, an effective public regulator.

If one accepts the premise that ungoverned profit-maximizing companies are no more philanthropic than their public sector counterparts, then state institutions become the weakest link in fighting corruption *regardless of the provider*. What tends to be lost in the debate over service reform is that regulatory integrity is the key to both effective public and private provision.

The 2004 World Development Report promotes the perspective of many private provision advocates who seek to 'separate the policymaker from the provider'. They argue that when the same government charged with delivering services must also monitor and regulate the service provider, an inherent conflict of interest weakens internal accountability. Accordingly, they maintain that increasing user fees and increasing choice will make consumers less tolerant of poor quality in general, and corruption in particular. Private provision and commercialization thus 'empower' consumers and force providers to behave in an accountable manner.

Critics of this perspective, however, respond that there is no substitute for effective regulation when it comes to essential services. Especially for natural monopolies such as utilities, the question of choice is moot; regulation is the only way to prevent a variety of market failures, including corruption. Even for such competitive services as health care and health insurance, public authority is required to protect consumers from fraud and abuse. Industrialized Western countries have created thousands of such regulations and an enormous regulatory apparatus for this purpose.

Yet even in countries with strong institutions, control over information provides ample opportunity for firms to cheat government and taxpayers. In the United States, the nation's second largest hospital chain paid $54 million to the government to settle claims that doctors at a California hospital performed hundreds of unnecessary heart operations and then billed government insurance programmes for reimbursement. In July 2003, a leading US medical laboratory paid over half a billion dollars in fines after pleading guilty to obstructing investigations over its conspiracy to defraud government health care programmes (*Financial Times* 2003).

The 'privatization paradox' described at the beginning of this paper is especially perplexing when it comes to good governance in developing countries with weak institutions. The same government officials that were too corrupt to deliver services to citizens are expected to be immune to the lucrative inducements of private firms. Public sector managers unable to control the behaviour of front-line government agencies must somehow enforce compliance with standards of corporate responsibility.

While public service employees may steal from consumers, supply warehouses and budgets, private providers also have numerous opportunities for corruption and regulatory capture. These include the bidding process for public contracts, the establishment of contractual terms, enforcement of contract compliance (including tariff changes), and anti-competitive collusion. Moreover, the more money is at stake, the greater the potential for corrupt behaviour. For example, according to the World Bank itself, 'transnational firms headquartered abroad are more likely than other firms to pay public procurement kickbacks' (Hellman and Kaufmann 2000). Corporate corruption is not an isolated phenomenon. In the United States, accounting scandals at Enron and WorldComm preceded record-breaking bankruptcies, while energy companies have been implicated in manipulation of the price of electricity in California's deregulated market (Palast 2003).

There are countless examples of corruption in privatizations undertaken in developing countries (Hawley 2000; Hall 1999). Among the best known is the infamous 'loans for shares' scandal in Russia, in which a large proportion of the country's most valuable assets were sold off to political insiders for a fraction of their worth (Johnson 1997). In Papua New Guinea, the national Ombudsman Commission investigated a Build-Own-Transfer concession to the Malaysian firm JC-KRTA. It concluded that the contract award involved favours from high-level politicians and was based on personal contacts with the government (Kaman 2003). In Orissa, India, a government-appointed committee reported illegal behaviour on the part of a major private generator, including non-payment to the transmission company, the refusal to provide concessional pricing arrangements stipulated by the regulatory commission, and non-compliance with regulatory judgements (Prayas 2003).

Rationale No. 4: Making Reform Irreversible

One of the most compelling rationales for private provision is that it helps make reforms permanent. The ebb and flow of the political system creates a certain degree of uncertainty. What one reformer accomplishes today may be undone by the next administration. Private provision is thus a useful way to remove policy from the political agenda. It is much easier to increase subsidies or reverse employment cutbacks than to re-nationalize private assets or expel private firms from the market.

Permanence has its attraction but it is important that only the right reforms be cast in stone. Unfortunately, policymakers often lack sufficient information and analysis to be able to predict the social and economic impacts of major reforms. In this sense, while making effective reforms irreversible is highly desirable, it would be dangerous to leave no exit door for policies that are poorly implemented, have far deeper negative impacts than initially believed, or have major unintended consequences that were not originally considered. Thus, before making decisions that preclude reversal or even significant modification, policymakers should undertake a focused analysis of expected impacts over time.

One implicit premise underlying the rationale for policy permanence is that the political system is inherently corrupt and responsive to rent-seeking interests. Thus, it is better to prevent anyone from making policy changes than allow policy to be constantly subject to manipulation and political calculus. Policymakers in many countries may have good reason to be sympathetic to such a premise. However, to the extent the existing system excludes the poor, rural people or other marginalized groups from essential services, policymakers should determine whether any permanent policy alternative is more likely to improve the status quo or lock in (or deepen) current inequities. Upon reflection, they may conclude that only by directly challenging political elites can government truly advance the public welfare.

The most common way that government can tie its own hands in service reform is through privatization or long-term private concessions. Expropriating private property (and to a lesser extent rescinding a legal contract) is typically considered a radical, populist and irresponsible act, especially by investors upon whom governments depend to generate jobs and economic growth. Such actions can bring the wrath of multilateral and bilateral lenders and lead private rating agencies to seriously downgrade sovereign credit risk. Because such pressures can lead to higher interest rates or even a cutoff of credit, private provision can effectively remove government from service provision for the foreseeable future.

Even in cases where it is politically feasible to take back control of essential services, private provision may over time make such an alternative impossible for more practical reasons. Especially when it comes to complex, integrated sectors such as utilities, surrendering the capacity to deliver services may make it impossible for the government to turn back the clock. As Gleick, Wolff, Chalecki and Reyes (2002) put it:

> When governments transfer control over their water system to private companies, the loss of internal skills and expertise may be irreversible, or nearly so. Many contracts are long-term – for as much as 10 to 20 years. Management expertise, engineering knowledge, and other assets in the public domain may be lost for good. Indeed, while there is growing experience with the transfer of such assets to private hands, there is little or no recent experience with the public sector re-acquiring such assets from the private sector.

Multilateral trading system and service. Governments can also make public service reforms permanent through legally binding constraints. Perhaps the most controversial of these is through the WTO's General Agreement on Trade in Services. (For an overview of the Agreement's provisions, see Box 5.) While GATS does not privatize services, it does limit the ability of governments to take actions that affect the competitive position of foreign investors. The impact of GATS therefore does not derive from the sale or contracting out of public assets, but rather from restricting government regulation or subsidizing service providers, especially in ways that provide advantages that might discriminate against an existing or potentially existing competitor (Hilary 2001; Krajewski 2002; Speed and Tuerk 2003).

Box 5
An overview of the General Agreement on Trade in Services

GATS went into effect as part of the World Trade Organization on 1 January 1995. Its purpose is the progressive liberalization of trade in services under four distinct 'modes':

1 *Cross-border supply*: the ability of non-residents to supply services within another member's territory.
2 *Consumption abroad*: the freedom to purchase services in the territory of another member.

3 *Commercial presence:* the opportunity for foreign suppliers to establish, operate, or expand a commercial entity in a member's territory, such as a branch, agency or wholly-owned subsidiary.

4 *Presence of natural persons*: permission for entry and temporary stay in the member's territory as foreign individuals in order to supply a service.

The Agreement calls for successive rounds of negotiation to extend GATS coverage into new service sectors, and to specify rules that affect governments' ability to regulate or participate in those sectors. GATS applies to all WTO members, which are subject to legally binding dispute settlement decisions.

GATS has potentially far-reaching effects, since a wide range of services may fall under its jurisdiction. The Agreement excludes services 'provided in the exercise of government authority', which means that the service must be provided on *neither* a commercial *nor* a competitive basis. Currently, however, it is difficult to determine the precise scope of the Agreement since there is a great deal of controversy over these important qualifications.

Once a government has made a commitment under GATS, it can be hard to reverse. If a government does choose to withdraw from a previous commitment, it must compensate other members whose service suppliers may be adversely affected. GATS protects foreign service suppliers and investors through several basic rules. Some of these rules apply only when approved by members for specific service sectors.

- *Most favoured nation.* Government must extend any regulation or financial measure that benefits one foreign service provider to all foreign providers. Most-favoured nation treatment applies automatically to all sectors unless a member explicitly excludes that sector from the MFN rule.
- *National treatment.* Government must offer 'best treatment' of domestic service providers to foreign providers. If competition is altered to favour domestic providers, even as an unintended consequence of promoting domestic social goals, a measure can be ruled as discriminatory. National treatment provisions apply only to sectors in which a country affirmatively lists commitments.
- *Market access.* Government may not restrict the number of service suppliers or employees in a sector, the value of transactions, or the types of legal entities that may supply a service. Like national treatment, market access provisions only apply when a country explicitly makes this commitment in a sector.
- *Monopolies and exclusive providers.* Governments may exercise monopoly for a service sector, but can only do so by listing the sector as a country-specific exception. Governments that make commitments in this area cannot use their power in a way that violates MFN, national treatment, or market access commitments.
- *Domestic regulation.* Still under negotiation in Geneva, these provisions could create some form of 'necessity test' to be applied to regulations such as professional qualification, technical standards and licensing procedures. Regulations determined to pursue non-legitimate objectives or to be 'more trade restrictive than necessary' by a dispute settlement panel would not be permitted.

Once a government has made specific sectoral commitments under the GATS, it may only reverse them by negotiating acceptable compensation with all affected parties – a costly undertaking that virtually ensures continuity. The WTO itself declares that 'because unbinding is difficult, [government] commitments [to a sector] are virtually guaranteed …' (WTO 2003). This means that if subsequent events reveal serious negative social or economic effects, it may be too late to take corrective action.

While WTO officials routinely deny that GATS applies to basic public services, the ambiguity of existing language suggests otherwise. GATS does exempt those services 'supplied in the exercise of governmental authority', but defines those services as being provided neither on a competitive nor commercials basis. Thus for services in which governments compete with private providers or charge cost-covering fees, they would appear to potentially fall under GATS jurisdiction. Moreover, in the current round of negotiations, Northern countries have already made numerous requests for opening up water, electricity, health and education services, making it quite clear that governments are now being pressured to make commitments on essential services that will be fully subject to GATS disciplines.

Even as Northern governments pressure Southern countries to open up their essential service sectors, citizens from these countries – including public service managers, local governments, and consumer advocacy and policy research organizations – have mobilized to demand that their government refrain from making irreversible commitments that could undermine government's ability to regulate or subsidize essential services. Indeed, the entire European Union has categorically excluded these services from its GATS commitments.[13]

The WTO and its supporters characterize opponents of GATS as uninformed and alarmist. Yet neither the WTO nor the multilateral lending institutions have prepared a framework for assessing even the economic – to say nothing of the social – impact of opening services under GATS.[14] The argument made here is not that liberalizing trade in essential services is always a bad decision. Rather, it is that policymakers are fully justified in demanding more information about the consequences of that liberalization before jumping in with both feet.

Many who are aware of WTO processes have observed that it may be impossible to apply traditional 'safeguard' measures to GATS commitments. While trade in goods is primarily about tariffs and quotas, trade in services is primarily about investment restrictions. A government facing negative balance of payment or employment impacts in manufacturing can temporarily raise tariffs and limit imports. It cannot, however, simply stop foreign firms with domestic investments from providing services, even for a limited time.

For many competitive services, safeguards may be intractably difficult to implement. Yet for *essential* services whose primary purpose is human welfare, governments should insist on greater flexibility for policy actions that affect foreign investors. One approach might be to create safeguards involving regulation and subsidy allocation – rather than direct expropriation or forced exit – and the development of objective indicators that make it possible to measure negative social impacts from liberalization.

With such a framework in place, it would be possible to specify an impact threshold for applying safeguards, enabling governments to respond quickly with policies that may not be normally WTO-consistent. While foreign investors may dislike any measure that could undermine their competitiveness or profitability, objective social impact indicators would help ensure that safeguards are not hijacked by protectionist interests.

Conclusion

While many of the rationales for private provision of essential public services are compelling, private provision in practice does not always deliver the benefits associated with these rationales. In some cases, private service delivery results in a fiasco while in other cases undeniable improvements are evident. In many of the latter cases, however, the economic logic underlying private provision of essential services can exclude or harm poor people, or force the government to assume costs that rival or vastly exceed those associated with public sector reform.

Moreover, the benefits of private provision are often most doubtful precisely where public services are performing the worst. Governments that already have strong institutions and accountability mechanisms are likely to be able to implement privatization policies quite effectively. However, they are also more likely to have effective service providers and low levels of corruption to begin with. On the other hand, rent-seeking public institutions and governments driven by special interests typically deliver poor-quality services or limit access to the privileged few. While there may be much room for improvement, such governments offer little hope for properly regulating private firms that deliver essential services.

Proponents of private provision often assume a 'counterfactual of inaction'. They compare best-case private provision scenarios with a continuation of failing public service. The implication in much privatization literature is that government is simply beyond hope. Yet there are often viable options for reforming public services, especially by increasing accountability to citizens and making budgets more progressive. In many cases, the constraints on these options are starkly political, while in others the need is for greater technical capacity or better organizational incentives. Before committing to private provision, especially with weak regulatory capacity, governments should assess the constraints to 'doing privatization right', the costs of doing it wrong, and options for reforming existing public sector services. Toward that end, this paper encourages policymakers to:

- Determine which *kinds of institutions* are needed for different provision options;
- Assess *the feasibility and time horizon* for strengthening or creating those institutions;
- Evaluate the *risks* of attempting different paths of reforms and ask whether those risks are acceptable;
- Estimate the potential *social and economic costs* of service provision while appropriate institutions are being built; and
- Consider *a range of roles* that the private sector might play in providing essential services.

Most participants in the debate over reforming services may agree with the idea of keeping policy options open until analysis and evidence are available. However, in practice much policy advice leaves room for only limited options within a single pre-determined approach. Yet policymakers must choose between 'all or nothing' as they consider alternatives for policy reform.

The pace and sequencing of policy reform are critical. Experience with 'big-bang' structural reforms has been disappointing, because the institutions required to make them work are usually not in place. A gradual, cautious approach can help governments avoid big mistakes and also enable learning that translates into subsequent policy action. In the case of essential services, full private sector management (or ownership) of service delivery may suddenly give government new responsibilities that it is not willing or able to fulfill.

Private provision contracts need not delegate wholesale management of complex services to a single provider. Within the private sector, large corporations contract out specific tasks to smaller firms in order to increase efficiency or production flexibility – while maintaining full control over finished products and services. Similarly, governments may continue to provide essential services directly while using contracts to produce important inputs into final service delivery (e.g. construction, installation of household utility connections, meter-reading and bill collection, etc.).

For example, there is an important distinction between a service contract that 'assigns responsibility for isolated tasks', and management contracts in which 'management authority is transferred to the private sector'. The more isolated the task, the less risk the private provider is expected to assume.

Privatization advocates point out that service contracts under weak public management are unlikely to result in significant improvement (Marek, Yamamoto and Ruster 2003). However, by the same token, where regulatory capacity is weak, governments are unlikely to enforce private sector compliance with terms of complex and sweeping management contracts.

Weak states therefore present obstacles to both public and private service delivery options. The challenge for policymakers is to determine how to structure and sequence reforms so as to enhance the government capacities needed to make chosen reforms effective. As they begin the reform process, governments can harness the efficiency and incentives of private provision without taking big risks. For example, private firms may bid on delivering specific elements of service delivery to government buyers, rather than delivering the entire service to households.

Particularly where institutions are weak, governments as customers (typically monopsonies) are likely to have far greater ability to hold private firms accountable than individuals. Greater efficiency in these areas may help improve service quality or financial sustainability, thereby contributing to effective public sector reform. Alternatively, as government learns how to monitor and regulate limited private provision activities, it may become better prepared to move on to more advanced stages of private provision.

Notes

1 This paper uses the term 'privatization' to connote variants of provision by non-state actors: private firms or non-profit organizations. Private provision refers to control over assets: direct ownership or authority over management and resource allocation decisions. Under private *provision*, the public sector plays primarily a regulatory role. However, many forms of private sector *participation* can exist under direct public provision. Some of these are discussed in the Conclusion.

2 In deference to the WDR authors' request to refrain from quoting the draft report, direct citations are not provided. The final report was to be issued on 20 September 2003.

3 For critical analyses of the PSD Strategy, see Leon Bijlmakers and Marianne Lindner, 'The World Bank's Private Sector Development Strategy: Key Issues and Risks', WEMOS, April 2003; Kate Bayliss and David Hall, 'A PSIRU Response to the World Bank's Private Sector Development Strategy', Public Services International Research Unit, October 2001; Nancy Alexander, 'Growing Dangers of Service Apartheid', *News and Notices for IMFF and World Bank Watchers*, Vol. 2 (5), Winter 2001–02.

4 Major international institutions have begun to oppose the use of cross-subsidies in principle, despite the fact that these are still the norm in wealthy countries. According the OECD, 'It is far preferable to fund non-commercial services through an explicit transfer mechanism than through hidden cross-subsidies because external funding mechanisms allow competition to develop in the potentially competitive services.' See OECD Directorate for Financial, Fiscal and Enterprise Affairs, 'Non-Commercial Service Obligations and Liberalization', Working Paper No. 2 on Competition and Regulation, 23 April 2003, page 3.

5 While Vivendi agreed to increase investment following the public protest, the World Bank subsequently questioned the project as too costly and non-competitively tendered. Bayliss, 2002.

6 Smith *et. al.* (op.cit.).

7 Penelope Brook Cowen, 1997, 'Getting the Private Sector Involved in Water – What to do in the Poorest of Countries?', *Public Policy for the Private Sector*, Note No. 102, World Bank.

8 For an exhaustive technical review of the PPA, see Prayas Energy Group, 'The Bujagali Power Purchase Agreement: A Study of Techno-Economic Aspects', commissioned by International Rivers Network, November 2002.

9 Corral *et al.* (op cit.).

10 Elliott Sclar, 2001, *You Don't Always Get What You Pay For: The Economics of Privatization*, Cornell University Press.

11 Robert Behn and Peter Kant, 1999, 'Strategies for Avoiding the Pitfalls of Performance Contracting', *Public Productivity and Management Review*, Vol. 22 (4), 471–478.

12 For an overview of the findings of the country reports, see Kessler 2003.

13 Several governmental bodies in the North have articulated concern over the risks of GATS in undermining regulatory authority, the ability to subsidize services, and public welfare. These include the government of British Columbia, the United States National Conference of State Legislatures, the US National League of Cities, and the State Senate of California. In addition, the Government of the Philippines recently announced its intention to keep all essential services off the table in GATS negotiations.

14 GATS Article XIX, Section (3) states: 'For the purposes of establishing such guidelines [for new rounds of negotiations] the Council for Trade in Services shall carry out an assessment of trade in services in overall terms and on a sectoral basis with reference to the objectives of this Agreement ...' Before the Doha Round, several developing countries called for completion of the assessment, but were ignored by the Quad countries. The USTR treated the request as untimely.

References

Arhin-Tenkorang, Dyna, 2000, 'Mobilizing Resources for Health: The Case of User Fees Re-visited', Commission on Macroeconomics and Health, 3 November.

Arteaga, Ana Maria, 2003, 'The brutal rationale of privatisation', *Social Watch Report*.

Augustus, Theresa, 1997, 'Pakistan Power Needs and Environment', *TED Case Studies*, Vol. 7, No. 1, January.

Baer, Werner and Melissa H. Birch (eds) 1994, 'Privatization in Latin America'.Cited in Yusuf Bangura, 2000, 'Public Sector Restructuring: The Institutional and Social Effects of Fiscal, Managerial and Capacity-Building Reforms', United Nations Research Institute for Social Development, Occasional Paper No. 3, February.

Bayliss, Kate and David Hall, 2002, 'Unsustainable Conditions: the World Bank, Privatization, Water and Energy', Public Services International Research Unit, 7 August.

Bayliss, Kate, 2002, 'Privatisation and Poverty: The Distributional Impact of Utility Privatization', Centre on Regulation and Competition, Working Paper No. 16, January.

Bayliss, Kate, 2002, 'Water Privatisation in Sub-Saharan Africa: Progress, Problems and Policy Implications', Paper presented at Development Studies Association Annual Conference, University of Greenwich, November, pp. 12–13.

Behn, Robert and Peter Kant, 1999, 'Strategies for Avoiding the Pitfalls of Performance Contracting', *Public Productivity and Management Review*, Vol. 22 (4), 471–478.

Bijlmakers, Leon and Marianne Lindner, 2003, 'The World Bank's Private Sector Development Strategy: Key Issues and Risks', Wemos/ETC Crystal, April.

Birdsall, Nancy and John Nellis, 2002, 'Winners and Losers: Assessing the Distributional Impact of Privatization', Global Center for Development, Working Paper No. 6, May.

Biswas, Trineesh, 2003, 'Enron's Investment in Indian Power Plant Still Embroiled in Legal Battles', *Investment Law and Policy Weekly News Bulletin*, June 20.

Bourbigot, Marie-Marguerite and Yves Picaud, 2001, 'Vivendi Water: Public-Private Partnership (PPP) for Municipal Water Services', Regional Conference on the Reform of the Water Supply and Sanitation Sector in Africa, Kampala, Uganda, February (quoted in Bayliss 2002).

Brook-Cowen, Penelope, 1997, 'Getting the Private Sector Involved in Water – What to Do in the Poorest of Countries?', *Public Policy for the Private Sector*, Note No. 102, World Bank.

Civil Society Consultation on the 2003 Commonwealth Finance Ministers' Meeting on Provision of Basic Services, Bandar Seri Begawan, Negara Brunei Darussalam, 22–24 July.

Corral, Violeta, Kate Bayliss and David Hall, 2001, 'FDI Linkages and Infrastructure: Some Problem Cases in Water and Energy', PSIRU, July.

Donahue, John, 1989, *The Privatization Decision: Public Ends, Private Means*, Basic Books, p. 45.

Dubash, Navroz, 2002, *Power Politics: Equity and Environment in Electricity Reform*, World Resources Institute.

Ellerman, David, 2001, 'From Sowing to Reaping: Improving the Investment Climate(s)', World Bank.

Equinet, Medact, World Development Movement, and others, 2003, 'The GATS Threat to Public Health: A Joint Submission to the World Health Assembly', May.

Estache, Antonio, Vivien Foster and Quentin Wodon, 2001, 'Making Infrastructure Reform Work For the Poor: Policy Options based on Latin American Experience', LAC Regional Studies Program, WBI Studies in Development, FPSI, World Bank, p. 19.

Estache, Antonio and Martin Rossi, 'How Different is the Efficiency of Public and Private Water Companies in Asia?', *World Bank Economic Review*, Vol. 16, No. 1.

Financial Times, 2003, 'Convictions for US healthcare fraud up by 22%', 11 August.

Finnegan, William, 2002, 'Leasing the Rain', *The New Yorker*, 8 April.

Fischer, Ronald, Rodrigo Gutierrez and Pablo Serra, 2003, 'The Effects of Privatization on Firms and on Social Welfare: The Chilean Case', Inter-American Development Bank, Research Network Working Paper No. R-456, May.

FT Energy Newsletter, 1997, Global Water Report, 26 March 1997 (quoted in Bayliss 2002).

Gleick, Peter, Gary Wolff, Elizabeth Chalecki and Rachel Reyes, 2002, *The New Economy of Water: The Risks and Benefits of Globalization and Privatization of Fresh Water*, Pacific Institute, Oakland, CA, February.

Gómez-Lobo, Andres and Dante Contreras, 2003, 'Water Subsidy Policies: A Comparison of the Chilean and Colombian Schemes', Department of Economics, University of Chile, May.

Haarmeyer, David and Ashoka Mody, 1998, 'Tapping the Private Sector Approaches to Managing Risk in Water and Sanitation', RMC Discussion Paper 122, World Bank, p. 13.

Hall, David, 2003, 'Water Multinationals in Retreat: Suez Withdraws Investment', Public Services International Research Unit, January.

Hall, David, 2001, *Water in Public Hands*, Public Services International, June, p. 16.

Hall, David, 1999, 'Privatisation, Multinationals, and Corruption', *Development in Practice*, Vol. 9, No. 5, November.

Hawley, Sue, 2000, 'Exporting Corruption: Privatisation, Multinationals and Bribery', *The CornerHouse*, Briefing No. 19.

Hellman, J., G. Jones and D. Kaufmann, 2000, 'Are Foreign Investors Engaging in Corrupt Practices in Transition Economies?', *Transition Newsletter*, May–June.

Hilary, John, 2001, *The Wrong Model: GATS, Trade Liberalization, and Children's Right to Health*, Save the Children.

Hsiao, William, 2000, 'What Should Macro-Economists Know About Health Care Policy: A Primer', IMF Working Paper WP/00/136, International Monetary Fund.

Johnson, Juliet, 1997, 'Russia's Emerging Financial-Industrial Groups', *Post-Soviet Affairs*, Vol. 13, No. 4.

Kaman, Julienne, 2003, 'Privatization of Water in Papau New Guinea-Eda Ranu', Paper presented at the Civil Society Consultation on the 2003 Commonwealth Finance Ministers' Meeting on Provision of Basic Services, Bandar Seri Begawan, Negara Brunei Darussalam, 22–24 July.

Kessler, Tim and Nancy Alexander, 2003, 'Vanishing Acts: How Downsizing Government Contract Out Water and Electricity Services', North-South Institute.

Kessler, Tim, 2003, 'From social contract to private contracts: The privatisation of health, education, and basic infrastructure', *Social Watch Report*.

Krajewski, Markus, 'Public Interests, Private Rights and the "Constitution" of GATS', Paper prepared for the Workshop 'GATS: Trading Development?'

Krina, Ada, 2002, 'Private Infrastructure: A Review of Projects with Private Participation 1990–2001', *Public Policy for the Private Sector*, Note No. 250, World Bank Group.

MacIntosh, Arthur, 2000, 'Privatisation of Water Supplies in Ten Asian Cities', January.

Marin, Philippe, 2002, *Output-Based Aid: Possible Applications in the Design of Water Concessions*, World Bank, Washington, D.C., p. 12.

McCully, Patrick, 2002, 'Avoiding Solutions, Worsening Problems: A Critique of the World Bank's Water Resources Sector Strategy', International Rivers Network, 27 May.

Meacher, Michael, 2001, Keynote Speech delivered at International Conference on Freshwater, Bonn, Germany, 4 December.

Megginson, William and Jeffry Netter, 2001, 'From State to Market: A Survey of Empirical Studies on Privatization', *Journal of Economic Literature*, Vol. 39, June.

Ninan, Ann, 2003, 'Private Water, Public Misery', *CorpWatch India*, 16 April, http://www.corpwatchindia.org.

Palast, Gregory, 2003, 'Power Outage Traced to Dim Bulb in White House', *Working for Change*, 15 August.

Pitman, Keith, 2002, *Bridging Troubled Waters: Assessing the World Bank's Water Resources Strategy*, World Bank.

Prayas Energy Group, 2003, 'Case Study of Reform of the Power Sector, Orissa, India', Paper presented at the Civil Society Consultation on the 2003 Commonwealth Finance Ministers' Meeting on Provision of Basic Services, Bandar Seri Begawan, Negara Brunei Darussalam, 22–24 July 2003.

Prayas Energy Group, 2002, 'The Bujagali Power Purchase Agreement: A Study of Techno-Economic Aspects', commissioned by International Rivers Network, November.

Raquiza, Maria Victoria, 2003, 'The Water Case: Increased Rates for Poorer Services', *The Poor and the Market*, Social Watch Report.

Santos, Eduardo, 2003, 'Privatization of MWSS a Big Success', *INQ7*, 29 April.

Sclar, Elliott, 2001, *You Don't Always Get What You Pay For: The Economics of Privatization*, Cornell University Press.

Singh, Ajit, 2001, 'Foreign Direct Investment and International Agreements: A South Perspective', Occasional Paper No. 6, South Centre, October.

Social Watch Report, 2003, 'The unacknowledged social implications'.

Speed, Robert and Elisabeth Tuerk, 2003, 'GATS and Water', Discussion Paper for Workshop on Trade and Water, Geneva, 3 March.

Tendler, Judith , 2000, 'Why Are Social Funds So Popular?', in Shahid Yusuf (ed.), *Local Dynamics in the Era of Globalization*, Oxford University Press.

Thompson, John, 2001, 'Private Participation in the Water Sector: Can It Meet Social and Environmental Needs?', World Summit on Sustainable Development Opinion, International Institute for Environment and Development, May.

Waelkens, Maria-Pia and Isaline Greindl, 2001, 'Urban Health: Particularities, Challenges, Experiences and Lessons Learnt: A Literature Review', Ecole de Santé Publique/Université Libre de Bruxelles, August (cited in Bijlmakers and Lindner).

Water Aid, 2003, 'The Paradoxes of Funding and Infrastructure Development in Uganda', available at www.wateraid.org.uk.

Winpenny, James, 2003, *Financing Water for All*, Report of the World Panel on Financing Water Infrastructure, World Water Council and Global Water Partnership, March.

World Bank, 2003, *Public Communication Programs for Privatization Projects: A Toolkit for World Bank Task Team Leaders and Clients*, World Bank External Relations Department.

World Bank, 2003, 'Bridging Troubled Waters', Annex C, World Bank Operations Evaluation Department, p. 16.

World Bank, 2004, *World Development Report*.

World Trade Organization, 2002, 'Trading Into the Future', online guide to the WTO Agreements, 1999, quoted in Scott Sinclair and Jim Grieshaber-Otto, *Facing the Facts*, Canadian Centre for Policy Alternatives, 2002, p. 34.

Zimbabwe Independent, 1999, 10 December (quoted in Bayliss 2002).

11

HOW WELL DO MEASUREMENTS OF AN ENABLING DOMESTIC ENVIRONMENT FOR DEVELOPMENT STAND UP?

Barry Herman

Abstract:

Official donors and private investors, let alone scholars, have increasingly focused on the role of institutions and policy quality in development. They have thus sought quantitative measures to assist management allocation decisions and to focus public attention. This paper examines three prominent indicators: the World Bank's Country Policy and Institutional Assessment, the World Economic Forum's Global Competitiveness Indices, and a set of governance indicators developed at the World Bank. The paper calls for appreciating the low reliability of such indicators. Nevertheless, when produced transparently and discussed openly, they can play a progressive advocacy role in strengthening governance.

Introduction

> *It's the institutions, stupid.*
> Guillermo Calvo and Frederic Mishkin[1]

There is a great sense among economists working on development today that the quality and robustness of domestic political and economic institutions matter greatly, both for the effectiveness of all types of policies (including exchange-rate management, the focus of Calvo and Mishkin in the quote above) and for the prospects for development itself. In this view, if societies get their institutions 'right' and also adopt the 'right' policies (which is supposed to be more likely when a country has the 'right' institutions), they will create an 'enabling environment' for development that will transform positive economic stimuli into long-lived virtuous circles of development.

Official donor and creditor agencies proclaim to their developing and transition economy clients the absolute necessity of building such an 'enabling' domestic environment for development. The phrase is a social science term of art in that it defines itself by its results rather than by its characteristics. However, a number of specific domestic policies and institutions have been advocated by the Bretton Woods institutions, and these have been especially important candidates for most lists of required qualities of an enabling environment. The converse is also true: the list has changed over time as the foci of mainstream donor thinking about development have changed.

The World Bank quantitatively assesses progress by its developing and transition economy member states in implementing those policies through their scores on its Country Policy and Institutional Assessment (CPIA). The Bank is not unique in stating the institutional and policy requirements for development and attempting to measure country performance in implementing them. Other organizations such as the World Economic Forum (WEF) and similar institutions (e.g. regional development banks) attempt to define and then measure what they regard as the 'essential' features. They use different indicators and get different country rankings and ratings, albeit with often high degrees of correlation. Moreover, some authors have combined the indicators developed by different authors into statistically derived synthetic measures, notably a team at the World Bank led by Daniel Kaufmann.

The remainder of this paper critically examines the World Bank's CPIA methodology, focusing on the CPIA exercise for 2003. It is contrasted with the two major annual indicator exercises undertaken by the WEF in 2003. Finally, the approach undertaken by the Kaufmann team is discussed. The aim is to gain insight into how such indicators are constructed and some notion of their reliability. In fact, the indicator methodologies are frequently revised, albeit within a continuing philosophy of what counts and broadly how to measure it.[2] The conclusion is that all such indicators should claim no more than to be windows into a partial and clouded picture of development. One should be wary of asking the indicators to do policy jobs for which they are weakly suited (admittedly, this begs the question of how such policy jobs should be done, but that is beyond the scope of this paper). Indeed, to motivate the more technical discussion, the following section looks at how such indicators enter into the policy realm.

Development Cooperation and Development Advocacy: Why the Indicators Matter

Statistical indicators of complex phenomena are so common in everyday life that we typically lose sense of their artificiality. However, national income accountants can convince you that gross domestic product is rife with theory, virtually arbitrary assumptions and leaps of faith, especially as some components must be estimated from very partial data. The consumer price index and the 'volume' of international trade are other examples. But the measurement difficulties in these indicators pale in comparison to efforts to measure such elusive and intangible concepts as the 'quality' of governance and the 'capacity' for macroeconomic management or the overall concept of 'enabling environment'. And yet these concepts are being measured by numerous authors around the world, albeit for two essentially different purposes.

Indicators for Management

For over 25 years, the World Bank has sought internally to measure implementation by developing countries of those policies and institutions that the Bretton Woods institutions deemed necessary for development. The chief motivation for the measurement exercise has from the beginning been the directive of the Bank's Board of Governors that management should take into account the 'policy performance' of borrowing countries as well as their need when allocating the concessional resources of its International Development Association (IDA). As the requirement to measure implementation was interpreted quantitatively, management of the Bank developed a set of numerical indicators for performance in different policy areas, which the staff scored for each country on the basis of personal judgements about the relevant policies in the countries concerned. The indicators were then combined into a single index. For most of the last quarter-century, the quantitative assessment exercise was fully confidential, kept even from the Bank's Executive Directors (although World Bank researchers were allowed to use the indicators on condition that confidentiality was maintained, making replication by other scholars impossible). However, beginning in 2000 the Bank revealed its methodology for creating its index, which by then had evolved into the modern CPIA, and published summary statistics of its measurements for groups of countries and for groups of components of the overall index. It also began to show individual countries their CPIA scores.

A major controversy in the Bank in recent years has been whether the CPIA scores for individual countries and for specific policy and institutional areas should also be brought into the public domain. This paper would argue they should not, because the methodology is too weak and unreliable for the scores to merit the attention they might receive if published. Indeed, greater confidence in the objectivity of CPIA-type assessments might be warranted were they undertaken by independent country-based scholars and not Bank staff. Nevertheless, it has apparently been agreed as part of the fourteenth replenishment of IDA funds that the numerical ratings will be fully disclosed for those countries that draw from IDA, beginning with the assessment to be undertaken in 2005 (IDA 2004, p. 38).

It should be appreciated that CPIA assessments are made and scores are calculated for all countries that borrow from the World Bank, but that the scores for non-IDA countries will remain fully confidential. The discriminatory treatment in publishing the Bank's quantitative assessments of the poorest countries of the world would be hard to justify were CPIA primarily for purposes of analysis or public discussion. In fact, its main justification is still for use in allocating IDA funds, a management function. Indeed, the published CPIA ratings will be called the 'IDA Resource Allocation Index' (IDA 2004a, p. 2n).

One way or another, management has to allocate IDA funds and the CPIA is a long-standing part of the guidance on how to do this that has been given by the intergovernmental overseers of management – namely, the Executive Board and the Governors that stand over it. The CPIA can reflect imperfect science and still carry out the management function (of course, the Board could decide to utilize a different tool or to make decisions on a different basis, but that is another story). In its favour, the CPIA embodies the honest effort of the staff to aid management in making its decisions. Against it, as will be detailed below, is its extreme complexity and lack of robustness. In fact, other multilateral banks also undertake exercises similar to the CPIA for allocating aid resources to their borrowing member countries. Their quantitative results are apparently somewhat similar but not the same as the CPIA, which is also the case for their methodologies.[3]

Once CPIA ratings are published, will they become *ipso facto* the one global standard around which the regional banks and other donors will align? It appears to be the most complex exercise of its type and the most expensive.[4] Indeed, the pressure for CPIA disclosure comes not from IDA countries but from donor countries, some of which might well adopt it as a ready-made factor to enter in their own aid allocations as they seek to be more selective in choosing which countries they assist and to what extent (see Hout 2003 and Koeberle 2003, pp. 257–260).

Nevertheless, it is noteworthy that when the United States recently set up its Millennium Challenge Account, which is highly selective in the countries to be supported, it decided not to apply a CPIA-style methodology nor the CPIA itself, but to utilize published indicators prepared by independent bodies.

The resulting selection differed significantly from what it would have been had CPIA scores been used instead, based on published CPIA quintiles (see Alexander 2004, p. 8). This is not to say the US criteria were right and the World Bank's wrong, only that they differed, reflecting different degrees of importance given to different components of an 'enabling environment', different ways to measure the components, and different ways to combine those measurements. In each case, the country ratings reflected the guidance given to management by the overseeing policymakers. There is no reason they should be the same.

Indicators for Advocacy

Numerous independent organizations and institutions have developed indicators of institutional and policy 'quality'. Most of them seek to measure a rather narrow range of aspects of what their authors take to be the 'enabling' environment for development (e.g. Transparency International on perceptions of corruption, Freedom House on political rights and civil liberties, PricewaterhouseCoopers on opacity in private and government policies and reporting). But whether narrow or broad, these indicators are transparent in their methodology and the author institutions make their results fully available (although some business-oriented indicators are sold to paying clients instead of being freely provided).

One prominent effort to produce a comprehensive indicator like the CPIA is the World Economic Forum's two Global Competitiveness indices. Like most of the independent producers of such indicators, WEF uses its indices to focus public attention on individual country performance in order to raise public debate about shortcomings, as it measures them. For sure, the developers of the WEF indicators have a particular perspective and the reader needs to be aware of what it is. However, that is not hidden from view, as the whole exercise hinges on transparency. Indeed, while this paper takes issue with some of the methodological decisions in the index, it can be said that the WEF does what it sets out to do – namely reflect the views on the 'enabling' environment of the internationally-oriented business community in poor and rich countries.

The CPIA also situates itself within the class of advocacy indicators, although it fits there uneasily, as data are not publicly available for individual countries. Sometimes, however, obscurity can be an advantage. A case in point is how the CPIA is used in the new series of joint annual reports of the World Bank and International Monetary Fund (IMF) on the implementation of policies and actions needed to reach the international development goals, such as are contained in the Millennium Declaration, adopted by the United Nations General Assembly in 2000. The restrictions on the CPIA that force the authors to appeal to aggregate figures actually serve the purpose of the advocacy, which is to say that 'on the whole' developing countries are making appropriate reform efforts and that the support of developed countries directly and through multilateral cooperation needs to be 'scaled up'. Indeed, one finds in the first report that 'Overall, there is an improving trend in developing country policies' (World Bank and IMF 2004, p. 51). The evidence is the improving average CPIA ratings for low- and middle-income countries and for different geographical regions, as shown in charts. There remains, of course, great scope for improvement, especially in low-income countries which score on average lower than middle-income countries, and the pace of reform will have to be accelerated (ibid., pp. 51–56). The whole weight of the CPIA exercise was not needed to reach those conclusions, and sceptical donor authorities (or their legislatures) might demand a more independent assessment to be convinced.

One should appreciate, more generally, that in all these exercises, whether done in-house by official agencies or by non-official sources, the indicators are quite weak. One should not put much faith in the precise numbers assigned by them. The best demonstration of this point seems to be in the conclusions coming from a research project developed by Daniel Kaufmann and colleagues at the World Bank that will be discussed below. They measure different parts of the domestic economic and political environment by drawing comprehensively on information from a large number of different exercises that attempt to measure various institutional and policy areas in individual countries. Some of the information is based on survey data, other parts are assessments by experts like the CPIA, and there are also 'hard data' indicators. The authors statistically combine all the information into a series of synthetic indicators in a way that is rich, in being based on the most information feasible, and also yields measures of how much confidence is warranted in the results derived. Kaufmann's results are sobering and should serve as a warning that individual measures – whether of the CPIA, the WEF indicators, or indicators of particular aspects of institutions or policy quality – are not able to discriminate reliably among countries except when their scores are quite far from each other (more precisely, the authors find 90 per cent confidence intervals are wide). The same warning would apply to drawing conclusions from scores for the same country at different points in time.

With this caveat, one can nevertheless say that the independent institutions that have been developing quantitative indicators of policy quality and institutional development by and large serve a useful function in focusing public attention on how one country's performance compares to another (their methodologies, being open to scrutiny, can also be critiqued publicly). True, this type of comparison, even when done objectively and well, must be understood to be a gross indicator, whose importance lies in the public discussion of the numbers rather than in the numbers themselves. Indeed, the best methodology for such advocacy work would seem to combine cross-country quantitative indicators with in-depth and well-informed narratives of each country's situation.[5] The view here is that when domestic political conditions permit it and when such exercises have credibility, they can help promote progressive reform of policies and institutions.

World Bank Country Policy and Institutional Assessments

The World Bank and the donor community have focused considerable attention recently on the CPIA as an index and as a process. As noted above, the indicator has evolved over time as part of an ongoing effort by World Bank management to formally take account of borrowing country policy performance in allocating IDA resources. From the beginning, the Bank's intention was to develop a summary indicator that it could use to allocate greater amounts of IDA resources relative to need-based allocation criteria to countries that scored well on the indicator and relatively smaller amounts to poor performers. This was meant both to put resources into policy environments where they were expected to be relatively effective and as a way to encourage borrowing governments to improve their 'performance'.[6]

Driven by donors, the CPIA has mainly reflected their view on what constitutes appropriate policies and institutions for development. In practice, the same staff members who are responsible for the Bank's programmes in each country and the policy reform conditionality attached to those programmes also make the CPIA assessments. This 'by definition indicates the normative judgement of the World Bank as to which policy environments [are] best-suited to development' (Collier and Hoeffler 2002, p. 26).

On the one hand, the CPIA is thus vulnerable to the civil society critique that it 'rates governments on how faithfully they adopt neoclassical policies' (Alexander and Kessler 2003). Indeed, a perusal of instructions to staff on how to grade countries gives much ammunition to this view (see World Bank 2003). On the other hand, a number of the items that the CPIA seeks to capture should also appear on the list of essential policy and institutional concerns of the most heterodox advisers. Thus, even analysts who are critical of the full package of World Bank prescriptions that are summarized by the CPIA might find useful components that the exercise is seeking to measure.

In practice, however, and in a notable departure from the transparency that the Bank strongly advocates to its borrowing member governments, none of the CPIA country information has thus far been released to the public and only that for IDA countries is programmed for the future. However, it will be argued here that there is reason enough in the weaknesses of the CPIA methodology for development analysts not to complain too loudly about this.

Development of the CPIA Methodology

The aim of the Bank is that the CPIA assess 'how conducive [a country's policy and institutional] framework is to fostering poverty reduction, sustainable growth and the effective use of development assistance' (World Bank 2003, p. 1). This has been accomplished by averaging scores on 20 aspects of a country's policies and institutions, the result being the CPIA index. In addition, the Bank clusters the 20 items into four sub-groups that are meant to summarize distinct categories of essential policy for development (see Box 1). In essence, these clusters represent short-term economic management, long-term economic management, anti-poverty policy, and overall domestic governance.

Box 1

Policy and institutional characteristics in the CPIA index, 2003

A. Economic management
    1. Management of inflation and macroeconomic imbalances
    2. Fiscal policy
    3. Management of public debt (external and domestic)
    4. Management and sustainability of the development programme

B. Structural policies
    5. Trade policy and foreign exchange regime
    6. Financial stability
    7. Financial sector depth, efficiency and resource mobilization
    8. Competitive environment for the private sector
    9. Goods and factor markets
    10. Policies and institutions for environmental sustainability

C. Policies for social inclusion/equity
    11. Gender
    12. Equity of public resource use
    13. Building human resources
    14. Social protection and labour
    15. Monitoring and analysis of poverty outcomes and impacts

D. Public sector management and institutions
    16. Property rights and rule-based governance
    17. Quality of budgetary and financial management
    18. Efficiency of revenue mobilization
    19. Quality of public administration
    20. Transparency, accountability and corruption in the public sector

Source: World Bank, 'Country policy and institutional assessment 2003': assessment questionnaire, March 2003, p. 1.

Both the four clusters and the 20 individual items in Box 1 seem to reflect less an overall coherent design than the history over a quarter-century of step-by-step revision and accretion of concepts that management sought to include in the CPIA. Over time, individual items in the CPIA have been added and subtracted, split and merged. The main constant seems to have been that there be 20 items, and that they be weighted equally in the CPIA average. Thus, as new items came into the CPIA index, other items had to be collapsed or dropped.[7]

The entry and exit of items has reflected both revisions in thinking about what are the most important elements of policy and changing pressures on management from IDA donors. One item in particular, 'IDA portfolio performance', had an especially checkered career and perhaps is indicative of some of the pitfalls that can arise in designing quantitative performance indicators. This element entered the CPIA in 1993 as a result of a request by IDA donors to measure how well countries utilized specifically their IDA resources. According to the Bank's independent Operations Evaluation Department (OED), the only measure of portfolio performance available at the time was in reports of IDA supervisory missions, and this entered into the CPIA index with a weight of 20 per cent. However, OED regarded the portfolio performance measure as 'often subjective and biased in a positive direction', compared to *ex post* OED evaluations (World Bank 2001, p. 30). OED also regarded the IDA evaluations as not adequately separating the World Bank's own from the borrower's shortcomings. Moreover, if a badly-performing project was dropped from a country's portfolio, the country's performance rating rose. In light of the above concerns, the weight of the portfolio performance indicator was reduced to 10 per cent in 1995 and 7 per cent in 1997, and it was dropped from the CPIA in 1998.[8]

It should be emphasized that from the start, the Bank sought to gauge policy measures taken and not development outcomes, which are not fully within the control of governments in developing or any other countries. The OED doubted that management succeeded in this regard and issued a warning against interpreting any internal Bank research as finding that 'good policies' as measured by the CPIA from 1977 to 2000 help explain good economic growth (World Bank 2001, pp. 16–18).

Perhaps the warning should be circulated (or re-circulated) to World Bank researchers, as they continue to use the CPIA as an explanatory variable in econometric exercises. For example, Kraay and Nehru (2004) use the CPIA from 2001 back to 1977 – indeed, extrapolated back to 1970, based on an association of the CPIA with the domestic inflation rate – and claim that they have found a significant inverse association of the quality of policies and institutions with the probability of debt distress. Perhaps they have, and perhaps they found an association between high inflation and debt distress, given that inflation and the CPIA have been highly correlated, as noted in their extrapolation exercise, and given the OED observation on the tendency of Bank staff to rate countries with good economic outcomes as having good CPIA scores.[9] In sum, while institutions undoubtedly matter as a determinant of vulnerability to debt distress, econometric results using the CPIA do not necessarily show it.

Moreover, although the index was substantially revised in 1998 (and again in 2001) and smaller revisions are made each year, neither the changes in the structure of the CPIA nor in the definitions of individual items seemed to cause significant changes in the rating scores, at least through 2000. Indeed, the OED found the scores to be remarkably constant, even though there is a general impression that developing country policy has improved on average from the 1970s to today (World Bank 2001, pp. 13 and 18).

The OED also found an unexpected shrinkage over time in the dispersion of CPIA scores, which it hypothesized resulted not from real policy movement toward the mean in the developing world, but from how the staff was coping with the increasing complexity of the CPIA scoring (World Bank 2001, p. 18).[10] In addition, OED made another important observation about the CPIA that exemplifies a general caveat in the design of index numbers. That is, if each item in the CPIA is intended to have the same weight in the overall index, it should be normalized to have the same mean. In practice, however, some items tended to have higher scores and thus systematically had higher average weight in the CPIA than items with generally lower scores (World Bank 2001, p. 20).[11]

The CPIA Methodology in 2003

In light of these and other concerns, the Bank has devoted considerable additional staff time and resources to trying to strengthen the CPIA, with particular emphasis recently in developing indicators of the institutional dimensions that it now includes in the index. The results thus far, however, seem instead to confound different issues and sometimes challenge understanding.

As can be seen in Box 1, some of the 20 items in the CPIA are policy indicators and others focus on institutions. However, not only are the two dimensions mixed in calculating each country's overall CPIA index number, but individual clusters also contain both institutional and policy dimensions. Cluster A, in particular, contains one fully institutional item (number 4), two essentially policy-related items (numbers 1 and 2) and one that is an equal mixture of both (number 3). In the latter case, the Bank instructs its country staff in assigning a score for the item to consider both 'debt service capacity' and 'debt management capacity' and weight each equally. Debt-service capacity pertains to the financial capacity to make timely payments to creditors, which depends on export earnings, capital flows, etc. and the policies regarding these variables that the government is pursuing. Debt management capacity pertains to having a central office to track and manage the government's financial obligations (see World Bank 2003, p. 5). These really are quite different and it is not clear why they are merged rather than scored separately, other than the seemingly artificial commitment to keep the number of items averaged in the overall index at 20.

Indeed, a case could be made not only to separate the policy and institutional elements of individual items in the CPIA, but also to split the CPIA itself into two separate measures, one for institutions and another for policies. Having the institutional capacity to assess options, undertake policies and deliver public services effectively and fairly is quite distinct from policy choices that a government actually makes. Countries with strong institutions may elect governments that make unfortunate policy decisions. Equally, governments of countries with weak institutions may make appropriate policy decisions, albeit without necessarily being able to follow through fully and effectively on their implementation. It was the latter concern that led to the greater emphasis on institutional features in what had originally been a policy indicator, but they are distinct. Thus, while the Bank reasonably wants to track both institutional capacity and policy choice in its continuing country assessments, the CPIA as now constructed makes it very difficult to disentangle them.

The scoring of each of the 20 items has been on a scale of 1 ('unsatisfactory for an extended period') to 6 ('good for an extended period'), with obvious gradations in between.[12] Staff members who make the assessments are given narrative guidelines that characterize the situations that should merit scores of 2 to 5 for each item. The staff are also given benchmark scores based on a subgroup of countries (19 in 2003), which are prepared as a preliminary round or pre-test of the CPIA assessment. To give the flavour of the guidelines, Box 2 reproduces the full scoring guidance for two items, 'Management and sustainability of the development programme' (item 4) and 'Property rights and rule-based governance' (item 16).

The written instructions for the staff also include hot links to background research related to each characteristic, which the staff may consult for additional guidance. These include 'objective indicators' that can serve as 'guideposts' for making the subjective assessments. For example, the guideposts for item 8, 'Competitive environment for the private sector', include such items as number of days needed and cost to register a business (World Bank 2003, p. 11). In other cases, the guideposts are as judgemental as the CPIA item

Box 2

Scoring guidelines for two items in the CPIA, 2003

Management and sustainability of the development programme (item 4)

Score	Guidance for score
2	Institutions and instruments for implementing economic and development policies and managing shocks are not effective. Actual or incipient economic, political or security obstacles make it unlikely that authorities will implement needed reforms or maintain existing achievements. The public and key stakeholders have no influence on, or do not support, key decisions. The Government does not rely on participatory processes to gather information or review plans.
3	Institutions and instruments for implementing policies and managing shocks are weak, but there have been occasional successes. There are several impediments/obstacles that reduce the chances of successful reform efforts. There is only limited consultation and participation with key stakeholders and civil society. Participatory processes are rarely used, and public support is low.
4	Institutions and instruments work fairly well, although there are problems. While there are some impediments/obstacles to policy reforms, the Government has demonstrated the ability in the past to overcome these obstacles in many, but not all, cases. Some consultation has taken place with stakeholders, and participatory processes have been used in a limited fashion. Government coordination is good, and there is moderate public support for reform efforts.
5	Tools are available to implement policies and manage events effectively. Policies and actions of key agencies are well coordinated. Authorities have a coherent programme of reform or a record of sustained good performance with broad public support. Participatory processes are often used as means through which the views of stakeholders can be heard and inform government decision-making .

Property rights and rule-based governance (item 16)

Score	Guidance for score
2	Enforcement of contracts and recognition of property rights depends almost entirely on informal mechanisms. Laws and regulations are applied selectively or changed unpredictably, for example through frequent and unpublicized executive decrees. Judicial decisions are not publicly available. Favouritism rather than equal treatment pervades dealings with the state. Obtaining a business licence can take an inordinate time and require numerous 'unofficial payments'. Crime and violence substantially increases the cost of doing business.
3	The law protects property rights in theory, but in fact registries and other institutions required to make this protection effective function poorly, making the protection of private property uncertain. Judicial decisions are sometimes publicly available. Rules are not changed

arbitrarily but may not be publicly available. Those without connections can secure a business licence, but the process is overly
bureaucratic and prone to delays. The state is able to provide a
modicum of protection against crime and violence.

4   Property rights are protected in practice as well as theory. Property
registries are reasonably current and non-corrupt. Rules are publicly available and a mechanism exists to resolve conflicts of rules.
Courts may be costly to use but judicial decisions are publicly available. Obtaining necessary licences is a small share of the cost of
doing business. The state is able to protect most citizens most of
the time from crime and violence.

5   A rule-based governance structure governs interactions between
all citizens and their government. The legal system is highly predictable. Laws and regulations affecting businesses and individuals
are transparent and uniformly applied; changes in them are publicly
announced and occur only after public hearings and deliberation. A
well-functioning and accountable police force protects citizens from
crime and violence.

Source: World Bank, 'Country policy and institutional assessment 2003': assessment
questionnaire, March 2003, pp. 6 and 23.

itself, or even more so. For item 17, 'Quality of budgetary and financial
management', the Bank staff member is directed not only to the IMF Code
of Good Practices on Fiscal Transparency, but also to a Checklist of
Budget/Financial Management Practices that includes 23 items, each of
which is to be assessed on a scale of 1 (inadequate) to 10 (excellent), including
items like 'Has medium-term perspective' and 'Based on accounting standards' (World Bank 2003, pp. 24 and 30). One must truly sympathize with the
staff members of the Bank who have to make these assessments each year.
The earlier observed regression to the mean in the scoring in the 1990s seems
a fully human response to what management is asking them to do.[13]

Moreover, while the 20 separate items in Box 1 are clearly named, the
actual content being measured is often not. For example, 'financial stability'
(item 6) seeks to capture three dimensions of policy believed to affect the
degree to which a country is prone to financial crises. These dimensions are
identified as (a) competition policy, (b) legal regime, and (c) regulatory regime.
The staff members are told in the instructions, furthermore, that one characteristic of competition policy that they should take into account is the degree
to which the external capital account is open (World Bank 2003, p. 9). But this
seems odd. Most analysts would see that as a part of macroeconomic policy
and neutral with respect to competition if applied appropriately (e.g. countries
that wish to limit the degree of opening of their capital accounts, particularly

regarding short-term flows, might still permit foreign-owned banks to operate in the domestic economy on the same basis as domestic banks).

One might also question if the dimensions identified in the instructions to staff for scoring a particular item are always the most relevant ones for that item. For example, if being more or less prone to financial crisis is the element that 'financial stability' is meant to capture, then the first two of the three dimensions noted in the preceding paragraph seem out of place. Also, in addition to prudential regulations (the third dimension), it seems that ability of the central bank to be an effective 'lender of last resort' would be significant. Indeed, the degree of openness of the capital account seems inversely related to the potential exposure to financial crises, especially for developing countries with thin financial markets.

By the same token, the competition and legal regime dimensions in item 6, as just cited, seem to fit better as dimensions of item 7, 'financial sector depth, efficiency and resource mobilization'. The focus in item 7, however, is on monetary and credit policies, tax policies and ownership policies. Regarding the first set of policies, there is one factor that one expects to see in such instructions – namely, to take account of the degree to which domestic interest rates are market-determined. That is standard 'Washington consensus'. But it seems curious to also include the extent to which 'the public sector borrowing requirement crowds out credit to the private sector' (World Bank 2003, p. 10). The latter is a key macroeconomic issue that is already covered by item 1. In fact, maybe it is also covered in item 2.

In other words, not only is it not clear that each of the 20 items actually measures what it sets out to measure, but it is not clear that there are 20 distinct items. Item 1 'assesses whether a country has a consistent macroeconomic programme (in terms of exchange rate, monetary and fiscal policy) that addresses inflation and internal and external imbalances'. Item 2 'assesses the size of the fiscal balance and the composition of government revenue and spending to assess their compatibility with adequate provision of public services for economic growth, favourable macroeconomic outcomes, and a sustainable path of public debt' (World Bank 2003, pp. 3 and 4). While there are aspects of item 1 that are not in item 2 and vice versa, the macroeconomic and debt sustainability aspects of item 2 seem part and parcel of the fiscal aspects of item 1. Much the same kind of overlap can be seen in the final two items (numbers 19 and 20) and for various items in between. However, if there are not 20 separate indicators in the CPIA, the index is not a simple average of 20 indicators but a weighted average of a smaller number of indicators in which the weights are the number of items that track a single factor.[14]

Whatever the assessment difficulties, scores are given for each item and are sent to the headquarters CPIA team, which checks for coherence and consistency in the scoring. This is important, as different staff members might well assign different scores to any one item for a country and a common standard would not necessarily result automatically. University teachers and students know this type of problem full well. Thus, a central team at Bank headquarters checks the scoring across countries of each individual item and reviews the narratives for assigning each specific score that now have to be sent to headquarters with the scores. The team also undertakes statistical tests for systematic bias in the scoring and examines outliers, assessing whether scores for such countries are warranted, possibly sending them back to country offices for revision.

Use of the CPIA Scores

When the staff agrees to a final set of item scores for each country, the CPIA index numbers are calculated. Since 2000, World Bank country managers are required to discuss the 20 final item ratings and overall index with their respective developing country counterparts. Each country's results are compared in a table to regional averages and to its own performance in the previous year (when the instructions may have differed, at least for some items). The narratives that the assessing staff produced are also shared, providing a written commentary to explain staff thinking in assigning the scores. Developing country officials are not supposed to challenge the scores. The conversation, which presumably takes place primarily with IDA countries, which have an incentive to care about their ratings as they affect their IDA allocations (see Appendix 1), would likely be about how to score higher next year.

Perhaps as a spur to low-performing governments of IDA countries to do better, the Bank has grouped these countries into quintiles by their CPIA scores, as noted earlier, and reported the average score for each quintile (see Table 1). Quintiles have similarly been calculated and reported for the four main clusters of items. Observers can thus know if the World Bank judges an IDA country to have relatively strong policies and institutions (defined as in the top fifth), relatively weak ones (bottom fifth) or something in between, and how 'good' or 'bad' each quintile is on average, based on the quintile mean.[15] One would not know from the data in Table 1, however, whether there were countries with ratings well below the mean of the lowest quintile or well above the mean of the highest quintile, nor whether the distribution of CPIA scores was still very much bunched in the middle.

The quintile report is a rather broad display of the CPIA results and one that World Bank management has sought for several years to improve upon. Indeed, as part of the previous replenishment of IDA resources, the Bank pledged to work to increase CPIA disclosure. As an intermediate step to eventual

Table 1. Country Policy and Institutional Assessment (CPIA) ratings, 2003[a]

First quintile Average = 3.69	Armenia, Bhutan, Cape Verde, Grenada, Honduras, India, Maldives, Mauritania, Nicaragua, Samoa, Senegal, Sri Lanka, St Lucia, St Vincent and the Grenadines, Tanzania, Uganda, Vietnam
Second quintile Average = 3.59	Azerbaijan, Bangladesh, Benin, Bolivia, Bosnia and Herzegovina, Burkina Faso, Ghana, Indonesia, Madagascar, Mali, Nepal, Pakistan, Rwanda, Republic of Yemen
Third quintile Average = 3.34	Albania, Cameroon, Dominica, Ethiopia, Georgia, Guyana, Kenya, Kyrgyz Republic, Lesotho, Malawi, Moldova, Mongolia, Mozambique, Serbia and Montenegro, Zambia
Fourth quintile Average = 3.01	Cambodia, Chad, Democratic Republic of Congo, Republic of Congo, Côte d'Ivoire, Djibouti, Eritrea, The Gambia, Guinea, Kiribati, Niger, Sierra Leone, Tajikistan, Tonga, Vanuatu
Fifth quintile Average = 2.58	Angola, Burundi, Central African Republic, Comoros, Guinea-Bissau, Haiti, Laos PDR, Nigeria, Papua New Guinea, São Tomé and Principe, Solomon Islands, Sudan, Togo, Uzbekistan, Zimbabwe

[a] Countries are listed alphabetically within each quintile. IDA countries not rated in the 2003 CPIA exercise were Afghanistan, Liberia, Myanmar, Somalia, and East Timor (Timor-Leste). *Source:* Information supplied by the World Bank.

full disclosure, management proposed in 2003 that it report country scores in half-point ranges (number of countries with scores from 3.0 to 3.4, 3.5 to 3.9, etc). However, when the IDA Deputies met in November 2003 and considered the matter of greater public disclosure, they were only able to agree to look 'to the [Executive] Board for further discussion and decisions in advance of IDA-14, taking account of the diversity of views on the subject' (IDA Deputies 2003). As noted earlier, it has since been agreed that full disclosure will begin with IDA-14.

The OED review of the CPIA asked back in 2001 why there was such controversy over full disclosure. Its answer was that 'CPIA data are not yet robust enough to withstand full disclosure' (World Bank 2001, p. 46). At that time, Bank staff did not have to write the narratives to explain their ratings and the OED thought that such an 'audit trail' would greatly enhance the credibility of the ratings. That would depend on the narratives' being of consistently high quality, which requires significant staff time in thinking them through and drafting them. Even so, there are probably limits to the confidence that countries would put into them. The assessing staff member comes to the exercise with all the experience of having worked closely with the country as a representative of the Bank. This is necessarily a partial perspective. The Bank staff members are in an asymmetrical power relationship with the government being assessed. This is not meant to impugn the integrity or competence of the staff in any way. It is about the ineluctable nature of the relationship.

Other Approaches to 'Enabling Environment' Indicators

It should be recalled that the initial and principal use of the CPIA was not analysis but allocating IDA resources, for which purpose, the views of the 'lending officers' of the Bank were a naturally germane and appropriately confidential source. That origin also seems to suggest an important hypothesis as to why the index grew over time to be so complicated and difficult to interpret. In other words, at first, perhaps, some donors or management wanted to take account of the 'quality' of macroeconomic policy in allocating IDA funds, and at a later time they or others may have wanted to add gender issues, and then property rights, and so on. In specifying the issues to include and agreeing to weight them equally, and even keeping a lid on the exercise by limiting the number of separate issues to 20, the concerns of various IDA donors and management could have been included in the allocation decisions in a practical way. If this is the process by which the CPIA was developed (and that history is not in the public domain), it would not be surprising if the average of the 20 items after 25 years was not easily interpreted in terms of an elegant or even coherent concept. But it also did not matter. Its purpose was resource allocation and not analysis. It had to produce an IDA allocation that seemed broadly correct to the donors and this it apparently did. At least, the IDA donors appear to want to retain it.

Other enabling environment indices seem to be more coherent by design. They have either a political aim to influence policy or an informational one to assist global investors or for research purposes. In all cases, these indices are for public (or client) consumption. This allows them – actually, requires them – to be transparent about their methodology and reveal their calculations, as well as their detailed results.

Global Competitiveness Indices of the World Economic Forum

The World Economic Forum (WEF) has developed two indices that are meant to compare national capacities for economic growth. One is based on a reading of the growth and development literature and the other draws upon the business and management literature (WEF 2004, Chapter sections 1.1 and 1.2). The first index is based on sub-indices of the macroeconomic environment, the quality of public institutions and the development of technology. The second looks at the ability of enterprises to operate effectively (see Box 3). These are

Box 3

**Policy and institutional factors in Global
Competitiveness Indices, 2003**

Growth Competitiveness Index

A Macroeconomic environment
   1 Macroeconomic stability
   2 Government waste
   3 Country credit rating
B Public institutions
   1 Contracts and law
   2 Corruption
C Technology
   1 Innovation
   2 Information and communication technology
   3 Technology transfer

Business Competitiveness Index

A Company operations and strategy
B Quality of the national business environment
   1 Factor (input) conditions
      a. Physical infrastructure
      b. Administrative infrastructure
      c. Human resources
      d. Technology infrastructure
      e. Capital markets
   2 Demand conditions
   3 Related and supporting industries
   4 Context for firm strategy and rivalry
      a. Incentives
      b. Competition

Source: World Economic Forum, *Global Competitiveness Report 2003–2004* (New
York: Oxford University Press, 2004), Chapter sections 1.1 and 1.2.

complementary approaches (and the two indices are highly correlated), but they
highlight different perspectives on requirements for development, reflecting the
different professional disciplines of the authors of the two indices.[16]

Together, the indices cover much the same area as the CPIA. The Business
Competitiveness Index compares broadly with cluster B of the CPIA, and the
Growth Competitiveness Index covers much the same ground as clusters A
and D of the CPIA. The main difference is the explicit focus on technological
advance and the absence of social indicators in the WEF, probably reflecting
its well-known corporate viewpoint. WEF is not a development bank.

Also, while the CPIA incorporates the views of a small group of World Bank
country experts, the WEF indices are based on both 'hard' data (statistical

time series, such as density of telephone lines as an indicator for ease of communication) and an Executive Opinion Survey. The latter is compiled by 'partner institutes' in 102 countries (in 2003), following common guidelines for purposes of comparability. The partners are 'typically leading national research or academic institutes committed to contributing to the growth potential of their respective economies' (WEF 2004, p. xi). All together, the partner institutes surveyed almost 8,000 'senior business leaders' on the situations in their domestic economies in 2003. When, as for some low-income countries recently added to the exercise, the local business people surveyed did not appear able to adequately compare their economy to the rest of the world, a sub-sample of foreign business executives in that country was used instead.[17] All the survey information is necessarily subjective opinion and usually there is no alternative to it (e.g. extent of corruption would be hard to measure from published data).

There is considerable art as well as room for politics in constructing such indices. An example from the Growth Competitiveness Index illustrates the point. In previous years, the macroeconomic environment cluster contained an expression for government expenditure as a share of gross national product with a negative sign, meaning smaller was better. While this might be true at some high levels of government spending, it did not signal what was really important, distinguishing effective from wasteful spending. Recognizing this shortcoming, the authors instead sought to find a proxy for wasteful spending and ended up with a sub-index made up on the following survey questions (WEF 2004, p. 28):

- Do government subsidies to business in your country keep uncompetitive industries alive artificially, or do they improve the productivity of industries?
- In your country, how common is diversion of public funds to companies, individuals or groups due to corruption?
- How high is the public trust in the financial honesty of politicians?

One can wonder if civil society advocates might have thought to ask respondents somewhat different questions, such as 'How common is diversion of public funds ... due to policy?' or 'To what extent does the business viewpoint in general guide economic and social policymaking?'

The WEF indices are also notable for rating all countries on a single scale, developed and developing. However, appearing on a single list is not the same as being on a single scale and the Growth Competitiveness Index also illustrates this well. In this case, the way technological progress was treated in the exercise undermined the technology cluster and the overall Index. Recognizing that technical change differs in advanced and developing countries, the authors divided up countries into more and less innovative economies, based on the number of US 'utility patents' (for innovation) that were registered per capita in 2002. They then weighted the components of the technology index differently for the 'core' (high-innovation) and non-core countries, and also weighted the three major components differently in the overall index.[18] Thus, the position of individual countries in the overall index depends both on how they score on individual sub-clusters of items and how the clusters are weighted. Whether or not one finds them convincing, the two specific sets of weights make up separate indices and should be shown as such.

The Business Competitiveness Index, in contrast, is derived in a way that relies more on statistical methodology. First, each apparently relevant survey question and quantitative indicator for each sub-cluster in the index is tested for a significant correlation with GDP per capita. All those that passed this hurdle were then implicitly assigned weights in their cluster index through a factor analysis. Finally, the two main cluster indices were combined in a weighted average, where the weights (including an interaction term) resulted from a regression of the two indices on GDP per capita. While the author chose the initial questions to include in the exercise, he can say that the data chose how they would be represented in the final index.

The WEF indices thus give two business-oriented perspectives on an 'enabling environment' for development. The surveys that underlie the indices are not of cross-sections of local country populations but of business leaders. This is an important segment of the population in every society, but not the exclusive one to sample, nor necessarily the one to rely upon, as Adam Smith implicitly warned us more than 200 years ago.[19] WEF then seeks wide dissemination of the business viewpoint captured in its indices to 'help pre-cipitate an internal debate within the country between government officials, business leaders, organizations of civil society and the academic community on key problem areas and how best to address them' (WEF 2004, p. xi).[20] There is a political agenda in the WEF indices and it is a fully transparent one.

The Kaufmann Methodology: Research-driven

The approach to constructing the WEF Business Competitiveness Index is part way to the more analytical research strategy followed by a group of World Bank researchers led by Daniel Kaufmann. They also generate an index – actually, indices – from subjective data, but they look for inputs from not one but 25 separate sets of data produced by 18 different organizations (Kaufmann, Kraay and Mastruzzi 2003). Some of the data are surveys (including by the WEF) and others are expert assessments (including the CPIA). Some are global in scope and some have more restricted country cov-erage. All together, 250 variables pertaining to 199 countries and territories were made candidates for indices on various hypothesized dimensions of 'governance', which is the part of the 'enabling environment' on which they focus.[21]

As in the CPIA and WEF exercises, the authors begin with assertions of what the important dimensions of governance are, based on their 'views of what constitutes a consistent and useful organization of the data that is concordant with prevailing notions of governance' (Kaufmann *et al.* 2003, p. 2). Thus, based mainly on the academic literature, they specify six indicators of governance: voice and accountability, political stability, government effectiveness, regulatory quality, rule of law, and control of corruption. These indices are not further combined into any overall concept of governance, nor do they feed into any overall 'enabling environment' measure. Moreover, readers are warned repeatedly and even precisely about large margins of error in the results. Researchers in this team have their hubris under control.

The statistical procedure for combining the many data points into estimates of the six indicators of governance is itself interesting. The approach assumes that the six indicators are six true and unobserved variables and that the actual data points are linear functions of the true variable and a disturbance term. They then estimate the unobserved true variable from the observed variables and are even able to give greater weight in the estimation process to the observed variables that have stronger statistical properties (less 'noisy signals'). In the Bayesian tradition, the authors also generate 'confidence intervals' (with 90 per cent probability) that the true and unobserved variable is within a specific range, as given by the probability distribution on the variable, conditional on the data used to generate it.

What is unique and highly important in this approach is that when the authors rank countries by their imputed scores from the estimated relationship, they not only can give the score itself, but also a confidence interval around it. Figure 1 shows this presentation for the 'control of corruption' variable. The length of the confidence intervals vary, depending on how many data sources included that country and how much precision was ascribed to each source, but all the intervals are relatively large. The authors emphasize that small differences in the mid-point estimates between countries that are ranked near each other do not convey reliable information. They are more confident in making comparisons of countries whose confidence intervals do not overlap.

Indeed, they suggest that users of their work 'focus on the *range* of possible governance values' for each variable for each country, rather than the point estimate (Kaufmann *et al.* 2003, p. 13). They express concern in particular about allocations of development assistance to countries on the basis of indicators such as these, citing in particular the allocation rules for the

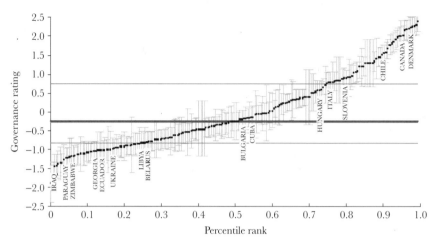

Source: Daniel Kaufmann, Aart Kraay and Massimo Mastruzzi, 'Governance Matters III: Governance Indicators for 1996–2002', Social Science Research Network Electronic Library, 30 June 2003, p. 55.

Note from the source: 'This graph shows estimates of the indicated dimension of governance (on the vertical axis) for all countries graphed against each country's percentile rank (on the horizontal axis) for 2002. The vertical bars show the statistically-likely range of values of governance for each country [90% confidence interval], with the midpoint of each bar corresponding to the best single estimate. Selected countries are labelled. As emphasized in the text, the ranking of countries along the horizontal axis is subject to significant margins of error, and this ordering in no way reflects the official view of the World Bank, its Executive Directors, or the countries they represent.'

Figure 1. Indicator of control of corruption across countries, 2002

Millennium Challenge Account of the United States and how the CPIA is used in IDA allocations (ibid. p. 24). Because those allocation decisions have to be made in any event, the import of this conclusion is not that the allocations are wrong in some sense, but that they are not as 'scientific' as they appear, however much quantified and formula-driven. They embody a certain amount of arbitrariness attributable to a large dose of uncertainty associated with the allocation methodology. Management is responsible for the allocation and should understand the low degree of robustness of the allocation process it uses.

Conclusion

The starting point in this paper was the observation as made by many writers on development that the quality of institutions are important determinants of successful policymaking and policy implementation for development. The next point was that somehow the quality of the institutions and of the policies could be measured. It seems that the main conclusion one might draw from the discussion above is that one should be very modest in what one claims regarding such measurements.

One may get experts to quantify their opinions about a country or one may undertake an opinion survey of a more or less representative sample of people or one may even select an existing quantitative data series to be a good proxy for some aspect of institutional development. None of that ensures that the numbers generated mean what the designer intends them to mean or with an acceptable degree of reliability to warrant an analytical conclusion. The Kaufmann team's results contained an important warning about reliance on indicators such as the CPIA in allocating aid resources. Countries are just too susceptible to misclassification, which does not remove the need to use some process or rule for making the allocation. The WEF effort reminds one to be sensitive to the policy agenda of entities promoting enabling environment indices. And from the CPIA exercise one sees the need for independent assessment and keeping the complexity of what one is trying to measure under control.

Certainly, one should be sensitive to the potential bias of experts making personal quantitative assessments,[22] or even of survey respondees (keeping in mind, for example, that the populations that the WEF sampled did not reflect the full range of public opinion in a country). Another place where bias can enter is at the starting point of the exercise, when the analyst considers the broad institutional requirements against which the country is going to be compared. Do we really know what is required in an enabling domestic environment? Certain countries that do not compare well against success indicators like 'rule of law' or 'transparency' in government nevertheless grow rapidly over an extended period, raise per capita real incomes substantially, and notably reduce poverty. This suggests that perhaps there are multiple sets of effective policies and institutions for development. At the same time, one also has to be suspicious of too quick a retreat into cultural relativism. Political leaders of countries that lack certain characteristics have argued that view, which has rightly been dismissed, as by Amartya Sen (2003), as a dodge to deny their populations true global values, in particular ones that should be regarded as human rights.

Finally, what is left? The negative conclusions should not go so far as to write off the entire effort to quantify any aspect of institutional and policy development, but rather to appreciate its limit. A more promising approach might be to combine the quantitative comparative approach with a traditional and still useful one that pre-establishes a framework or set of questions within which to carry out the country analyses and then request independent experts to examine particular countries, utilizing the framework to structure their reports. Quantitative measures of aspects of the situation might usefully complement the structured narrative. Such a dual approach would allow the expert to be as nuanced as he or she is able in the narrative and to bring in features that would escape a quantitative approach, while the quantitative indicators can serve as a check on the analysis in selected topic areas that admit of such measurement. As our understanding of what really is needed in an 'enabling environment' is quite limited, the goal of the exercise should be to foster debate in countries, which might lead to effective advocacy for strengthening those aspects of the institutional and policy environment on which citizens find they can agree.

Appendix 1

The Performance-based System for Allocating IDA Resources

Not only is the CPIA today a complex indicator that challenges interpretation, as was argued above, but the IDA allocation formula into which it is inserted also looks like a kind of 'Rube Goldberg' invention. First of all, the CPIA does not enter directly into the allocation formula but is initially used to calculate a 'Country Performance Rating' (CPR). The square of the CPR is then entered into the formula for allocating IDA funds (see IDA 2003, p. 2).[23]

There are several steps in calculating the CPR. The first is to calculate a weighted average of two indices, one of which is the CPIA. The other index seeks to track implementation of each country's active IDA projects and programmes (the score is the percentage of products deemed 'at risk', converted to an inverted 6-point scale). It is based on the Bank's overall Annual Report on Portfolio Performance (see World Bank 2002).[24] In calculating the weighted average of the two indices, the CPIA is given a weight of 80 per cent and portfolio performance receives 20 per cent. The combined score is then multiplied by a 'governance factor' which either raises or lowers the score, depending on whether the governance factor is greater or less than one. The result is the CPR.

The governance factor has been calculated from the scores on CPIA items 4 and 16–20, plus a 'procurement practices criterion' from the portfolio performance review. The possible score on each of the seven items ranges from 1 to 6 and the first step is to calculate the simple average of the seven scores. This average is then divided by the average of the midpoint of the possible ratings of each item – i.e. 3.5. The resulting number is raised to the power of 1.5 and the result of that calculation multiplies the weighted average of the CPIA and portfolio performance. Thus, if a country's average score on the seven items lies above 3.5, the governance factor will raise its CPR above the weighted average of the CPIA and portfolio performance indicator. If the country's average score on the governance items is below 3.5, its CPR is lowered. Also, since the governance factor contains an exponent, the amount by which it raises or lowers a country's score increases exponentially, the greater the distance from the 3.5 'norm' (albeit only by a factor of 1.5). In sum, the expression for the CPR can be given as follows,

$$CPR = [0.80CPIA + 0.20PP](gov/3.5)^{1.5}$$

where 'gov' is the average of scores on the seven governance items and PP stands for the IDA portfolio performance measure.

It may be seen that the governance elements of the CPIA can count rather heavily in the allocation exercise. In fact, the Bank acknowledges that as the governance elements enter into both the CPIA and portfolio performance ratings indices and again in the governance factor, they are double-counted. Moreover, the exponent in the governance factor makes the IDA allocation quite sensitive to changes in the governance items. More precisely, the Bank calculated that a one-point drop in one of the seven individual governance items would, *ceteris paribus*, reduce the Country Performance Rating by 7.5 per cent and that would drop the country's IDA allocation by 15 per cent (IDA 2003a, p. 2).[25]

How the Bank's staff members rate the governance items thus matters a lot. A relatively 'easy grader' brings more resources to his country, albeit within the limits given by the CPIA headquarters consistency check. By the same token, the government will have a monetary incentive to undertake the governance reforms (or appear to undertake the reforms) that will score well in the CPIA. One may only wonder if there is a governance reform counterpart to the observation in United States school districts of 'teaching to the test', so the average scores look as good as possible to the authorities and the voters. Unfortunately, that has not been the same as producing well-educated children.

Notes

Views expressed are those of the author and not necessarily the views of the United Nations. Research assistance on the CPIA by Daniel Cohen is much appreciated. We both express our appreciation to Rui Coutinho of the World Bank for patiently explaining how the CPIA process works. Appreciation is also due to Pingfan Hong for econometric consultations and to Nancy Alexander, Ariel Buira, Paul Collier, Tim Kessler, Andrew Kuper, Agosto Lopez-Claros, Cristián Ossa, Ejeviome Otobo, Shang-Jin Wei and John Williamson for reading earlier drafts. If the paper is not much better as a result, it is my fault.

1 Calvo and Mishkin, 2003, p. 106.
2 The World Bank commissioned an external panel of experts in 2004 that recommended changes in the CPIA, some of which were to be implemented in the 2004 CPIA exercise, which was postponed until late in the year for that purpose (World Bank 2004). The WEF is working on a major revision of its indicators, which are to be utilized in its 2005 assessment (WEFa 2004, p. xix).

3 The aforementioned external review panel called on the multilateral banks to 'harmonize [their] different rating systems to the extent possible' so as to 'reduce the burden of ratings exercises on country counterparts and to decrease inefficiencies associated with each agency having a different rating system' (World Bank 2004, p. 14). But are the different ratings necessarily a sign of 'inefficiencies', or could they also reflect different views of the relative importance of various components of an enabling environment?

4 The review panel reported that Bank staff estimate the cost of an annual CPIA exercise as $1.5 million, which has not been explicitly budgeted in the past, although management has agreed to the panel's recommendation to do so in the future (World Bank 2004, p. 12).

5 This is the approach of a project of the Centre for Public Integrity called 'Global Integrity' that combined cross-country assessments of the functioning of governments, particularly in regard to susceptibility to corruption, based on detailed questionnaires, complemented by substantial individual country narratives by social scientists and investigative reporters (see Centre for Public Integrity 2004). The project covered 25 countries and could be expanded in future years (truth in advertising: the author was a member of the Methodology Advisory Committee for the project).

6 The quantitative ratings were never applied mechanically, but served to guide lending and to help management defend against pressures from individual borrowing countries and their bilateral supporters to increase allocations. In practice, the normative allocations were not always matched by programme outlays, and exceptions to the general allocation methodology were regularly applied – for example, to limit allocations to the largest countries that might otherwise have absorbed most of what IDA had available to lend (see Kapur, Lewis and Webb 1997, Vol. 1, pp. 1151–1157).

7 However, mainly based on the recommendations of the external review panel, there will henceforth be only 16 items in the index and they will be more consistently grouped than before (on that, see text below). Moreover, each cluster will be weighted equally, rather than each item (IDA 2004, pp. 38–39).

8 However, it still features in the performance-based allocation of IDA resources, as is described in the Appendix to this chapter.

9 To be fair, the authors also experiment with a separate institutional quality measure prepared by the Kaufmann team, of which Kraay is part (see below), although it was only available for 2002, which gives them significant but weaker results than with the CPIA time series.

10 One curious comment of OED in this context, which this author has seen repeated in other World Bank papers, is that the staff making the CPIA assessments in the 1990s saw the exercise 'as a means of establishing a rank order among countries rather than absolute scores' (World Bank 2001, p. 18). This is peculiar because the country staff did not send ordinal rankings to CPIA management but cardinal scores. Presumably they knew that the ultimate use of the scores was in allocations of dollars, not to first place, second place, third place finishers, but to every IDA-eligible country, and for that an allocation based on ordinal rankings for some 80 countries would have been incredibly cumbersome.

11 By the same token, the items with higher variance of their scores have greater influence in the distribution of overall CPIA scores, which may be important for researchers with access to CPIA data to consider.

12 Possible scores are 1, 2, 2.5, 3, 3.5, 4, 4.5, 5 and 6, with 2 being 'unsatisfactory', 3 being 'moderately unsatisfactory', and equivalently for 4 and 5. The written instructions do not explain when or how to use the half-point scores. The 'extended period' in scores

of 1 and 6 is defined as at least three years. The scoring instructions will also be changed on the recommendation of the external panel to redefine the scores of 1 and 6 as extreme assessments and not protracted good or poor performance, and to allow half-point scores of 1.5 and 5.5 (World Bank 2004, p. 8).

13 The external panel on CPIA noted that staff 'lack an effective system of incentives' for paying adequate attention in preparing their contribution to the CPIA and called in their summary of recommendations (but without an explanatory text in the body of the report, as for every other recommendation) for the Bank to adequately recognize staff contributions 'so that due diligence can be ensured and accountability is present even when subjective assessments are inescapable' (World Bank 2004, pp. iv and 3). Management agreed to do so.

14 There are more and less precise statistical ways to ask how many separate items are really in the CPIA. At the more informal end of the spectrum, the OED reported finding substantial correlations, especially notable between the new governance items added in 1998 and the standard policy items (World Bank 2001, p. 20). In addition, in an early draft of an important paper arguing that aid should be targeted more on countries with good policies and high poverty, 'good' was variously defined as relatively high scores on CPIA, cluster averages, and individual items in the CPIA. Each cluster alone 'worked' in the growth and aid-effectiveness equation, as did 10 of the individual items, which the authors took to mean that the 10 contained almost all the information in the 20 (Collier and Dollar 1998, Appendix). This was dropped in the published version of the paper and confidence in CPIA reliability as an indicator was placed instead on its having significance in a growth regression with common quantitative proxies for 'good' policies, which were not significant (Collier and Dollar 2002, p. 1499). This is a faith-based statement and not statistical inference, given the correlations among 'independent' variables in the exercise.

15 In an effort to emphasize that this is a grading of governments, one non-governmental organization has translated the quintiles into letter grades (A,B,C,D,F) and published the result on the Internet (Citizens Network on Essential Services 2003). The letter grades, however, go beyond what the data contain, as they assume the Bank is grading on a C curve and that the tails of the quintile distribution can be interpreted as 'excellent' and 'failing'.

16 Jeffrey Sachs and John McArthur developed the first index and Michael Porter the second. Xavier Sala-i-Martin and staff of the WEF now produce the first and Porter continues on the second.

17 The criterion for rejecting the local business views was when the standard deviation of their replies on a survey question significantly exceeded that for the global sample (WES 2004, p. 36).

18 In the technology index, technology transfer has no weight in the core countries and the other items are weighted equally, while for the non-core countries, the innovation sub-index counts for 1/8, technology transfer for 3/8 and the weight of the rest is 1/2. In the overall index, the weight for the technology component is 1/2 for the core countries (the other components have 1/4 each), while each of the three components receives equal weight for the non-core countries (WEF 2004, pp. 5 and 27).

19 'People of the same trade seldom meet together, even for merriment and diversion, but the conversation ends in a conspiracy against the public ...' (Smith 1937, p. 128).

20 Again, later in the report: 'In the coming years, our aim is to work more and more closely with country leaders to improve the objectivity of the data collected in this

Report, disseminate it more broadly, and create forums and other mechanisms to inform and catalyse local action' (WEF 2004, p. 54).

21 This was for the 2002 estimates; as some of the data were not available in earlier years, smaller data sets were used to generate estimates for exercises covering multiple years.

22 Kaufmann, Kraay and Mastruzzi tested systematic bias of expert assessments from different institutions compared to results from sample surveys and found a consistent right-wing bias in Heritage Foundation assessments. Moreover, in every instance in which a significant bias was found on any item, including in the CPIA on the issue of regulatory quality, it was in the right-wing direction. To be fair, the size of the effect was quite small. (Kaufmann *et al.* 2003, pp. 22–23.)

23 The formula also contains a slowly decreasing function of gross national income per capita (exponent of –0.125) and there is also a basic fixed allotment for every IDA country, which helps increase the share of small economies. In addition, 'blend' countries get a lower allocation than the norm given by the standard formula in order to take account of their access, albeit limited, to other financial resources. Also, post-conflict countries and countries suffering from major natural disasters can receive larger allocations than given by the standard formula (IDA 2003, p. 2). For the first time that this author is aware of, the formula was released into the public domain through the report of the external panel on CPIA (World Bank 2004, p. 7n).

24 Recall that this was a component of the CPIA from 1993 to 1997. When it was dropped from the CPIA in 1998, it immediately reappeared as a separate factor that would be averaged with the CPIA in allocating IDA funds, as it remains today.

25 In addition, more volatility was observed in the CPR than was intuitively expected, which was traced to the governance factor and in particular to the high variance of the procurement practices item in it (IDA 2004a, p. 3); as a result, annual values of this item will be replaced by three-year moving averages in allocations under IDA-14 (IDA 2004, p. 40).

References

Alexander, Nancy, 2004, 'Country Ownership Undone', Citizens' Network on Essential Services, Silver Spring, Maryland. Unpublished manuscript (23 February).

Alexander, Nancy and Tim Kessler, 2003, 'The Millennium Development Goals (MDGs) in an Unaccountable Global Order', December (on the web page of Citizens' Network on Essential Services at www.challengeglobalization.org).

Calvo, Guillermo A. and Frederic S. Mishkin, 2003, 'The Mirage of Exchange Rate Regimes for Emerging Market Countries', *Journal of Economic Perspectives*, Vol. 17, No. 4 (Fall), 99–118.

Centre for Public Integrity, 2004, *Global Integrity, 2004: Public Integrity Index and Country Reports*, CD-ROM, Washington, D.C.: Centre for Public Integrity.

Citizens' Network on Essential Services, 2003, 'World Bank Scorecard: Tool to Allocate Resources Among Low-Income Countries in 2002', November (see http://www.servicesforall.org).

Collier, Paul and David Dollar, 2002, 'Aid Allocation and Poverty Reduction', *European Economic Review*, Vol. 46, No. 8 (September), 1475–1500.

——, 1998, 'Aid Allocation and Poverty Reduction', World Bank, 20 October draft (see http://www.worldbank.org/research/aid/background/bg98_allocation.htm and http://www.worldbank.org/research/aid/background/bg98_allocation_tables.pdf).

Collier, Paul and Anke Hoeffler, 2002, 'Aid, Policy and Peace: Reducing the Risks of Civil Conflict' (see http://econ.worldbank.org/programs/conflict/topic/12198/library/doc?id = 12418).

Development Committee, 2003, 'Achieving the MDGs and Related Outcomes: A Framework for Monitoring Policies and Actions', Background Paper prepared by the staff of the World Bank and International Monetary Fund (DC2003-0003/Add.1), 28 March.

Hout, Wil, 2003, 'Good Governance and the Political Economy of Selectivity', Working Paper No. 100, Asia Research Center, Murdoch University, October (see http://wwwarc.murdoch.edu.au/wp/wp100.rtf).

IDA, 2004a, 'IDA's Performance-Based Allocation System: IDA Rating Disclosure And Fine-Tuning the Governance Factor', September (see http://siteresources.worldbank.org/IDA/Resources/PBAFINAL.pdf).

——, 2003, 'Allocating IDA Funds Based on Performance: Fourth Annual Report on IDA's Country Assessment and Allocation Process', March (see http://siteresources.worldbank.org/IDA/Resources/PBAAR4.pdf).

——, 2003a, 'IDA's Performance-Based Allocation System: Current and Emerging Issues', October (see http://www-wds.worldbank.org/servlet/WDSContentServer/WDSP/IB/2003/10/27/000160016_20031027122520/Rendered/PDF/27082/pdf).

IDA Deputies, 2003, 'Chairman's Summary', IDA-13 Mid-Term Review, Washington, D.C. 5 November (see http://siteresources.worldbank.org/IDA/Resources/IDA13MidTermReview.pdf).

International Development Association [IDA], 2004, 'Additions to IDA Resources: Fourteenth Replenishment – Working Together to Achieve the Millennium Development Goals', draft for public comment, 16 November (see http://siteresources.worldbank.org/IDA/Resources/webdraftreport.pdf).

Kapur, Devesh, John P. Lewis and Richard Webb, 1997, *The World Bank: Its First Half Century*, 2 volumes. Washington, D.C.: Brookings Institution Press.

Kaufmann, Daniel, Aart Kraay and Massimo Mastruzzi, 2003, 'Governance Matters III: Governance Indicators for 1996–2002', Social Science Research Network Electronic Library, 30 June (see http://ssrn.com/abstract = 405841).

Koeberle, Stefan, 2003, 'Should Policy-Based Lending Still Involve Conditionality?', *The World Bank Research Observer*, Vol. 18, No. 2 (Fall), 249–273.

Kraay, Aart and Vikram Nehru, 2004, 'When Is Debt Sustainable?', Policy Research Working Paper No. 3200, World Bank (see http://econ.worldbank.org/files/32872_wps3200. pdf).

Sen, Amartya, 2003, 'Human Rights and Asian Values', 2nd edition, Sixteenth Morgenthau Memorial Lecture on Ethics and Foreign Policy, Carnegie Council on Ethics and International Affairs, New York, 1 May 1997.

Smith, Adam, 1937, *An Inquiry into the Nature and Causes of the Wealth of Nations*, New York: Modern Library Edition.

World Bank, 2004, 'Country Policy and Institutional Assessments: An External Review Panel Recommendations and Management Follow-Up', 10 June (see http://siteresources.worldbank.org/IDA/Resources/CPIAExpPanRepSecM2004-0304.pdf).

World Bank, 2003, 'Country Policy and Institutional Assessment, 2003': Assessment Questionnaire, March (see http://siteresources.worldbank.org/IDA/Resources/CPIA2003.pdf).

World Bank, 2002, 'Annual Report on Portfolio Performance, Fiscal Year 2002', 2 volumes, 12 December (see http://siteresources.worldbank.org/QAG/Resources/

arppfy02report.pdf; see also http://siteresources.worldbank.org/QAG/Resources/ arppfy02Definitions.pdf and http://siteresources.worldbank.org/QAG/Resources/ arppfy02statsappendix.xls).

World Bank, 2001, 'OED IDA Review: Review of the Performance-Based Allocation System, IDA 10–12', 14 February (see http://wbln0018.worldbank.org/oed/ oeddoclib.nsf/View+to+Link+WebPages/310529285EC4A83685256A680079BC9F/ $FILE/PBA.pdf).

World Bank and International Monetary Fund, 2004, *Global Monitoring Report, 2004: Policies and Actions for Achieving the Millennium Development Goals and Related Actions*, Washington, D.C.: World Bank.

World Economic Forum [WEF], 2004, *Global Competitiveness Report 2003–2004*, New York: Oxford University Press.

WEF, 2004a, *Global Competitiveness Report 2004–2005*, Basingstoke, England: Palgrave Macmillan.

12

THE COCOA MARKET UNDER NEOLIBERALISM

Irfan ul Haque

Abstract:

This paper considers the case of cocoa to illustrate the problems faced by primary commodity producers. We examine the impact of market liberalization in cocoa-producing countries as well as consuming industrial countries on the cocoa price and cocoa farmers. We show that market liberalization is not responsible for such improvements in productive efficiency as occurred over time, one of its two stated goals. Nor is there convincing evidence that the producers' share in the export price increased, the other stated goal of liberalization. A serious consequence of the preoccupation with market liberalization, rather, was that it diverted attention from cocoa producers' main concerns – viz. market volatility, low prices and the declining producers' share in the value chain. We then go on to explore possible measures to address these issues, notably filling the institutional vacuum created as a result of the abolition of state marketing authorities in several cocoa-producing countries. We finally attempt to show that the conditions are favourable for cocoa producers to coordinate their production policies in order to maintain satisfactory cocoa prices. This would also arrest the erosion of the incomes of cocoa producers.

Introduction

There was a time when commodities figured prominently in discussions of international trade, financial, and development issues. Already in the early 1940s, John Maynard Keynes, in conceptualizing what has emerged as the twin Bretton Woods institutions, devoted a great deal of thought to the commodity issue and its close links with international financial stability (Keynes 1943).

He laboured in the shadow of the Great Depression, when commodity prices plummeted to depths not seen before, and was well aware of the commodity shortages during and after World War II.

At that time, the volatility and unreliability of commodity markets was of concern to industrial as well as to developing countries. The disjuncture of interest in commodities came later, as the industrial countries succeeded in reducing their dependency on commodity imports with the development of synthetic substitutes and other means. They also put in place a formidable structure of agriculture protection, even as commodities remained major providers of livelihood and foreign exchange for a large part of the developing world.

Thus, the interest in international solutions to the commodity problem on the part of the industrial countries waned over time, turning into virtual hostility under the sway of the neoliberal ideas, to global cooperative actions. International commodity agreements, buffer stock schemes, and other state interventions are now widely regarded as failures, never to be repeated again.

But the commodity problem persists. It afflicts particularly the poorest countries, threatening their livelihood and jeopardizing their national economic management through strains on government budgets and exchange earnings. World forums concerned with issues of trade and finance are reluctant to take up the subject of commodities and explore possible solutions. Jacques Chirac has called it 'a sort of conspiracy of silence'.[1] While the world development community rightly worries about the external debt burden on the very poor countries, it gives little thought to what is arguably the other half of the problem.

This paper aims to contribute to the current efforts launched by several non-governmental organizations (NGOs) and others to restore the issue of commodities to the world trade, finance and development agenda. We examine the case of cocoa, a commodity that has been subjected to market liberalization at both domestic and international levels. We first describe the structure of the cocoa market and identify the factors that are deemed to explain price formation. This provides the necessary background to a discussion on the impact of neoliberal policies on cocoa producers. We then address the generic issues and explore the remedies that might be considered in the light of past experience, before offering conclusions.

The Cocoa Market and Price Formation

Three generic issues arise in the context of primary commodities: the world market volatility, the declining trend in commodity prices, and the relatively small share of primary producers in the 'value chain'.[2] These issues arise out of the way primary commodity markets are structured, function, and behave. Since at the core of the commodity problem is the struggle to bring world supply and demand into balance over the short as well as the long term, who produces what and at what cost is central to its resolution.

Cocoa Production

Cocoa is among the more important commodities exported by developing countries, with a world total of about US $2.5 billion in recent years. Four countries – Côte d'Ivoire, Ghana, Nigeria and Cameroon – account for about two-thirds of world production and for three-quarters of world exports of cocoa beans. Cocoa producers are a rather diverse group. Brazil and Malaysia are relatively high-income developing countries, while Ghana, Nigeria and Indonesia are lower-income. Côte d'Ivoire and Cameroon fall somewhere in the middle. For the four largest economies (Brazil, Indonesia, Malaysia, and Nigeria) the cocoa sector is a rather insignificant source of income, employment or foreign exchange earnings. On the other hand, for Côte d'Ivoire and Ghana, more than 30 per cent and 25 per cent of the total earnings, respectively, come from cocoa exports. Thus, what happens in the world cocoa market is of critical interest to these two countries; similarly, developments in these two countries have a great impact on the world market.

The structure of production – how production is organized – also differs among countries. Whereas production in West Africa is heavily concentrated in very small farms, cocoa farms in Brazil tend to be bigger (ranging between 10 to 100 hectares), while Malaysia has mostly large estates. Significant differences remain, however, between the two modes of production. Large private estates are run rather like commercial firms – that is, profitability is given much greater weight in production decisions. For smallholders, profits do not have a clear meaning since they also provide labour. Large estates are therefore less wedded to producing cocoa and more prepared to withdraw when market conditions turn unfavourable. Cocoa is quintessentially a smallholder crop that requires substantial labour input to harvest and dry the crop, which gives smallholders considerable advantage over the larger estates (Ruf and de Milly 1990).

The 1990s witnessed a sharp slowdown in overall cocoa production, mainly the result of declines in Malaysia and Brazil. Ghana and, to a much smaller extent, Cameroon were the only major producers whose production rose faster than in the previous decade (Table 1). Although Indonesia's rate of expansion also slowed (which was to be expected, considering the very small base from where it started), its production nevertheless continued to expand, at an astounding rate of 13 per cent a year. In terms of yields, the

Table 1. Growth rates of production and area harvested (annual percentage trend rates of growth)

Countries	Production		Area harvested
	1980–89	1990–99	1990–99
Brazil	1.9	−2.8	−0.1
Cameroon	1.7	2.2	0.6
Côte d'Ivoire	8.8	6.7	5.2
Ghana	0.8	5.7	8.3
Indonesia	28.4	12.8	7.7
Malaysia	23.8	−12.4	−14.2
Nigeria	4.5	1.0	2.1
World total	5.2	2.1	

Source: FAO Database.

West African countries lag far behind the two Asian producers, Malaysia and Indonesia. Brazil's yields and overall output in recent years suffered from 'witches' broom' disease.

The availability of a suitable natural environment is critical for the expansion of cocoa production. According to an International Cocoa Organisation (ICCO) study, soil and climate conditions are particularly favourable for cocoa production in Malaysia and Indonesia, but because the harvest cannot be dried naturally, the quality of Asian cocoa is inferior (Ruf and de Milly 1990). Conditions in the other cocoa-producing countries range from average to good. Indonesia is the only major producer with considerable land availability, although Ghana too has good potential.

Cocoa Prices

The behaviour of cocoa prices has been typical of other primary products, showing wide fluctuations and a declining secular trend. Table 2 gives the estimates of price volatility (after adjusting for inflation)[3] for cocoa and a few selected groups of agricultural products. As they have been averaged over the year, these indices underestimate the price volatility on a day-to-day basis. The year-to-year fluctuations, however, are likely to convey a better sense of the fluctuations in farmer income, since the price on any single day affects only the trades of that day.

During practically each of the past four decades, the cocoa price was more unstable than that of the entire group of tropical beverages to which cocoa belongs (the other commodities in the group are coffee and tea) as well as the other commodity groups, 'vegetable oilseeds and oils' and 'agricultural raw materials'. During the 1980s, however, the cocoa price was just a little less

Table 2. Price volatility index for cocoa and selected commodities 1960s–1990s (as adjusted for inflation)

	1960–1969	1970–1979	1980–1989	1990–1999
Cocoa	16.3	22.0	20.3	11.5
Tropical beverages	5.2	21.0	18.5	17.9
Vegetable oilseeds and oils	6.4	17.0	22.7	7.5
Agricultural raw materials	4.0	11.6	6.2	5.9

Source: UNCTAD.

Table 3. Cocoa prices and the stock ratio (10-year-period average)

	Stock ratio %	World price SDR2002/ton
1960–69	40.1	2,875
1970–79	27.5	4,375
1980–89	43.0	2,582
1990–99	54.1	1,063

Source: ICCO.

volatile than vegetable oilseeds and oils, and during the 1990s it was more stable than its own group average.

The data suggest that price volatility tends to rise in periods of high global inflation –the 1970s and the 1980s – even though inflation as such seems to have little influence on the volatility of individual prices. The instability indices relating to current prices (not shown) are of an order of magnitude similar to those for prices adjusted for general inflation. What is significant, however, is that there is no indication that the economic liberalization and globalization of the 1990s made agricultural prices more unstable. In fact, the instability index in each case was lower than in previous decades, in some cases considerably so.

Thus, despite their stated objectives, the operations of the international cocoa agreements and state marketing authorities appear not to have had any discernable impact on the cocoa market. It is, therefore, basically the interaction of supply and demand – as reflected in the movements of world stocks of raw cocoa – that seems to have largely determined the world cocoa price. Table 3 gives the 10-year average for both stock levels and prices over the last four decades. On the face of it, the high prices during the 1970s can be explained in terms of the low stock levels, and the low prices of the 1990s in terms of the high stocks. Similarly, comparing the situation during the 1960s and the 1980s, prices were 11 per cent lower in the latter period when the stock ratio was about 8 per cent higher. Thus, the negative relationship between the stock-to-grinding ratio and the world price appears to hold rather well over the last four decades.

Table 4. Regression results (price as dependent variable)

	Intercept	Time	Stock-ratio	R^2
1961–2001	50.74	–0.02	–0.03	0.75
		(4.75)	(6.84)	
1961–70	90.40	–0.04	–0.03	0.87
		(2.95)	(5.99)	
1971–80	–195.82	0.10	–0.03	0.86
		(5.03)	(3.25)	
1981–90	153.1	–0.07	–0.02	0.99
		(17.56)	(18.38)	
1991–2001	170.82	–0.08	–0.03	0.29
		(1.71)	(1.38)	

Note: The regressions are least-squares, semi-logarithmic in prices. The parentheses give the *t* values.

Nevertheless, a closer examination of the relationship is warranted, since the price decline during the 1990s is hard to explain exclusively in terms of the movement of stocks *within* the decade. In order to determine how the relationship held up over time, regressions were run for the data on prices and stocks including and excluding the time trend.

Taking the period 1961–2001 as a whole, a fairly robust relationship seems to hold between the cocoa price and the stock-to-grinding ratio, although also showing a statistically significant long-term declining trend in the price of 2 per cent a year (Table 4). In other words, the stock levels have an impact on cocoa prices in addition to an underlying long-term declining trend. On an average, each percentage point increase in the stock-ratio is associated with a price decline of 3 per cent. The time trend and the stock-ratio together explain some 75 per cent of the variation in price over the entire period. This relationship holds well for the first three sub-periods (covering 1961–90); in fact, the relationship for individual decades is even stronger. The coefficient of the stock-ratio is remarkably stable, at about 3 per cent, whether the decades are taken together or severally. The price trend over these three periods, however, shows wide fluctuation; after declining 4 per cent a year during 1961–70, it rises 10 per cent a year during the 1970s, only to decline again by 7 per cent annually during the following decade. In short, while the sensitivity of the price with respect to changes in the stock-ratio is quite stable, the time trend captures the impact of factors specific to the period in question.

The 1990s, however, marked a sharp break with the past in that the explanatory power of the two independent variables was greatly diminished. Neither the stock-ratio nor the time trend had a coefficient significant at a 95 per cent level of confidence, although the coefficient for the stock-ratio still remains at 0.3. This suggests that the depressed prices of recent years call for an explanation that goes beyond the factors seen to be historically important. At the same time, we need to explain the factors responsible for the secular decline in cocoa prices, which seem to be independent of the forces of supply and demand. It would be one thing if the price decline were due to improvements in overall productive efficiency; quite another if it resulted from declining real wages and general living standards.

The Impact of Neoliberal Policies

The rise of neoliberalism had a profound influence on the functioning of commodity markets, their control within producing countries, and the discussion of the commodity problem itself. International commodity agreements have now been all but abandoned; the few that exist exclude 'economic clauses' – that is, clauses relating to control and regulation of production and exports with a view to maintaining or stabilizing prices. In countries with state marketing authorities, the liberalization measures focused primarily on their dismantlement. Market liberalization and deregulation also occurred in the industrial countries, although protection of agriculture and other activities of interest remained strong.

Earlier international cocoa agreements (ICAs) relied on buffer stocks to defend prices within specified bands. However, prices could not be stabilized during the 1970s, as there were no stocks that could be unloaded in the market; besides, producers faced with high cocoa prices had lost interest in price stability. In the late 1980s, on the other hand, the collapse of the cocoa market could not be avoided since the maximum level of buffer stocks, specified in the ICA, was reached quickly, and the efforts at price stabilization were abandoned. The 1993 and later cocoa agreements dropped the provisions for buffer stocks or price ranges altogether.

To determine how cocoa producers have been affected by market liberalization, it is necessary to examine developments both within producing developing countries and in consuming, industrial countries.

Market Liberalization in Producing Countries

When discussing the measures to liberalize economies, the focus has basically been on the West African cocoa producers – viz. Côte d'Ivoire, Cameroon, Ghana and Nigeria – as these were the producers whose governments played a dominant role in the cocoa trade. In other respects, the state's role in economic activity or promoting economic development has not been too different from cocoa producers in East Asia or Latin America. Besides marketing, the state institutions – marketing boards in the anglophone countries (Ghana and

Nigeria) and some sort of centralized funds in the francophone countries (Côte d'Ivoire and Cameroon) – played a role in quality control, research on plant breeding, market intelligence and extension service.

Typically, the marketing boards managed the entire marketing process, buying cocoa directly from producers and selling it to traders and processors at a specified, guaranteed price, at least for the whole cocoa season if not longer. The *caisse de stabilization* system, on the other hand, did not involve ownership or direct handling of the crop at any stage, but instead relied on private licensed traders for domestic purchase and export. The state authority, however, did guarantee a producer price and established a scale for all payments involved from the farm to export and another scale for the difference between the f.o.b. and c.i.f. prices for main destinations. As a result, depending on the difference between the world market price and the guaranteed producer price, the fund, in principle, could accumulate or run down financial reserves. Another difference was that the state trading authority under the *caisse* system was administratively not a part of the government.

The state marketing institutions were established by the colonial powers with the aim of regulating trade in primary commodities, and they served their purpose more or less satisfactorily during the colonial time (Williams 1985). As in the case of other public bodies in developing countries, however, their performance after independence deteriorated. They became large bureaucracies, influenced by politics, and increasingly inefficient in their designated functions. All this was reflected in the high cost of their operations, which, given the way the system worked, was borne largely by cocoa farmers. The francophone institutions actually became insolvent, as they were unable to build up reserves in the face of high costs of operations and low world prices.

The liberalization programmes aimed to improve productive efficiency by aligning domestic prices with world prices and to give cocoa farmers a higher share of the f.o.b. price. There was, in fact, some contradiction between the two goals since the increased production from liberalization could lower the world price, thereby raising the possibility that the price the cocoa farmer actually received would also be lower.

Evaluating the impact of market liberalization measures presents a number of conceptual and practical difficulties. There are significant differences among the four major producers as to the timing and nature of the measures taken. Nigeria dismantled its marketing boards virtually overnight in 1986, largely in response to domestic political pressures. Although it also devalued its currency at about the same time, Nigeria remained hesitant to deregulate and liberalize other spheres of economic activity.

Ghana, on the other hand, started on economic reforms under an IMF/World-Bank-supported structural adjustment programme in the early

1980s. It brought its fiscal situation under control and adjusted its exchange rate, and generally liberalized the economy. After more than a decade of neglect, cocoa production and exports started to recover. The government took a number of other policy measures in the early 1990s, notably introducing private sector competition in domestic procurement and transportation and privatizing Produce Buying Company, a subsidiary of Ghana's Cocoa Board (COCOBOD). Later on, Ghana began allowing private companies to export directly 30 per cent of their domestic purchases (Varangis and Schreiber 2001). However, while the Ghanaian authorities drastically reduced the workforce and generally streamlined the COCOBOD's activities, they did not agree to its abolition.

The measures taken in the cocoa sectors of the two francophone counries – first, Cameroon, and later, Côte d'Ivoire – were more far-reaching. Cameroon started its reforms in 1990 with the abolition of its public marketing body, while adjusting domestic cocoa price and marketing margins to eliminate the need for subsidies. Liberalization in Côte d'Ivoire was initiated in the mid-1990s; it consisted of increasing competition in the procurement and export of cocoa, improving transparency and accountability of its stabilizing fund – *Caisse de Stabilization* (CAISTAB) – while increasing the returns to farmers (Varangis and Schreiber 2001). In 1999, CAISTAB was abolished, and in its place the government set up a much smaller agency.

In short, market liberalization and deregulation had taken place in all of the four West African countries over the last two decades, though with significant differences. Thus, while Ghana continues to have a marketing board, its overall economic system is no less market-oriented than (say) that of Côte d'Ivoire or Nigeria. Nevertheless, in evaluating the impact of liberalization, the researchers have focused basically on one factor – the producer's share in the f.o.b. price (see, for example, Varangis and Schreiber 2001; Gilbert and Varangis 2003). They point out that the countries free of state marketing – Brazil, Cameroon, Indonesia, Malaysia, and Nigeria – had significantly higher farmgate prices as a proportion of the export price (70–90 per cent) than those of Ghana or Côte d'Ivoire (less than 50 per cent), which did have state marketing in 1994–95, the year to which the data relate. Furthermore, the researchers attempt to show that the abolition of the state marketing authority significantly lowered domestic marketing costs and taxes.

These two conclusions are actually interrelated since the producers' share in the export price does depend on marketing costs and taxes. Indeed, data in Gilbert and Varangis (2003) show that the observed differences in the producers' share were due largely to the much higher implicit or explicit taxes in Ghana and Côte d'Ivoire; the marketing costs proper differed little across the countries covered (Figure 4 in their paper). But to the extent that the state institutions provided public services (such as quality control and extension service), the reduction in taxes may not have been an entirely positive development. Indeed, the quality of cocoa exported by Cameroon and Nigeria deteriorated sharply following the liberalization. But the most serious weakness of the conclusion that the producers' share improved following liberalization is that it rests basically on the findings for just one year. Given that export prices are highly unstable, the producers' share in any one year may not provide a reliable guide to the actual situation.

To remedy that weakness, Table 5 provides the data on the producers' share in the export price averaged over five-year segments covering 1981–2000. In both Indonesia and Brazil, where there is no state trading, the producer share in the export price is indeed generally higher, although it shows considerable variation over time. The extraordinary high shares in Nigeria and Ghana during 1981–85 are questionable; the cause was probably their grossly overvalued currencies. One thing, however, seems clear: abolishing the marketing board in Nigeria did not have an unambiguous impact on the share. In the case of Cameroon, the share was already on the high side just prior to liberalization, but declined to 62 per cent during 1996–2000. Côte d'Ivoire embarked on market reforms only toward the end of the 1990s, but it too shows that there was an actual decline in the share, relative to earlier periods.

In short, there is no firm evidence that cocoa farmers actually benefited from market liberalization. The liberalization process seems to follow a set pattern. During the first year or so, a number of private companies enter the cocoa trade, which temporarily pushes up producer prices. But this phase is followed by a period of consolidation and restructuring when the outcome for the producer depends on a host of other factors (Fold 2001). In any case, the cocoa farmers are not concerned about their share as such but rather about the actual price they obtain and how it relates to their production costs, which vary considerably across countries.

The estimates of production costs are given in Table 6, relating to the 1995–99 period, which helps even out yearly variations. They have been

Table 5. Producer prices as a percentage of export unit values (averages for the period)

	Brazil	Cameroon	Côte d'Ivoire	Ghana	Nigeria	Indonesia
1981–85	72.8	55.4	55.1	113.8	120.9	78.9
1986–90	68.6	70.9	59.9	37.3	96.1	74.7
1991–95	78.9	85.7	65.6	48.2	101.2	84.7
1996–2000	82.0	62.1	50.5	52.4	89.0	82.6

Source: ICCO and UNCTAD.

Table 6. Estimates of costs of production for major cocoa producers

	Production costs $/kg		Producer price	Export price	Cost producer price ratio %	Cost export price ratio %
	1989	1995–99		1995–99		
Brazil	1.00	1.62	1.18	1.44	137	112
Cameroon	0.83	0.60	0.82	1.34	73	45
Côte d'Ivoire	0.66	0.60	0.68	1.36	87	44
Ghana	0.48	1.27	0.78	1.48	163	86
Indonesia	0.60	0.36	1.17	1.14	30	31
Malaysia	1.00	0.85	1.20	1.20	71	71
Nigeria	0.50	2.16	0.92	1.34	235	161

derived by taking into account three factors: the estimates of costs for producing one kilogram of cocoa beans in 1989, provided by an ICCO study (Ruf and de Milly 1990); an adjustment for the improvements in yields between 1989 and 1995–99, taking it as an approximation for productivity improvements across countries (derived from the FAO database); and an allowance for the effects of domestic inflation and exchange rate changes during the period in question on the basis of the IMF data. The resulting estimates do not take into account the costs of replanting and new planting and are at best a rough approximation.

Indonesia's production cost – 36 US cents a kilogram – is far and away the lowest. Although its yields improved greatly during the 1990s, the catastrophic decline in the rupiah exchange rate consequent to the Asian financial crisis of 1997 was a far more important factor. On the other hand, the estimates for Ghana and Nigeria are on the high side, probably for the opposite reasons: domestic inflation was not adequately compensated for by an adjustment in the exchange rate, although both also suffered large declines in yields. Despite the weaknesses of the estimates, it is probably safe to say that Brazil and Nigeria have now become the highest cost producers, though their reasons are different. In Brazil, the major cause for the rise in cost was the deterioration in yields following the outbreak of a plant disease. In Nigeria, neglect and general mismanagement are the main causes: cocoa production is not a priority sector in that country and there has been considerable migration of young working-age population out of cocoa areas.

Overall, the variations in yields across countries appear to be the most important variable in production costs, where market liberalization did not have much impact. There is also no systematic evidence that the cocoa growers in countries without state marketing enjoyed a higher financial surplus. On the face of it, Brazil, Ghana and Nigeria operated at a loss, although in Ghana's case costs were lower than the export price by a significant margin. The ratio of production cost to producer's price was roughly similar for Cameroon, Côte d'Ivoire, and Malaysia.

Structural Changes in the World Cocoa Market

Dismantlement of government regulations and market liberalism were not confined to the cocoa-producing countries. Significant changes also occurred in the industrialized countries (the main consumers of cocoa) that had a profound impact on the structure of the market and price formation. The recent behaviour of international cocoa prices, which seems to break with historical trends, can be explained to a large extent by these developments. The change in the market structure had in particular two consequences for the formation of cocoa prices:

- there was an evident decline in the level of cocoa stocks needed to carry on the processing and chocolate manufacturing activities in the European countries (the principal market), but also elsewhere; and
- the world market price appears to have become rather less sensitive to the forces of supply and demand.

Four developments have had a significant influence on the functioning of the cocoa market in recent years, even though they evolved over a longer period of time.

1 A few large transnational corporations have now come to dominate the cocoa trade (as in other commodities), having taken over, replaced, or merged with the smaller companies engaged in trading physical cocoa. This development has benefited from the dramatic improvements in communications, which enable individual companies to develop efficient market intelligence and facilitate the management of large-scale transnational operations.
2 The old distinction between trading and processing companies has become blurred, as most large trading companies are now also engaged in cocoa processing, sourcing beans directly from exporting countries to exploit the scale economies in transport, storage and processing. This occurred because the large chocolate manufacturers decided to hive off the less profitable processing of cocoa into intermediate products (cocoa liquor, cocoa butter, and cocoa powder) from their core activities. At the high end, however, chocolate manufacturers continue to do their own processing

to ensure quality. By the mid-1990s, some 70 per cent of all grindings was done by the top 10 firms, with the three largest cocoa-processing companies – Archer-Daniels-Midland (ADM), Barry Callebaut and Cargill – dominating the market. These companies account for some 40–50 per cent of world grindings at present and may reach the 75 per cent mark within a few years (Fold 2001).

3 The third development is linked to the second. With the disappearance of the state-dominated marketing structures in cocoa-producing countries, large transnational companies have, to a considerable extent, also taken over the exporting functions in the producing countries. According to a recent ICCO report (ICCO 2001), some 90 per cent of cocoa exports from Côte d'Ivoire are now handled by companies that are subsidiaries or have close links with the international companies engaged in cocoa trade. Similarly, in Sulawesi – the cocoa-producing area of Indonesia – some 60 national traders were engaged in cocoa exports as recently as 1998; by 2000 only two were left, the rest having been taken over by foreign companies (Humphrey 2002). This process of corporate integration and concentration has also been driven by economies of scale in transportation. Cocoa is no longer shipped in bags but in large containers directly to end-users, which has considerably reduced handling costs at both ends of the shipment.

4 Finally, the chocolate manufacturing industry has experienced increased concentration, itself a result of globalization and of the increased impor-tance of brand recognition and marketing strategies. Following some 200 takeovers in the chocolate industry during 1970–90, only 17 firms have come to control about half of the world market in chocolate, five firms – Nestlé, Mars, Hershey, Kraft-Jacob-Suchard and Cadbury-Schweppes – enjoying dominant positions (Fold 2001). The ICCO (2001) study notes: 'The process has involved takeovers of smaller companies by the large international concerns, mergers to form larger combined entities and incursion of the international companies into new or developing mar-kets' (p.7). This mirrors the developments on the retail side, where market concentration has also increased, large supermarkets essentially turning into renters of shelf space.

The overall result of these developments has been that cocoa producers face a monopsony situation on the sale side (i.e. they can sell to only a few buyers). On the retail side of the finished product, consumers face a near-to-a-monopoly situation. The consequence of the increased concentration along the supply chain – trade, processing, and manufacture of chocolate – is that the procurement and provision of intermediate products is not governed wholly by 'arm's-length' arrangements but by long-term inter-corporate agreements, contracts or understandings. Apart from the issue of who benefited from these developments (discussed in the next section), they have implications for both the need for carrying stocks and price formation.

Two parallel developments have reduced the need for stocks. One, because there are now much fewer firms at each level of the activity, the need for stocks to carry on normal business activity has declined considerably. This results from the fact that, relative to their turnover, larger firms tend to carry a lower level of stocks than do smaller firms. At the same time, traders and processors now face relatively stable and reliable demand from their partners and associates in business, which also reduces the level of stocks to be held. The second development is of a technological nature. As in other manufacturing activity, chocolate manufacturers have started to rely on modern management techniques and practices to reduce their costs; in particular, manufacturers have adopted the just-in-time inventory management practice, where supplies of inputs are obtained as required in manufacturing. Within Europe – the biggest market for chocolate – a handful of processors (mostly based in the Netherlands) have delivery vehicles working virtually round the clock, responding to demand from manufacturers all over the continent.

The decline in the requirements for stocks by itself could suffice to explain the generally depressed prices in recent years. Throughout the 1990s the stocks-to-grinding ratio remained in excess of 55 per cent, compared with the long-term average of roughly 40 per cent for the four decades 1961–2001. The ratio declined during 1995–99, but it did not fall much below 50 per cent. Thus, two factors appear to be keeping the cocoa price low: the stocks have been at a historically very high level in recent years, while the *need* for stocks for carrying on business has also declined quite substantially. The result is a large overhang of unwanted stocks that has continued to depress cocoa prices.

The question then arises as to why stock levels have not been adjusted downward, which is to say why cocoa supplies have persistently outstripped demand, despite low prices. Some influences have certainly limited output, given that it has remained more or less stagnant at about 2.8 million tons since 1995. The key, however, is the behaviour of individual producers, which has sharply diverged. Overall, production from the seven major cocoa producers rose by less than 15 per cent between 1990 and 2000. However, two countries dominated the expansion: Côte d'Ivoire and (the low-cost) Indonesia together accounted for virtually the entire increase (63 per cent and 35 per cent, respectively), while the output increases in Ghana and Nigeria just about offset the declines in Brazil and Malaysia.[4] It was noted earlier that despite low world prices, the production costs in Indonesia particularly but also in Côte d'Ivoire allowed producers a significant margin.

In short, some producers continued to be willing to supply cocoa at the low price. The increased productivity could partly be the reason, but the higher yields were realized only in some of the cocoa-producing areas. A major reason must have been that smallholder farmers accepted a sharp decline in their incomes rather than moving out of cocoa production. In some countries, depreciated exchange rates and depressed wages helped the process. There is, however, scant information on wages and incomes earned by cocoa growers. According to one study on Côte d'Ivoire (Bonjean and Chambas 2001), there is evidence of increasing poverty and declining incomes in cocoa-producing areas.

Revisiting the Generic Issues

Cocoa is a representative commodity: its world market price is highly volatile and has been on a declining trend, and the producers do not appear to have benefited from the technological and other productivity-enhancing improvements, whether in their own countries or along the value chain. These have been perennial problems, but the neoliberal policies were not aimed at dealing with them. It was a basic tenet of neoliberalism that the commodity problem must not be addressed by interfering in the market. Freely functioning markets would ensure that supply and demand reach a balance and arrest the downward price trend not related to productivity improvements.

The search for solutions has now become more difficult, for it must be carried out in an environment where there is widespread suspicion of public action and institutions. In particular, there is little support today for a revival of international commodity agreements or reestablishment of state marketing authorities. Nevertheless, we attempt here to revisit the generic issues from a perspective that is generally lacking today.

Price Instability

In dealing with the issue of volatile markets, the measures designed to stabilize prices or producers' income should be distinguished from those intended to somehow compensate for the consequences of such occurrences. The STABEX is a well-known example of a scheme designed to provide compensation, on an *ex post* basis, for unforeseen export earnings shortfalls to a number of African, Caribbean, and Pacific (ACP) countries under the various Lomé Conventions on EU-ACP cooperation. The IMF's Compensatory Financing Facility (CFF) was also designed to provide short-term financing as balance of payments support to producer countries that faced adverse developments in their export markets. Neither of the two schemes is currently operative. STABEX was abandoned when the last Lomé Convention was negotiated, although thought is now being given to its revival in some form.

The main reason why the CFF has been little used over the years is that the financing under the scheme is contingent on the country concerned being able to satisfy the IMF as to the temporary nature of the price fall, a condition that primary producers have found difficult to fulfil. Funds are not available if the price fall is seen as following a secular trend. In addition, in 1983 the Fund tightened the conditionality for drawings under the CFF; this discouraged drawings.[5]

With respect to stabilizing prices, a distinction can be drawn between measures that aim to stabilize producer prices within producing countries, as was attempted by the state marketing authorities, and measures that stabilize world market prices, as was intended under the early International Cocoa Agreements (ICAs). At the national level, the goal of price stability can be either short-term – that is, confined to stabilizing intra-year prices – or covering a longer term.

The abolition of the state marketing authorities inevitably meant abandoning efforts at stabilizing producer prices, which evidently resulted in increased price instability. Export prices during the 1990s became more volatile in Cameroon (without the state marketing authority), while Ghana experienced the opposite. Gilbert and Varangis (2003) show that producer prices, following market liberalization, were considerably more unstable in Cameroon, Côte d'Ivoire, and Nigeria, though not in Ghana, the only country that kept its marketing board.

The only recent efforts to address the continuing problem of price instability has come from a few experts in the World Bank and UNCTAD (though so far without institutional endorsement), promoting the idea of 'market-based risk management' instruments (e.g. Dehn 2000; Larson, Verangis and Yabuki 1998). Insofar as hedging instruments are concerned, there is nothing new in the proposal, as traders have long been hedging against price uncertainty through the futures market. Traders with physical stocks of a commodity routinely protect themselves against price decline by selling futures contracts. Thus, if the price actually falls, they can recover the loss by buying back the futures contract; the opposite occurs if the price rises. In short, a hedged trader's gains or losses in the physical market are offset through losses or gains in the futures market.

Where the new proposals differ, however, is in tapping the interest in options trading on the part of large commodity funds. Options trading can be a more attractive instrument against uncertainty than straightforward hedges; they enable traders with stocks to protect themselves against a price fall without forgoing the possibility of taking advantage of a rising market. This is done by buying a put option, giving the trader the right to sell the product at a specified price, which is exercised if the price declines. The payoff on the bet turning out favourably can be quite considerable, unlike the ordinary hedge which basically offsets gains or losses. But several things have to be considered. First, the use of options and hedges as protection against price uncertainty, as with any insurance, has a cost, which is directly proportional to the risks involved. The cost of options, as indeed of ordinary hedges, tends to rise both with the length of time covered and with the market's volatility. These instruments are therefore useful only for covering a relatively short period of time (around three months), without the cost becoming prohibitive. To state the obvious, these instruments, like conventional hedges, simply offer protection against price uncertainty; they do not deal with the volatility itself.

Second, options are a particularly risky instrument if they end up being used as bets on the market behaviour – that is, the risk of a hedger turning into a speculator. Options trading is notorious for its vulnerability to irregularities of all kinds. There have been many instances where an institution engaged in options trading has been rendered bankrupt through the actions of a lone trader (UNCTAD 2003 provides a useful list of avenues for fraud in trading). In short, adequate regulation and supervision of options trading, as well as high personal integrity of professionals engaged in trading, would be crucial to protect farmers against mismanagement or fraud. These are governance requirements that seem to go well beyond the skills required to successfully manage a state marketing authority.

Finally, individual cocoa farmers do not have the sufficient means, size, or expertise to purchase hedging instruments. The promoters of the idea do recognize this problem, but some believe that in the absence of a state authority, the problem could be overcome by local institutions – notably, farmers' cooperatives. Cooperatives enjoy an appeal for a variety of reasons, but there are few examples in developing countries of success. A major problem relates to their establishment. Ideally, they should arise out of some grassroots movement, but options trading is unlikely to be high on the movement's list of priorities. On the other hand, state-sponsored cooperatives have their own problems, most serious being the question of ownership with respect to their functions and policies. In any case, there is still no assurance that the cooperative would be of a size, financial strength and capability to manage options trading. All in all, the chances of a cooperative movement in any of the West African cocoa-producing countries becoming a force capable of marshalling the needed expertise and resources appear rather slim.

Nevertheless, hedges and options do have a place in commodity trade. Given the recognition that the abolition of state marketing authorities created an institutional vacuum, there is a place for streamlined quasi-state bodies that are independent of the government but are answerable to it for their performance. They are required in order to undertake some of the neglected tasks, such as quality control, handling of storage and transportation, and research and extension service. There is also a need to take advantage of buyers' need for insurance against price instability, which should result in sharing, if not complete elimination, of the cost of a hedge. Provided there is adequate supervision and regulation, these bodies could be allowed to use hedging instruments to facilitate their management of stocks and trading activities. The financial performance of the old marketing authorities could conceivably have been improved with greater, but judicious, use of such instruments.

With respect to stabilizing world prices, a mechanism appears unlikely to emerge in the foreseeable future. The memory of the failure of past cocoa agreements to stabilize prices is too fresh and the industrial countries have no interest in a mechanism to stabilize prices. As Gilbert (1996) put it: 'The commodity agreement movement is effectively dead'(p.1).[6]

The ICAs suffered from problems common to other commodity agreements. The earlier agreements, as noted, relied on buffer stocks to keep the market price within specified ranges. There were, however, no stocks to release in order to arrest the steep price rise of the 1970s while the situation was just the opposite when the stipulated stock level was insufficient to prevent cocoa prices from falling. A lack of adequate financing was a related problem that stymied the market operations under the third agreement that became operational in 1981. Matters were not helped by the fact that the largest cocoa producer – Côte d'Ivoire – did not join the first three agreements, nor did a major consumer, the United States.

Possibilities for Price Maintenance

Price stabilization and maintenance are closely related, for they both turn fundamentally on the producers' ability to regulate their supplies. While an *international* agreement might be unrealistic at this stage, the prospects of regulating cocoa supplies by the cocoa producers – either under the umbrella of ICCO or on their own – seem promising even though there are serious difficulties to over-come. In fact, the 1993 ICA contained a provision (Article 29) for producers to organize production curtailment arrangements to over-come market imbalances. Similarly, the 2001 ICA, while not mentioning production curtailment, provides for coordination of national production policies (Article 34). This suggests that at least those consuming countries that are signatories to the ICAs are not averse to measures to maintain prices. In fact, there is a vocal civil society in industrial countries that advocates 'remunerative prices' for primary producers.

Prices of primary products can remain below production costs over long periods, which causes hardship to producers and difficulties for government. When faced with similar problems, the industrial countries have tended to be remarkably pragmatic in giving protection and financial aid to the troubled sector. Primary-producing countries can take a leaf from this experience: if arrangements to regulate production or exports are not possible under an international agreement, producers could come together with the aim of improving on their own the markets for their products. Such cooperation is also needed for strengthening their bargaining position vis-à-vis transnational corporations engaged in trade in commodities in question.

A number of attempts have been made to achieve producers' alliances, the most well known being OPEC (the Organization of Petroleum-Exporting Countries). Others have included coffee, tin and natural rubber. A cartel-like action was also attempted for aluminium, a manufactured product, in the early 1990s, to deal with the threat of supplies from the former Soviet Union disrupting the market (Gilbert 1995). The experience of these alliances indicates that, for their success, at least two prior conditions must be fulfilled, or at least substantially fulfilled. The first is that all major producers share a common interest and vision in controlling production or exports so that collective action has sufficient support. The problem arises because the costs of the action are borne by the alliance members (i.e. withholding production or exports), but the benefits are shared by all producers. This 'free-rider' problem can more easily be tackled if there are only a few producers of the commodity in question.

Second, a price level completely divorced from market forces can only be maintained for a very limited period of time. The bigger the difference between the price that the alliance members want and the free market price, the more difficult it becomes to maintain the target price. The payoff on cheating is directly proportional to this difference, and under pressure an alliance risks its breakdown. There is also the consideration that higher the target price, the more likely that non-alliance sources of supplies would emerge.

Cocoa appears to be an ideal candidate as far as the first condition is concerned: the number of major producers is very small and all agree that some degree of supply regulation is needed. As seen earlier, seven producers account for virtually the entire world output, of which three – Côte d'Ivoire, Ghana and Indonesia – account for close to three-quarters. Côte d'Ivoire is far and away the biggest producer and could enjoy the status of a 'swing voter', rather similar to Saudi Arabia's role in OPEC. This means that its vote could be decisive in situations where other producers are divided on a particular issue (Gilbert and Smit 2003).

Four of the largest producers are in the same region and geographically more or less contiguous, which should make monitoring of production and exports somewhat easier. At the same time, two producers – Brazil and Malaysia – appear to have lost interest in cocoa. Cocoa is expensive to produce in these countries and is not particularly vital to their economic interests. Since basically large estates are involved, the switchover to alternative opportunities should be easier.

Thus, if the three big producers – Côte d'Ivoire, Indonesia and Ghana – were to agree on a scheme to regulate production and/or exports, it should not be too difficult to get the other two producers, Cameroon and Nigeria, on board. As far as Nigeria is concerned, it has neither the available land nor a particularly favourable environment for cocoa production (Ruf and de Milly 1990). At any rate, cocoa is only of minor importance to that country, accounting for less than 1 per cent of its total exports. Cameroon, on the other hand, has both land and a suitable environment, and cocoa remains a major export, accounting for close to 15 per cent of its export earnings. Being a relatively small producer, however, it poses little threat to the big three and its needs or interests should not be too difficult to accommodate.

It remains possible, however, that newcomers – as has happened in the coffee sector – could free-ride the market. This cannot be ruled out, but the threat may not be exaggerated. With a depressed world market, cocoa is not a particularly attractive crop for newcomers, considering that it takes several years before the investment starts to pay. The important thing is that the producers respect the second condition mentioned above – that is, they should aim at a price that can be realistically maintained and defended. In any case, production or export-regulating mechanisms cannot be expected to last indefinitely; periodic revisions of the maintained price are necessary if market forces are not to overwhelm the situation.

In sum, the success in managing production to maintain prices turns essentially on the three largest cocoa producers. They do at present have internal political problems to deal with, while also needing improvements in their respective cocoa sectors (particularly, in Ghana, but also Côte d'Ivoire), but agreeing on each other's share in the world market need not be an insurmountable problem. A common position among the key producers could also strengthen their bargaining position vis-à-vis the transnational corporations that they must deal with.

Cocoa Producers and the Value Chain

As cocoa moves from the farmgate to the port for export and then on to the final consumer, it goes through both a process of handling (i.e. grading of output, packaging, domestic transport, paperwork, trade finance, etc.) and actual physical processing; the processing consists, at the earliest stage (usually carried out by the grower), of drying the fruit and preparing the beans, and later of producing the finished product, usually in the form of chocolate. Talbot (2002) provides a stylized sketch of the value chain for cocoa as follows:

cocoa pods → 'rest' → 'remove seeds' → ferment → dry → cocoa beans →
roast → shell → cocoa nibs → grind → chocolate liquor → press → cocoa
butter and powder → chocolate (along with the input of sugar and milk).

Basically, the commodity moves from the grower to a collector or a village-level
trader after having been dried and fermented. The commodity is then
acquired by a national trader, which could be a state marketing authority,
which does the grading and quality control before its being exported. In some
cases – but only to a very small extent in West Africa and Indonesia – cocoa
beans are processed into intermediate products (cocoa liquor, butter, or powder) for export. The product is then either taken over by an international
trader or processor, which typically has long-term arrangements with established large chocolate confectioners, or gets traded in the world commodity
market. The chocolate manufacturer then arranges the retailing of the
finished product. Cocoa generally constitutes less than 10 per cent of the cost
of manufactured chocolate.

The question arises as to how various steps along the value chain are
controlled and coordinated, especially when national boundaries are crossed.
In particular, how are improvements in productive efficiency shared between
producers of primary products in developing countries and final consumers
in industrial countries? In the case of cocoa, as for some other primary products, producers have been hit hard by the depressed prices, but this has had
little impact on the price of the finished product. This means that cocoa producers have faced price declines without benefiting from the increased sales
that would have followed from a decline in chocolate price (Morisset 1997).
Thus, from the perspective of economic advancement, the distribution of
value-added between primary producing, developing countries and the consuming, industrial countries has become no less an important issue than the
level and instability of the price.

The distribution of value-added and the appropriation of profit at each
stage of the chain depend on the market structure, the rules governing commercial transactions and the corporate relationships that develop at each
level. In the case of agricultural commodities, in addition, the ecology, specific
processing requirements (including phytosanitary considerations), and the
ease of mechanization, storability and transport all play a role in structuring
transnational commercial relationships (Talbot 2002). If atomistic competition prevailed (i.e. if all sellers and buyers were so insignificant that they could
not individually influence the market price) and if the bargaining power did
not depend on agents' economic status, the market could be relied upon to
settle more or less satisfactorily the question of who gets what at different
stages. In the case of primary commodities, however, that is far from the case,

and it is one reason why globalization and market liberalization are viewed with suspicion by those who have little control over how markets function.

Smallholder cocoa farmers must sell what they produce at pretty much the price they can get. They depend on village traders for temporary finance and typically they can go to no more than one or two traders. As the product moves to the port for export, it goes through various handlers, none of which operates in a competitive environment. In the past, the state marketing authority enjoyed a monopsonist's position; today, the situation with respect to reward-sharing between local agents and overseas monopolies has become quite opaque. As the intermediate product moves to its final destination in the consuming countries, the market structure is characterized by high corporate concentration. All in all, only a fraction of world cocoa supplies actually gets traded in the world market; an undetermined but large portion is not traded on the basis of arm's length arrangements.

In short, the cocoa value chain is held to be 'buyer-driven': that is, the buyer – the international trader, typically a transnational – decides where to purchase and process the raw material (Raikes, Friis and Ponte 2000; Talbot 2002). A number of factors have contributed to keeping cocoa producers' control rather limited in the value chain. A major contributor to the increased dependence on foreign companies has been the general deterioration of infrastructure (rural roads, seaport facilities) and the disappearance of local capabilities in marketing and quality control following the abolition of state marketing authorities. This situation is in sharp contrast to colonial times, when colonial powers invested heavily to build local infrastructure as well as state institutions in pursuit of their trade interests (Fold 2001).

The evident unfavourable economics of producing intermediate products has been another reason keeping cocoa producers at the low end of the value chain. The process is highly capital- and energy-intensive, while the intermediate products do not enjoy an advantage in transport over cocoa beans (ITC 2001). Given these handicaps, the increasingly high duties on processed products in the industrial countries would seem to be unnecessary. Certainly, the productivity-improving developments in industrial countries have given cocoa producers a better share in the value chain. For example, a supplier in a cocoa-producing country is just not able to supply the intermediate products on a just-in-time basis to a chocolate manufacturer in Europe, even if all other handicaps are somehow overcome.

Some leading chocolate manufacturers have, however, invested in processing capacity in a developing country, especially in processing organic chocolate. In response to the pressure from civil society, transnational corporations have begun to show interest in 'fair trade' (i.e. ensuring that cocoa is produced where environmental and labour standards are respected) and signed a protocol at the ILO against child labour in cocoa production, even though there is little evidence that the problem is serious or widespread. These developments may be deemed desirable from some perspectives, but they are unlikely to help the vast majority of cocoa producers. The problem is that these otherwise legitimate concerns serve only to divert attention from producers' immediate concerns, and the pursuit of fair trade in practice has come to mean unfair trade for all but a few.

The conclusion from all these qualifications, however, is not that cocoa producers cannot improve their status in the value chain. After all, two cocoa producers – Brazil and Malaysia – have developed considerable domestic processing capacity and import cocoa beans from other producers for processing purposes. This has ocurred not as a result of the freely functioning market but through active government support and direction at an early stage. The availability of local enterprise and the existence of domestic demand for chocolate were seen as other factors favouring processing, although Malaysia did not fulfil the latter condition (Talbot 2002). Whereas other cocoa producers do have some processing capacity, they are, at least for now, handicapped for reasons given above, and the examples of Brazil and Malaysia may not be replicable. For them, an improvement in their position in the value chain could be realized through a careful regulation of production and exports to the world market as well as better quality control and investment in infrastructure.

Conclusion

The real fault with the neoliberal policy prescriptions is that they fail to target the fundamental problems of concern to cocoa-producing countries. The problems they do address – improving productive efficiency and producers' share in the price – while important are not the ones that have preoccupied most cocoa producers. A more serious consequence of neoliberalism, however, seems to be the creation of an intellectual environment of do-nothing, laissez-faire. Hence any search for solutions to unstable and low primary goods prices is dismissed as a waste of time. In these circumstances, the most important step to be taken to bring commodities back on the trade-finance-development agenda is to challenge this mindset and open up the debate to a freer exchange of ideas. Application of free market principles may very well be useful here.

Even within their limited stated goals, market liberalization measures do not appear to have been a resounding success. There is little evidence that they have helped improve productive efficiency in cocoa-producing areas. Indeed, the increase in yields that occurred in Cameroon and Côte d'Ivoire resulted from investments made before the measures were adopted. In Nigeria's case, efficiency actually deteriorated. Little attention was given to investment in infrastructure and delivery systems that would have raised productive efficiency. Improving cocoa growers' share in the export price was indeed a worthy goal, but here too the results were mixed. In any case, the producer's share on its own provides little indication of the benefits for the cocoa grower, but little interest was shown in examining this matter relative to production costs and the market price.

While market liberalization measures did not quite achieve their stated objectives, however, they do not appear to have done much harm either, at least as far as cocoa is concerned. There is no evidence that these measures increased price instability; equally, it would be wrong to credit them with the evident reduction in the price instability. Prices were more stable during the 1990s simply because they had come closest to the bottom. Nor can the market liberalization be held responsible for the depressed prices, but only if this paper's conclusion that the recent output increase had little to do with those measures is held to be valid.

There is little doubt that the state marketing authorities suffered serious problems, some of which were aggravated by the depressed cocoa prices as well as a poor macroeconomic environment in the producing countries. But it now seems doubtful that the remedy lay in abolishing them altogether. The counsellors of liberalization gave little consideration to revamping the state institutions before deciding on their dismantlement. Though far from perfect, Ghana's recently improved Cocoa Board offers an example that can be replicated elsewhere.

The need for a public body to assure cocoa quality and provide other public goods (market intelligence, research and extension) is now widely appreciated. Consideration is also being given to regulating cocoa output to arrest the continuing decline in prices. If there is to be a producers' alliance, a public agency that can control exports, manage stocks and regulate production would be a *sine qua non*. Then, too, there is the question of improving the position of cocoa producers in the value chain, where state action and promotion would be vital.

Finally, as noted earlier, the possibility of any future international cocoa agreement to help stabilize and maintain prices is not on the cards. Notwithstanding the inherent difficulties in managing price bands and buffer stocks, we do not see any support for such a scheme in the industrial countries emerging in the foreseeable future. But this should not stop the producers from exploring ways of managing the cocoa market on their own. The prospects for a producers' alliance in cocoa appear at least as good as in natural rubber or coffee, although other difficult issues must be addressed.

Notes

This paper, benefited from the advice and comments of a number of persons, particularly Mehmet Arda, Alan Brewer, Olivier Matringe, Erich Supper, Henning Terwey and Jan Vingerhoets. To all of them, I am most grateful. Thanks are also due to Arunas Buktevisius for his help in accessing key data bases and to Yusuf Haque for a tutorial on how futures markets function in reality.

1   President Jacques Chirac, speaking to the 22nd Summit of the Heads of State of Africa and France, Paris, 20 February 2003.
2   'Value chain' basically refers to the chain of value added as a commodity moves and is processed all the way from the farm to the final consumer.
3   The instability index has been derived by taking the average of the deviations from the trend-line estimated by means of least-squares.
4   This would appear to dispose of the hypothesis in Gilbert and Varangis (2003) that the market liberalization caused cocoa production to increase and depress prices. Leaving aside Indonesia, the production increase occurred mostly in countries that did not liberalize.
5   Editor's note: Drawings under the CFF were made subject to conditions similar to those required for a stand-by arrangement in the first credit tranche, and for credits that would take the country's indebtedness into the upper tranches, that the country should have a satisfactory balance of payments situation (apart form the export shortfall) or a Fund supported program in effect, or a program that would qualify for Fund support in "the credit tranches" if requested. See Executive Board Decision No. 7528-(83/140) of Sept. 14, 1983.
6   The movement may be dead, but this author believes that at least it is not yet buried. For one thing, the international commodity agreements were far from being a total failure. In virtually each case the commodity agreement failed for specific but different reasons. Second, the commodity agreements never enjoyed the wholehearted support of the consumers for rather narrow, self-interest reasons. And finally, a comprehensive approach to the commodity problem, covering all major commodities – as envisaged by Keynes or in UNCTAD's Integrated Programme – was never tried.

References

Bonjean, Catherine Araujo and Gérard Chambas, 2001, 'Impact du mode d'organisation des filière agro-alimentaires sur la pauvreté: La filière cacao en Côte d'Ivoire', CERDI-Université d'Auvergne, France, September.

Bedford, Ally, Mick Blowfield, Duncan Burnett and Peter Greenhalgh, 2001, 'Value Chains: Lessons for the Kenyan Tea and Indonesian Cocoa Sectors', Infocus Report No. 3, Natural Resources Institute, University of Greenwich.

Fold, Niels, 2001, 'Restructuring of the European Chocolate Industry and its Impact on Cocoa Production in West Africa', *Journal of Economic Geography*, Vol. 1, 405–420.

Dehn, J., 2000, 'Commodity price uncertainty in developing countries', World Bank Policy Research Working Paper 2426, World Bank, Washington D.C.

Gibbon, P., 2001, 'Upgrading Primary Production: A Global Commodity Chain Approach', *World Development*, Vol. 29, No. 2, 345–364.

Gilbert, C., 1987, 'International Commodity Agreements: Design and Performance', *World Development*, Vol. 15, No. 5, 591–616.

Gilbert, C., 1995, 'International Commodity Control: Retrospect and Prospect', Policy Research Working Paper No. 1545, November, World Bank, Washington D.C.

Gilbert, C. L., 1996, 'International Commodity Agreements: An Obituary Notice', *World Development*, Vol. 24, No. 1, 1–9.

Gilbert, C. L., and Hidde P. Smit, 2003, 'Producer Agreements in Agricultural Commodities', Paper prepared for FAO Commodity Consultation Meeting, Rome, 17 March.

Gilbert, C. L. and Panos Varangis, 2003, 'Globalization and International Commodity Trade, with Specific Reference to the West African Cocoa Producers', NBER Working Paper No. 9668, April, Cambridge, Mass.

Humphrey, John, 2002, 'The Value Chain Approach – Linking National Producers to International Buyers and Markets', Executive Forum on National Export Strategies, Institute of Development Studies, University of Sussex, Brighton, UK.

ICCO, 2001, 'Structural Changes in the Cocoa Sector and Price Formation on World Markets', Report No. EX/109/4, 9 March, International Cocoa Organisation, London.

ICCO, 2003, 'Trends in Global Supply and Demand for Cocoa', Report No. EX/116/7, 20 February, International Cocoa Organisation, London.

ITC, 2001, *Cocoa: A Guide to Trade Practices*, Geneva: International Trade Centre.

Keynes, J. M., 1943, 'The International Regulation of Primary Products', reprinted in D. Moggridge (ed.), 1980, *Collected Writings of John Maynard Keynes*, London: Macmillan and Cambridge University Press.

Larson, D., P. Varangis and N. Yabuki, 1998, 'Commodity Risk Management and Development', World Bank Policy Research Working Paper 1963, World Bank, Washington D.C.

Morisset, Jacques, 1997, 'Unfair Trade? Empirical Evidence in World Commodity Markets over the Past 25 Years', April, World Bank, Washington D.C.

Raikes, Philip, Michael Friis Jensen and Stefano Ponte, 2000, 'Global Commodity Chain Analysis and the French *Filière* Approach: Comparison and Critique', Working Paper Subseries on Globalisation and Economic Restructuring in Africa, No. IX, CDR Working Paper 00.3, February, Centre for Development Research, Copenhagen.

Ruf, F. and H. de Milly, 1990, 'Comparison of Cocoa Production Costs in Seven Producing Countries', Paper presented at ICCO Advisory Group on the World Economy, VII meeting, Accra, Ghana, 18–20 June.

Talbot, J. M., 2002, 'Tropical Commodity Chains, Integration Strategies and International Inequality: Coffee, Cocoa and Tea', *Review of International Political Economy*, November, 9: 4, 701–734.

Varangis, P. and G. Schreiber, 2000, 'Cocoa Market Reforms in West Africa', in Akiyama, Baffes, Larson and Varangis (eds.), *Commodity Market Reforms: Lessons of Two Decades*, Washington D.C.: World Bank.

Williams, G., 1985, 'Marketing With and Without Marketing Boards', *Review of African Political Economy*, 34, 4–15.

UNCTAD, 2003, 'A Primer on New Techniques Used by the Sophisticated Fraudster', UNCTAD/DITC/COM/39, March, UNCTAD, Geneva.

INDEX